Wordsworth and the Victorians

𝔚𝔬𝔯𝔡𝔰𝔴𝔬𝔯𝔱𝔥—𝔯𝔞𝔩 𝔐𝔬𝔲𝔫𝔱—𝔄𝔪𝔟𝔩𝔢𝔰𝔦𝔡𝔢.

MR. JOHN BURTON,

Respectfully announces to the LITERATI of EUROPE and AMERICA,
that, in pursuance of instructions from the Executors, he

WILL SELL BY AUCTION,

IN THE THIRD WEEK OF JULY NEXT,

AT THAT HAUNT OF HALLOWED MEMORIES, RYDAL MOUNT,

NEAR AMBLESIDE, WESTMORELAND,

THE SELECT LIBRARY

𝔒𝔣 𝔱𝔥𝔢 𝔩𝔞𝔱𝔢 𝔳𝔢𝔫𝔢𝔯𝔞𝔱𝔢𝔡 𝔓𝔬𝔢𝔱-𝔏𝔞𝔲𝔯𝔢𝔞𝔱𝔢,

WILLIAM WORDSWORTH, ESQ. D.C.L.

LAST, NOT LEAST, OF THE LINE OF "LAKE MINSTRELS."

ALSO,

A FINE GALLERY PICTURE,

"VULCAN PRESENTING TO VENUS THE ARMOUR FOR MARS."

A capital specimen of the Neapolitan School, by one of its most
consummate Masters,—*Lucca Giordano.*

Catalogues are in preparation, and will be duly forwarded, on application, (inclosing Postage stamps,) addressed to Mr. JOHN BURTON,
Auctionier & Accountant, 38, Avenham Lane, Preston.

April 25th, 1859.

WORDSWORTH
AND THE
VICTORIANS

STEPHEN GILL

CLARENDON PRESS · OXFORD
1998

OXFORD
UNIVERSITY PRESS

Great Clarendon Street, Oxford OX2 6DP

Oxford University Press is a department of the University of Oxford.
It furthers the University's objective of excellence in research, scholarship,
and education by publishing worldwide in

Oxford New York

Athens Auckland Bangkok Bogotá Buenos Aires Calcutta
Cape Town Chennai Dar es Salaam Delhi Florence Hong Kong Istanbul
Karachi Kuala Lumpur Madrid Melbourne Mexico City Mumbai
Nairobi Paris São Paulo Singapore Taipei Tokyo Toronto Warsaw
and associated companies in Berlin Ibadan

Oxford is a registered trade mark of Oxford University Press
in the UK and in certain other countries

Published in the United States
by Oxford University Press Inc., New York

© Stephen Gill 2001

British Library Cataloguing in Publication Data
Data available

Library of Congress Cataloging in Publication Data
Data available

ISBN 0-19-818764-5

1 3 5 7 9 10 8 6 4 2

Typeset by Cambrian Typesetters, Frimley, Surrey
Printed in Great Britain on acid-free paper by
Bookcraft Ltd, Misomer Norton, Somerset

To the Memory of

WILLIAM KNIGHT AND EDWARD DOWDEN

there are only two people I can think of this side of Paradise who would think of giving a Christmas present in *eight volumes*. It is a most beautiful and usable W. I am particularly glad to have it, as he seems to suit me. His love of nature, and his constant use of it are a link to higher things which I greatly love . . . so his poetry rests and refreshes me with a new strength of head and heart, of thought & love. I shall often take a volume about with me.

(Edward King, Bishop of Lincoln, 23 December 1897)

. . . in estimating for ourselves the greatness of a poet we have to take into account the history of his greatness. Wordsworth is an essential part of history.

(T. S. Eliot in *The Use of Poetry and the Use of Criticism*)

Acknowledgements

I WISH to thank the British Academy and the Leverhulme Trust for the award of a Research Fellowship, and Lincoln College and Oxford University for sabbatical leave and research funds, all of which have greatly assisted me in the writing of this book.

During my research I have been helped by the librarians and staff of the following institutions and I gratefully acknowledge their courteous attention: the Bodleian Library, the English Faculty Library, and Pusey House Library, Oxford; the Pierpont Morgan Library, New York; the Memorial Library of the University of Wisconsin, Madison; Cornell University Library; the Huntington Library, Pasadena; Dr Williams's Library, London; the Wordsworth Library, Grasmere; the Cumbria County Record Office, and the Carnegie Public Library, Kendal.

I owe especial thanks to Mark L. Reed, Paul F. Betz, and Michael Jaye for allowing me access to their Wordsworth collections, whose holdings supplement in important ways those of the institutions named above.

For permission to quote from copyright material in their care, I thank the Trustees of Dove Cottage, the Pierpont Morgan Library, Division of Rare and Manuscript Collections, Cornell University Library, the Council of Alexandra College, Dublin, and Professor Jonathan Wordsworth. Some of the material spread across Chapters 1–3 has already appeared elsewhere. Material from 'England's Samuel: Wordsworth in the "Hungry-Forties" ' is reprinted by permission of SEL Studies in English Literature 1500–1900, 33/4 (Autumn 1993), 841–58; material from 'Wordsworth and "Catholic Truth": The Role of Frederick William Faber', Review of English Studies, NS 45 (1994), 204–20 is reprinted by permission of Oxford University Press; material from 'Copyright and the Publishing of Wordsworth, 1850–1900', Literature in the Market-place: Nineteenth-Century British Publishing and Reading Practices, ed. John O. Jordan and Robert L. Patten (Cambridge, 1995), 74–92, is reprinted by permission of Cambridge University

Press. For illustrations I acknowledge with thanks the help of Jeff Cowton and Michael Jaye, the Trustees of Dove Cottage and Leeds City Art Gallery.

A book of this kind cannot be written without the help of friends and I would like to thank the following, all of whom have provided information, advice, and encouragement: Reggie Alton; Dinah Birch; David Bradshaw; Chris Brooks; James Butler; John Carey; Jeff Cowton; Jared Curtis; Peter Howell; Cecil Y. Lang; Stephen Parrish; Ian Reid; Christopher Ricks; Nicholas Roe; William St Clair; Robert and Pamela Woof; Jonathan Wordsworth. My debt of gratitude to Clare Tilbury is immeasureable.

Contents

List of Illustrations

Frontispiece The 'Haunt of Hallowed Memories': advertisement for the sale of Wordsworth's library at Rydal Mount, following the death of Mary Wordsworth in 1859. Reproduced by courtesy of Michael Jaye.

A Note on Texts

THE STANDARD edition, *The Poetical Works of William Wordsworth,* ed. Ernest De Selincourt and Helen Darbishire (5 vols.; Oxford, 1940–9), is being superseded by *The Cornell Wordsworth,* General Editor Stephen Parrish (16 vols. continuing, Ithaca and London, 1975–). All quotations from Wordsworth's poems are taken from the 'Reading Text' in the relevant volumes of *Cornell* where they have appeared, otherwise from the Oxford edition, but every quotation from famous poems such as *Tintern Abbey* has not been solemnly footnoted. As the 1850 text of *The Prelude* was the only one available in the Victorian period all quotations in this book are drawn from the text of it in the *Cornell* volume, *The Fourteen-Book Prelude,* ed. W. J. B. Owen (Ithaca, 1985), unless there is reason to quote from the actual first edition.

Abbreviations

Abbreviations for works or the names of individuals cited frequently within a chapter, but only in that chapter, are given at their first mention in a note. What follows is a list only of works or persons referred to across the whole book.

DW	Dorothy Wordsworth
HCR	Henry Crabb Robinson
HCR: Books	*Henry Crabb Robinson on Books and Their Writers*, ed. Edith J. Morley (3 vols.; London, 1938).
HCR: Corr.	*The Correspondence of Henry Crabb Robinson with the Wordsworth Circle*, ed. Edith J. Morley (2 vols., London, 1927)
Prose	*The Prose Works of William Wordsworth*, ed. W. J. B. Owen and Jane Worthington Smyser (3 vols.; Oxford, 1974)
PW	*The Poetical Works of William Wordsworth*, ed. Ernest de Selincourt and Helen Darbishire (5 vols.; Oxford, 1940–9)
STC	Samuel Taylor Coleridge
W	William Wordsworth
WL	*The Letters of William and Dorothy Wordsworth* (8 vols.; Oxford, 1967–93). Individual volumes: *The Early Years 1787—1805*, ed. Chester L. Shaver (1967); *The Middle Years*, pt. I: *1806–1811*, ed. Mary Moorman (1969); *The Middle Years*, pt. 2: *1812–1820*, eds. Mary Moorman and Alan G. Hill (1970); *The Later Years*, pt. 1: *1821–1828*, ed. Alan G. Hill (1978); *The Later Years*, pt. 2: *1829–1834*, ed. Alan G. Hill (1979); *The Later Years*, pt. 3: *1835–1839*, ed. Alan G. Hill (1982); *The Later Years*, pt. 4: *1840–1853*, ed. Alan G. Hill (1988); *A Supplement of New Letters*, ed. Alan G. Hill (1993). The edition is referred to serially as *WL*, I–VIII.
WL	The Wordsworth Library, Grasmere

Introduction

I

Wordsworth's *The White Doe of Rylstone* opens at Bolton Abbey, a strikingly romantic ruin in Yorkshire on the banks of the river Wharfe where it runs through the estate of the Duke of Devonshire. In June 1882 Abraham Stansfield, poet, botanist, and dedicated Wordsworthian, made a pilgrimage to the spot and he later described his visit for the *Manchester Quarterly*. A chance conversation with 'a stalwart man of the fells', he records, elicited

much interesting information, the most important item of which was that 'the late duke' . . . had assiduously sought, but vainly, to naturalize on his Bolton estate another white doe! How many attempts were made, how many white does, after varying fortunes, found their way to Bolton, we forget, but the result was uniform: utter failure to naturalize so rare an animal.[1]

This encounter may serve to introduce the subject of this book and to indicate something of its nature—and whether the countryman was just pulling Stansfield's leg hardly matters.

Thirty or so years after his death Wordsworth is a marketable name. His Grace wants to introduce a white doe at Bolton Abbey not from an interest in breeding rare strains but because Wordsworth has identified Bolton Abbey as the place where one ought to see a white doe. A much earlier tourist knew as much. In 1841 Tennyson had paced nine miles along the Wharfe, his 'imagination inflamed' by Wordsworth's poem, not expecting but no doubt devoutly wishing to catch a glimpse of the legendary creature. The medium of Stansfield's account is also significant. His journey was a *literary* pilgrimage and his record, for the organ of the Manchester Literary Club, was written for the growing number of people with an appetite for anecdotes about literature and literary celebrities. This book is, in part, about the various ways in which Wordsworth was honoured in the Victorian period, but it is also about the ways in which he was constructed as as a marketable commodity.

Late twentieth-century readers might make a pilgrimage to Grasmere or to Tintern Abbey, but not to Bolton Abbey. *The White Doe of Rylstone*, absent from all current selections and anthologies, is unread. But it retained its place in Victorian awareness of Wordsworth's *œuvre*. In 1855 it inspired John William Inchbold's Royal Academy painting, *At Bolton: The White Doe of Rylstone*, and it was issued twice separately in 1859 and 1867 in handsome illustrated editions.[2] The Victorian sense of what constituted Wordsworth was different from ours and in part this book is also a study of what it was. *The Excursion* was regarded as Wordsworth's great work. Counselling those who wished through private study to become well informed in the central branches of humane learning, James Pycroft insisted on one Wordsworth poem only in his *A Course of Reading* (1844): 'Read *The Excursion*'.[3] A single-volume edition was what Elizabeth Gaskell recommended as the best companion for a young friend making a first trip to the Lake District—and quotations from it stood as epigraph to *Modern Painters* in 1843 and *Adam Bede* in 1859. Circulation of *The Prelude*, on the other hand, in Great Britain was limited by copyright restrictions until 1892 and *Home at Grasmere*, the first book of *The Recluse*, now a central poem in the Wordsworth canon, was almost unknown since it was not published until 1888. Even after Matthew Arnold had argued that selection from within Wordsworth's massive output was a necessity if he was to survive, Victorian taste was more catholic than ours. The representative selection issued under the auspices of the Wordsworth Society in 1888 exemplifies Wordsworth's poetry right up to 1846.[4] Even the Victorian sense of the periods of Wordsworth's career was different from ours. A selection entitled *Early Poems of William Wordsworth* would now signal work up to 1798, *Lyrical Ballads* being recognized as the beginning of the 'great decade' of maturity. John Ramsden Tutin's 1889 selection under that title begins with a poem dated 1786 but concludes with a sprinkling of the *River Duddon* sonnets of 1820.[5]

Opening with Stansfield's narrative also indicates the kind of book this is. Without, I hope, being merely anecdotal, I have drawn heavily on individual testimony and history and have not eschewed the anecdotal. Acts of cultural transmission are committed by human beings from various impulses and in various ways. The preacher who invokes *Tintern Abbey* from the pulpit; the publisher who spots a niche in the gift-book market; the critic whose visibility is enhanced by a full-dress reappraisal of Wordsworth's contemporary significance; novelists and poets who draw on Wordsworth; environmental activists who summon Wordsworth to their cause; and solitary readers whose motions of heart and imagination are recorded only in a diary entry or a letter—all are involved in constructing and diffusing 'Wordsworth', and it is their acts that are the substance of this study.

II

Wordsworth and the Victorians originated in my work on *William Wordsworth: A Life* (1989). What struck me as inviting further exploration was Wordsworth's cultural significance during his last twenty-five years. At a time when indisputably Wordsworth's creative powers were waning, his importance grew. Wordsworth the radical, whose history remained undivulged in manuscripts of *The Prelude*, was, of course, unknown to the world at large, but the voice of Wordsworth the conservative-radical, the humanitarian and morally concerned Wordsworth, that was listened to with increasing respect. Churchmen, social reformers, and educationalists canvassed his support. Rather like the later T. S. Eliot, the later Wordsworth became a cultural icon, to be visited, written about, and, by disciples, revered. In so far as the constraint imposed by the length of a single-volume biography allowed discussion of this phenomenon, it was in terms of the impact his growing fame had on Wordsworth. In this book I have expanded a little on material touched on in the biography, but have dealt more extensively with Wordsworth's impact on the Victorian age, both during his lifetime—he was a Victorian for over a quarter of it—and posthumously.

Work on the biography also brought me close to other material that is of historical importance. All students of Victorian culture are aware of the high place afforded to literature, especially poetry, and of the seriousness with which critics assessed literature in relation to the conduct of life and the establishment of moral principles. In Wordsworth's case the almost unanimous judgement that his work was of the soundest led, on occasion, to such extraordinary hyperbole as Henry Hudson's ranking of Wordsworth as 'the most spiritual and the most spiritualizing of all the English poets, not Shakespeare, no, nor even Milton, excepted: indeed, so far as I know or believe, the world has no poetry outside the Bible that can stand a comparison with his in this respect', or James Russell Lowell's declaration that 'Wordsworth's better utterances have the bare sincerity, the absolute abstraction from time and place, the immunity from decay, that belongs to the grand simplicities of the Bible'.[6]

But it was not just critics and moralists, all of whom had in a sense a vested interest in the elevated construction of Wordsworth, who acknowledged the moral worth of his writing. Preserved in the correspondence files at the Wordsworth Library in Grasmere are the testimonies of many people who wrote to tell the poet what his work had meant to them. Their tone is one of intense gratitude. Wordsworth's poetry, they witness, has helped them, even saved them in life's crises. Some of the letters are overblown, though none the less sincere for that, but others are very moving in their candour. They offer insight into the unmisgiving directness with which many Victorians looked to literature for instruction and the comfort of spiritual guidance. I have tried to explore their witness without condescension. Within university departments of English such a mode of reading is regarded as old-fashioned at best, suspect and misguided at worst, but it is still more common, and more valued in the wider world than professors suppose.[7]

III

What has evolved from these originating impulses is an essay in two kinds of literary and cultural history. The first tries to document as fully as possible, consonant with still being readable and interesting, the ubiquity of Wordsworth. In part this attempt entails marshalling fragments of evidence which are slight in themselves, but substantial in aggregate—for example, the fact that in Coventry Patmore's house hung portraits of Wordsworth and Faraday, 'the two greatest men of our time'; that having gone through *The Excursion* twice, Darwin read attentively across the whole corpus of Wordsworth's poetry;[8] that *Nature*, T. H. Huxley's 'Weekly

Illustrated Journal of 'Science', carried a quotation from Wordsworth at the mast-head of its first issue on 4 November 1869 and
continued to do so.[9] Some of Wordsworth's formulations became
common coin. In 1853, for example, Dickens protested against any
alteration of fairy stories, 'which are so tenderly and humanly
useful to us in these times when the world is too much with us early
and late', and E. B. Ramsay, Dean of Edinburgh, invoked the same
poem in 1862, when he warmly endorsed a comment from the
Quarterly Review that after hearing *Messiah* we feel 'as if we had
shaken off some of our dirt and dross, as if the world were not so
much with us'.[10] 'The light that never was on sea or land' was
another happily usable line in discussion of visual art. Both Burne-
Jones and Hardy summon it, without feeling required to identify
the source of such familiar words.[11]

Evidence of this sort is plentiful and many Victorian scholars
have cited examples since Katherine Peek made a pioneering survey
over fifty years ago.[12] To translate general acknowledgement of
Wordsworth's ubiquity into a form that can be of scholarly use,
however, more detail is needed. What Wordsworth did people
actually read, for instance? What editions were in circulation
and how far did copyright restrictions affect the contents of
popular, cheap volumes? The importance of the great critical
pronouncements—Arnold's and Pater's, for example—is well
known, but what impact on the developing construction of
Wordsworth did academic scholars have? What were the most
significant achievements of the Wordsworth Society and what did
they have to do with the rise of organizations whose remit still
affects the daily lives of those who live and work in or visit the Lake
District? These issues underlie various chapters in this book and an
attempt is made to address them carefully in the conviction that
if these factual questions are not answered in detail they are
not, for purposes of literary and cultural history, worth raising at
all.

The second form of literary history essayed is of a more familiar
kind, the study of Wordsworth's 'fecundating of later works of
literature'.[13] The kind of critical enquiry adverted to in Christopher
Ricks's observation about the vitality of literary transmission (and
marvellously exemplified in his own work) has been denigrated and
its necessary death foretold. Andrew Elfenbein's recent *Byron and
the Victorians*, however, demonstrates the continuing possibilities

of the form and I hope that the critical chapters in this book contribute to our appreciation of those writers for whom Wordsworth was a presence not to be put by.[14] Discussion is limited to the relationship of Wordsworth and the writer in question and as tunnel vision and forced claims are the besetting sins of this kind of study I have erred on the side of caution, maintaining the tenor of the rest of the book by sticking as far as possible to documented or otherwise solid evidence.

The two kinds of literary history are not, however, quite as separate as the preceding paragraphs and the book's chapter divisions suggest. Ricks is right to insist that 'the most important and enduring rediscovery or reinvention of a book or of a writer comes when a subsequent creator is inspired by such to an otherwise inexplicable newness of creative apprehension', but the inspiration is not necessarily and always through direct contact with the originating work of art. In 1864, for example, John Campbell Shairp contributed a long article on Wordsworth to the *North British Review*, which was later revised for his collection *Studies in Poetry and Philosophy* (1868). The essay is touched on below in the survey of major critical writings after Wordsworth's death. It is good criticism, which helped establish Shairp as a substantial literary figure whose election as Professor of Poetry at Oxford was not undeserved. But its greatest and most lasting value was undoubtedly that it came to the attention of the young Gerard Manley Hopkins, who entered into his notebook part of Shairp's exposition of 'Wordsworth's recognition of the relationship between an onlooker and the "heart" or "character" of a scene'. Here, as Hopkins's biographer Norman White observes, 'is more than a foretaste . . . of "inscape" and "instress" '.[15] Or, to take another instance, staying with Hopkins: On 7 August 1886 Hopkins wrote a wonderful letter to Richard Watson Dixon, whose main thrust about the inadequacy of rhetoric in English poetry flows from observations about Wordsworth's '*charisma*'.[16] What had prompted Hopkins's thoughts was the presidential address to the final meeting of the Wordsworth Society on 9 July 1886, delivered by Lord Selborne, which Hopkins can only have known from newspaper reports. As is noted in discussion below of the Wordsworth Society, the meeting at which the Society dissolved itself was a melancholy affair, with old men in reminiscent mood, but the tedium of the presidential address is more than compensated for by the richness of Hopkins's response to it. Seed even as poor as Lord Selborne's falls on fertile as well as stony ground.

IV

Early in *The Prelude* (1805, II. 213–15) Wordsworth reflects on the difficulty of pin-pointing influence:

> Who that shall point as with a wand, and say
> 'This portion of the river of my mind
> Came from yon fountain'.

Throughout this book I have been mindful of this caution, eager to chart Wordsworth's tributary flow into the river of Victorian literature and culture, but very hesitant about identifying it as the originating spring.

Consider, for example, the following morsel of evidence. When prospecting for the purchase of the Balmoral estate, Prince Albert enthused about the countryside and observed that 'the people are more natural, and are more marked by that honesty and sympathy which always distinguish the inhabitants of mountainous countries, who live far away from towns'.[17] Strong indication, surely, for the vigilant Wordsworthian that the poet's influence reached to the apex of Victorian society. But it is more than doubtful that Prince Albert was consciously rehearsing the Preface to *Lyrical Ballads*. Enthusiastically reporting what he believed he had observed, Albert was endorsing one of his period's notions about rural integrity which Wordsworth had played a large part, but not the only part, in creating. In such a case the most that can sensibly be claimed is that the link is one of similarity or analogy, or that Wordsworth has contributed in some unquantifiable measure to this or that phenomenon.

There could be almost no circumference to a study which sought to map all such examples as Albert's effusion. What was Wordsworth's part in the centrality of children and childhood in Victorian literature and art? No account of it could omit the Wordsworthian poetic child, but in examination of specific novels, poems, and pictures, evidence of Wordsworth's direct agency for the most part evaporates. Or again, in *Sacred Tears: Sentimentality in Victorian Literature*, Fred Kaplan rightly observes that 'Wordsworth's fascination with sentiment made him a pervasive presence among the Victorians', but what 'pervasive' indicates is that to weigh Wordsworth's contribution to Victorian sentiment would itself require a book-length study, in which moving beyond generalities would be difficult.[18]

Even where there is evidence of intellectual relationship the temptation to assert actual influence often needs to be resisted. Consider, as one example that must stand for many, Wordsworth, Dickens, and education. In a letter of 1829 Wordsworth protested: 'Natural history is taught in infant schools by pictures stuck up against walls, and such mummery. A moment's notice of a redbreast pecking by a winter's hearth is worth it all.'[19] Bitzer, Sissy Jupe, and the definition of a horse are strikingly prefigured here and the link of Wordsworth and *Hard Times* reminds us that shortly after the poet's death *Household Words* for 25 May 1850 carried a tribute to his right-mindedness about education. The affinity is there, but that is all it is. Wordsworth's most important statements about education were made in private letters Dickens could not have known, or in essays which he was not likely to have read, and in *The Prelude*, not published by May 1850. In short, Dickens and Wordsworth were close in spirit on many aspects of educational practice and the closeness is important for our sense of intellectual allegiances in the period, but even the most ardent Wordsworthian has to acknowledge that Dickens's convictions about school-rooms would have developed as they did had Wordsworth never written a line.

V

The limits on speculation and assertion just outlined are self-imposed, an attempt to avoid the kind of single-vision special pleading which too often distorts studies of this kind. Other limits have also been observed, however, largely for reasons of space, which are regrettable. *Wordsworth and the Victorians* concludes at the close of the nineteenth century. A case could be made for pursuing the theme to the end of the Great War, during which Wordsworth's virtue as a specifically *English* poet was fervently promoted. But why stop there? Wordsworth's advocacy of imaginative literature as a countervailing force to many threatening tendencies of the age underpins much of the thinking of the Newbolt Report, *The Teaching of English In England* (1921), about the place of English Literature in modern life and, with D. J. Palmer and Chris Baldick as guides, one could fruitfully pursue Wordsworth's place in the rise of English studies in the twentieth century.[20]

Even within its Victorian limit, however, this book is not inclusive. During the excursion to the Marabar Caves in *A Passage to India*, Ronnie and Adela draw momentarily closer together through a shared memory: ' "Do you remember Grasmere?" ' Wordsworth's own landscape, 'Romantic yet manageable', rises up between them and the alien, unassimilable, Marabar Hills. But what image of Grasmere was formed by the children in Indian schools, for whom Wordsworth's poetry was part of the curriculum, or by readers in Australia or Canada or the West Indies? Gauri Viswanathan's *Masks of Conquest* is a justly acclaimed pioneering study, but it lacks the kind of detail that could provide a sense of the imaginative experience of such readers encountering at several thousand miles distance the Englishness of English Literature.[21] *Wordsworth in the Empire* is a book waiting to be written, as is *Wordsworth in America*. Wordsworth's poetry was being freshly set by American printers from as early as 1802; his first editor, during his lifetime, was an American, Henry Reed; *The Prelude* and Christopher Wordsworth's *Memoirs of William Wordsworth* were better received in America than in Great Britain; American admirers contributed substantially to the Wordsworth memorial in Ambleside Church; the greatest private collectors of Wordsworth books and manuscripts were (and still are) Americans. But apart from the line through Emerson and Thoreau, Wordsworth's presence in American literature and art has not been fully explored,[22] and how much remains to be done can be indicated by the fact that at the time of writing no comprehensive bibliography exists of the publication of Wordsworth in America.

After admission of so many limits and exclusions, it hardly needs saying that *Wordsworth and the Victorians* is meant to open the subject up, not close it down. It is dedicated to the memory of two great scholars, whose work I have come more and more to admire, who must stand as exemplars of all those whose contribution to the construction and diffusion of Wordsworth in the Victorian period is examined in this book.

Fame

Never forget what I believe was observed ... by Coleridge, that every great and original writer, in proportion as he is great or original, must himself create the taste by which he is to be relished; he must teach the art by which he is to be seen ... and if this be possible, it must be a work of *time*.

I

'The king-poet of our times'

In 1841 Elizabeth Barrett dispatched John Kenyon north on a delicate mission. She wanted something from 'the king-poet of our times', Wordsworth, an emblem of him both as high-priest of Nature and as domestic being at home amongst the Lakes.[1] Kenyon returned, to her delight, with 'a slip of green' from the garden at Rydal Mount, the poet's dwelling since 1813. It is fortunate that shrubs grow abundantly in Cumbria, for Wordsworth's garden was clearly suffering depredations. In September 1836 a newly-married couple were observed approaching Rydal Mount. As they lingered at the gate, the lady was heard to whisper to her husband, 'We must not go in; but do you get on the wall & snatch a sprig of laurel, or anything; we *must* take something away.'[2] On the way back down the hill to their carriage they most probably passed others on a similar quest, for Rydal Mount had already become a shrine.

> Fair Rydal Mount, thy bowers are meet
> To be a poet's chosen seat;
> By him thy lawn, and waving woods,
> Thy views of mountain, vale, and floods,
> Will wake the deep and thrilling glow,
> Which bids the stream of song to flow.

Thus Mrs Bourne in 1832, sentimental herald of a remarkable phenomenon.[3] For the first time in English history a writer's home had become a place of general pilgrimage while its saintly incumbent was still alive. The faithful could even buy an icon. In 1840 Edward Moxon published an engraving of a drawing by William Westall, *Room at Rydal Mount*, which depicts the 70-year-old poet standing in solemnly meditative pose.[4] The image, which was issued widely in large postcard size, conveys both dignity and domesticity. Oil-paintings, walls of books, and a bust in a niche, testify to a life of successful literary endeavour, while his wife, Mary, seated comfortably at a work-table just away from the fire, reminds the observer that this is the poet who as long ago as 1815 had announced in prefatory verses to *The White Doe of Rylstone* how much he owed to his 'Beloved wife' and her companionship 'beside our blazing fire'. One figure is missing, the other constant in Wordsworth's domestic life, his sister. Now suffering from

FIG. 1 William Westall, *Room at Rydal Mount* (1840)

Alzheimer's disease, Dorothy occasionally alarmed the curious
peering over the wall at Rydal Mount, but she could have no place
in Westall's picture. When she did appear in the memoirs of those
who visited the poet, it was only to emphasize how splendid was his
devotion to the 'dear, dear Sister' of *Tintern Abbey*.

For many visitors a detour off the main road up to Rydal Mount
and an imagined reception in the gracious drawing-room of the
Westall print was enough. A sprig of laurel made a lasting souvenir.
Or one might hope to catch a glimpse of the poet in public, as John
Ruskin and his parents did in 1830: 'We went to Rydal Chapel in
preference to Ambleside as we had heard that Mr Wordsworth
went to Rydal ... We were in luck ... We were rather
disappointed in this gentleman's appearance especially as he
seemed to be asleep the greater part of the time.'[5] An enormous
number of people, however, called to see the poet in person. Some
sent a note in advance from a neighbouring inn, requesting the
favour of a brief audience. Others, like the Chartist poet Thomas
Cooper, author of *Purgatory of Suicides*, just turned up, in his own
words, 'a dust-covered pilgrim'. (Cooper addressed Wordsworth
afterwards as 'Venerated Sir'.[6]) Robert Montgomery, ambitious
poet of *The Omnipresence of the Deity* (1828), was so moved by
his reception by the elderly 'bard of Rydal' that he memorialized
the occasion in 130 lines of dreadful verse, beginning:

> A thought the Universe in worth outweighs
> Viewed as dead matter, meaningless and dumb:
> Hence, on some form where intellect is shrined
> And genius dwells in purity of power
> To God and wisdom dedicate, we gaze
> With no cold glance, by common love inspired.
> And thus on him, that venerable bard!
> The laurelled priest of poetry and truth,
> August with years, by mournful calm subdued,
> With filial reverence my spirit looked
> When first I heard him in his mountain-home
> My entrance welcome.[7]

But it was the letter of introduction from a friend, or the friend of
a friend, that brought most visitors to the presence. A message from
Sir William Boxall is a typical specimen. Having met two ladies,
friends of his hosts, 'true & sincere worshippers', Boxall wrote to
Wordsworth in 1836 to prepare him for a visitation:

every evening is passed in reading aloud something out of your volumes. I cannot tell you how truly sincerely they love you and I verily believe that there is no Book but the Bible that is to them so full of inspiration. You would be delighted to see the beautiful appreciation with which they read you & I believe nothing short of a pilgrimage to Rydal Mount will suffice them that they may themselves tell you how much gratitude they feel towards you.[8]

Neither the intention of this letter, nor its reverential tone, were unusual. During the last fifteen years of his life Wordsworth was besieged by visitors, whose passage to Rydal Mount was eased by friends from his extensive and overlapping circles of acquaintance. In 1846, for example, George Dawson, a charismatic preacher and lecturer from Birmingham, went on honeymoon to the Lake District. Trading on his friendship with Harriet Martineau, whose house in Ambleside he had borrowed, Dawson introduced himself to the poet and was given the usual tea and tour of the library and grounds.[9] Wordsworth had not met him before and was never to meet him again, but Dawson had his hour and returned to preach the Wordsworthian gospel to his large following.

Dawson arrived through the Martineau connection, but he and others like him might come from many directions. In popular image Wordsworth was still what he had announced himself to be in the Preface to *The Excursion*, namely, 'a Poet living in retirement', but in fact he dined when he chose with an impressive number of the most accomplished, powerful, and well-connected people of his time—and they all had friends. There was the London world of artists and writers, actors and lawyers, bankers and politicians, in which he moved easily. Through Henry Taylor he met the circle of young intellectuals, most notably John Stuart Mill, whom the author of *Philip van Artevelde* liked to foster. Wordsworth was a vital agent in drumming up support for Talfourd's copyright agitation in the late 1830s because he was on friendly terms with so many titled and influential people in or on the fringes of government. Through his brother Christopher, Master of Trinity College, Wordsworth became acquainted with grand ecclesiastics and academics at Cambridge, but it was his Oxford admirers who engineered an honorary degree in 1839. A complex web of relationships brought Wordsworth into contact with Southwood Smith, Hugh Tremenheere, and others active in social reform. And there was, finally, the less easily classifiable group of substantial people, comfortably off, intelligent, socially concerned, many of whom were his neighbours, or their friends, such as the Fletcher family, the Gregs, and the Arnolds. The Rydal Mount Visitors Book, kept for most of the last decade of Wordsworth's life, contains over two thousand names.

Many of them were American.[10] Professor George Ticknor of Harvard was an early visitor in 1819, who called again in 1835, 1838, and 1849, and introduced many friends. The noted Bostonian William Ellery Channing was the forerunner in 1822 of many Unitarians, such as Orville Dewey, who was astonished in 1833 by the energy with which the poet discoursed not on poetry but on politics.[11] The year 1833 also saw the first visit from Emerson, who came again in 1848 and described his visits in *English Traits* (1856). Emerson, whose estimate of the poet is indicated by his comment that the *Intimations Ode* is 'the high-water mark which the intellect has reached in this age', was disappointed by the man on his first visit, but none the less he returned. Wordsworth was too important to pass by.[12]

Simply seeing the author of *Tintern Abbey* in the flesh was itself a prize. 'My dear Hillard, I have seen Wordsworth!', Charles Sumner wrote in 1838. 'How odd it seemed to knock at a neighbour's door, and inquire, "Where does *Mr.* Wordsworth live?" Think of rapping at Westminster Abbey, and asking for Mr. Shakespeare, or Mr. Milton!'[13] But the Senator was rewarded with more than a handshake. Wordsworth and he conversed 'on a variety of topics', particularly memorably on copyright and slavery. Politicians, educationalists, clergymen, writers, and publishers, Wordsworth's American visitors were serious people, for the most part the New England intelligentsia at its most representative, and he seems to have responded to them with appropriate gravity.

The stream of callers testified to Wordsworth's fame. So did his post-bag. Some of the letters and offerings which Wordsworth received were absurd. In 1836 T. Fitzjames Price sent a Latin version of *Yarrow Visited* ('Anne hac Arrovia est? an hocce flumen'), with an obsequious note excusing the intrusion: 'there is a pleasure in connecting one's self, however slightly, with one whose greatness one *feels*'.[14] But this tribute was mild compared to others. The dedication to John Peace's *An Apology for Cathedral Service* (1839), 'as a mark of his veneration for a poet "only not divine" ', is more than matched by a series of letters through the 1840s from

Charles Lamb's former schoolfellow, the Reverend Charles Valentine Le Grice. Having prised a walking-stick as a souvenir from the reluctant poet, Le Grice continually refers to his treasure as if it were a piece of the true Cross.[15]

The source of the discomfort provoked by such tributes is easily identifiable. Price's letter shows massive self-regard. Peace's dedication simply goes too far. It is disturbing to think of Le Grice, an Anglican clergyman, venerating one of Wordsworth's possessions as if it were a religious relic. Some of the letters sent to Wordsworth, however, are discomfiting in a different way. In 1841, John Simon, a medical tutor at King's College, summed up in a letter to Wordsworth what the poetry had come to mean to him:

Instruction in all, which it chiefly behoves to know—humbler reliance in the Divine rule—fuller love of Man—deeper & holier sympathies with Nature—in success, self-diffidence—in trial & suffering the stay and comfort of religious wisdom—are lessons which I, in common with thousands—owe to those works.[16]

It is difficult to enter imaginatively into the frame of mind of anyone responding to a body of poetry in quite this way, or to reconstruct a cultural milieu in which such terms could be used. Difficult but not impossible, for Simon's declaration is clearly a carefully worded, dignified statement. Other letters, however, whose intent is the same as Simon's, test to the limit a reader's powers of empathy. This, for example, an extract from a very long letter from Thomas Powell in 1836, which Mr Micawber would have been proud of:

As I have named 'Tintern Abbey' I cannot tell how that poem has haunted me: it however has been the Angel & not the Demon-haunt. How often has the spirit led me, when I have been well nigh bowed down by the weight of world of heart and brain—how often has it led me to rest in this silent Abbey of Thought. Now all these feelings and recollections rushed over me while reading your letter: thoughts which I deemed had long been crushed by the iron hand of *Matter*—(not reality but rather unreality, seeing that it is perishing)—now thronged around me, like a burst of sunshine long buried in a shroud-like cloud—the captive song seemed released from its bondage, & the music was tears.[17]

Or this, from Frances Ogle, who was moved in 1840 to tell Wordsworth how his work had rescued her. She recalled that she had come to his writings, at a time when, wearied with painful excitement and worn with increased conflict her mind greatly needed the benefits of such a restorative, such a strengthening, yet calm-giving balm. And here she found it—here she first began to drink those waters of peace, of comfort, of quiet yet earnest joy, which (with reverence be it spoken) she has found no where else in such rich abundance, excepting at the Fount of Life itself. Here she gladly learned the 'cheerful faith, that all which we behold is full of blessing'; a faith from which she hoped never again to depart.[18]

This is not parody, nor did Wordsworth respond to it with embarrassment. Her letter, he wrote, 'could not but be grateful to me, expressing so feelingly as it does the salutary effect my writings have had upon your mind'.[19] One might wonder about Miss Ogle's psychological state and have a view as to whether it was good for the poet to be told that his work was akin to the Bible, but what has to be registered is that Frances Ogle poured out this effusion in evident seriousness; that the poet replied to it respectfully; and that he was able to do so because he was by this time getting used to receiving tributes of this kind.

II

Varieties of Fame

Such letters, and the increasing flow of visitors to Rydal Mount, confirmed by the late 1830s that Wordsworth's fame was widespread and assured.

It had been slow in coming. Contrary to belief, which the older Wordsworth and his disciples did little to dispel, his career did not follow a single trajectory from neglect to acclaim. *Lyrical Ballads* went through four editions between 1798 and 1805, establishing at least the beginnings of a reputation which *Poems, in Two Volumes* of 1807 ought to have consolidated. The unsparing attack on most of the 1807 poems, however, voiced most tellingly by the *Edinburgh Review* but disseminated, even down to the *ad hominem* tone, by most other reviews, silenced Wordsworth. No further volume of poetry appeared for seven years. More important, it ensured that he became the property of a coterie. Whereas Scott sold thousands of the *Lay of the Last Minstrel* and *Marmion*, securing a comfortable relationship with a public whose taste he rightly felt he knew, Wordsworth comforted himself with the knowledge that at least Lady Beaumont, a few discerning friends, and a tiny body of readers recognized his genius.

When the silence was broken it did little in the short term for his reputation. *The Excursion*, a finely produced quarto which announced itself in 1814 as only part of a projected great philosophical poem, *The Recluse*, had not cleared its 500-copy printing twenty years later.[20] The first collected poems of 1815 was sluggish. Copies of *The White Doe of Rylstone*, another fine volume also issued in 1815, cumbered Longman's warehouse for fifteen years. *Peter Bell* and *The Waggoner* in 1819 sold rather more briskly, but still in relatively small numbers. For example, 701 copies of *Peter Bell* were sold in the year of publication. John Murray sold 12,000 copies of the opening cantos of *Don Juan* in three months (which Byron thought disappointing).[21]

That Wordsworth mattered was of course recognized by those best qualified to judge. Scott never doubted Wordsworth's powers, though he thought his stiff-necked refusal to attune his work more to public taste was culpably foolish. Keats and Shelley absorbed, criticized, and eventually threw Wordsworth off, but his work was instrumental in shaping not only their own poetry but their conception of the poetic life. Even Byron's goading in *Don Juan* of the Lake District madman, the metaphysical obfuscator, the political apostate, is testimony to his sense that Wordsworth, in some malign way, counted. But a reputation with one's poetic peers remains a coterie reputation and ardent proselytizing, such as Talfourd's 1815 panegyric in *An Attempt to Estimate the Poetical Talent of the Present Age*, only confirmed the fact. 'To the consideration of MR WORDSWORTH's sublimities we come with trembling steps, and feel, as we approach, that we are entering upon holy ground'.[22] Such a tone was to become unremarkable in the 1840s. In 1815 it is strikingly discordant. Most reviewers up to the 1820s still came to scoff and they did not remain to pray.

It is usual to ascribe Wordsworth's doldrum years to the influence of the *Edinburgh Review*. In part this is certainly right. From 1803 to 1822 (when he pronounced the Lake School of poetry 'pretty nearly extinct'[23]) Francis Jeffrey fought a campaign against Wordsworth which was not confined to reviews of his poetry alone—articles on Crabbe or Burns served as well. It was sustained, intelligent, and witty. The openings to Jeffrey's reviews are justly famous. 'This will never do', on *The Excursion*, and on

The White Doe, 'This, we think, has the merit of being the very
worst poem we ever saw imprinted in a quarto volume'.[24] But
Jeffrey's reviews counted not just because they read well. They
added up, over many years, to a consistent and not undiscriminating
probing of all the most difficult aspects of Wordsworth's poetic
project—his metaphysics, his choice of 'low and rustic life' for
subject-matter, his egotism, his diction, his attitude to learning,
civilization, refinement, to 'society' in short.

During the 1830s the situation changed. It is difficult to say why.
No doubt sheer survival was an important factor, as it is in the
recuperation of nearly all writers who live long enough and
continue to produce. The deaths of Keats, Shelley, and Byron left
Wordsworth indisputably in command of the field. As their poetic
careers blazed and were extinguished, his simply went on.
Whatever its merits, his poetry continued to appear. At Coleridge's
death in 1834 memoirs and critical appreciations, most notably De
Quincey's articles in *Tait's Edinburgh Magazine*, began the
mythologizing of the two great poets whose writing lives stretched
back to the now distant time when the French Revolution was a
recent event.[25] Everything De Quincey revealed suggested that both
artistically and biographically the survivor, Wordsworth, was a
much more interesting figure than had been generally supposed.

The spirit of the age also played its part. It is usually a sign of
desperation when historians invoke this elusive power, and so it is
here, but some such term seems indispensable when one tries to
account for certain social or cultural events whose contemporary
impact now seems mystifying. Take, for example, Henry Taylor's
Preface to *Philip Van Artevelde: A Dramatic Romance* (1834).
Taylor was a member of the Colonial Office particularly active in
slavery matters, who was in love with literature and the literary
world. Hospitable to young talent and generous, he won for himself
a considerable reputation as a poet of large-scale ambition.[26] In the
Preface to his best-known work, Taylor arraigns the poetry of
recent decades for promoting feeling over thought. Dazzling
imagery and intoxicating verse there has been in abundance, but 'a
want of any views or reflections which, if unembellished by
imagery, or unassociated with passionate feelings, it would be very
much worth while to express'. 'No man', Taylor declares, 'can be a
very great poet who is not also a great philosopher.'

The Preface is not strikingly written nor judiciously illustrated, but it was received by many as if it had been uttered by Dryden or Dr Johnson. Felicia Hemans applauded 'the putting forth of really strengthening and elevating views respecting the high purposes of intellectual power', and this was the tone adopted by most of *Philip Van Artevelde*'s many reviewers.[27] Here was noble, inspiring, elevating work. Even critics who resisted the fashion enough to whisper that perhaps the poem was not first-rate, joined in the chorus of approval for the Preface.

Taylor's polemic spoke to and for the intellectual arbiters of the coming age—Tennyson, Carlyle, A. H. Hallam, John Sterling, R. C. Trench, F. D. Maurice, R. M. Milnes, J. S. Mill. But it also voiced the concerns of a wider public whose growing welcome for spiritually uplifting books, for greater seriousness in religious matters, and for social conscience in political and economic affairs was to determine both the tone and substance of English writing into the mid-century. And it was these readers who found that Wordsworth was their poet. Denominational magnifying glasses might find flaws in *The Excursion* or *Ecclesiastical Sketches*, but the overall moral tendency of these poems could hardly be doubted, and Wordsworth's recent publications confirmed his place as pre-eminently the poet for the age. The collected editions of 1827 and 1832 consolidated a lifetime's work, but *Yarrow Revisited* in 1835 went further. With its 'Postscript', a major statement on the New Poor Law and other social issues, and its body of new poems, this volume asserted quite freshly, as the collected editions did not, that the living Wordsworth could contribute to contemporary debate quite as trenchantly as Carlyle. *Yarrow Revisited* was the first of Wordsworth's publications to sell widely—new editions were called for in 1836 and 1839—and it certainly confirmed his own sense, as well as his readers', that at last his time had come.

The award of an honorary degree at Oxford in 1839 was the high point of this decade of growing fame. It was not the greatest public tribute paid to him—that must be the Laureateship conferred in 1843 accompanied by generous words from the Queen herself— nor was it his first honorary degree—Durham University had recognized him the previous year—but it was the most richly significant, simply because of the constellation of people involved. The scene in the Sheldonian Theatre might be that of a great historical painting, academical dress being substituted for classical or period costume. On 12 June the Professor of Poetry, John Keble,

whose *The Christian Year* had established him as a more widely
read Wordsworthian poet than Wordsworth was to be in his
lifetime, delivered the Creweian Oration at the presentation of the
degree. To Wordsworth's poetry, he declared, must be referred all
those 'who sincerely desire to understand and feel that secret and
harmonious intimacy which exists between honourable Poverty,
and the severer Muses, sublime Philosophy, yea, even, our most
holy Religion'.[28] The Arnolds, who had made the journey from
Rugby to be present at this notable occasion, would have agreed. So
perhaps too the young Arthur Hugh Clough, who was also there,
but as he had a hangover from the night before it may be doubted
whether he joined in the enthusiastic cheering of the unusually large
assembly.[29] Once robed as honorary Doctor of Civil Law, the 69-
year-old poet awarded the prize for the Newdigate Prize Poem to
the undergraduate John Ruskin. The following morning, in a
quieter but no less significant gathering, Wordsworth breakfasted
with Newman and Keble in Francis Faber's rooms in Magdalen.

   One aspect of the praise now being heaped on Wordsworth calls
for attention. It is that by the late 1830s what were once derided as
his follies are being identified as the true sources of his strength.
Wordsworth's retirement to his native mountains had once been
seen as an affected and culpable refusal to draw nourishment from
the common stock of culture and civilized life. 'Above all things',
the *Critical Review* had declared in 1807, 'we would intreat Mr.
Wordsworth to spend more time in his library and less in company
with the "moods of his own mind" ', a sentiment echoed by Lucy
Aikin in the *Annual Review* for 1808, who believed that the poet
'appears ... to starve his mind in solitude'.[30] Now it was
commonplace to invest with a spiritual aura a lifetime apparently
spent secluded from the follies and temptations of the world in
solitary pursuit of a personal vision of truth. Wordsworth was now
credited with the power of the seer, whose visions were supremely
worthy of poetic utterance, whereas once he had been contemned
as an egotist in thrall to his own delusions, who insisted on
'connecting his most lofty, tender, or impassioned conceptions,
with objects and incidents, which the greater part of his readers will
probably persist in thinking low, silly, or uninteresting'.[31] Wordsworth's impassioned lines on God and Nature, once characterized
as 'a tissue of moral and devotional ravings',[32] were now
welcomed, because of their very lack of doctrinal specificity, as

profound explorations of spiritual mysteries. Even his formal, metrical experiments had been revalued. An 'open violation of the established laws of poetry', Francis Jeffrey called them, which encouraged others to 'lawless outrage and excess'.[33] No such condemnation is heard in the 1830s. In so far as commentators mentioned the lyrical experiments at all, they tended to take at face value Wordsworth's own assertion in the Preface to *Lyrical Ballads* and the *Poems* of 1815 that the revivifying of poetry at which he aimed entailed wrenching it free from prevailing notions of poetic diction and literary decorum.

Not everyone, of course, joined in the swelling anthem. At the second reading of Lord Mahon's Copyright Bill on 6 April 1842, Thomas Wakley, Coroner for West Middlesex and MP for Finsbury, delivered a long speech. Wakley, founder of *The Lancet* and a champion of medical reform, was a courageous, humane man, but he had little time for the pretensions of literary people, and after declaiming some of Wordsworth's lyrics, he declared, 'I myself could string such compositions together by the bushel, I could write them by the mile'.[34] Laughter in the House, but not much in the country. Wakley was used to battling against popular opinion, but even he can hardly have expected the storm of chastisement and lampooning that blew up. What he said would barely have raised an eyebrow when the judgement of the *Edinburgh Review* prevailed, but Wakley was out of touch with what had been happening to Wordsworth's reputation in the previous decade. The penalty was that he was treated as if he had been caught defacing a national monument.

When his career had been at its nadir, Wordsworth had written that a true poet must labour on, 'cheered by encouragement from a grateful few, by applauding Conscience, and by a prophetic anticipation, perhaps, of fame—a late though lasting consequence'.[35] Various kinds of evidence attest the nature and extent of the fame he lived to enjoy in his last fifteen years.

The most important evidence from the literary historian's point of view was not at the time the most visible. It was not until later in the century that it became clear that the Wordsworth who had become a national monument continued to claim readers as a vital force and to influence seminally those who were to become intellectual forces themselves. Wordsworth, in short, mattered to such as Elizabeth Gaskell, Charles Kingsley, Tennyson, Matthew

Arnold, Ruskin, even Charles Darwin, who as a young man read *The Excursion* twice with high enthusiasm.

There is the evidence of public tribute in other people's books. The most famous, certainly the most significant in view of Ruskin's later importance, is the epigraph to the first volume of *Modern Painters* in 1843: one of the Wanderer's loftiest declarations about Nature and Truth from *The Excursion* (Book IV. 978–92). William Whewell's *Elements of Morality*, is less famous now than *Modern Painters*, but in its time it was quite as weighty, and it too was dedicated to Wordsworth.[36]

Dedication, however unsought or even unwanted by the dedicatee, is never a one-way transaction. Acknowledgements in substantial work such as Ruskin's or Whewell's, where the affinity between Wordsworth and the dedicated book is strong and evident, disclose the author's intellectual indebtedness, but they also confer something on the dedicatee. As Wordsworth put it rather pompously on receiving Whewell's work, the transaction was 'honourable to both parties'.[37] Even dedications such as the one by John Peace mentioned earlier share in this cultural transaction. A minor figure he certainly was, but Peace added his groatsworth to the dissemination of Wordsworth's name and of the image of Wordsworth as a giant among the living.

So it was with quotation. I want to exemplify deliberately from an obscure example, precisely because it is the intention of this chapter to indicate just how widely Wordsworth was being promoted into visibility. Many 'Wordsworthians'—the revealing title was in general use by the 1830s—are well-known names. Many, however, are only footnotes to cultural history, yet in their day they made an impact. Take the work of Gideon Mantell.

Mantell was no Darwin, but in his lifetime he was respected as a proven medical researcher, as a geologist, and as a writer with a gift for popularizing geology. He was elected Fellow of the Royal Society in 1825 and held other distinguished offices. In the 'Concluding Remarks' to his most successful book, *The Wonders of Geology* (1838), which went through ten editions, Mantell affirmed his conviction that there is an indissoluble bond between 'enduring love and admiration for natural knowledge' and 'that intellectual light, which once kindled can never be extinguished, and which reveal to the soul the beauty, and wisdom, and harmony of the works of the Eternal'. The first edition ends with a quotation from

Felicia Hemans's *To the Poet Wordsworth*. For the 1839 reissue, however, Mantell revised his conclusion. Here, after a sentence about 'inexhaustible fields of inquiry' which may 'prove a never-failing source of the most pure and elevated gratification', which is itself full of echoes of *Tintern Abbey*, Mantell quotes ten lines from the poem (126–35), the hymn to Nature which attests the poet's 'chearful faith, that all which we behold | Is full of blessings'.[38]

The transaction was mutually beneficial. The quotation from Wordsworth reassured any nervous reader that this scientific work was in no way irreligious; on the contrary, that the overall significance of these facts and diagrams could be summed up in a poet's 'prayer'. It also, however, served to insert Wordsworth into the world of science. Although professedly a popular book, the two-volume *Wonders of Geology* is, like many another nineteenth-century 'popular' book, dense with evidence and argument. It is clearly written by an expert. By quoting *Tintern Abbey* Mantell implied that poetic utterance is evidence, too, that Wordsworth has something to offer the man of science.

I am not suggesting, of course, that Mantell was consciously claiming Wordsworth as an ally. Other contemporaries, however, were and their desire to recruit the poet, so to speak, is further testimony to his standing in the early years of Victoria's reign. On 7 November 1844, for example, Archdeacon Thomas Thorp, President of the Cambridge Camden Society, the ecclesiological group founded in 1839, declared of their visitor that 'He (Mr Wordsworth), might be considered one of the founders of the Society. He had sown the seed which was branching out now among them, as in other directions, to the recall of whatever was pure and imaginative, whatever was not merely utilitarian, to the service of both Church and State.'[39]

There were those, on the other hand, who believed that the elderly poet could exercise most beneficial influence in the temporal sphere. In 1845 Hugh Seymour Tremenheere, an Inspector of Schools and assistant Poor Law Commissioner, approached Wordsworth with a request. The letter is such an exemplary early Victorian document that it deserves generous quotation. Telling the poet that he has arranged for him to receive various official papers on the condition of the labouring poor, Tremenheere launches into an essay:

All the Educational and General Inquiries of late years, into the state of the labouring classes, prove convincingly that one of the most effective means towards ameliorating even the physical condition of the poor, is to afford them the opportunity of having their minds opened by a more enlarged and useful, as well as their hearts affected by a religious education. They want more than ever an increase of intelligence, to enable them to cope with the increasing difficulties of their condition, arising from the constant multiplication of their numbers and the altered relations of modern society. And in my opinion the state of the agricultural labourers in many parts of the country presents quite as formidable considerations regarding the future peace of the Kingdom, as that of the lower classes in our large towns.

I am well aware that no one is more alive to these matters than yourself. May I take the liberty of adding that an impulse might be given to the serious consideration of them, by a few words from yourself.

In 1816, in the Advertisement to the Thanksgiving Ode, you expressed a wish that 'knowledge, civil, moral, and religious,' might be improved 'in such measure that the mind, among all classes of the community, might love, admire, and be prepared to defend that country under whose protection its faculties have been unfolded, and its riches acquired.' The 'martial spirit' which was then under your consideration, has not declined; but the deficiency or utter blank of all knowledge 'civil, moral, or religious,' among large masses of the community, has since that time become more glaring and more dangerous.

Having hinted at his request, Tremenheere now makes it explicit. He has heard, he says, that Wordsworth is proposing to issue a volume of selections:

May I so far presume to say that, (if you have not already acted on a similar idea,) an addition, however brief, in prose or verse, embodying your present impressions on the subject of elementary education for the lower classes, would be of much value, and would greatly help to increase that growing sense of responsibility, which has been so long in abeyance among those whose positions, whether as Landlords or Manufacturers, make them answerable to a great extent for the condition of the lower clasees on their estates or in their neighbourhoods. Happily, your voice is now more and more listened to; and (permit me to add) you may feel conscious that it will be more so yet. A word or two from you, in the present stage of public opinion on this subject, would not, I am sure, be in vain.

Half a century of so-called progress, marked by the uncontrolled growth of industrialization, commerce, and colonization, has degraded the lower orders:

This degradation is a source of danger, and a disgrace. The force of mind which has enabled the upper classes to do so much, would find no difficulty, if it would set about it in a Christian spirit, in aiding the lower classes to place themselves in a position, mentally, morally, and physically, more in harmony with the present requirements of civilized life, and therefore in a safer state in regard to the interests of the upper classes and of society in general. These notions, I venture to believe, are not far from an accordance with your own.[40]

Tremenheere's sentiments are not surprising. His letter is an identikit portrait of the spectres which haunted the middle class throughout the 1840s and 1850s—recognition that the benefits of 'progress' have been unevenly distributed; acknowledgement that the higher orders have selfishly neglected their duties; conviction that physical improvement in the condition of the poor is not enough by itself to bring about genuine amelioration; fear that the ever-multiplying masses, in the country as well as the towns, will soon threaten social order unless their lot is improved. What is surprising is that these sentiments should have been voiced in an appeal to a 75-year-old *poet*.

Tremenheere was no crank. During thirty years of public service, largely as a commissioner on various boards of inquiry, he reported on schools, the state of the mining population, conditions in certain trades, the employment of women and children in agriculture, and so on.[41] By 1845 he had already investigated at first hand the state of schools in England and Wales, the administration of the 1834 Poor Law, and the living and working conditions amongst miners. Unlike Disraeli, who plundered Blue-Books for *Sybil* in 1845, Tremenheere made his assessment of the 'Two Nations' from first-hand knowledge, being one of the writers in fact of the kind of reports Disraeli used. Nothing in these grim documents would lead one to suppose that their authors might see a role for poetry as an instrument in social regeneration. And yet Tremenheere wrote to Wordsworth.

He was responding to an idea of Wordsworth which had been gaining currency since the 1830s. It was strengthened by the unexpected resurrection in 1838 of an important early Wordsworth document. On 14 January 1801 Wordsworth had written to Charles James Fox, drawing his attention to *Michael* and *The Brothers* in the second edition of *Lyrical Ballads*, on the grounds that the poems contributed to contemporary debate about the condition of the poor.[42] This letter, however, had a second life, when Sir Henry Edward Bunbury edited *The Correspondence of Sir Thomas Hanmer, Bart.* and in it not only included Wordsworth's letter to Fox but emphasized its importance in his preface. In a note to Wordsworth apologizing for having acted without permission, Sir Henry explained that he had acquired the letter through his first wife, who was Fox's niece, and that he had for over twenty years 'been accustomed to turn to it with undiminished pleasure' as a wise statement 'with regard to the condition of our labouring classes'.[43]

The date is significant. Southey's Jacobinical play of 1794, *Wat Tyler*, surfaced in 1817 to his great embarrassment, he now being an outspoken Tory, but Wordsworth's letter to Fox was no such spectre. When it was broadcast with Sir Henry's earnest commendation, it was generally agreed, in the chilling words that open Carlyle's *Chartism* (1839), 'that the condition and disposition of the Working Classes is a rather ominous matter at present'. But Wordsworth had anticipated Carlyle some years earlier in the 'Postscript' to *Yarrow Revisited*, where he questions the 1834 Poor Law and the unfeeling application of 'systems of political economy', and argues that the Act throughout 'proceeds too much upon the presumption that it is a labouring man's own fault if he be not, as the phrase is, beforehand with the world'.[44] What Sir Henry's disclosure of Wordsworth's early views revealed—or rather, confirmed—is that however much Wordsworth's political complexion may have altered since *Lyrical Ballads*, his radical humanitarianism had remained constant.

Keble fostered this image of Wordsworth as the poet for the times when he praised him in the 1839 Creweian Oration for exhibiting 'the manners, the pursuits, and the feelings, religious and traditional, of the poor', and in the dedication to his Oxford *Lectures on Poetry*, for championing 'the cause of the poor and simple'.[45] But the image was fostered too by the poet himself. Commenting on his topical poem, *The Warning*, he declares himself to be more troubled by the complexion of contemporary social affairs than at any time since the Napoleonic war and claims the right to speak about issues touching 'the poor & humbly employed' among whom 'the greater part of his life has been passed'.[46] Wordsworth's last separate collection, *Poems, Chiefly of Early and Late Years* (1842), was presented overtly as a contribution towards social healing, at a time,

When unforeseen distress spreads far and wide
Among a People mournfully cast down,
Or into anger roused by venal words
In recklessness thrown out to overturn
The judgement, and divert the general heart
From mutual good . . .[47]

When these words were published, Chartism was a force manifesting itself in many ways, all of them threatening, and reports into conditions of employment for some of the labouring masses had indicated the source of its energies. In July 1842 the *Manchester Times* reported that 'hungry and half-clothed men and women are stalking through the streets begging for bread'. Their distress might well be the result of the operation of the 'laws' of Political Economy, but as individuals they served to witness none the less to a breakdown in society that had no precedent. And it was precisely because the visible phenomena of distress were so bewilderingly widespread and various, that Wordsworth was heeded. The touchstone of his radical humanitarianism, the assertion in *The Old Cumberland Beggar* 'That we have all of us one human heart', pointed to a truth deeper than those of Political Economy, namely, that beneath the economic and social *malaise* lay a deeper *malaise* still. Men had lost sight of that mutuality of respect and concern which was fundamental to social coherence in a rapidly changing age.

It became, in fact, commonplace to declare that Wordsworth's poetry serves 'to break down . . . the conventional barriers that, in our disordered social state, divide rich and poor into two hostile nations'.[48] In 1846, for example, George Dawson claimed that by

drawing lessons of wisdom and instruction from the poor; by showing that amongst the poor there often dwell noble souls; by putting into the lips of men, externally mean, sentences and sentiments of wisdom; this great poet has done much to overthrow the mere vulgar respect for rank, which inquires not often whether that rank be sustained and supported by true nobility.[49]

One commonplace has replaced another. To Shelley, Keats, Byron, and Hazlitt, Wordsworth had been the lost leader, who had betrayed his early radicalism. By the 1840s the circumstances against which his apostasy had been measured had so changed that to the new generation political apostasy mattered less than the evidence, consistently threaded throughout his work, that Wordsworth was 'a leader in that grandest movement of modern times, care for our humbler bretheren; his part being not to help them in their suffering, but to make us reverence them, for what they have in common with us, or in greater measure than ourselves'.[50]

For the poet celebrated as a prophet for the age and honoured for a lifetime's commitment to his art, one final honour remained. On the death of Southey in 1843 Wordsworth was appointed Poet Laureate. On the face of it there is little to be said about a gift from one's sovereign. It is clearly an honour. The stately *pas de deux* which took place over the appointment, however, is amusing and quite revealing. On 30 March 1843 Lord De La Warr, the Lord Chamberlain, sent Wordsworth a gracious letter offering him the Laureateship, declaring that he was glad to be able to 'propose this mark of distinction on an Individual whose acceptance of it would shed an additional lustre upon an Office in itself highly honourable'. This can have come as little surprise to Wordsworth, even though he had received a letter a day or two before from John Kenyon, retailing the London gossip that Campbell and Tennyson were also contenders. He replied at once that he was too old for the duties of the post. On 3 April the Lord Chamberlain expressed his unfeigned regret and assured Wordsworth that the Laureate's duties, now nominal, would not be allowed to interfere with his 'habits of country retirement'. At this juncture the Prime Minister, Sir Robert Peel, joined in, with a personal letter undertaking that 'you shall have *nothing* required of you', and emphasizing that it was the Queen's wish that he should be appointed.[51] Wordsworth could no longer refuse. But he had established that it was he who was conferring lustre on the Laureateship, not the other way round, and that he had accepted only because it was his sovereign's conviction that as long as he lived no one else could claim the title of preeminent national poet.

III

An Image for Posterity

After Wordsworth's death on 23 April 1850 three events began the process of transmitting an image of Wordsworth for posterity—the appearance of *The Prelude*, the publication of the official biography, and the erection of public monuments.

The Prelude, or Growth of a Poet's Mind had been long awaited. Wordsworth had completed a thirteen-book version in 1805 and had revealed its existence in the Preface to *The Excursion* in 1814. There he informed readers that his autobiographical work was preparatory to a philosophical project, *The Recluse*, and that it would not be published until that work (of which *The Excursion* was a part) was complete. Even as *The Recluse* became increasingly unrealizable Wordsworth stuck to his position, though he could not resist excerpting passages from the unpublished *Prelude* for separate publication from time to time. Towards the end of his life it was common knowledge, bewailed by his admirers, that Wordsworth was withholding a substantial poem for posthumous publication. Once they were empowered, his executors did not delay. The latest revised manuscript, now in fourteen books, was rushed through the press and published on 27 July.

Although it was overshadowed by the instant success of *In Memoriam* in the same year, *The Prelude* made an impact.[52] A few readers saw at once that the most interesting aspect of the poem was its politics. Macaulay concluded with disgust that they explained the poem's posthumous publication: 'The plain truth is that he wrote it when he was a Jacobin and was ashamed to print it after he became an exciseman. He goes all the lengths of Thelwall or Tom Paine.' Making the plain truth even plainer in his journal, he declared: 'The poem is to the last degree Jacobinical, indeed Socialist.'[53] The *Examiner* agreed, only it marked these tendencies to Wordsworth's credit. Despite patronage and puffing 'by the champions of old abuses', Wordsworth remained 'the child and champion of Jacobinism . . . Even in the ranks of our opponents Wordsworth has been labouring in our behalf.' Insights like these, however, were rare. Most reviewers simply praised in general terms: 'sustained interest and great, we had almost said unequalled, beauty' (*Fraser's*); 'among the most remarkable poems in our language' (*British Quarterly*); 'continuous power and richness of expression' (*Prospective Review*); 'exquisite beauty' (*North American Review*). *The Prelude* was absorbed without damaging shock to the prevailing image of the lately dead, great poet.[54]

Simple explanations for this come to mind readily enough. Reading a fourteen-book poem let alone assessing its full significance

takes a lot of time and not even the most conscientious reviewers
can be expected to have made the effort. Wordsworthians tend to
regard the publication of *The Prelude* as one of the most important
literary events of the nineteenth century, but readers in 1850 who
bought *David Copperfield*, or *Alton Locke* or *In Memoriam* can be
forgiven for thinking otherwise, not least because there had been so
much Wordsworth recently. With editions in 1845, 1847, 1849
(two different editions), Moxon exploited Wordsworth's late fame
to the full. The market was not yet saturated as the next decades
would show, but a Wordsworth publication was not a rare event.

Two more substantial factors, however, need to be taken into
account. The first is that by 1850 general perception of Wordsworth
had settled into a form that would not easily be shaken. Once he
had been attacked as a dangerous radical. Later he was denigrated
as an apostate. Wordsworth's politics had mattered to Francis
Jeffrey and to Shelley, Byron, and Hazlitt. And they continued to
occupy that Victorian survival from the Romantic era, De Quincey,
who made them in 1845 the centre-piece of one of the finest critical
essays published in Wordsworth's lifetime.[55] But, as has already
been suggested, to most other older admirers, who had outlived
alarums and excursions about Napoleon, and to the younger
generation who had not known them, what Wordsworth's politics
were at the end of the previous century was of little moment. His
early poetry was comprehensively de-historicized—*Lyrical Ballads*
was rightly viewed by Jeffrey as subversive, but by the 1840s the
early poems were being read as universal statements of a Christian's
humanitarian duty—and the later poems caused no difficulty to
those who wanted to believe that humanitarianism was all that
Wordsworth's politics had ever amounted to. His poetics, of
course, were a different matter. No one doubted that Wordsworth
had lofty views on Imagination and the power of poetry, but these,
it was understood, tended to direct the mind to regions of truth
higher than politics. When Keble hymned Wordsworth as one who
'whether he discoursed on Man or Nature failed not to lift up the
heart to holy things [and] tired not of maintaining the cause of the
poor and simple', couching his tribute in generalities which no one
would want to quibble with, he summarized and added strength to
a construction of Wordsworth as prophet and teacher which
prevailed until well into the next century.[56]

The second factor is that nothing in *The Prelude* threatened

Keble's assessment. It could be put more positively—the fourteen-book poem, being published in 1850, strongly reinforced it. For what was the story of the 'Growth of a Poet's Mind' which *The Prelude* had to tell? A story of one of God's elect—artistically speaking—who is beguiled out of his proper sphere, betrayed by the ardour of his youthful humanitarianism into the delusion that politics might bring about a new, juster world. From this delusion he is rescued by Nature and human love, emerging more fitted for high endeavour in his proper sphere, the realm of the imagination, precisely because he has been tested.

Had readers in 1850 been able to pull off their shelves *Salisbury Plain* (1793–4), *A Letter to the Bishop of Llandaff* (1793), Wordsworth's letters to William Mathews of 1794–5, and the *Imitation of Juvenal* (1795–6), they might have felt less comfortable about *The Prelude*'s account of history and politics. But they could only judge on the published evidence, which indicated that barely out of university Wordsworth had published two loco-descriptive poems in 1793 and that nothing of any value had followed until 1798, when in the first edition of *Lyrical Ballads* he had presented his claim to be the poet of the humble and lowly. Careful readers of *Biographia Literaria* (1817) with long memories would know that Wordsworth had written something in that gap which had deeply impressed Coleridge, a poem set on Salisbury Plain, and in 1842 they might have thought they could read it when Wordsworth published *Guilt and Sorrow; or, Adventures on Salisbury Plain*. What in fact he issued was a version of this early poem so altered that it revealed nothing about the radicalism of Wordsworth's thought after 1793, despite being presented by the poet as a work largely of biographical interest only.[57] Now *The Prelude* explained the missing years. Between 1793 and 1798, when he discovered that God had destined him for Art not Politics, Wordsworth was being tested. Nothing in Wordsworth's later life or writings known to the public might suggest that more could be said about Wordsworth's radical years. That *The Prelude* (1850) is a variant on the familiar narrative pattern of transgression and salvation, made it easy to assimilate. As far as contemporary readers were concerned, it also fitted the known facts.

The authorized biography published in 1851 disclosed nothing that might unsettle a comfortable view of the Poet Laureate. The production of the *Memoirs of William Wordsworth* by the poet's nephew, Dr Christopher Wordsworth, Canon of Westminster, caused a good deal of family friction. Although he had been the poet's choice for whatever biographical writing might be thought expedient after his death, he was very busy with church politics at a time of crisis, and there was some doubt about his fitness for the task. Wordsworth's son-in-law Edward Quillinan, himself a poet and writer, certainly felt slighted not to have been asked and for a while it was questionable whether he would co-operate in gathering materials. Christopher Wordsworth also muddied the waters by negotiating with his own publisher John Murray rather than Moxon, whose long-term stability he doubted, until he was checked by a severe rebuke from the executors. But none of this showed in 1851. Issued from the familiar publishing house, the two-volume *Memoirs* told their story with a massive display of authority. Christopher Wordsworth printed an autobiographical memorandum dictated by the poet in his seventy-seventh year, quoted from Wordsworth's previously unpublished commentary on his whole *œuvre*, referred to and excerpted extensively from unpublished letters and of course emphasized that he was a member of the family writing with its *imprimatur*.[58] A surprising amount of biographical information was already in circulation, but all previous accounts of the poet's life looked flimsy, or evidently partial, compared with this solid presentation of documents and verified evidence.[59]

Up to a point this impression was true. As literary criticism the *Memoirs* are nugatory. Mary Wordsworth privately observed that 'C.W. knew less of W's poetry than almost any of her aquaintance, & his wife nothing at all',[60] and the biography bears out her suspicion. Christopher Wordsworth declares that his uncle had interdicted any 'critical review of his Poems . . . or exposition of the principles on which those Poems were composed', but even so the absence of any literary sensibility in the organization of the volumes is astonishing. But as an account of the Life and Works the *Memoirs* are substantial and their mass of documentary material was to be pillaged by all other writers of introductions and biographical notices for the next twenty years. Although Christopher Wordsworth effaced himself as literary commentator, however, there was nothing neutral about his presentation of his uncle's life and opinions. At the outset he made clear what the premises were which would determine the presentation of these materials. His uncle's works, he declared, 'must be taken as a whole', it being 'very unjust and erroneous to cite any one poem, or a few lines, composed in his earlier years, as a deliberate expression of his maturer judgement'. All of the poet's works, moreover, in verse and prose 'must be read with habitual reference to the time in which they were composed'.[61] In practice these propositions licensed an extremely tendentious biography. Under their aegis whatever was disconcerting could be explained away either as an aberration attributable to historical context, or as an aberration which becomes insignificant once glossed by the poet's maturer reflections.

Not surprisingly this tendentiousness is most marked in the narrative of the poet's radical years. In a two-volume work of sixty-four chapters just two are devoted to 1791–5. In them it is not disguised that Wordsworth espoused republican theories, but what is emphasized is that they were only theories; that he always abhorred violence; that the republican phase soon passed, leaving only a lifelong commitment to justice and truth. The reader is assured, moreover, that however close the idealistic youth came to despair, he never 'lapsed into scepticism. No! His early education, his love of the glories and beauties of creation protected him from any approach to that.'[62]

The tendentiousness of this account of Wordsworth's radical years was to a large extent hidden from its readers, for the reason already given, namely, that they could not read the *Letter to the Bishop of Llandaff*, for example, or the early *Salisbury Plain*. Another area of tendentiousness, however, was more obvious to contemporaries. Quillinan, a Roman Catholic, found the whole biography 'poisoned' by 'Dr. C.W.'s High Church Dogmatism', and it is not difficult to see why,[63] As Christopher Wordsworth was writing, the Church of England was reeling from self-inflicted wounds and from perceived attack from without. Barely had the wretched business of the Gorham Case been settled to no one's full satisfaction when the onslaught of 'Papal Aggression' was felt. The Prime Minister, Lord John Russell, had written his ill-advised letter to the Bishop of Durham about the Catholic threat and Christopher Wordsworth himself had preached on the topic in Westminster.[64] Possibly the exposition of Wordsworth's opinions in the *Memoirs* would have been the same without these national events focusing opinion on the Catholic Question, but they can hardly have been

out of the biographer's mind as he sifted through his uncle's
remains. The Wordsworth who emerges is one near-obsessed with
worries about Catholics. Declaring that Wordsworth's opinions on
national subjects are of great importance, Christopher Wordsworth
devotes pages to full quotation of letters—notably to Francis
Wrangham and the Bishop of London—which spell out the poet's
objections to Catholic Emancipation in all its forms and reveal his
concern for the Church of England and Christian education. The
injunction to read everything in the light of historical circumstances
is ignored, as Christopher Wordsworth prints Wordsworth's most
intemperate utterances as if they are the settled opinions of a
lifetime. The Canon of Westminster presents his uncle in his own
image.

This image-making is buttressed by one deliberate act of
exclusion: no mention is made of Annette Vallon and Wordsworth's
illegitimate daughter, Caroline.

Wordsworth's widow, his son-in-law Edward Quillinan, and his
intimate friend Henry Crabb Robinson—at least these all knew
about Annette, but astonishingly his sons did not.[65] Christopher
Wordsworth was thus in an impossible position. Were the sons to
learn now what their father had not chosen to confide in them?
Now that he was a respectable clergyman, John Wordsworth's
position in particular had to be considered. Concealment on the
other hand was risky, even if the offence against the truth could be
justified. The anxiety in family conferences 'as to the expediency of
mentioning a delicate subject in the forthcoming Memoir'[66] was
intensified by receipt of a letter from the French family which had
(or was interpreted as having) a whiff of blackmail.

Christopher Wordsworth wanted to give the facts. He told
Quillinan that as the matter had been mentioned to him casually in
a London street he was certain 'that the *truth will out*'.[67] He was,
moreover, confident that he could present them sympathetically by
dwelling on the youth of the poet, the turbulent situation in France,
and on Wordsworth's responsible attitude to his obligations later in
life.[68] But suppression carried the day. The family's game-plan,
agreed in August 1850, was that he would not mention 'the French
entanglement' unless 'compelled in self defence'.[69] As fears of
French intervention proved unfounded, Annette was not mentioned
in the *Memoirs*, and Christopher Wordsworth even went so far as
to assure readers that the poet 'wrote as he lived, and he lived as he

wrote. . . . It is very necessary that Posterity should be assured of this, in order that it may have a firmer faith in his principles. And no such guarantee can be given of his sincerity in enunciating those principles, and no such evidence can be afforded of their results, as is supplied by the records of his life.'[70] Further evasion was inevitably entailed. Christopher Wordsworth could not mention the reason why Wordsworth visited France in 1802—to settle affairs with Annette prior to his marriage—or that at the end of the European tour of 1820 he stayed in Paris and strolled with Mary, Annette, and Caroline in the Jardin des Plantes.

Only once does Christopher Wordsworth hint at something. During the narrative of Wordsworth's residence in France he comments on the 'very critical' condition of the young man 'inexperienced, impetuous, enthusiastic, with no friendly voice to guide him', in a country in a state of revolution, where,

The most licentious theories were propounded; all restraints were broken; libertinism, if we may so speak, was the received law of society. He was encompassed with strong temptations; and although it is not my design in the present work to chronicle the events of his life, except so far as they illustrate his writings, I cannot forgo a notice of the dangers which surround those who in an ardent emotion of enthusiasm put themselves in a position of peril without due consideration of circumstances of place, time, and person which ought to regulate their practice.

A marginal note in the proof copy of the *Memoirs* now in the Wordsworth Library reads: 'passage much objected to by Mrs W'. Not surprisingly, for it is an open invitation to conjecture.[71] But Christopher Wordsworth dug his heels in, and with only slight changes the passage stayed.

There are, of course, other reticences and questionable emphases in the *Memoirs*, but none so important as the skimpy and tendentious treatment of Wordsworth's life 1790–5, the presentation of him as a die-hard upholder of the National Church, and the exclusion of Annette Vallon. Christopher Wordsworth diminished almost to vanishing point a period of political radicalism which Wordsworth was never completely to disavow. By erasing Annette he also conveyed the impression that Wordsworth's anguish over the course of the French Revolution was entirely a matter of principles and theories, that the Poet had been concerned for Man, but that his own feelings had not in any other way been engaged.

And this suggestion meshes comfortably with the rest of the biography. Wordsworth stands clear as a man of exceptional purity,
whose period of trial, which was itself essentially honourable, only
served to ground him more firmly in principles which he was to
spend the rest of his life expounding. Never a sceptic, his faith
rested in the God who had spoken to him through Nature during
his formative years, and in the (High) Church of England. The
source of his power was contemplation. His influence for good
stemmed from the unity of his life and art. His biographer, one
cannot help suspecting, believes he might have made an excellent,
if unworldly, Bishop.

By finally authorizing the text of his poems in the six-volume
edition of 1849–50 Wordsworth had raised his own monument. By
issuing *The Prelude* and the *Memoirs* his family had raised theirs.
It was inevitable that his friends and admirers would wish to mark
Wordsworth's death in a similarly substantial, public manner.
Within a month of his death the Bishop of London chaired a meeting at the home of Sir John Taylor Coleridge, at which it was
resolved to raise a subscription to 'do honour to the Memory of
William Wordsworth'. An executive committee was formed, which
included Archdeacon Julius Hare, William Butterfield the architect,
Royal Academicians William Dyce and Charles Eastlake, the actor
William Charles Macready, John Ruskin, and other friends of the
poet, and it decided at a meeting on 10 June that the objects of the
subscription were to be:

I To place a whole-length effigy of Wordsworth in Westminster Abbey.
II If possible to erect some monument to his Memory in the neighbourhood of Grasmere, Westmoreland.

The pamphlet in which the aims of the subscription were
announced named the Committee and those who had already made
a donation. They are remarkably weighty lists. The Committee
begins with the Chairman, the Bishop of London, and then mores
through other bishops, peers and baronets, MPs and QCs, the
masters of four Cambridge colleges, professors, artists, and poets.
Arnold and Tennyson are included—and this is just the Committee.
The subscription list is much longer. The Queen and Prince Albert
top the giving with £50. Next comes John Kenyon, whose £25
looks generous against the standard £10 given by such figures as
the Marquis of Landsdowne and William Gladstone. Amongst the

niggardly are Thackeray and Messrs Bradbury and Evans—one guinea apiece. Both lists are roll-calls of a good part of the English establishment, which testify to Wordsworth's standing in the worlds of Church and State.

One entry deserves to be rescued from oblivion. It reads:

William Powell, Esq.	£1	1	0
Mrs. Powell	1	1	0
Master Powell	1	1	0
Miss Powell	1	1	0

Bleak House comes irresistibly to mind. Did Master and Miss Powell have any more choice, one wonders, than Mrs Pardiggle's Egbert, 'who sent out his pocket-money, to the amount of five-and-threepence, to the Tockahoopo Indians', or Alfred, who at five 'voluntarily enrolled himself in the Infant Bonds of Joy, and [was] pledged never, through life, to use tobacco in any form'?

Quarrels and hurt feelings are endemic to such ventures and this one was no exception. A rift opened up between the Lake District faction, headed by Dr John Davy, and the London group, when northern subscribers started to ask for their money back so that it could be devoted to their local cause. But Cumbrian energy got things done. Harriet Martineau's suggestion that the most appropriate monument would be cottages for the poor was brushed aside in favour of a more permanent monument in the only possible place.[72] In August 1851 a profile medallion of Wordsworth by Thomas Woolner was placed in Grasmere Church, and above it the long tribute from Keble's *De Poeticae Vi Medica: Praelectiones Academicae Oxonii Habitae* about Wordsworth, the specially chosen of God.[73] Tennyson growled to Woolner at such needless long-windedness: 'Is Wordsworth a great poet? Well then don't let us talk of him as if he were half known,' but his protest went unheeded.[74] And there was still money available, much of it raised by Wordsworth's American editor, Professor Henry Reed.[75] Two years later a memorial window was dedicated in Gilbert Scott's new church at Ambleside, which recorded this first of many generous American contributions to the poet's honour: 'partim Angli partim Anglo-Americani'.[76]

Events in London did not proceed so briskly. Nine sculptors submitted models. Woolner's plan was for a monument with the poet in the centre on a pedestal, flanked by two groups, 'symbols of the two great principles he strove to inculcate. 1. Control of Passion (Being the basis of LAW) . . . 2. Nature contemplated to the glory of God (Being the basis of RELIGION)'.[77] Front-runner though this ambitious design was, Frederick Thrupp's was preferred—largely, it was rumoured, because he had been prepared to accept almost any fee provided he won the competition—and in disappointment Woolner left for Australia. The competition winner, however, proved dilatory in executing the commission and the effigy was not unveiled until 1854, and only then after unseemly wrangling with the Dean and Chapter of Westminster Abbey about where it was to be placed. Its positioning in the baptistery pleased no one save the sculptor.

The marble statue itself, however, was unexceptionable. Taking the likeness from Haydon's life-mask of the poet, from an 1819 Haydon drawing and from Haydon's *Wordsworth on Helvellyn*, Thrupp's creation conformed to the now well-established tradition of what an image of Wordsworth should be.[78] The poet in middle-age is seated, legs crossed and shoulders rounded a little forwards, in an attitude of intense contemplation. His head is slightly bowed. The whole suggests what Hazlitt had long before identified as most characteristic about Wordsworth: 'It is as if there were nothing but himself and the universe. He lives in the busy solitude of his own heart; in the deep silence of thought.'[79]

All of the major portraits of the poet, in fact, seem to be variations on Hazlitt's observation. Wordsworth on Helvellyn in Haydon's 1842 oil is as craggy and solid as the rocks against which he is placed. But, arms folded and head bowed, he is definitely in contemplative repose. It does not look as if it cost him any effort to get up the mountain. Millais's depiction of Ruskin in his 1853–4 portrait makes a striking contrast. Ruskin stands like a man ready at any minute to stride on and his gaze is outwards, as if he is really taking in the prospect before him. In Pickersgill's 1850–1 full-length oil Wordsworth looks incapable of any effort at all. By placing the poet against a rocky landscape the artist has clearly aimed at something like the effect of *Wordsworth on Helvellyn*, but he has missed the air of contemplative austerity. This elegantly clad and shod, white-haired gentleman, sitting with pencil in hand, looks like an elderly clergyman with a taste for improving verses. None of the extant portraits, save possibly Haydon's of 1818 nicknamed 'The Brigand', conveys any sense of the Wordsworth who walked over two thousand miles across Europe, taking in the Alps on the way, who climbed Snowdon at the dead of night, and who had, when Hazlitt met him, 'a convulsive inclination to laughter about the mouth'.[80]

2

England's Samuel: Wordsworth as Spiritual Power

A great poet ... ought to a certain degree to rectify men's feelings, to give them new compositions of feeling, to render their feelings more sane, pure and permanent, in short more consonant to nature, that is to eternal nature, and the great moving spirit of things. He ought to travel before men occasionally as well as at their side.

I

England's Samuel

In a sonnet entitled *Poets are Nature's Priests* the anti-slavery campaigner Thomas Pringle likened Wordsworth to Samuel.[1] Just as Israel, misled by Phineas and Hophni, mocked its priests and profaned its God, so England has erred from the path of righteousness. But God's voice can still be heard:

> Men highly privileged are prone to ill:
> Yet Israel then had SAMUEL—we have WORDSWORTH still.

It is an arresting claim, that Wordsworth was chosen by God to be an instrument for the salvation of His people, but not an uncommon one. Pringle was unusual in tracing the poet's Old Testament lineage so directly, but not at all unusual in celebrating the priest of Nature as a source of spiritual power.

Spiritual power is an almost infinitely elastic term and what people found in, or constructed from Wordsworth, differed greatly. Quakers thought him a Quaker. Anglo-Catholics hailed him as one of themselves. For others it was precisely because it resisted all sectarian labelling that Wordsworth's poetry was so nutritious. But what links all the numerous tributes is the conviction, born of first-hand experience, that Wordsworth—both the work and the example of the life—was a spiritually active, empowering force. With the decline in his reputation in the 1860s, the first, energetic phase of the construction of Wordsworth ended,[2] but an image had been created which persisted, challenging revision or refinement from those who contributed to the extraordinary Wordsworth renaissance later in the century. That first phase is the subject of this chapter.

II

Four Witnesses

In his *Reminiscences* William Charles Macready recalled how he first became acquainted with Wordsworth. Around the supper table in their lodgings, he and the other boarders joined in a 'depreciating chorus' about his poetry. Only one of the party defended it, and all he could remember to quote in evidence was the last line of the Westminster Bridge sonnet—'And all that mighty heart is lying still!' But it was enough. Thrilled by the line, the young Macready at once 'purchased the poet's works, and, reading them was converted to an enthusiastic love of his writings, ever after being eager to acknowledge my gratitude to him for having made me in some respects a wiser, and excited in me the aspiration to become a better man'.[3]

Looking back as a celebrated actor to his tyro days in the green room and theatrical boarding houses, Macready singles out a moment when he was 'converted'. Not just impressed or moved, but converted. Life divides into before and after Wordsworth. And, as with all converts, Macready feels the obligation laid on him by gratitude to bear witness. The power that converted him remained a force in his life, endowing him with wisdom and the humility to want to be a better man. Aptly recalling *The Ancient Mariner*, Macready pin-points the moment when he was unexpectedly held by another's power and his life changed.

Macready, 'eager to acknowledge [his] gratitude', serves to introduce the main concerns of the first part of this chapter. Other reminiscences might have been chosen, for his was only one testimony amongst many. Differing substantially in how they characterize the nature and the effect of the power they acknowledge, they agree broadly in their language of gratitude and in their affirmation. Wordsworth's poetry, they declare, was a beneficial agent in their lives, not just a source of pleasure, a superior pastime, but a transforming power and a force for good.

In 1835 Wordsworth received a letter from Sir William Gomm, which read in part:

Some years have passed, My Dear Sir, since I first made Acquaintance with your Writings.—It was when I was other than I am today; in a season when I bore about a bleeding heart; stricken with the heaviest Calamity that can befal our Nature.—It was my good Angel, I believe, that prompted me to open your Volumes, and breathed in me a presentiment that in them I might find my balm. They were my Companions in a lonely Pilgrimage over the North of Germany;—undertaken mainly, because I found rest intolerable;—and if you could see those Weather-worn Volumes;—how they are scarr'd about with my pencil-marks where passages delighted me through immeasurable portions of them;—but particularly in that invaluable and most glorious portion of the Excursion 'Despondency Corrected':—you would there discover better than I shall ever find words to express to you whether I owe them a Debt or not.—[4]

Sir William Maynard Gomm (1784–1875), son of a lieutenant-colonel who was killed in action, was gazetted ensign in the army, in honour of his father, before he was 10 years old. He fought in the Peninsula War under Wellington, served under Sir John Moore at Corunna, was wounded twice and saw action in all of the major Peninsula campaigns, distinguishing himself particularly at Salamanca. In 1815, now decorated and knighted, Gomm fought in the battles of Quatre Bras and Waterloo. Eventually he became Commander-in-Chief in India and rose to Field Marshal. He received an honorary degree from Oxford five years earlier than Wordsworth. Despite being on campaign more or less continuously for fifteen years, Gomm wrote excellent letters and much poetry. The sonnet he composed on revisiting the battlefield at Waterloo in 1868, which was published in his *Letters and Journals*, demonstrates a high level of accomplishment.[5] After first meeting Wordsworth in the early 1830s, he regularly sent him verse for comment.

An exceptional man, but Gomm's need when he found Wordsworth was one felt by most human beings at some point in their lives. As an orphan, Gomm was brought up with his brother and sister by an aunt and her friend, a Miss Goldsworthy, to both of whom, as his letters home indicate, he was devoted. Having survived fifteen years of war, however, Gomm was battered immediately after the peace by a series of deaths. He lost first his brother in 1816, then his dearly-loved sister the following year. Both his surrogate parents were dead by 1822 and his wife died in 1827. Mourning, alone, and without immediately pressing occupation, Gomm looked for relief to the great Romantic resource, travel, and to poetry for spiritual nourishment.

It is impossible to say, of course, precisely or confidently what Gomm found in Wordsworth, but both the language of his testimony and what it explicitly points to give some idea. The letter uses the language of religion, but stops short of religion itself. Employing the trope common to all Christian witness literature, Gomm records that it was providence which led him to the comfort he most needed, when he most needed it. Even in his darkest hour, his 'good Angel' was watching over his destiny, guiding him to a boon which suffering had fitted him to receive. But although couched in religious terms, the letter does not gesture towards the Bible or revealed religion. Whereas Frances Ogle, in the letter quoted in Chapter 1, flutteringly invokes 'the Fount of Life itself' as the ultimate spiritual resource of even a Wordsworth devotee, Gomm does not.

By acknowledging particular indebtedness to the fourth book of *The Excursion*, 'Despondency Corrected', moreover, Gomm was focusing on just that part of Wordsworth's *œuvre* which caused some Christians most anxiety. In Book III the Solitary relates how suffering, in particular the loss of his wife and two children, brought him to his present state, a melancholy recluse among the mountains. Book IV consists of the Wanderer's struggle to raise him from despondency. Nothing can sustain us, he avers, but absolute faith in the divine order, submission to duty, and attention to conscience. What rouses the Wanderer to eloquence, however, is the attempt to reawaken the Solitary's imaginative response to the natural beauty surrounding him. Whether it be 'Chaldean Shepherds, ranging trackless fields, | Beneath the concave of unclouded skies', or the 'lonely herdsman' seeing in 'the blazing chariot of the sun, | A beardless Youth, who touched a golden lute, | And filled the illumined groves with ravishment', Man has always found in Nature, the Wanderer declares, intimations of divinity. When we are deaf to all other voices, Nature's 'inarticulate language' can still speak to us.[6]

The Wanderer's theology is capacious enough to have pleased

even Keats, who loved passages in this book above all the rest of the poem.[7] It views pagans kindly and does not invoke Christ, revelation, or doctrine. James Montgomery was justified in observing when *The Excursion* first appeared: 'We do not mean to infer, that Mr. Wordsworth excludes from his system the salvation of man, as revealed in the Scriptures, but it is evident that he has not made "Jesus Christ the chief corner-stone" of it.'[8] But this is why so many, like Gomm, found in *The Excursion* the balm they sought. Nothing in it was incompatible with Christianity, but here was consolation, spiritual counsel, and imaginative succour unattached to doctrine or sect.

To many readers Wordsworth's poetry offered not quite a substitute for religion but an alternative realm in which religious sensibilities could operate. Compassion towards the humble, reverence for the primary affections of our nature, life as a term of trial in which our souls are formed, beauty in the meanest thing, the spirituality of the universe—all of these religious *topoi* are stressed in lyric and dramatic forms which quicken imagination and emotion by investing incidents of everyday life with a spiritual aura. Response to Wordsworth's 'sense sublime | Of something far more deeply interfused, | Whose dwelling is the light of setting suns', required no understanding of, or assent to, the doctrine of the Incarnation.[9]

As far as John Stuart Mill was concerned the transcendental aspects of the poetry were of no account. Describing himself as 'one who has, not thrown off religious belief, but never had it', Mill was prepared to dismiss the 'mysticism', the talk of 'holding communion with the great forms of nature ... finding a grandeur in the beatings of the heart & so forth' as 'nonsense'.[10] Yet Mill, too, witnessed to Wordsworth's saving power.

His testimony in his *Autobiography* is made in a work that is in many ways remarkably akin to *The Prelude*.[11] Both autobiographies are retrospects, drawn up when their subjects were anxious as to their future direction. Mill and Wordsworth had already established themselves. When *The Prelude* was completed in 1805, *Lyrical Ballads* had gone through four editions. Mill had published *A System of Logic* (1843), *Essays on Some Unsettled Questions of Political Economy* (1844), and *Principles of Political Economy* (1848), when he composed the first version of the *Autobiography* in 1853–4. But both writers were in an uncertain period when they formally took stock of their lives. Looking back, *The Prelude* and the *Autobiography* identify a moment in the past when outside agencies intervened to redirect momentum which had stalled. Both autobiographies, moreover, though undergoing revision in the subject's lifetime, were published posthumously, and so were received into an intellectual milieu quite different from what it would have been had they been published when first written.

Mill's *Autobiography* also resembles *The Prelude* in another important respect. It is an act of self-understanding and self-projection, and as with all such documents its evasions and omissions are as revealing as its emphases and inclusions. For Mill's biographers its silences and hesitancies are, of course, eloquent. It has been argued that Mill's detailed account of how much his father put into his education masks his anger at being so controlled that even his career was determined for him. Another scholar has discerned within the *Autobiography*'s apparently 'unquestioning acceptance of his role as a speculative thinker', an 'uneasy recognition of the marginality of the theoretical thinker in Victorian society', while another, as a historian, finds it necessary to supplement the *Autobiography* substantially in attempting to give a balanced account of the context of Mill's earliest public activities.[12] Such considerations, however, fundamental though they must be to any biographical account of John Stuart Mill, are not relevant to this chapter. For once narrative testimony can be taken at face value, since the concern of this study is with what individuals claimed to find in Wordsworth, not with what those claims may reveal about their psychology if assessed against other evidence.

In the opening chapters of the *Autobiography* Mill chronicles the progress of his education from the age of 3. It is an astonishing narrative, which his father, James Mill, might have commended, not only because of what it witnesses—the success of a project to shape a reasoning machine—but because of the manner of its witness. It is a dry, sequential account of intellectual ascent. When feelings are mentioned, love and fear for example, it is because Mill has something to say about their place in an ideal scheme of education, not because he wishes to evoke with any Dickensian intensity particular moments of love or fear. Mill's mother is barely mentioned. From Greek to Arithmetic, Latin, History, Logic, Political Economy, Law, the narrative proceeds through childhood and youth to its first climax, when Bentham's exposition of the 'principle of utility' illuminates the vista of the young Mill's future. It 'fell exactly into its place as the keystone which held together the detached and fragmentary portions of my knowledge and beliefs. It gave unity to my conceptions of things. I now had opinions; a creed, a doctrine, a philosophy; in one (and the best) sense of the word, a religion' (p. 68).

Mill's narrative so far is a triumphant one, which acknowledges fully what his father had given him. Reservations are expressed about James Mill's methods and about his self-inflicted emotional mutilation, and also about the neglect of imaginative culture in his educational programme, but nothing forewarns of the extent or the acuteness of the crisis which irrupts as unexpectedly into the narrative as it did into the life of its subject.

From 1821 Mill, in his own words, something of a 'dry, hard logical machine' (p. 110), was a man with 'what might truly be called an object in life; to be a reformer of the world', whose 'conception of happiness was entirely identified with this object' (p. 136). Energetic public activity combined with intellectual work became the staple of life, a diet which led by 1826 to 'a dull state of nerves, such as everybody is occasionally liable to, unsusceptible to enjoyment or pleasureable excitement' (p. 136). Then came the crisis:

> In this frame of mind it occurred to me to put the question distinctly to myself, 'Suppose that all your objects in life were realized, that all the changes in institutions and opinions which you are looking forward to, could be completely effected at this very instant; would this be a great joy and happiness to you?' and an irrepressible self-consciousness distinctly answered 'No!' At this my heart sank within me; the whole foundation on which my life was constructed fell down. All my happiness was to have been found in the continual pursuit of this end. The end had ceased to charm, and how could there ever again be excitement in the means? I had nothing left to live for. (pp. 136–8)

Mill spoke to no one about his state of mind, aware especially that his father 'was the last person to whom in such a case as this I looked for help' (p. 138), and he carried on working as the cloud of dejection grew thicker and thicker.

In such a condition the supreme endowment of Mill's training, analytical power, was rendered impotent. As is evident from the description of the crisis, an analytical formulation, remorselessly applied, had triggered the collapse, but it could not effect a cure: 'to know that a feeling would make me happy if I had it, did not create the feeling' (p. 142). Assistance had to come from without and it had to come unsought.

It came by accident. Reading in Jean François Marmontel's *Mémoires d'un père* (1804), Mill was moved to tears by the account of Marmontel's feelings on the death of his father, and he seized on this as evidence that he was not, after all, 'a stock or a stone' (p. 144), but one who had capacities for feeling.

Relieved from an 'ever present sense of wretchedness' (p. 144), Mill was now open to a second, more powerful intervention of grace. In the autumn of 1828 he read some Wordsworth out of curiosity, and though expecting little found 'the precise thing for my mental wants at that particular time' (p. 150):

In the first place, these poems addressed themselves powerfully to one of the strongest of my pleasurable susceptibilities, the love of rural objects and of natural scenery . . . In this power of rural beauty over me there was a foundation laid for taking pleasure in Wordsworth's poetry; the more so, as his scenery is mostly among mountains . . . my ideal of natural beauty. But Wordsworth would never have had any great effect on me if he had merely placed before me beautiful pictures of natural scenery. A collection of very second rate landscapes does this more effectually than any books. What made Wordsworth's poems a medicine for my state of mind was that they expressed, not outward beauty but states of feeling, and of thought coloured by feeling, under the excitement of beauty. They seemed to be the very culture of the feelings which I was in quest of. By their means I seemed to draw from a source of inward joy, of sympathetic and imaginative pleasure, which could be shared in by all human beings, which had no connexion with struggle or imperfection, but would be made richer by every improvement in the physical or social condition of mankind. I seemed to learn from them what would be the perennial sources of happiness when all the greater evils of life should be removed. And I felt myself at once better and happier as I came under their influence.

Mill goes on to say that his present (i.e. 1853–4) estimate of Wordsworth is very far below what it was, but this passage reveals how completely he had absorbed him. It is a tissue of echoes of the Preface to *Lyrical Ballads* and the Preface and Supplementary Essay to the collection of 1815. That poetry is not a copy of nature but an imaginative engagement with it; that it is an expression of joy; that poetry binds together human beings; that it searches for the permanent over the transitory; that poetry can make men better and happier—all of these are Wordsworth's own propositions. To which need only be added his declaration in the 1800 note to *The Thorn*, that poetry is 'the history or science of feelings'. Mill has omitted the transcendental aspect of the poetry, but otherwise his account in the *Autobiography* of what Wordsworth did for him is formulated in terms of which the poet would have approved, for he supplied them.

If the *Autobiography* stood alone, a commentator would have to ask, to what extent is its account of crisis and rescue a fiction? For what usually bedevils discussion of such retrospective narratives is the paucity of *contemporary* documentation. Biographers would give a good deal, for example, to discover contemporary evidence about the state of Dickens's mind while he was working at Warren's blacking factory, or about Wordsworth's during the period he dramatized so vividly, ten years later in *The Prelude*, as one in which he abandoned moral questions in despair. But evidence is lacking and conjecture is determined by the immensely powerful formulations already given by the subject, who is best placed to know, but also to invent.

In Mill's case however, contemporary evidence does exist. There is the speech he made defending Wordsworth against Byron at the London Debating Society on 30 January 1829, and the long letter to John Sterling, 20–2 October 1831, in which Mill records the impression he gained when he visited Wordsworth during a recent tour of the Lake District.[13] Together they corroborate the *Autobiography*'s account of what Wordsworth meant to Mill in the late 1820s.

The speech, in reply to J. A. Roebuck's in favour of Byron delivered the previous evening, lasted for over two hours, but only once does Mill indicate the degree of his personal investment in it. Underscoring an exposition of one aspect of Wordsworth's poetry, Mill refers to 'My own change since I thought life a perpetual struggle—how much more there is to aim at when we see that happiness may coexist with being stationary & does not require us to keep moving' (p. 441). For the most part, however, his advocacy is formally structured and low-key, as if aiming to win assent through persuasion rather than by passionate avowal.

Mill starts with the proposition that poetry is an important branch of education of the intellect and of the feelings: 'Folly of supposing that the first suffices without the last' (p. 434). He establishes criteria for judging the highest poetry and outlines reasons for placing Wordsworth in that class. He then examines the poetry under three heads. It is to be valued for its power of describing objects 'in some light or viewed in some manner which makes them excite different emotions from what a naked delineation would' (p. 436). Second, Wordsworth's poetry records a wide range of human feelings. It also awakens the reader to previously unexperienced feelings and 'must be considered as having enlarged our knowledge of human nature by having described to us most powerfully & movingly a state of feeling which very few if any of us previously knew to exist' (p. 440). Third, Wordsworth's thoughts are valuable, because they 'comprise a better & a more comprehensive morality than all other poets together—& alone of all poets he seems able to make moralizing interesting' (p. 441). Mill concedes that Wordsworth the metaphysician on occasion swamps the poet, but excuses this as the unfortunate by-product of Wordsworth's desire to explain the origins and significance of his deepest feelings.

Two aspects of this speech are particularly noteworthy. The first is that Mill draws heavily on the Preface to Wordsworth's 1815 collection, so heavily that it must be assumed he was gambling on few of his audience having read it. He repeats Wordsworth's commendation of the lines from *Resolution and Independence*, 'Over his own sweet voice the Stock-dove broods', and cites, as Wordsworth does, the stone and sea-beast passage from the same poem. Mill remarks that a poet labours under 'the necessity of in some measure educating his reader's mind to make him susceptible of those feelings' (p. 440), which is also pointed out by Wordsworth, who at least owns up that the observation is Coleridge's. Mill's rather shaky attempt to define higher and lower classes of poetry according to the effect it makes on higher and lower orders of minds also originates in the 1815 Preface. Being captious one might say that such borrowing shows that the young Mill was no more averse to lifting material than most people with a speech to prepare. No doubt it does. But it also demonstrates how deeply the Wordsworthian convert had been affected not only by the poet's language but also by his characteristic strategies for defending his work.

The second notable feature of the speech confirms this point, but it also marks out what is original in Mill's presentation, original in the sense that it is evidently the product of a personal response. By stressing the poetry's 'culture of the feelings', Mill affirms what Wordsworth had long before declared the element which distinguished his from popular poems of the day: 'that the feeling therein developed gives importance to the action and situation, and not the action and situation to the feeling'.[14] This declaration, from the Preface to *Lyrical Ballads*, is one which the poet never rescinded, but by 1829 most devotees, when advocating Wordsworth, would not have turned for evidence to the ballads to which it applies. What were more usually brought forward to exemplify the loftiness of feeling in the poetry and its elevating power were those passages in *Tintern Abbey*, *Ode to Duty*, the *Ode: Intimations*, some of the sonnets and, above all, *The Excursion*, which tended to connect feeling with aspiration towards unity with the 'Wisdom and Spirit of the Universe, | Thou Soul that art the Eternity of Thought'. Mill will have none of this. Whenever Wordsworth 'philosophizes over' his feelings and 'endeavours to account for them', the poetry is, Mill uncompromisingly asserts, 'bad' (p. 440). Where it is strong is in the range of feeling evoked, as in such poems as *The Kitten and the Falling Leaves*, *The Mad Mother*, *The Female Vagrant*, *Complaint of a Forsaken Indian Woman*, *The Last of the Flock*, *The Sailor's Mother*, *Poor Susan*, *The Farmer of Tilsbury Vale*, *To A Highland Girl*, and *The Solitary Reaper*. This is a very interesting list. Not many speakers would care to try to win over an audience with most of them as examples of Wordsworth's power. But they matter to Mill because they express basic human emotions, not always but generally, it should be noted, arising from loss or isolation. When Mill does cite *Tintern Abbey*, *Resolution and Independence*, *Ode: Intimations*, and the *Ode to Duty*, it is with a similar emphasis. He dwells on these poems because they register the common human sense of loss, or of the precariousness of our sense of stability and identity, and because they suggest the compensation that can be found in this world, if experience is rightly understood.

Mill's account of actually meeting Wordsworth is epilogue to this speech. As his journal indicates, Mill saw the Lake District through the lens of Wordsworth's poetry and became convinced that the only proper place to encounter the poet was, as he wrote to Sterling, 'in his own kingdom—I call the whole of that mountain region his kingdom'. The king did not disappoint him, being 'still more admirable & delightful a person on a nearer view than I had figured to myself from his writings' (p. 82). He was struck by 'the extensive range of his [Wordsworth's] thoughts and the largeness & expansiveness of his feelings' and by the 'extreme comprehensiveness and philosophic spirit which is in him' (pp. 80–1). Unlike Southey, whom Mill found narrowly opinionated, Wordsworth 'seems always to know the pros and cons of every question' (p. 81). To Mill Wordsworth seemed a level-headed, well-informed, capable man, at peace with himself and his surroundings, perhaps, to use Mill's phrase out of context, 'the poet of unpoetical natures'.[15] What is clear from this 'somewhat enthusiastic' letter is that Mill went to the Lake District with a formed idea of the Wordsworth he wanted to find, and that he found him.

William Hale White—better known as Mark Rutherford—also 'found' Wordsworth, but his circumstances could hardly have been more different from Mill's. Whereas Mill grew up without being trammelled by codified religious belief, Hale White was in its straitjacket from birth.

His parents were devout members of the dissenting congregation of the Old Meeting, later called the Bunyan Meeting, in Bedford. There was nothing of the Murdstone or Pontifex about either of them—William White was notably courageous and intellectually flexible—and the childhood of their son, who was born in 1831, seems to have been a very happy one. But it was lived within the faith, not just coloured by it, but permeated to a degree inconceivable to anyone not brought up in a dissenting household. Prayer-meetings, Sunday-school, and a Sunday strictly kept for worship—these were not additional to the life of the week, but its foundation.

Parental hopes, particularly his mother's, years of religious nurture, and want of any other obvious route to a profession, determined that Hale White would train for the Congregational ministry. In 1848 he entered the Countess of Huntingdon's College at Cheshunt, Hertfordshire, and three years later the recently established theological college, New College, in St John's Wood. Early in 1852 he and two others were expelled for expressing opinions which were, in the view of the College Council, 'incompatible with their retention . . . of their position as Students for the Christian ministry'.[16]

The immediate cause of the expulsion was local and specific. Increasingly dismayed at the narrow repetitiveness of the teaching at New College, where Paley and the argument from design were still taught as if they constituted the latest learning, Hale White and his friends had circumspectly tried to widen discussion about the origin of the biblical record, but not circumspectly enough. The Principal smelt heresy and acted to eradicate it. The real cause, however, was unknown to the college authorities. 'It was Wordsworth', Hale White later wrote, 'and not German research which caused my expulsion from New College.'[17]

After a vain stab at schoolmastering, Hale White secured a post in Somerset House, and later in the Admiralty, and buckled down to a life of unremitting administrative labour. A need to possess his own earlier existence, however, to make a bridge between the servant of the Admiralty and the youth whose determination to follow truth had cost him so dear, inspired a series of fictions in his later middle age. In *The Autobiography of Mark Rutherford* (1881), purportedly 'edited by his friend Reuben Shapcott', Rutherford describes his experience of Wordsworthian conversion. Confessing that though a theological student he had no knowledge of God 'and could not bring my lips to use the word with any mental honesty', he recounts an event 'I remember as well as Paul must have remembered afterwards the day on which he went to Damascus'. Chancing on *Lyrical Ballads*, Rutherford was possessed by Wordsworth's God, 'the God of the hills, the abstraction Nature':

Instead of an object of worship which was altogether artificial, remote, never coming into genuine contact with me, I had now one which I thought to be real, one in which literally I could live and move and have my being, an actual fact present before my eyes. God was brought from that heaven of the books and dwelt on the downs in the far-away distances, and in every cloud-shadow which wandered across the valley. Wordsworth unconsciously did for me what every religious reformer has done,—he re-created my Supreme Divinity; substituting a new and living spirit for the old deity, once alive, but gradually hardened into an idol.[18]

This is one of the most striking accounts of spiritual renewal in Victorian literature, and it is much quoted. But it was not Hale White's only evocation of his road-to-Damascus experience. In old age he returned to it, in an account written for his children, in which the fictional persona is laid aside:

The most important changes in life are not those of one belief for another, but of growth, in which nothing preceding is directly contradicted, but something unexpected nevertheless makes its appearance. On the bookshelf in our dining-room (at Bedford) lay a volume of Wordsworth. One day when I was about 18 I took it out and fell upon the lines

> Knowing that Nature never did betray
> The heart that loved her.

What they meant was not clear to me, but they were a signal of the approach of something which turned out to be of the greatest importance, and altered my history.

It was a new capacity. There arose in me an aptness for the love of natural beauty, a possibility of being excited to enthusiasm by it, and of deriving a secret joy from it, sufficiently strong to make me careless of the world and its pleasures. Another effect which Wordsworth had upon me, and has had upon other people, was the modification, altogether unintentional on his part, of religious belief. He never dreams of attacking anybody for his creed and yet it often becomes impossible for those who study him to be members of any orthodox community. . . . His poems imply a living God, different from the artificial God of the churches. The revolution wrought by him goes deeper and is more permanent than any which is the work of Biblical critics, and it was Wordsworth, and not German research which caused my expulsion from New College . . . For some time I had no thought of heresy, but the seed was there and was alive just as much as the seed-corn is alive all the time it lies in the earth apparently dead.[19]

Late in life Hale White observed: 'Much of the religion by which Wordsworth lives is very indefinite.' But, he added, 'Because this religion is indefinite it is not therefore the less supporting'.[20] What Wordsworth offered the fledgling theological student was not a specific alternative to the God of the New College, but a vision of alternative possibilities. The alpha and omega of Hale White's early experience of God had been Calvinist systematic theology, in which was unfolded the 'scheme of redemption from beginning to end'.[21] *Lyrical Ballads* playfully but insistently urged an end to the 'dull and endless strife' of books and disputation, in favour of the wisdom available to 'a heart | That watches and receives'. Turn away from certainty to the blessedness of a receptive 'wise passiveness'; feed the body with the 'blessing in the air' of a March day; tune the music of the soul 'to love'—these are the commandments of the *Lyrical Ballads*.[22] They formed 'a hidden conduit open into an unknown region whence at any moment streams may rush and renew the desert with foliage and flowers'.[23]

The poem to which Hale White refers in the autobiographical note, *Tintern Abbey*, must have struck him, in one respect, as the kind of utterance with which he had long been familiar. Adult members of the Old Meeting who sought full entry to the Church, were required to testify to their conviction of salvation before being received as one of the 'elect'. *Tintern Abbey* is a passionate testimony of salvation which, for all its equivocating ifs and buts, hymns the joy of certitude that in the 'sense sublime | Of something far more deeply interfused' and 'all the mighty world | Of eye and ear', the poet finds his guide, guardian and 'soul | Of all my moral being'. Wordsworth's appeal to Hale White was not only that he belonged, evidently joyously, to a different elect, but that he could make his testimony intelligible and, through the power of his language, available.

Hale White's search for the 'living God' preoccupied him to the end of his life and took him well beyond Wordsworth—most notably to Spinoza—[24] and there is some evidence that in middle life he bitterly questioned the value of a Nature creed which seemed to have so little connection with the life of regulated urban drudgery which most people, including himself, were forced to endure.[25] In later life, however, he seems to have rediscovered Wordsworth. Hale White became a textual scholar with all of Housman's severity and rigour and contributed significantly to the textual controversies which flared up during the late-century Wordsworth renaissance. In 1898 he published *An Examination of the Charge of Apostasy Against Wordsworth*, which deploys extraordinarily detailed knowledge of Wordsworth's writings to refute the notion that his was a fractured life. His 'sole aim', Hale White declares, 'is to show that he was no apostate, and that to the last he was *himself*'.[26] A year later he fulfilled a long-felt desire for pilgrimage to the hallowed ground of the *annus mirabilis* of Wordsworth and Coleridge. Here he walked in the imagined company of those he spoke of, according to his second wife, 'as of personal friends, with all the intimacy, love, and reverence'.[27] Hale White was as obsessed as Wordsworth was with the search for continuity and wholeness of life, so it is appropriate that the last entry in the *Diary on the Quantocks* should connect directly with the feelings of the 18-year-old who was possessed by *Lyrical*

Ballads: 'Wordsworth has a singular power of expressing articulately that which would be mere mist without him, but is of vital importance.'[28]

The next witness is rather different from all those mentioned so far. One evening in 1817–18 the party in Macready's lodgings struggled to be hospitable to the guest of one of the boarders. It went against the grain, as he was 'clownish in his build and deportment and brusque in his manners, over-bearing and dogmatic to absolute rudeness in the superciliousness of his remarks and his apparent contempt for the understandings of those around him'.[29] More than a quarter of a century later this intellectual hobbledehoy, now Master of Trinity College, Cambridge, published *The Elements of Morality, including Polity*.[30] He dedicated it, through the form of an open letter, to Wordsworth:

My dear Mr. Wordsworth,

I am very desirous that, if the present book finds its way to the next generation, it should make known to them that I had the great privilege of your friendship. And there is no one to whom I could with more propriety dedicate such a work: since in your Poems, at the season of life when the mind and heart are most wrought on by poetry, I, along with many others, found a spirit of pure and comprehensive morality, operating to raise your readers above the moral temper of those times. I shall rejoice if it appear from the following pages, that such influences have not been wasted upon me.

That you may long enjoy the reverence and affection with which England, on such grounds, regards you, is the wish and prayer of

My Dear Mr. Wordsworth
Your cordial friend and admirer
W. Whewell.

Trinity College, Cambridge.
April 14, 1845.

In the years since he had made such a bad impression on Macready, William Whewell had come a long way. An energetic polymath, Whewell had become a lecturer in mathematics at Trinity, then Professor of Minerology, then Professor of Moral Philosophy, and eventually Master of Trinity. Publishing weightily on mathematics, geology, and astronomy, he was elected to the Royal Society and to the Geological Society, of which he became President in 1837. His major works in science are the *History of the*

Inductive Sciences (1837) and *Philosophy of the Inductive Sciences* (1840). *The Elements of Morality* is the most important treatise from Whewell's later period, when his interest was primarily engaged in ethics and theology. Sydney Smith quipped 'science is his forte and omniscience his foible', which was accurate, but not just. Throughout his career Whewell—who also wrote poetry and published on Gothic architecture—amassed information in different fields, driven not by restlessness or an eye to the main chance, but by an intense desire to unify knowledge. His philosophical work does not abandon science, but builds on it, in an attempt to integrate scientific with moral and theological discourse.

As a young man, with ambitions for a career in mathematics, Whewell had been hostile to Wordsworth's poetry. By the early 1820s, however, he was numbering himself amongst the 'Wordsworthians', no doubt in part because he had warmed to the poet on a recent meeting.[31] Visiting and corresponding regularly, Whewell came to regard Wordsworth as an important influence on his intellectual and spiritual development and, though by no means a humble or even gracious man, he was ready to acknowledge his debt. Writing to Wordsworth in 1841, he declared that 'if there be any thing good' in his moral speculations, 'I am persuaded that I have been led to it in no small degree by the lessons which in former times I learnt from your writings, to which I always ascribe a considerable portion of the formation or reformation of my intellectual character'.[32]

Any one of a number of Whewell's friends might have written this letter—Julius Hare, for example, Archdeacon of Lewes. Hare, one of Whewell's intimates from his early days in Cambridge, was an energetic champion of good causes, with a high public profile.[33] He also was a Wordsworthian. For 'thirty years', he told the poet in 1849, he had 'revered [him] as my Master and Moral Teacher'.[34] Or John Sterling, sometime curate to Hare and close friend of John Stuart Mill, who regarded Wordsworth as one of his spiritual guides. Or Professor Adam Sedgwick, the geologist, one of Whewell's staunchest allies in Cambridge battles, who showed his respect for Wordsworth by contributing a substantial geological essay for later editions of his *Guide to the Lakes*.

Wordsworth's initial contact with all of these people came about, of course, through chance. As his brother Christopher established himself in Cambridge, becoming Master of Trinity in 1820,

Wordsworth had occasion to meet his colleagues. That Whewell and Sedgwick were northerners helped friendship ripen, as did Whewell's marriage to the daughter of the Marshalls of Hallsteads, Ullswater, lifelong friends of the Wordsworth family. The regard in which Wordsworth was held by this group, however, rested on something more substantial than accident of personal contact. He was valued as a bold precursor, and a current companion in arms, in a battle for nothing less than the soul of a generation.

In December 1832 Sedgwick delivered an address consisting in part of an attack on the teaching of philosophy at Cambridge. Whewell was enthusiastic about it to Julius Hare, and he also commended a sermon by Thomas Rawson Birks on 'Mathematical and Moral Certitude'. In the words of one historian of Victorian moral philosophy, 'These two attacks on Paley and the support given by Whewell mark the point at which philosophy at Cambridge began its public resistance to empiricism and utilitarianism.'[35] The contention that this was a turning-point is reinforced by a letter Whewell wrote to Wordsworth in 1834, also about Birks's address. Seeing about him nothing but the mischief of 'our unhappy utilitarian morality and despairing politics', wrought in great measure by the influence of Cambridge philosophers speculating about the 'gravest interests of men' in an 'ignoble and hopeless tone', Whewell declares his belief that only if the 'tendency of thought' represented by Birks were to prevail, could much of the mischief be undone.[36] From this time on Whewell became the acknowledged leader of those who were determined that it should prevail.

Through their lectures, sermons, and other writings, and strongly through personal advocacy, this group battled against philosophical empiricism and all modes of thought stigmatized as utilitarian, determined to restore moral teaching to its rightful place and to elevate the tone of intellectual debate. Whewell's *Elements of Morality* is one of its most significant documents. They built on others than Wordsworth, of course—Coleridge's later work, for example, was a heavily mined resource—but reverence for his poetry was a common bond. That Whewell dedicated the *Elements of Morality* to him indicates his stature as the one who had begun the fight and encouraged its continuance through his whole life's work. The personal note of the dedication, in addition, suggests that the Master of Trinity acknowledged not just an intellectual indebtedness, but that Wordsworth's writings and the example of his life had served to determine the course of his own.

What is perhaps most striking about this parade of testimony is that Wordsworth could be of use to such opposed figures. Mill's professional disdain for Whewell's work verged on the contemptuous. 'It can scarcely be counted as anything more than one of the thousand waves on the dead sea of commonplace, affording nothing to invite or reward a separate examination,' was his devastating judgement on the *Elements of Morality*.[37] Whewell recognized Mill as the enemy, regarding him as only the cleverest of those whose every thought tended to worldliness and moral debauchery. Yet both men constructed from Wordsworth something that answered to their needs.

A further striking example of such construction is to be found in the life and work of the Reverend Frederick William Robertson. His name almost certainly means little to any reader of this book who is not also a church historian or a researcher into Sussex local history. He wrote little save sermons and addresses. He did not convert to Rome in a blaze of notoriety like F. W. Faber, nor suffer the well-publicized obloquy which was J. A. Froude's portion. And yet for a few years he was as famous—a figure 'never to be mentioned without interest and respect' was Matthew Arnold's judgement.[38] A memorial in the chapel of Brasenose College, Oxford, and a bust in the Bodleian Library testify to his contemporary fame. The fact that his lectures were still in print in 1906, fifty-three years after his death, indicates that it was not ephemeral.

Robertson's fame rested on a six-year period only, his ministry at Brighton. Deeply influenced by Dr Arnold, Robertson was ordained in 1840.[39] During a curacy at Cheltenham this ascetic, somewhat reclusive man was so increasingly tormented by doubt as to his efficacy as a priest and the faith he professed, that he fled to the Tyrol. He returned to the charge of St Ebbes, in the poorest part of Oxford, before leaving in 1847 for the incumbency of Trinity Chapel, Brighton. Here, at last Robertson found his role. His eloquence and directness attracted a large congregation. But what made him notorious was that he became the champion of Brighton's working class and offended most establishment interests. As he supported education for the poor, better housing and more leisure, and was unsound on the question of keeping the Sabbath,

Robertson was accused of being a Socialist and sceptic. He was certainly a nuisance. A bitter struggle with the Vicar of Brighton darkened the last years of his ministry, and he died in 1853, aged only 37, worn out. Upwards of two thousand mourners followed his coffin to the grave.

The nature of Robertson's Brighton ministry was determined by his spiritual crisis. The ingredients themselves of the crisis are so familiar that it would be easy to condescend to it as one more example of Victorian 'faith and doubt'. Robertson's agonized letters, however, and his moving account of struggling with bottomless depression, check condescension.[40] So profound were his doubts about the value of his vocation that Robertson might easily have followed Hale White in flight from organized religion. Fifty years later he would probably have relinquished the Christian Faith altogether. But Robertson did neither. Testing and abandoning everything save the conviction that the Christ figure (whoever or whatever the historical Jesus might have been) was man's surest guide, he reconstructed a basis for belief and conduct:

I know but one way in which a man may come forth from his agony scathless; it is by holding fast to those things which are certain still—the grand, simple landmarks of morality. In the darkest hour through which a human soul can pass, whatever else is doubtful, this at least is certain. If there be no God, and no future state, yet, even then, it is better to be generous than selfish, better to be chaste than licentious, better to be true than false, better to be brave than to be a coward.[41]

Throughout this crisis, fought through amongst the mountains, Wordsworth was, appropriately, Robertson's second gospel.[42] In the last year of his life he publicly declared himself to be,

one who has for years studied Wordsworth and loved him, and year by year felt his appreciation and comprehension of Wordsworth grow, and has during all those years endeavoured to make Wordsworth's principles the guiding principles of his own inner life.[43]

Professing a faith which fused Christian ethics with Wordsworthian humanitarianism, and which had covert sympathy with pantheism, it was inevitable that Robertson's ministry would be notable for its contribution to social rather than ecclesiastical affairs. What shaped it, however, and engendered the suspicion and hostility which eventually ground him down, was the date at which his ministry began.

Robertson reacted to the French Revolution of 1848 as Wordsworth had done in 1789—'Bliss was it in that dawn to be alive'. Privately he rejoiced: 'The world has become a new one . . . To my mind, it is a world full of hope, even to bursting . . . I could almost say sometimes, in fulness of heart, "Now let Thy servant depart in peace".'[44] In public he was similarly unrestrained. A course of Sunday afternoon lectures on the book of *Samuel* turned into discourses on the rights of property and the rights of labour, on the limits of authority, and on the nature of kingship, that were so unsettling that he was denounced to his Bishop 'as a Revolutionist and a Democrat'.[45]

No wonder Robertson frightened the worthies of Brighton: a Church of England minister who echoed the Nunc Dimittis because he glimpsed in the dawn of the age of labour the harbinger of the kingdom of Christ. But his denouncers were quite wrong. Robertson was no Revolutionist and, judged against the demands of the Chartists, no Democrat. He was conspicuous, however, in responding so positively to events which others saw only as calamitous. As reaction to 1848 set in he wrote:

What appals me is to see the way in which persons, once Liberal, are now recoiling from their own principles, terrified by the state of the Continent, and saying that we must stem the tide of democracy, and support the Conservatives. Why, what has ever made democracy dangerous but Conservatism? The French Revolution! Socialism! Why, these men seem to forget that these things came out of Toryism, which forced the people into madness.[46]

A new self-consciousness in the working man, an awakened desire for self-betterment, the stirrings of conscience in the rich and powerful—if the events in France promoted these, they were to be welcomed. And if welcoming them meant that one was labelled a Chartist or a Socialist or even a Communist, then this was the cross to be borne. What mattered most, since new energies could not be dammed up, nor the new era rolled back, was that the working man should be raised to be worthy of his coming power.

Robertson unstintingly involved himself in the one activity open to him to promote this aim locally, education for the labouring classes. He was instrumental in founding a Working-Man's Institute in Brighton, which quickly attracted over a thousand penny-a-week subscribers, and he was, by request, the principal speaker when it was opened on 23 October 1848. When it foundered, largely because of disagreements over policy among committee members, Robertson unreproachfully assisted in the dissolution of the one society and the formation of another. Despite increasing exhaustion simply from over-work, and continual disappointment, the result both of being attacked in the local press and being let down by men he had trusted, Robertson remained tactful, considerate, and hopeful.

The purpose of this biographical account has been to emphasize that, like H. S. Tremenheere, Robertson worked in the world and not just in the study. He knew at first hand the people he hoped to serve. Wrangling committees met in unlovely rooms, unreliable co-workers, ceaseless cajoling for funds—these were the realities of Robertson's service to the cause of education for the poor, and they indicate how strikingly he resembled another contemporary 'Chartist' cleric, Charles Kingsley. Late in life Kingsley declared that his 'soul had been steeped from boyhood in [Wordsworth's] poetry', and just before he entered the most heroic phase of his activity in the late 1840s he wrote:

I have been reading Wordsworth's 'Excursion', with many tears and prayers too. To me he is not only poet, but preacher and prophet of God's new and divine philosophy—a man raised up as a light in a dark time, and rewarded by an honoured age, for the simple faith in man and God with which he delivered his message; whose real nobility is independent of rank, or conventionalities of language or manner, which is but the fashion of this world, and passes away.[47]

But from the point of view of this study the difference between Robertson and Kingsley is what matters. Kingsley's test of a good man was that he 'attacks the evil and the disgusting the moment he sees it',[48] but in his attack on the London sweat-shops, in his campaigns for sanitary reform, and in his writings as 'Parson Lot' in *Politics for the People*, Kingsley made little use of Wordsworth. The contemplative poet, who appealed profoundly to the nature mystic in Kingsley, was no ally for battle in the city. With Robertson this was not the case. By the time of his death in 1853 the Simeon vision of 1848 had certainly faded, but the convictions which underpinned his ministry had not and the most remarkable of these was the conviction that Wordsworth could speak to the working man.

That Robertson was a Wordsworthian was apparent in his two lectures to members of the Mechanics' Institution in February 1852 on *The Influence of Poetry on the Working Classes*. In the course of a wide-ranging and quirkily original exposition of the place of poetic imagination in daily life, he quotes Wordsworth in set-pieces and alludes to him continuously.[49] It was not until shortly before his death, however, that Robertson gathered together all his thoughts on Wordsworth, in a lecture delivered to the Brighton Athenaeum on 10 February 1853.

As were all of Robertson's lectures, this one is lucid, economical, and focused on essentials, but much of what he says is familiar. Wordsworth is presented as an unworldly poet, not, that is, a milksop who could not face the world, but as one who knew it too well to believe that the things of this world—especially politics—mattered. Robertson makes the case for the value of contemplative natures and at one point declares to any sceptic in his audience that, 'There is a sweat of the brain and a sweat of the heart, be well assured—working-men especially—as much as there is sweat of the brow'.[50]

So far, so predictable. At three points, however, Robertson reveals attitudes which explain why others of his cloth and caste in Brighton thought him pernicious. The first is when he quotes with fervent approval *Excursion*, I. 196–218, a rhapsody about communion with the 'living God' through Nature, in which every element of Christian Revelation is disregarded.[51] The second is a passage in which Robertson inveighs against the degrading pursuit of wealth which characterizes the age and invokes Wordsworth's vision of the essential worth of the individual, with arguments against mechanization of labour which strikingly anticipate *Unto This Last*. The final one is the section in which it is argued, tortuously, that Wordsworth was always a democrat—an aristocratic democrat—who saw in the poor 'the stately nobles of nature'. What is the higher truth, Robertson demands: 'to say that the lower classes are degraded, and evil, and base; or to say there yet slumbers in them the aristocratic and the godlike, and that *that*, by the grace of God, shall one day be drawn forth?'[52]

III

Christians for Wordsworth

Each of the witnesses summoned so far valued Wordsworth for his power to operate in the realm of the spirit. His poetry excites the 'aspiration to become a better man', simultaneously enriching a person's affective life while suppressing egotism through its stress on 'relationship and love'.[53] None of them, however, felt pressed to investigate with any nicety Wordsworth's relation to any one branch of the institution of spiritual power, the Christian Church.

There was no doubt, of course, that he was a stalwart Anglican. *Ecclesiastical Sketches* (1822) and the 'Postscript' to *Yarrow Revisited* (1835) manifested his reverence for the traditions of the Church and his respect for its social function. Keble's Sheldonian oration in 1839 broadcast the conviction of the group promoting his Honorary Degree that it was, in the words of John Peace, a 'Christian Poet who stood before them'.[54] Two years later John Henry Newman lauded Wordsworth as seminal to the 'great progress of the religious mind of our Church to something deeper and truer than satisfied the last century',[55] a recognition which took another form when the Cambridge Camden Society welcomed him as a founding father. The elderly poet was hemmed in by divines. His brother Christopher, Master of Trinity College, Cambridge, was a man so 'red-hot' in orthodoxy that Southey claimed he believed 'in forty articles, thirty-nine not being enough for his capacious conscience'.[56] His nephew was climbing fast towards a bishopric, one of his sons was a clergyman, his friends and correspondents were such pillars as John Keble, Hugh Rose, Henry Alford, and William Sewell. Anglicanism, as Katherine Peek puts it, 'was woven into the fabric of his thought and life'.[57]

If the white-haired gentleman strolling in the courts of Trinity seemed the epitome of the Anglican layman, his work, however, was not so entirely satisfying. One almost unknown publication can introduce the point. In 1842 a pamphlet called *Contributions of William Wordsworth to the Revival of Catholic Truths*, compiled by Samuel Wilkinson, was published in a series, *The Christian's Miscellany; Conducted by Members of the Church of England*.[58] Wordsworth's contributions include *The Poet's Epitaph*

and *The Old Cumberland Beggar*, but consist mainly of extracts
from *The Excursion*, under such headings as 'Utilitarian Knowledge', 'The Difficulties of Reason', 'The Sciences', and from much
later poems such as *Bruges, At Albano 1837, Musings Near
Aquapendente*. Prose extracts from the *Yarrow* 'Postscript' conclude
the little anthology.

The range and kind of poetry represented are predictable. What
makes the pamphlet such a fascinating document is the setting in
which the extracts are placed. Modest though it is in size, the
Contributions is a polemical intervention at a critical moment in
the history of the Oxford Movement. After the publication in
February 1841 of *Tract No. 90, Remarks on Certain Passages in
the Thirty-nine Articles*, reaction against Tractarianism, which had
been burning on a slow fuse, ignited. The tract was censured by the
Heads of Houses; the Tractarian candidate for the Professorship of
Poetry was defeated; and in May 1842 the Bishop of Oxford
delivered his famous charge. Wilkinson's Wordsworth selection
appeared when the progenitors of Tractarianism were under the
most damaging attack yet in their Oxford home.

The pamphlet is both aggressive and defensive. The title given to
the selection is calculatedly challenging. From the beginning of the
Movement the Tractarians had used the word 'Catholic' freely, in a
manner certain to alarm orthodox churchmen already agitated by
the Catholic Emancipation Act of 1829, but they had used it
carefully. The Catholic Church was the one Church of Christ,
instituted by Him. By 1841, however, the suspicion that the
Tractarians were tending Romewards was so well rooted that when
Newman in *Tract No. 90* used 'Catholic', with upper and lower
case initial letter, no matter how subtle his discriminations, he was
convicted at once. As Owen Chadwick observes in *The Victorian
Church*, 'Not even the university was accustomed to the word
Catholic as not meaning Roman Catholic. They knew that
Newman disliked the word Protestant and read in the tract that no
Catholic need hesitate to subscribe the articles. The obvious
meaning suggested that the articles were no barrier to Roman
Catholic dogmas.'[59] By invoking *Catholic Truths* in his pamphlet in
1842, Wilkinson was insisting, in opposition to Newman's assail-
ants, on the legitimacy of the term as it had become current in
Tractarian discourse.

The rest of the editorial matter, on the other hand, is defensive. It inserts Wordsworth not only into Tractarianism, but into the Movement at this particular moment of crisis. The title-page carries a substantial quotation from Newman's open letter of self-defence to Dr Jelf about *Tract No. 90* (quoted in part above), together with lines from the 'Prospectus' to *The Recluse* which seem to support Newman's contention.[60] The last page reprints the recently published note to *Musings Near Aquapendente*, strongly supportive of the Oxford Movement, under the eye-catching heading 'Mr. Wordsworth's Opinion of the Oxford Divines'.[61] All of this additional material, which acts as an interpretative gloss on the extracts, is brought into focus in the editor's prefatory remarks. The pamphlet, he declares, will fulfil his purpose should it help convince

any timid Churchman that the doctrines, which are now branded as Popish, were a few years ago held without persecution, or even without reprehension, by men whose zeal for the Anglican Church none suspect. They may prove that these doctrines have been expressed by others as strongly as by the Oxford Divines; and show the folly of those, who are disturbing the Church with their weak-minded alarms. . . .[62]

Wordsworth co-operated in the preparation of the pamphlet and approved these remarks, but he would not make quite the affirmation Wilkinson hoped for. Exactly what it was is not known, but in one letter the poet tells him that he wants 'to abstain from what you recommend. It would seem to enroll me as a partisan.'[63] That, of course, was exactly what Wilkinson had in mind and as far as Henry Crabb Robinson was concerned, he succeeded. He was appalled by the whole production, but the Preface in particular, 'from which one might infer he [Wordsworth] went all lengths with them [the "Oxford Divines"]', disgusted him. It was, he declared, simply 'dishonest.'[64] And one can see why. Not only the Preface, but also the dates appended to some of the passages, certainly imply that Wordsworth had always held to 'Catholic Truths'. But had Crabb Robinson read the pamphlet a little more calmly, he might not have been so dismayed, for what the Preface reveals is that its compiler was in difficulties. His intention was clear, but as he looked over Wordsworth's *œuvre* remarkably few passages struck him, he admits, as unequivocally right. The poet's 'power and influence', he falls back on suggesting, have been 'effectually exercised by the *feeling of truthfulness and reality*, which he has infused into those possessed by his spirit' and hence the

tone of Mr. Wordsworth's writings has perhaps done more to the restoration of a sounder state of feeling on religious truths, than his direct allusion to Catholic doctrines. And though the whole of his works might receive the title given to these extracts, the latter are not such striking examples as we might have expected to find in an author, whose influence in the Catholic movement has been so great.

Wilkinson is surprised that he cannot quite put his finger on the core of Wordsworth's Catholic teaching, but is so convinced that in general he is at one spiritually with the Oxford Divines that he entertains no serious misgivings. Many, however, did, amply bearing out what Crabb Robinson would only confide to his journal: 'Wordsworth's own religion, by the bye, would not satisfy either a religionist or a sceptic.' Convinced that 'Wordsworth is too upright a man to be guilty of any wilful deception', Crabb Robinson generously supposed that 'perhaps he is himself not perfectly clear on the subjects on which his mode of thinking and feeling is anxiously inquired after by his religious admirers'.[65] Others were not so indulgent. For them a question remained. It was not whether Wordsworth was a force for spiritual good—that was agreed—but rather, from what authority did this beneficent force emanate? To put it bluntly, what exactly did Wordsworth believe?

For some this forthright question deserved a forthright answer and they could not see that anywhere in his writings Wordsworth had provided one.[66] Repeating claims made ever since the publication of *The Excursion* in 1814, and which he had himself voiced in 1828, John Wilson asserted in 1842 that Wordsworth 'certainly cannot be called a Christian poet'. Though *The Excursion* contains many a 'well-merited encomium on the Church of England', he declares, 'it would puzzle the most ingenious to detect much, or any, Christian religion.' More specifically, the 'utter absence of Revealed Religion, where it ought to have been all-in-all', in the story of Margaret in Book I, promotes 'an unhappy suspicion of hollowness and insincerity in that poetical religion, which at the best is a sorry substitute indeed for the light that is from heaven'.[67]

Even after the offending passages had been substantially revised in 1845, perhaps in part as a response to Wilson's animadversions, the charge continued to be made. In 1862, in an otherwise notably warm-hearted appreciation, Alexander Patterson laments that 'a religion somewhat vague and indeterminate' precludes Wordsworth from being considered 'an eminently Christian poet'. Two years later an altogether more substantial intellectual figure revealed similar reservations. In a long article in the *North British Review*, John Campbell Shairp presented Wordsworth as a poet whose 'peculiar wisdom' was sorely needed 'by this excitement-craving, unmeditative age', but even he felt that in expounding his beliefs in the 'sanative power of nature' Wordsworth had neglected his highest duty: 'we cannot help thinking there was not only room, but even a call for a fuller enforcement of the Christian verities.'[68]

The quite different anxiety of one of Wordsworth's most ardent supporters contrasts with these demands for expository fullness. In one or two places Wordsworth's doctrine seemed all too worryingly clear.

Richard Perceval Graves became the resident clergyman in Windermere in 1835, partly through Wordsworth's influence, and for thirty years he was close to the poet and then to his surviving family. When he moved on to higher office as sub-Dean of the Chapel Royal in Dublin Graves remained eager to proselytize, on the basis of a Wordsworthian faith which he spelt out at length in *Recollections of Wordsworth and the Lake Country*. Save that he stresses more than is usual Wordsworth's all-round intellectual capability, his grasp of public affairs, and his inclination towards action (attributes not discernible in the Pickersgill portrait, whose wide circulation he deplores), nothing that Graves says in praise of the poet is new or worth recapitulating. Recommending Wordsworth as a poet of moral excellence, Graves is on home ground and the quotations and exposition roll out seamlessly—until he considers Wordsworth's religion. Suddenly Graves falters. After quoting the long passage from *Tintern Abbey* in which the poet declares himself

> well pleased to recognise
> In nature and the language of the sense,
> The anchor of my purest thoughts, the nurse,
> The guide, the guardian of my heart, and soul
> Of all my moral being.

Graves twists and turns to repel the charge that he has himself introduced—that this smacks of Pantheism.[69]

No doubt it was Graves's own scrupulosity that impelled him to face the issue, but the well-publicized bruising Frederick Robertson had earlier received, when he was vilified for not denouncing Pantheism vigorously enough as wholly incompatible with Christianity, was possibly a warning how best to treat it. Whilst defending Wordsworth, Graves also had to cover himself, and so he piles up explanations for the *Tintern Abbey* passage: (1) pantheism, which 'denies to Deity personality and will' is, of course, detestable, but often what is so stigmatized is 'only the meeting of the soul in its legitimate excursions with one presentation of that vast idea of the infinite and incomprehensible God'; (2) the concluding lines of the *Tintern Abbey* passage 'taken by themselves, can scarcely admit of a satisfactory justification', but the poet was unformed when he wrote thus; (3) *per contra, The Prelude* proves that 'at no time did [Wordsworth] identify God and Nature'; (4) orthodoxy is not to be expected in *all parts* of a poet's output. Indeed, the record of a poet's progress towards truth and certainty might be the most valuable constituent of his work.[70]

What is remarkable about this parade of uneasily assorted justifications is that they are there at all. Graves has already established so fully Wordsworth's general moral healthfulness that he could easily have continued with sonorities about the poet's all-embracing spirituality and left it at that. But Graves cannot, precisely because he understands and fears the purport of the *Tintern Abbey* lines. For him a belief in something whose dwelling is the light of setting suns is not no belief, but dangerous belief. Wordsworth's wisdom is a vital resource for the age, but it must be shown to rest in—not merely be congruent with—belief in a personal God. And, as another committed but also troubled Wordsworthian put it, explication must prove that the 'Christianity so zealously asserted in Wordsworth's maturer poetry [is] so obviously implied in the whole of it'.[71]

Graves gets into difficulties simply because he is determined to claim Wordsworth, *in his entirety*, as the national poet of the thirty-nine articles by law established. Those who occupied positions aslant the established Church were free to employ bolder strategies of recuperation, confident that their construction was not the 'established' Wordsworth, whose effigy reposes in Westminster Abbey, or anything like it.

In *Homes and Haunts of the Most Eminent British Poets* (1847),

William Howitt exalts the very poem which so troubled Graves. The 'see into the life of things' passage from *Tintern Abbey* Howitt interprets as 'perfect Quakerism', and insists that Quakerism is not the 'casual doctrine of one or two casual or isolated poems', but the 'great theme everywhere pursued. Of his principal and noblest production, *The Excursion*, it is the brain, the very backbone, the vitals, and the moving sinews. Take away that, and you take all.' As evidence Howitt quotes *The Excursion*, I. 197–218, the description of the youth's silent rapture amongst the mountains, commenting that this is the 'state to which every true Quaker aspires; which he believes attainable without the mediation of any priest or the presence of any church . . . It is that state of exaltation, the very flower and glorious moment of a religious life, which is the privilege of him who draws near to and walks with God.'[72]

Selecting passages which dwell on the possibility of direct, personal communion with the 'Wisdom and Spirit of the Universe', and only these, Howitt proves Wordsworth a Quaker. Essentially, that is. Howitt knew perfectly well that Wordsworth was not a Quaker. His argument is that essentially he was, and that the poetry demonstrates it. In other hands, however, this interpretative method could produce a very different result.

Though Wordsworth himself had vigorously opposed Catholic Emancipation, the nervous found some of his later poems worryingly sympathetic to Roman Catholic tradition. The *Eclectic Review*, for example, declared it its 'duty' in 1842 to protest against the sonnet *At Albano*, as tending to 'sanctify the grossest superstition by representing it as flowing from the same principle as enlightened faith, and to invite the conclusion that the darkest ignorance and delusion, if but founded on a religious element, cease to have their proper nature'.[73]

The challenge implicit here was not at once taken up. Reviewing the *Memoirs of William Wordsworth* in 1851 the *Dublin Review* only remarked that Wordsworth had of course seen 'the beauty and the merits of that Church which alone had preserved Christianity', not least because as a poet he could not but respond to the 'pure and impassioned poetry' of ritual 'which appeals so powerfully to the imagination'.[74] In 1855 the first Cardinal of the restored English hierarchy, Nicholas Wiseman, yoked Wordsworth with St Francis of Assisi and Dante in a lecture *On the Perception of Natural Beauty by the Ancients and the Moderns*, but in claiming

Wordsworth as the 'modern poet of nature and nature's soul', whose special power was that of 'awakening . . . higher and better feeling', Wiseman made no dramatic move of appropriation.[75]

A year later, however, the *Dublin Review*, now more committed than ever to its mission of winning converts from High Anglican waverers, decided to have done with caution and equivocation. Reviewing the Cardinal's lecture and Moxon's latest edition of Wordsworth's poetry, W. F. Finlason exploited Howitt's strategy of selective quotation and dogmatic assertion to the limit. Early in his long article he asserts that 'Wordsworth, though Protestant by education, was Catholic in character; Protestant by accident, he was Catholic by instinct; and thus his poetry owes its beauty to his unconscious sympathies with Catholicity'. Quoting extensively from *The Excursion* and then much later poems, Finlason makes a number of propositions which cannot but lead to the same triumphant conclusion. He accepts of course that Wordsworth was a Protestant, but this, he argues, was the result of 'false education and early prejudice', not 'the spontaneous growth of his mind'. Theologically Wordsworth is often shaky, but at such moments it is his intellect in command. Generally 'his heart was better than his head'. Finlason's strongest proposition is more inclusive still. It is simply that since 'Beauty and truth are always allied', Wordsworth 'was great in poetic beauty only when his muse sang in harmony and sympathy with Catholicism'. Quotation of true passages confirms their beauty: quotation of beautiful passages confirms their truth.[76]

IV

Wordsworth and Faber

This chapter has been concerned with acts of interpretation, construction, and appropriation in the early Victorian period. It concludes with perhaps the most striking of them all, an act of appropriation so concentrated and successful that it actually affected Wordsworth's poetry during its creation and thereby influenced which 'Wordsworth' was available to posterity. The agent was Frederick William Faber.

Faber (1814–67) first met Wordsworth in 1830 when he called at Rydal Mount, two years before going up to Balliol College,

Oxford. In 1837, now a Fellow of University College, he was ordained deacon and came closer to the poet during a period in which he assisted the incumbent at Ambleside. It was Faber's brother Francis who wrote to Wordsworth in 1839 enquiring whether he would accept an Honorary Degree,[77] and who hosted the breakfast party in Magdalen the day after the ceremony, at which Frederick Faber, Newman, and Keble were present. In 1840 Faber became tutor in a family in Ambleside connected with Wordsworth through marriage and after a foreign tour in 1841— undertaken partly to keep his charge, the eldest son, from 'vice'—he returned to Ambleside and to still closer intimacy with the poet and his circle.[78] After he had become Rector of Elton in Huntingdonshire Faber welcomed Wordsworth and his wife in 1844 on one of their visits south. A year later, however, the friendship came to an abrupt end. On 17 November 1845, Faber sent a brief note to Rydal Mount announcing his reception into the Roman Catholic Church.

Although Faber continued to correspond with Edward Quillinan, Wordsworth's Roman Catholic son-in-law, and to protest that his feelings for 'all the Wordsworths' were unchanged, Wordsworth broke with him completely.[79] Crabb Robinson was prepared to accept that while an Anglican Faber had not been 'conscious of being in heart a member of the Church of Rome',[80] but Wordsworth was incapable of this generous construction. He felt betrayed and his bitterness is an indication of how far the elderly poet had yielded to the personal and intellectual appeal of this extraordinary young man.[81]

That Faber had charisma is widely attested,[82] but there can be no greater proof than the fact that Crabb Robinson could not resist him. Finding him 'a flaming zealot', from whose views on everything he registered 'utter dissent', Crabb Robinson nevertheless admitted that Faber pleased him very much—by his spirited talk, his candour even in his prejudices, and, of course, his admiration for Wordsworth.[83] The poet's family was charmed. When he was in the Lakes Faber was attentive and when away he amused them with spirited letters about foreign adventures, or with accounts of his warfare against rabid dissenters in his new parish, which were tonic to the somewhat staid circle at Rydal Mount.[84]

What attracted the poet was something in addition to personal charm. The young priest displayed the kind of intellectual vigour Wordsworth had admired in Coleridge and Sir William Rowan

Hamilton and, unlike many clever young men, he could dispute with his elders without causing offence. He used his eyes, and although his sacramental vision of Nature differed essentially from Wordsworth's, the divergence inhibited neither conversation nor observation as they walked the hills around Ambleside. 'He had not only as good an eye for Nature as I have, but even a better one; and he sometimes pointed out to me on the mountains effects which, with all my great experience, I had never detected', Wordsworth admitted, impressed.[85] And Faber was a poet. Having won the Newdigate Prize in 1836, he published three volumes before becoming a Roman Catholic, which were bound to appeal to Wordsworth almost irrespective of their merits, as many of the poems celebrate named Lake District mountains and rivers in a manner closely akin to much of his own later verse.[86]

Faber's poetry is witness enough to Wordsworth's importance for him—to which one might add that a 19-year-old who eagerly plans to read *The Excursion* in its entirety twice is showing uncommon commmitment.[87] But, however it might have looked to the family at Rydal Mount, Faber was not just another Wordsworth disciple. Tested against his unyieldingly high Anglo-Catholic standards, most of Wordsworth's early poetry was found wanting. *Tintern Abbey* in particular Faber 'disliked' because of his 'great horror of Pantheism',[88] and though the later poetry fared better, it too was unsatisfactory in some respects. Wordsworth had been a force for good—that much Faber acknowledged when he described him as a '*Perirrhanterium*' or 'Sprinkler of Holy Water'—but he could not but 'mourn over his not having known Cath[olic] Truth when he was young'.[89] From the outset of his personal relationship with the poet Faber regarded himself as duty bound to bring Wordsworth closer to Catholic Truth now that he was old.

Many of Wordsworth's friends were elderly like himself and did not, or could not, share his passion for walking. Faber did. This may seem a trivial point to make in an account of an intellectual engagement, but it is, in fact, very important. Wordsworth had always unconsciously tested people by their willingness to get out and walk and the habit had not changed in old age, as many visitors to Rydal Mount discovered. Faber passed the test on all counts. He enjoyed walking whatever the season and, like the poet, he reckoned to use pedestrian time productively. In January 1843, for instance, Crabb Robinson, who was passing the Christmas season at Rydal Mount, was dragged away from his book to accompany Wordsworth and Faber on a walk during which Transubstantiation was the subject under discussion. He noted Wordsworth's 'deference towards his younger and more consistent friend'.[90] When Faber dedicated his *Sights and Thoughts in Foreign Churches and Among Foreign Peoples* (1842) to Wordsworth what he thanked him for in addition to personal kindness was 'Many Thoughtful Conversations on the Rites, Prerogatives, and Doctrines of the Holy Church'.[91]

Wordsworth's 'deference' towards his young friend, and his confidence in him, too, are evidenced by the fact that on one occasion he allowed him to speak on his behalf. During 1841 Wordsworth completed the poetic memorials of his 1837 Italian tour with *Musings Near Aquapendente*, a wide-ranging meditation on past and present, which purports to be the musings of the poet as he rests on a slope of the Apennines. As befits a poem written at the beginning of the 'hungry-forties', *Musings* is a melancholy piece, which rises to something like eloquence when the vigour of primitive faith is contrasted with that of the present

> chilled age, most pitiably shut out
> From that which *is* and actuates, by forms
> Abstractions, and by lifeless fact to fact
> Minutely linked with diligence uninspired,
> Unrectified, unguided, unsustained,
> By godlike insight.[92]

Feeling that a note was called for to situate this rather bleak assessment against more hopeful signs, Wordsworth entrusted the task to Faber, with the result that when the poem appeared in 1842 in *Poems, Chiefly of Early and Late Years*, what the public read *as by Wordsworth* was:

It would be ungenerous not to advert to the religious movement that, since the composition of these verses in 1837, has made itself felt, more or less strongly, throughout the English Church;—a movement that takes, for its first principle, a devout deference to the voice of Christian antiquity. It is not my office to pass judgment on questions of theological detail; but my own repugnance to the spirit and system of Romanism has been so repeatedly and, I trust, feelingly expressed, that I shall not be suspected of a leaning that way, if I do not join in the grave charge, thrown out, perhaps in the heat of controversy, against the learned and pious men to whose labours I allude. I speak apart from controversy; but, with strong faith in the moral temper which would elevate the present by doing reverence to the past, I would draw cheerful auguries for the English Church from this movement, as likely to restore among us a tone of piety more earnest and real, than that produced by the mere formalities of the understanding, refusing in a degree, which I cannot but lament, that its own temper and judgment shall be controlled by those of antiquity.[93]

It is hardly surprising that Crabb Robinson grew increasingly alarmed at Wordsworth's Puseyite drift.

Two years later—with *Contributions of William Wordsworth to the Revival of Catholic Truths* already in circulation—Faber made a more public act of appropriation. Preparing a life of St Bega for the *Lives of the English Saints* edited by Newman, Faber obtained Wordsworth's permission to append his *Stanzas Suggested in a Steamboat off Saint Bees' Heads*. Published in 1835 in *Yarrow Revisited*, the poem had been written in 1833, the year which Newman declared he always thought of as the beginning of the Oxford Movement.[94] The coincidence was not lost on Faber. Asked by the poet to ensure that the date of the poem's composition was printed, Faber took the opportunity to point out in a note that such an early date was 'a fresh instance of the remarkable way in which his poems did in divers places anticipate the revival of catholic doctrines among us'. While Faber acknowledges that Wordsworth's poetry 'prove[s] him to be very little in sympathy with Roman doctrine on the whole', the acknowledgement seems almost a concession rather than a positive point, given that what follows is renewed emphasis on the poet's 'affectionate reverence for the catholic past, the humble consciousness of a loss sustained by ourselves, the readiness to put a good construction on what he cannot wholly receive'.[95] The note was written by one whose vacillation was nearly at an end. 'I seem to grow more Roman daily,' Faber confessed to Newman in the same year.[96]

The acts of appropriation in these notes involved no more than highlighting some of Wordsworth's later poetry rather than his earlier and interpreting it in widely embracing statements which imply that the main body of the work has long since tended towards the promotion of Catholic Truth. In three instances, however, Wordsworth revised existing poems into greater conformity with an Anglo-Catholic interpretation. In two cases there is documentary evidence that Faber was the specific cause and in the third it is most likely that his influence was at work.

Ecclesiastical Sketches, first published in 1822, traced the progress of Christianity in Great Britain from its introduction to the present time. Additions were made to the original sequence in 1827, 1835, and 1845, either by sonnets composed for the series or by the inclusion of some which had appeared discretely elsewhere. Although the sequence is not historically inclusive—Mary Moorman has pointed out its notable silence about forms of dissent[97]— overall it stresses evolution and continuity and so Wordsworth acceded readily to suggestions from American admirers that the establishment of the American episcopacy was an appropriate subject for inclusion. Three sonnets on 'Aspects of Christianity in America' duly appeared in 1842.[98] Perhaps encouraged by this evidence that the poet was open to suggestion, Faber urged further additions which would own 'more explicitly our debt to the papacy' and so 'help to trim the balance (not very steady) of that series'.[99] Wordsworth responded with three sonnets which he said would serve 'to qualify or mitigate the condemnation which by conscience I am compelled to pass upon the abuses of the Roman See', and with a further six upon church services, which he thought 'wanting to complete the notice of the English Liturgy'.[100] Though Faber complained that they did not come up to his wish, the new sonnets colour the latter part of the sequence strongly, revealing how far the poet had moved towards Faber's goal that he should become 'more affectionately disposed towards authority & dogma'.[101]

The additional sonnets are the bulkiest testimony to Faber's influence on Wordsworth's poetry, but they almost certainly pleased him less than one further success, unnoticeable to all but most careful readers, yet astonishing in its significance.

High-churchmen were generally hostile to Milton. Not only were his republican politics of course anathema, but his theology too was suspect. *Paradise Lost* and *Paradise Regained* were no doubt great poems, but it was mainly dissenters who thought them great *Christian* poems. Orthodox Trinitarians held that both were evasive to the point of being effectively anti-Trinitarian and the recently discovered *De Doctrina Christiana* did nothing to alter their view. To those who admired Milton 'Publication of the treatise occasioned no little shock and disappointment . . . The *Christian Doctrine* revealed him an erring theologian, whose deviations now became apparent in *Paradise Lost*.' But for those who detested him, it was a welcome event—in Hurrell Froude's

gloating words, 'a final demolisher to his fame'.[102] Ten years after
its publication it was Clough's opinion that 'Were it not for the
happy notion that a man's poetry is not at all affected by his
opinions or indeed character and mind altogether, I fear the
Paradise Lost would be utterly unsaleable except for waste paper in
the University'.[103]

Incapable of being lukewarm about anything, Faber went far
beyond a simply intellectual disapproval in his response to Milton.
To him he was a living enemy, whose malignity must be countered
at every opportunity, and he vehemently repudiated the commonly
made distinction between the man and the work to which Clough
alludes:

I cannot understand the nice distinction of the man and the poet, pure
passages and impure. If a man wronged the person of my love, I could not
receive aid or pleasure from him; and I cannot conceive how anything like
a delicate and ardent love of the Saviour can enjoy the works of the
Saviour's enemy. Milton (accursed be his blasphemous memory) spent [a]
great part of his life in writing down my Lord's Divinity, my sole trust, my
sole love.[104]

Wordsworth, to the contrary, was steeped in Milton. In 1802 he
had summoned him as a flame to burn off the miasma of spiritual
degeneration:

> Milton! thou should'st be living at this hour:
> England hath need of thee: she is a fen
> Of stagnant waters . . .

and in 1814, in the 'Prospectus' to *The Recluse* published in the
Preface to *The Excursion*, he had disclosed that it was Milton who
was shaping his lofty conception of his own life's work:

> Of blessed consolations in distress;
> Of joy in widest commonalty spread;
> Of the individual Mind that keeps her own
> Inviolate retirement, subject there
> To Conscience only, and the law supreme
> Of that Intelligence which governs all;
> I sing:—'fit audience let me find though few!'
> So prayed, more gaining than he asked, the Bard,
> Holiest of Men . . .

The opening to *The Prelude*, had the public known it, would have revealed even more clearly that Wordsworth could not represent himself in his role as poet without evoking his great precursor.

Faber's opposition to Wordsworth's attitude to Milton was root-and-branch. It is difficult to credit his report, but by late 1842 he was claiming that tutored by him the poet 'already expresses strong distaste of the *opening* of Par. Lost'.[105] But Faber wanted more than a change of heart in the poet: the work needed to be changed. In private he railed against the 1802 sonnet:

England has no 'need' of Milton: how can a country have need of anything, policy, courage, talent, or anything else which is unblessed of God, and how can any talent in any subject be blessed by the Eternal Father for one who in prose and verse denied, ridiculed, blasphemed the Godhead of the Eternal Son?[106]

but though in the past Wordsworth had withdrawn poems from his canon in response to criticism,[107] it was not likely that he was going to withdraw one of his finest sonnets now. It may be, too, that Faber accepted that the damage the sonnet might do would be limited by its explicitly historical reference, that is, by the fact that it belonged to a moment in England's history now thankfully past.

Trans-historical, religious, or philosophical poetry, however, was another matter, and Faber looked for public recantation of at least the one utterance which gave such sharp offence to Anglo-Catholics that no less an admirer than Aubrey de Vere called it the 'worst line in Wordsworth'.[108] ' "So spake the bard, holiest of men"—if my tears could wash out those words, and the word "divine", the Excursion would go down to posterity free from that burden which now makes so many good men, at Oxford and elsewhere, look at it with coldness and distrust, when they might feed upon its Catholic grandeurs', Faber wrote to his brother in the letter already quoted. In a letter to Keble he was more optimistic of success. As Wordsworth became 'more affectionately disposed towards authority & dogma', Faber hoped that, 'we may at least be spared the pain of seeing Milton handed down in Wordsworth's verse as "holiest of men" '.[109] And his hope was fulfilled. In 1845 the objectionable line in the passage quoted above, which had been reprinted unchanged for thirty years, was emended to:

So prayed, more gaining than he asked, the Bard—
In holiest mood . . .

and this was the reading 'handed down' in all authorized editions thereafter.

Though the change in phrasing is slight, its significance is not. It is astonishing that, after his particular lifetime's endeavour, Wordsworth's orientation towards Milton can have changed, however slightly. But the edition of the collected poems of 1845 also contained further revision, bigger in itself and of greater significance, in that it substantially affected the 'Wordsworth' transmitted to the later nineteenth century.

1797–8 is known rightly as the *annus mirabilis*. During it an assured and productive poet composed *Tintern Abbey*—Faber's stumbling-block—many of the *Lyrical Ballads*, a great deal of meditative, quasi-philosophical blank verse, and *The Ruined Cottage*, whose final setting was Book I of *The Excursion*. (A brief introduction over familiar ground cannot be avoided here.) In *The Ruined Cottage* the Pedlar—a Wordsworthian persona—tells the story of the decline and death of Margaret to the poet-listener, who grieves as he learns the human meaning of the ruined walls and the overgrown garden which are all that remain. His tears are an appropriate, natural response to the tale the Pedlar has unfolded, but not the finally or fully appropriate one. The Pedlar invites his listener to share the wisdom he has attained:

> 'My Friend, enough to sorrow have you given,
> The purposes of wisdom ask no more;
> Be wise and chearful, and no longer read
> The forms of things with an unworthy eye.
> She sleeps in the calm earth, and peace is here.
> I well remember that those very plumes,
> Those weeds, and the high spear-grass on that wall,
> By mist and silent rain-drops silvered o'er,
> As once I passed did to my heart convey
> So still an image of tranquillity,
> So calm and still, and looked so beautiful
> Amid the uneasy thoughts which filled my mind,
> That what we feel of sorrow and despair
> From ruin and from change, and all the grief
> The passing shews of being leave behind,
> Appeared an idle dream that could not live
> Where meditation was. I turned away
> And walked along my road in happiness.'[110]

Clearly there are problems about this passage. They arise chiefly from questions which might be raised about the nature of the Pedlar's authority, and they drove Wordsworth to repeated reorganization of the whole poem before he embedded it in the dramatic structure of *The Excursion* in 1814. But although in the larger work the Pedlar's becomes only one voice in dialogue with the Solitary and the Pastor, his remains the dominant one and for thirty years this exposition of 'natural wisdom' remained unmodified. In 1845, however, the Pedlar's admonition to the poet was radically altered. His declaration now is that Margaret would not have wanted tears, for she was one

> Who, in her worst distress, had ofttimes felt
> The unbounded might of prayer; and learned, with soul
> Fixed on the Cross, that consolation springs,
> From sources deeper far than deepest pain,
> For the meek Sufferer.

Now when he picks up his own question about reading the 'forms of things with an unworthy eye', the Wanderer declares that 'sorrow and despair | From ruin and from change' are

> an idle dream, that could maintain,
> Nowhere, dominion o'er the enlightened spirit
> Whose meditative sympathies repose
> Upon the breast of Faith.

Wordsworth might have changed the Pedlar's exposition at any point after 1820, for protest had been made at its lack of explicit Christianity from the moment it was published, and he had himself drawn closer to the Church over the years. But he had not done so. Why did he change it now? Perhaps for many reasons. He was 74 years old and this, he must have known, would be his last chance. John Wilson's recently republished strictures were possibly a goad.[111] But the most likely reason *for this specific revision* is that Wordsworth was under Faber's sway.

Faber hated whatever smacked of Pantheism and he hated the vague. The Pedlar's exposition of 'natural wisdom' would have offended on both counts. More important, Faber dwelt passionately on the figure of Christ crucified and during his 1843 tour of Italy scoured Rome for a crucifix, acquiring one 'of ebony and ivory, so beautiful as to excite the envy even of my Roman Catholic friends from the absence of violent anatomy and distress. It was my joy and consolation in all my misery at Rome.' This is surprising, but much more so is the fact that the previous year he had persuaded Wordsworth to have a cedarwood Cross 'nailed up in [his] bedroom above his window, where the good old man's pleased eye rests on it first thing when he wakes'.[112] It is difficult now to register the full significance of this act. In the late 1830s and early 1840s the reappearance of the Cross on the altar of English parish churches was vehemently denounced as evidence of an insidious drift towards Rome. Clergymen who wore stoles with discreet embroidered crosses were at risk of being denounced as closet Papists. And the use of private aids to devotion beyond the Prayer Book and Bible was the clearest sign that a man's religion was becoming fevered.[113] But Faber clearly hoped that the poet would die, as Margaret does in the 1845 text, 'with soul | Fixed on the Cross', and the wooden Cross was nailed up.

How long it remained in place is not known, but it was probably soon removed, for by the time the 1845 edition was in circulation Faber had become a Roman Catholic and Wordsworth was in violent reaction against him. According to Crabb Robinson, he even intended 'introducing in the new edition a note expressing his regret that he had ever uttered a word favourable to Puseyism'.[114] But the note was never written and would have made little difference if it had been. Wordsworth's later work was easily absorbed into high Anglicanism and he had revised his earlier into conformity with it in the philosophical poem which mattered most to mid-Victorian readers, *The Excursion*. All that remained was that his biography should be written, in Bagehot's mordant words, 'with the apparent view of establishing that the great poet was a believer in rood-lofts, an idolator of piscinae'.[115]

3

'Fit Audience':
The Marketing of Wordsworth

Copyrights need be hereditary, for genius isn't.
(Dickens, on meeting William Wordsworth Jr., 1839)

I

Copyright and 'Pirates'

With Wordsworth buried, the posthumous *Prelude* published, and public memorials in place, the transmission of his influence entered a new phase. During the last fifteen years or so of the poet's life two Wordsworths had worked in conjunction. There was 'Wordsworth', the identifying term for an ever-increasing body of poetry and prose, some of which reached back to the end of the previous century. What constituted this 'Wordsworth' was of course strictly controlled by the poet and his publishers. He determined what the revised form of each new volume should be. They ensured that at least in Great Britain unauthorized publication was stopped. But there was also William Wordsworth, Esq., of Rydal Mount, latterly, as title-pages proudly announced, 'D.C.L., Poet Laureate, etc etc.'. This Wordsworth was accessible, either to the visitors at Rydal Mount, or to his many friends, particularly in London, whom he was still visiting in his late seventies. Reviews and articles up to 1850 dealing with 'Wordsworth' habitually referred to the Lake District sage in person, as if cherishing his continuing existence among the living.

A little after his death the situation was quite different. A few acquaintances recorded their meetings with the poet, but none of his friends rushed into print. As the sense of the poet as a living presence faded, Wordsworth became the published work, and it became a source of income, a commodity to be exploited, whose continuing value was inextricable from the skills of those who promoted it and the vagaries of the market. No one knew this better than Wordsworth's sons. Proud of their father's standing in the literature of his country and sensible of their duty as its custodians both to his memory and to the public he sought to reach, they were equally aware of the coarser facts of life—that their father's writings were worth money, that others wanted a share of it, and that their power to hold on to what they had inherited would not last long. The story of the transmission of Wordsworth until late in the century is bound up with their engagement, and that of others, with these commercial realities.

In 1814 in the Preface to *The Excursion* Wordsworth invoked Milton's 'fit audience let me find though few!', but the emphasis fell on 'fit' rather than 'few'. Despite occasional rodomontade about being hostile to publication, Wordsworth wanted readers and it was a solace in his old age to know that they stretched from North America to India. Pleasure was alloyed by the fact that readers who bought unauthorized editions contributed not a penny to the housekeeping at Rydal Mount, but before his death even this irritation was partly assuaged by the passing of copyright legislation which at least secured the position in the home market. William and John Wordsworth inherited a substantial literary property.[1]

Its value to them, however, was seriously diminished by the shape of Wordsworth's poetic career. The Act which was eventually passed after long campaigning in 1842 established copyright for the period of forty-two years from the date of a work's publication, or until seven years after the author's death, whichever was the longer, and Wordsworth died in 1850. But almost all of his best poetry had been published as far back as 1807, the date of his second great lyrical collection, *Poems, in Two Volumes*, and the two further volumes issued in 1815 marked the end of his great period. Wordsworth himself regarded them as a milestone. *The Excursion* had been published the previous year and now all the lyrical poetry, classified according to a scheme of the poet's own devising, was presented in a substantial Collected Works. To the poet, however, the edition was a milestone on a continuing way. Posterity may have judged that Wordsworth's creative life was over by 1815, but he emphatically did not. In the two collected volumes he was tidying up, not making an end, and he went on steadily issuing new volumes of original poetry until 1842 and substantially revised versions of the Collected Works until the very last year of his life. In 1849–50 a six-volume set appeared as the poet's final authorized edition. And ready for posthumous publication he left *The Prelude*. Amongst his papers was also *The Recluse*, Book I, the poem now known as *Home at Grasmere*, not fully prepared for publication, but publishable.

So the position was this. According to agreements entered into by the poet himself in 1836 and renegotiated by his literary executors in 1856 and again in 1877, Edward Moxon and Company, followed by Ward, Lock and Tyler, had exclusive rights to all Wordsworth's copyright material, published and unpublished.[2] Until 1892—forty-two years after the final authorized edition— they alone could claim to publish the *complete* poetical works. But this claim was more valuable in appearance than in fact, for after 1857—that is, seven years after the poet's death—anyone could publish the *best* of Wordsworth—the *Lyrical Ballads*, the 1807 poems, *The Excursion*—and they did.

Until 1892 Wordsworth's authorized publishers continued to issue the Complete Poetical Works, but they, and Wordsworth's heirs, were haunted by the clock. One by one Wordsworth's collected editions and separate volumes of original poetry came out of copyright protection. In 1857 the 1815 two-volume Collected Poems came out of copyright; in 1869 the 1827 five-volume Collected Edition; in 1877 the popular *Yarrow Revisited* volume of 1835; and in 1884 the last original volume, the 1842 *Poems, Chiefly of Early and Late Years*. Even the posthumous *Prelude* came into the public domain in 1892. On 4 June 1866 J. B. Payne of Moxon and Co. remarked in a gloomy letter, 'we must not, however, shut our eyes to the melancholy fact that each year renders our hold on the copyrights more slender, & the literary pirates more bold & successful in their depredations.'[3] It was not necessary for him to spell it out: John and William Wordsworth Jr. were all too well aware of their situation.

What little they could do to strengthen their position they did, but not before an ugly quarrel between the brothers had revealed how different were their attitudes to their inheritance. Ever since 1832 Moxon had been issuing collected editions of Wordsworth— each one with new poems and revisions to old—in a format which became a sort of Moxon–Wordsworth trade mark. Available since

1836 in uniform binder's cloth these multi-volume sets have an air of discreet authority about them. As the agreement their father had made with Moxon in 1836 neared expiry, however, John Wordsworth advocated a complete change. Moxon aimed at the middle classes, but it was their duty, John argued, to disseminate their father's poetry not to the few but to the many. At least as important in his thinking was the conviction that more money was to be made by more agressive and flashy marketing than Moxon was capable of. Moxon should be thrown over in favour of George Routledge, a publisher of the new breed who wooed 'the patronage of the masses'. Cautious, unconvinced that the masses were clamouring to buy poetry, and sensitive that John's suggestion smacked of the ungentlemanly, William resisted and, after a bitter exchange of letters, carried the day.[4] He was supported in his stand by his co-executor, who did not care to do business with such as Routledge: 'he is not the man I should wish to have the publication of your father's poems.'[5] A new agreement was signed with Moxon, which resulted in the publication in 1857—that is, when competitors were first free to enter the market—in a freshly edited six-volume edition.

It was prepared and seen through the press by John Carter, who had been Wordsworth's clerk since 1813. Carter was thorough to the point of fussiness over correcting the text and wilful in the matter of punctuation. As Jared Curtis puts it: 'In punctuation and spelling . . . [he] considered himself more expert than his late employer.'[6] But the prefatory 'Advertisement' to the edition did not announce these changes. What it dwelt on was that for the first time the notes which Wordsworth had dictated in 1843 were being published as headnotes to the poems, because although the poet had not intended their release, his Trustees could see no 'valid reason why the pleasure and benefit to be derived from the Notes should not . . . be more widely diffused'.[7] What the preface did not disclose was that the loyal Carter had also worked through the notes, excising whatever might conceivably give offence or reveal Wordsworth warts and all. A caustic comment here, an unguarded remark there—all were removed. As Curtis concludes, 'the moral and dignified poet perceived by the Victorians, and received by later generations of readers, was in significant measure a Wordsworth constructed and presented by John Carter, the *executor* of his literary estate.'[8]

In one respect the collected edition of 1857 was a shrewd piece of business. Christopher Wordsworth's *Memoirs* had given glimpses of the 'Fenwick' Notes; now they were being published.[9] The edition put the text of the poems which had been in any way revised back into copyright and it established copyright in the notes. Appearing with the imprimatur of Wordsworth's Trustees and revealing extensive material previously unpublished, the edition also affirmed that Rydal Mount remained the source of authority for Wordsworthian matters and that the family retained its interest in its literary property. Both of these implied affirmations were to emerge as troubling realities to editors later in the century.

For the rest of the copyright term six-volume sets appeared in stately procession, either reprints of the 1849–50 edition or versions of the 1857, which continued to carry the title-page vaunt, 'A New Edition' until the end of the line. They were complemented by large-format one-volume editions, redactions of the edition first issued in 1845, which graduated over time from the splendid to the magnificent. By 1889 the one-volume 'Complete Copyright Edition' was available in various versions, the most sumptuous of which, illustrated and printed on heavy untrimmed paper, is a fine example of the quality of design and printing which commercial publishers could attain.

As the copyright term neared its end, the Wordsworths acceded after initial reluctance to a request from Professor William Knight of St Andrews University to be allowed to publish a scholarly edition of the Complete Works, including all unpublished material. Between 1882 and 1889 Knight issued eleven majestic volumes, the result of extraordinary labour, which mark the beginning of a new phase in Wordsworth's publishing history as the poetry passed into the control of academics and became a subject for research.[10] Knight believed he was performing a once-for-all labour, but, as a later chapter demonstrates, he actually prompted an avalanche of scholarly publishing and began a dispute about the canon and the state of Wordsworth's text which continues to this day.

Over the decades between Wordsworth's death and the appearance of Knight's first volume, Moxon and then Ward, Lock dominated the field and other publishers had no option but to let them occupy the main ground. But other areas were there to be won and as soon as the law of copyright permitted they swarmed in to take them. Wordsworth was disseminated in astonishing quantity and across a wide range of publishing styles. Between 1858 and 1882 more than thirty substantial editions appeared in Britain and America and more than twenty editions of selections or single works.[11] There was keen competition between one-volume editions, which until late in the century were generally handsome books. Casings in blue or red shone with elaborate motifs in gold. The text was often framed within marginal rules, also in colour. A memoir of Wordsworth's life, a frontispiece plate, and illustrations to the poems were customary. The volumes issued by Routledge, 1858, Gall and Inglis, 1858, Nelson, 1861, and Nimmo of Edinburgh, 1863, set the standard.

Unwrapping, handling, reading these books must have given pleasure. The same cannot be said of publications at the other end of the market, the school texts. Paper-covered editions of the first book of *The Excursion*, 'The Wanderer', were published in 1863 (James Gordon, Edinburgh, Hamilton Adams, London), 1864 (Longman) and 1874 (Rivington, London, Oxford, Cambridge). If the illustrated editions tended to stimulate the airy-fairy imaginings of a Sissy Jupe, these unlovely little books were aimed at Bitzer. As Ian Michael has pointed out in his authoritative study of instructional manuals and anthologies, the establishment of public examinations from the 1850s onwards opened commercial possibilities for texts in which poetry is subjugated to the pedagogic function.[12] In 1863 Wordsworth's lines are presented as an opportunity for 'Grammatical Analysis and ... Paraphrasing' by the Revd H. G. Robinson,[13] and even more crushingly by the Revd C. H. Bromby in 1864 as exemplification of his own prefatory essay on 'Analytical Syntax'. In the notes to both editions practically every line is remorselessly parsed. The slim tract-style issue of the same book of *The Excursion* put out by the Society for Promoting Christian Knowledge in 1865, which at least lets the poetry speak as poetry, looks inviting by comparison.

The single volumes issued by Routledge, Nimmo and others, though attractive as objects, were books to be read. They printed as fully as copyright allowed the text of the poems in the order Wordsworth had specified. Other volumes, however, unequivocally aimed at beauty. The finest of them all was the selection by Robert Aris Willmott issued by Routledge in July and November 1859 in two printings of 5,000 and 3,000 copies respectively and reissued in August 1866 in a run of a further 3,000 copies at a guinea each.

Finely printed on good paper, cased in elaborately stamped, heavy boards, designed by Albert Warren, the poems are a vehicle for the illustrations by Birket Foster, Joseph Wolf, and John Gilbert, engraved on wood by the Dalziel brothers. The engravings alone cost the publisher £1,025.[14] Equal second place must go to *Wordsworth's Poems for the Young*, illustrated by John Macwhirter and John Pettie, with a vignette by John Everett Millais (Alexander Strahan, 1863, 1866, 1870) and *The White Doe of Rylstone*, illustrated by Birket Foster and H. Noel Humphreys (Longman, Brown, Green, Longmans and Roberts, 1859), reissued in smaller format by Bell and Daldy in 1867. The front-cover designs on both are splendid in various colours, the centre-piece of the latter in both issues being an embossed doe in white.[15] *The White Doe* was also available in a composition binding imitating green malachite, which shimmers in the light. Its marbled endpapers masquerade as silk and all edges are heavily gilt.[16]

Although executors and publishers customarily referred to these rivals as 'pirates', they were not really pirates. They respected the copyright position and in exploiting the market within the law they could not be convicted of robbing the executors of anything that was strictly theirs. Any breach of copyright, however, was a piratical act, which had to be countered. In theory this might seem a straightforward matter. Permission in all copyright materials is simply denied to anyone other than the authorized publisher. In practice it proved vexatious and far from straightforward.

In 1864, for instance, a certain A. W. Bennett asked and received permission to print some copyright pieces in his forthcoming *Our English Lakes, Mountains, and Waterfalls, as seen by William Wordsworth.*[17] When this very handsome book came to their notice, however, the Wordsworth camp was horrified. True, Bennett had only printed a few copyright pieces and had courteously acknowledged his obligation to Moxon for permission, but he printed *nothing but Wordsworth*. His book was a beautifully presented Wordsworth reader, strikingly illustrated with photographs of the Lake District. The compiler's introduction brazenly referred to it as a 'Selection from Wordsworth's Poetical Writings'. Worse still, Bennett had included a facsimile of the poet's autograph from a scrap of manuscript he had inherited and which, making a common mistake, he believed he could reproduce, since he owned the document itself. This was the most piratical publication the executors had encountered and they reacted with vigour.

William Wordsworth Jr. felt on safe ground. He recollected giving Bennett permission for a list which 'did not appear to contain any poems but those out of copyright, & I remarked at the time "that if that were so, as we could not bite, it was no use barking & we might as well make a virtue of necessity—and not refuse his application" '.[18] But Bennett had disgracefully exploited this generosity, so William thought, and he asked for Strickland Cookson's help in suppressing at the very least 'his most impudent facsimile'. On 22 December 1864 Bennett was threatened with a Chancery injunction to prevent the sale of his book unless he undertook to remove the facsimile and all copyright pieces. The executors' position was clear. Or rather, it was until William began to waver. Bennett's book was a *fait accompli* and it had, moreover, apparently sold 1,350 copies in only a few months. Instead of suppressing it, why not make money out of it? And so on 6 January 1865 he proposed that in return for being allowed to use a few more copyright pieces should he so wish, Bennett should hand over one-third of his existing and future profits to Moxon and the Wordsworths, and add Moxon's name to the title-page. Copyright, it seems, was not sacrosanct provided the sale price was right. Not surprisingly Bennett refused to countenance William's outrageous proposal. With some protest he swallowed the executors' withdrawal of permission that had been granted and suppressed the copyright pieces, but he still had a handsome book, and it went through three further editions without the Court of Chancery being disturbed.[19]

At one point in the correspondence Bennett unwittingly touched on the executors' most sensitive nerve. Expressing his hope on 30 August 1865 that they would not hinder another edition, he remarked to William: 'should you think well to renew your permission for any or all of them to be included in a new edition, I believe it will give real pleasure to many admirers of Mr Wordsworth's poetry.' The Wordsworths were all in favour of pleasing admirers of their father's poetry, but they wanted them to buy authorized editions, not scissors-and-paste productions. When William sent a kindly letter in the same year to another would-be anthologist, a Mr Evans from Manchester, J. B. Payne, writing on

26 July on behalf of Moxon, chided him for his generosity and urged him to hold the line of self-interest:

Mr Evans appears to be a person anxious to make his fame out of an appreciation of others' work, & to make money by a shrewd use of paste and scissors. Of all classes of pirates, this is the most dangerous to authors & publishers; the plausibility of its members, & the half-injured tone these assume as if in deprecation of refusal, are to the inexperienced, irresistable [sic]—while collections & selections do more harm to copyright books than anything else.

William Wordsworth was not 'inexperienced', and he knew how to turn down requests, but as the century rolled on a note of desperation enters his correspondence, as he recognizes that his position is growing weaker every year.

Adventurers could be combatted by the timely threat of a Chancery injunction, but the 'pirates' could not be stopped. The only strategy that might reclaim some of their gains was a counter-offensive. Moxon's first attempt was not auspicious. In 1857—that is when other publishers were first free to enter the market—a one-volume *The Earlier Poems of William Wordsworth* was issued concurrently with the six-volume complete works. Edited by William Johnston, who provided some textual apparatus and a serviceable account of Wordsworth's early career, the book was well printed and laid out, but it was unfortunately titled, 'earlier poems' suggesting juvenilia rather than 'poems up to 1814', and it was rather drab. It looks like a volume so conscious of its own distinguished lineage that it does not need to woo buyers. The contrast when Routledge entered the market a year later could not have been greater. His one-volume Wordsworth also carried an introduction and it included more poetry than *The Earlier Poems*, but its main appeal was to the eye. Illustrated by Birket Foster, the poems are printed within a red single-line border on the page, and cased in brightly coloured, gilt-embossed boards. This book had a long life, whereas *The Earlier Poems* was a commercial failure, written off in 1868 as having 'no probable chance of . . . recouping itself'.[20]

Moxon and Co. could produce beautiful books—*The Princess* (1860), for example, is a high-spot in any Victorian collection—but it was not until 1865 that an eye-catching production complemented the firm's stately but rather austere multi-volume sets of Wordsworth. A strikingly beautiful book, *Selection from the Works of William Wordsworth*, edited and introduced by the now well-known name, Francis Turner Palgrave, ought to have been a success. In *The Golden Treasury* (1861) its editor had already established his credentials both as an anthologist of sensibility and tact and as a Wordsworthian, and his selection for Moxon, in the publisher's judgement, could only enhance Palgrave's reputation as 'a judicious critic & as an elegant scholar'. But sales never took off.²¹ Moxon remained hopeful, but the Wordsworths had to grow used to disappointing statements of account accompanied by assurances that the selections would soon 'do something for us, & tend to make the balances more respectable' (28 March 1866).

Nor was another venture much luckier. In 1870 Moxon decided to launch a new edition which was to 'prevent these pirates from having it so much their own way as heretofore' (17 February 1870) by an assault on three fronts. The book was to be sumptuous, all edges gilt, its boards illuminated, with a fleur-de-lis device, in blue, cream, and gold; it was to carry full-page 'artistic etchings' by Edwin Edwards; and it was to be prefaced by an essay by William Michael Rossetti.²² This latter was important. Ever since Routledge's edition of 1858 it had been common for editions to carry a biographical-critical notice. Material gleaned from Christopher Wordsworth's *Memoirs* and from De Quincey were glued together with platitudes about the poet as philosopher and moral sage. Their standard of accuracy can be gauged from the fact that over successive printings editions put out by three different publishers, Gall and Inglis, Nelson, and Milner and Sowerby, gave two different dates for Wordsworth's death, both wrong. Now Wordsworth's authorized publisher was going to offer a Complete Works with a Preface that would set a new standard.

When they saw it, however, the Wordsworths were incensed. Nothing about the volume could compensate for the outrage of the Preface. Not only had Rossetti too made factual errors, claiming for example that Wordsworth had taken an MA at Cambridge and that he had married his cousin, but, much worse, he had drawn on De Quincey for comments such as, 'he was not to be called a practically self-denying or generous man', and had dwelt at such length on Wordsworth's 'defects'—personal, poetic, political—that what came over most clearly was that Rossetti certainly did not find him 'in the large sense, a fascinating or attractive writer'. Charles Wordsworth, Bishop of St Andrews, spoke for the whole family when he declared the tone of the piece 'so low and bad throughout that it is impossible to correct or improve it' (10 June 1871). The Preface had to go. That Palgrave's Preface might be substituted for Rossetti's, was one suggestion made. That the family might be forced to publish a repudiation if the Rossetti offence were not suppressed, was another.

Moxon and Co. weakly defended themselves, claiming that Rossetti was 'admittedly one of the best—if not the best—among English critics of the present day'—and their legal right to resist suppression was undoubted,[23] but they could not withstand massed family and episcopal displeasure and eventually a revised Preface was issued. The factual errors were corrected and the opprobrium for the remarks about Wordsworth's lack of generosity was shifted on to De Quincey by the deft introduction of a reference to him as a 'disputable authority'. But the tenor of Rossetti's essay was unchanged and it remained a source of bitterness to the Wordsworth family, particularly as both the revised and unrevised versions of the Preface remained current in the 1870s, despite Moxon and Co.'s stated willingness to accede to family wishes.[24]

II

The Open Market

The moment at which publishers other than Moxon were free to market Wordsworth coincided with the beginning of the golden age of British book illustration.[25] Routledge and Gall and Inglis in direct competition in 1858 set the standard for one-volume editions—Routledge's carrying superior illustrations by Birket Foster—and it immediately became all but obligatory for editions other than Moxon's to boast illustrations—head-pieces, roundels, vignettes, and full-page plates. Routledge raised the stakes with the lavish *Poems of William Wordsworth*, edited by Robert Aris Willmott, already mentioned and with *The Deserted Cottage* (1859), also illustrated by Foster, Wolf and Gilbert, engraved by the Dalziels. The challenge was taken up by Sampson Low, Son, and Marston with Wordsworth's *Pastoral Poems* (1859), carrying twenty plates, and by the very beautiful volumes already mentioned,

Bell and Daldy's *The White Doe of Rylstone* (1867), and Alexander Strahan's *Wordsworth's Poems for the Young* (1863). These were the high points, but many other publishers claimed a share of the market for illustrated editions—Thomas Nelson, Milner and Sowerby, William Nimmo, and Frederick Warne being the most established firms.

Wordsworth's offical publishers could not remain aloof, ignoring an important sector of the market. In 1871 Moxon issued the sumptuous edition, already touched on, illustrated by Edwin Edwards with W. M. Rossetti's preface, and subsequently issued another 'Only Complete Edition', which retained the head-piece illustrations of the 1871 while replacing the full plates with illustrations by Henry Dell.[26] Having broken with past austerity of design, the firm now upgraded the large-format one-volume edition by introducing a pot-pourri of illustrations by various (largely unidentified) artists.[27]

Illustration was not confined to the traditional media. As poet of famously beautiful landscapes Wordsworth cried out for photographic treatment and as the railway network made access easier, photographers were soon hauling their cumbersome equipment to scenes previously recorded only in the sketch-book. A. W. Bennett seems to have been the earliest to exploit Wordsworth and the new technology in his *Our English Lakes, Mountains and Waterfalls* (1864, 1866, 1868, 1870), photographer Thomas Ogle of Penrith. Later in the century Warne's 'Albion Edition' was issued with photographs by Payne Jennings of Lake District scenes. Another version appeared under the imprint of Peacock, Mansfield and Britton, with photographs, by an unidentified photographer, of scenes in harmony with quotations from Wordsworth, such as 'Calm is all Nature as a resting wheel'.

This brief bibliographical excursus is sufficient to establish a simple fact: from the middle of the century readers browsing through the solid mass of text in their new volume of Wordsworth could rest the eye on pictures. Many of the illustrations did long service, appearing over decades in successive editions, and, following the cavalier, common practice of the trade, they sometimes migrated between publishers. In some cases it is evident that little care was taken over the choice of illustration. Engravings that were to hand or could easily be bought in were used with scant regard either to stylistic consistency in the volume overall, or to the closeness of their relation to the text. Take, for example, the illustration to *The Waggoner* in Warne's 'Lansdowne Poets' edition. Wordsworth's Benjamin rumbles along a precisely identified road in the Lake District. Helm Crag, Dun-mail raise, Rydal Mere, Helvellyn, Wytheburn—all of these place-names plot his course in the poem. But Wordsworth's topographical specificity counts for nothing in one of the issues of the 'Lansdowne Poets' volume. In the illustration to *The Waggoner* a milestone reads 'To Lon[don]'.

Cobbling together illustration and text produces a still more ludicrous result in the frequently reprinted Gall and Inglis volume. The title-page depicts a woman in possibly seventeenth-century costume, seated at a desk, who is gazing up to huge, latticed windows through which light is streaming. The room is panelled and ceiling to floor curtains enclose the window embrasure. And this is meant to illustrate lines from Wordsworth's most poignant lament for loss of the sense of 'splendour in the grass, of glory in the flower':

> It is not now as it has been of yore.
> Turn whereso'er I may,
> By night or day,
> The things which I have seen I now can see no more!

The lady is certainly gazing, which is about the best that can be said for this wholly inappropriate image. Other illustrations, not inappropriate in themselves, simply waste paper. In Ward, Lock's 1889 volume, for example, a whole page (opp. p. 200) is given over to illustrating Wordsworth's sonnet, 'Written Upon a Blank Leaf in "The Complete Angler" '. The image does not interpret the poem, for there are no interpretative possibilities in it. But it is an agreeable picture of a man fishing.

In many editions a closer match of image and text made for a more pleasing overall effect. Naturally, commissioned artists searched the poems for a peg on which to hang the kind of image they were most skilled at. The merest mention of a bird or lamb was a sufficient prompt for a highly detailed, close-up drawing for the 1859 Willmott edition from Joseph Wolf, whose forte was such images of the natural world. In the same edition Birket Foster plucked out the line, 'This sea that bares her bosom to the moon', from the sonnet, 'The World is too much with us', as an opportunity for a fine sea and cloudscape. Henry Dell later

The
Poetical Works
of
William Wordsworth

It is not now as it has been of yore,
Turn wheresoe'er I may,
By night or day
The things which I have seen I now can see no more
Ode - Immortality p 494

EDINBURGH. GALL & INGLIS. LONDON

FIG. 2. Title-page to the Gall and Inglis *Poetical Works*

achieved comparable effects to Foster's, with louring skies, the sea, and mountains. But although the occasion for the particular image is often very slight, these illustrations do evoke an appropriately Wordsworthian atmosphere. By no means invariably picturesque in composition, the images of lakes and mountains convey a sense of distance, of potential sublimity, and in the twilight scenes, of the brooding and elegiac.

Many of the engravings, however, did make some attempt to attend to the essential human situation of a passage or a whole poem. The little girl being questioned in *We Are Seven*; Luke taking his farewell in *Michael*; the boy luxuriating before he begins his pillage in *Nutting*; the Wanderer from *The Excursion* visiting Margaret or telling her story to the poet; the Solitary Reaper bending over her work—such figures appear repeatedly. But generally what extraordinary figures they are. In the Gall and Inglis

And all the neighbours as he passed their doors
Came forth with wishes and with farewell prayers.
Michael p. 331

FIG. 3. Luke's farewell in 'Michael' in the Gall and Inglis *Poetical Works*

edition, for example, Luke is depicted saying goodbye to 'all the neighbours'. Dressed in part-medieval, part-Scottish tunic and plaid, he is standing outside the trellised porch of a *thatched* cottage, in a village street of thatched cottages. It might be the Cotswolds or Dorset, but it is a long way south from the landscape of slate and stone and isolated cottages such as 'The Evening Star'.

Nutting is a poem in which calm is followed by ravage. Illustrators tended to prefer the calm. In the Gall and Inglis edition a chubby little boy, accoutred in 'medieval' tunic with a curved dagger at his belt, stands with face so rapt, in a bower so dense with foliage and waving grasses, that he must be communing with fairy-folk. His expression is shared by the boy in the Sampson Low *Pastoral Poems*, but this lad is still more luxuriously dressed in velveteen tunic and bonnet and looks quite incapable of rising from his repose, let alone committing rapine on a grove of hazels.

the hazels rose
Tall and erect, with milk white clusters hung.
A virgin scene! . . A little while I stood,
Breathing with such suppression of the heart
As joy delights in.

Nutting p. 359

FIG. 4. Illustration to 'Nutting' in the Gall and Inglis *Poetical Works*

FIG. 5. Illustration to 'Nutting' in the Sampson Low *Pastoral Poems*

In all of the figure compositions children, especially young maidens, dominate. They are invariably healthy and decently dressed, only a bundle of sticks under the arm or some such sign indicating that they are rustics. Boys, when they appear, are generally feminized, both in dress and facial characteristics. Adult males are usually gentlemen in appearance, or elderly and stooping, or both, and they always look benign. There are no urban scenes. Birket Foster in 1859 depicts Poor Susan in her reverie as a maiden with bonnet and shawl, who would not be out of place among the ladies in Millais's illustrations to Trollope. By choosing to illustrate Susan's dream rather than the reality of her situation, Foster is enabled, of course, to place her amidst thatched cottages and wattle hedges rather than in Lothbury and Cheapside.

Landscape, animals and birds, some human beings, these are the limits of the illustrations to Wordsworth. The Solitary's sufferings are not depicted, nor the anguish of the Sailor in *Guilt and Sorrow*. No attempt is made to suggest the poetry's philosophical or religious dimension. The political Wordsworth is ignored, as is whatever is disquieting or threatening. What Wordsworth in *Michael* calls the 'homely and rude' is domesticated and sentimentalized. The engravings and photographs promote Wordsworth essentially as the celebrant of an idealized English rural life, of domestic virtues, of children and old age, and of benignity. Most insistent of all is the suggestion conveyed through the sheer number of the images of specific places that Wordsworth's was not a landscape of the imagination, but the Lake District, a paradise to be regained by anyone at the cost of a rail ticket. One edition even crossed the line dividing a volume of poems from a guidebook. Nelson's 1865 *Poetical Works* contains numerous unassuming, flatly representational topographical engravings. Above the one depicting Grasmere Lake (opp. p. 264) are the names of the mountains and above the village an arrow is all but drawn in to the words, 'Grasmere Village, the burial place of Wordsworth'.

III

The Question of Text

In the struggle for a share of the market in illustrated or beautiful gift-books Moxon had to compete on equal terms with other publishers. Only in the matter of textual authority did the firm occupy a superior position. Moxon's rivals, as this chapter has indicated, did not let this cramp their entrepreneurial activity, a fact of publishing history which raises a further issue. It can be stated very simply. Wordsworth was presented to Victorian readers in a variety of packagings, but what were they getting? George Eliot, Mill, Ruskin, and Tennyson—these all read Wordsworth in editions published in his lifetime and of course many other Victorians did too. But which of Wordsworth's words did someone read who bought an edition published after the poet's death in 1850?

A slight recapitulation brings the issue into focus. Wordsworth compulsively revised his poems. His latest comprehensive revision was in 1845, but the edition of 1849–50 contained a little more tinkering and as the final volumes appeared more or less as he died, this is the edition which bears the stamp of final authority. Slightly tidied up, its text remained the basis for all of the Moxon and later Ward, Lock Complete Poetical Works later in the century, and for all serious editions until the appearance of the still ongoing *Cornell Wordsworth* in the 1970s.[28] Victorian readers who cared about these matters and wanted the genuine article, so to speak, bought a Moxon or Ward, Lock edition. Those who preferred a cheaper book, however, or a more attractive one, or who wanted a selection rather than a complete works, were confronted by textual anarchy.

Routledge in 1858, 'availing ourselves of every piece which expired copyright places within our reach', reprinted Wordsworth's two-volume collection of 1815, with *The Excursion* added, and continued to do so in subsequent issues.[29] Warne's 'Chandos Classics' in 1872, reprinted the heavily revised five-volume Collected Edition of 1827, but when it was reissued as 'The Arundel Poets' in 1880 the 1835 *Yarrow Revisited* poems had been incorporated.

For his magnificently illustrated and produced selection in 1859 Robert Aris Willmott chose to print *An Evening Walk* not from a first edition of 1793, nor from the last, nor from any single intervening one, but in a text he constructed himself.[30] Other editors of selections exercised similar creative freedom. They excerpted passages and printed them as poems. They chose pieces from this edition or that and so produced a textual hybrid. They ignored Wordsworth's classification of his poems, preferring to group them according to systems of their own, and, perhaps more damaging, they often embellished extracts with titles entirely of their own invention. Aris Willmott favoured simple, descriptive titles, such as 'The Rivulet' or 'Greek Superstitions', for passages whose source and context he conceals. Another swashbuckler, Andrew James Symington, preferred the sonorous, heading extracts from *The Excursion* with titles such as 'Life under the British Constitution' and 'Loyalty to Church and State'.[31] The future President of the Wordsworth Society was no more scrupulous. Matthew Arnold showed concern for the aesthetics of his *Poems of Wordsworth* (1879), chivvying his publisher about details of typography and layout, and although the ordering of the poems was not Wordsworth's, it was the result of deliberation—'I have always wished to arrange these poems in some natural and logical order', Arnold told Macmillan.[32] His approach to the text of what he selected, on the other hand, could not have been more cavalier.

In the early stages of production, when the volume was being assessed for length, the printers were instructed to set up from a version of the 1845 single volume, against which Macmillan proposed to check readings from the 1832 four-volume edition, borrowed from 'some public or private library'. But Arnold also wanted to include some of the notes from the 1857 edition and to take some readings from the two-volume collection of 1815. It was in keeping with the spirit of the book's textual integrity that Arnold felt free to alter the titles of poems or to make up titles of his own.

What did this textual anarchy mean in practice? Those who bought the very attractive Gall and Inglis one volume in 1858 read the following lines in *Michael*:

> There is a comfort in the strength of love;
> 'Twill make a thing endurable, which else
> Would break the heart:—old Michael found it so.[33]

But thirty-eight years previously Wordsworth had changed these lines in inspired revision to:

> There is a comfort in the strength of love;
> 'Twill make a thing endurable, which else
> Would overset the brain, or break the heart.

And this was the version which anyone enjoying the poem in a Moxon edition in 1858 would have read. Scores of similar examples could be given, but reading even a representative list would be tedious. One substantial illustration must serve.

Book I of *The Excursion*, the story of the suffering and death of Margaret, which is now most commonly read in its original form as *The Ruined Cottage*, was a Victorian favourite. Routledge issued it in 1859 as a separate volume called *The Deserted Cottage*, with illustrations by Birket Foster, Joseph Wolf, and John Gilbert,[34] and it was frequently reprinted in pamphlet form for use in schools. It appeared in its proper setting in *The Excursion*, of course, in all Moxon complete and rival so-called complete editions. The conclusion to the story of Margaret, however, is an especially important case in the history of Wordsworth's revisions. As has been observed, the text of its first appearance in *The Excursion* in 1814 provoked exacting Christians to object that it failed to offer explicitly the consolations of Christianity—and one can see why. When the Pedlar attempts to place Margaret's suffering and death in a larger context, what he offers to his listener, the poet, is a purely 'natural wisdom', as he closes his story with an evocation of that tranquillity which the dead woman now shares. So the poem stood for thirty years, but in 1845, as has been discussed in the previous chapter, it was radically changed. Now the poet is told not to grieve for Margaret, for she had felt the 'unbounded might of prayer', and had drawn deepest consolation from the Cross. Whereas in 1814 the Wanderer's 'uneasy thoughts' and 'sorrow and despair | From ruin and from change' were tempered by meditation on the natural scene, in 1845 they are dismissed as,

> an idle dream, that could maintain
> Nowhere, dominion o'er the enlightened spirit
> Whose meditative sympathies repose
> Upon the breast of Faith.

These were the Christian words printed in all Moxon editions, of course, and in many others. But by no means in all. Reprinting *The Excursion* from pre-1845 unrevised texts, some editions continued to promulgate the 'natural wisdom' version the poet had so decisively altered. This was even true of the little booklets issued for schools. In 1865, if your school was using the text put out by the SPCK, not surprisingly you encountered the Christian version. But if your school in 1865 had decided to order the Reverend C. H. Bromby's edition ('With Full Notes and a Treatise Upon the Analysis of Sentences'), what you read was the 'natural wisdom' text.

On the visit to the Quantocks which moved him so deeply, Hale White reread *The Excursion*, Book I, and made the comment already quoted in Chapter 1: 'Much of the religion by which Wordsworth lives is very indefinite. Look at the close of this poem ... Because this religion is indefinite it is not therefore the less supporting.'[35] What he entered in his journal was the conclusion of the Pedlar's 'natural wisdom' in its pre-1845 version. In the revised text the religious consolation offered is not the least 'indefinite'.

Hale White was a textual scholar and a learned Wordsworthian, so we may perhaps assume that he was consciously choosing to read Wordsworth in the text in which he first encountered him as a young man. But for others, whether they found the religion of *The Excursion*, Book I, 'indefinite' or not depended on which edition they had bought.

IV

Anthologies and Selections

Victorian readers relished weighty books, but even the most ardent must have been daunted by Moxon's Complete Works. The single-volume edition consisted of around 700 pages of double-column text. The alternative for most of the copyright term was an edition in six volumes. Wordsworth's poetry invited, perhaps demanded, sifting.

'Gems' from Wordsworth had, of course, long been offered in anthologies. Some of these were organized around a theme, such as *The Language of Flowers* (c.1850), or *The Heart's Ease: A Choice Wreath of Poetry* (c.1850), a gathering of poems of sentiment. Others with titles such as *Beauties of the Modern Poets* (1826), *The Casquet of Literary Gems* (1828), *The Beauties of Poesy* (1826), or *The Talisman, or, Bouquet of Literature and the Fine Arts* (1831), offer a Wordsworth poem or two in gift-book packaging. *The Pious Minstrel* (1831) includes some Wordsworth in a garnering of 'Sacred Poetry'. Generations of children first encountered Wordsworth in Lindley Murray's *Introduction to the English Reader* (from 1801; many times reprinted), where 'The Pet Lamb' was, in the words of the full title, one of 'a selection of pieces, in prose and poetry, calculated to improve the younger classes of learners in reading; and to imbue their minds with love of virtue', or in collections such as the SPCK's *Readings in Poetry* (1833), or *The Juvenile Kaleidoscope; Containing Narratives, Sketches, &c. for the Instruction and Amusement of the Young* (1834). Richard Batt, a teacher at The Friends' School in Lancaster, included Wordsworth in *Gleanings in Poetry* (1836), a collection which is prefaced by an important essay on the place of poetry in genuine education.[36] As Ian Michael has established in his pioneering study of 114 anthologies from 1802 to 1870, by late in the period Wordsworth had displaced such stalwarts as Cowper and Campbell to become the second most anthologized poet after Shakespeare.[37]

Wordsworth's poetry was disseminated all over the English-speaking world in literally hundreds of annuals, keepsakes, casquets, and readers, but while some of these often very pretty books were no doubt precious to their owners, who perhaps read a Wordsworth poem for the first time in them, neither they, nor the schoolbooks being thumbed in the farthest reaches of the empire had any significant impact on the way Wordsworth was perceived. As commercial ventures they were offshoots of the work of construction already taking place and they ministered to received notions of the poet.[38] One anthology, however, certainly did have an impact, perhaps the most successful book of its kind of all time—Francis Turner Palgrave's *The Golden Treasury* (1861).

The idea for a presentation of the English lyric tradition was hatched with Tennyson in 1860, and two friends, Thomas Woolner and George Miller, were recruited to aid in the severe process of winnowing the initial selection. For this was to be a treasury of 'Of the Best Songs and Lyrical Poems in the English Language' and, as their working papers show, for these arbiters best had to mean best. Tennyson's was the decisive voice: 'He read almost everything twice over generally aloud to me [Palgrave]. The book as it stands fairly represents his taste, as his opinion was the final verdict: but so severe and strict was his judgment, that if the scheme of the book had been his, it would probably have held less.'[39]

But this was not be yet another casquet of gems. Wanting to convey a sense of the history of the English lyric, Palgrave organized the poems that survived the final selection into four books, each with a brief historical introduction, and the poems in the final book—largely from the first thirty years of the nineteenth century—were presented as the finest flowering of a tradition: 'to what was . . . inherited they added a richness in language and a variety in metre, a force and fire in narrative, a tenderness and bloom in feeling, an insight into the finer passages of the Soul, and the inner meanings of the landscape, a larger sense of Humanity,— hitherto scarcely attained, and perhaps unattainable even by predecessors of not inferior individual genius'.[40] In the selection that justifies this claim, Wordsworth figures more largely than any other poet. He, says Palgrave, gives this portion of the anthology 'its distinctive character', so that it might be called the 'Book . . . of Wordsworth'.[41]

Commending his 'little Anthology' to Christopher Wordsworth Palgrave observed: 'You will see that WW. has given us more numerically & quantitatively than any other poet. That our selection from him was not twice as long as it is, was due partly to the fact that several magnificent things like Hartleap Well & Laodamia appeared more properly *narrative* than *lyrical*: partly to

Tennyson's own strong feeling that we shd. admit nothing which did not exhibit his honoured predecessor in his fullest strength & glory.'[42] The constraints of the anthology inevitably determined that Wordsworth's fullest strength and glory should appear to be in his lyrics, but it was not only dramatic and narrative poems that were excluded by the compilers' working definition of 'lyric'. Anything tending towards the didactic was also excluded, which allowed a question mark to hang over *Elegiac Stanzas* before they were gathered in.[43] Only the *Ode to Duty* and the *Ode: Intimations of Immortality* were permitted entry from the mass of Wordsworth's lyrical-didactic output. Lines such as 'Wisdom and Spirit of the Universe', which the poet had printed as a free-standing effusion, were excluded, as was any verse touching on religion. Beginning a construction which Arnold was later to theorize and confirm, the *Golden Treasury* offered a Wordsworth quite unlike 'England's Samuel', a poet of strong and elemental feelings—joy in simple pleasures, of love and loss—freed from metaphysical, philosophical, and political baggage.

Genuine selections devoted entirely to Wordsworth were, of course, quite different from anthologies. As early as 1819 the *Eclectic Review* put the case for selection on aesthetic grounds, arguing that if his 'best pieces could be collected into one volume . . . while his ideots [*sic*] and waggoners were collected into a bonfire on the top of Skiddaw, the "Sybilline leaves" would form a most precious addition to our literature'.[44] Allan Cunningham's grounds were bizarrely different. Inviting Wordsworth to make a selection aimed specifically at 'the Scotch peasantry', he even offered to do the work when the poet confessed himself, not surprisingly, 'wholly at a loss' as to what the principles for such a selection might be.[45] Others urged the needs of the poor, arguing justifiably that the cost of the Complete Works put the poems beyond their reach. But Wordsworth resisted. His poems might appear within a volume—in, for example, R. W. Chambers's *Cyclopaedia of English Literature* (1844)—but separate publication of a selection was another matter. Picking out the plums of the collected works could only damage sales. It went, moreover, against the grain. Convinced that his poems were one, as the 'little cells, oratories, and sepulchral recesses' are in unity with the main edifice of 'a gothic church', he did not favour the exhibition of a buttress here or a fine example of vaulting there.[46]

Only twice in his lifetime was his resistance seriously breached and in each case the circumstances were exceptional. The first was in response to a proposal from a schoolmaster, Joseph Hine, that he be allowed to prepare a selection for classroom use. Wordsworth— whose lifelong interest in education has not yet received its due— approved of the project in general and of Hine in particular, as one whose high estimation of a poem such as *The Idiot Boy* indicated his moral fitness for the task.[47] The volume appeared in 1831 as *Selections . . . Chiefly for the Use of Schools and Young Persons*, with a very flattering prefatory essay on the educative use of such poetry as Mr Wordsworth's, and it was reissued in 1838.

The second occasion, however, was in response to very different pressure. In 1843 Wordsworth was astounded by the appearance of *Select Pieces from the Poems of William Wordsworth*, published by a certain James Burns. Having been approached by another schoolmaster, the Revd Henry Gough, for permission to compile a selection of poems 'principally intended for circulation among his own Scholars' at St Bees School, Wordsworth had given it, prompted no doubt by tenderness for this old foundation on the north-western edge of the Lake District.[48] He expected a simple publication consisting chiefly of poems on north-country subjects. What Burns actually published, from London, was a very pretty little gift-book, with a title-page vignette of Rydal Mount and numerous pictorial embellishments in the text, elaborate border decoration to all pages, and a fulsome dedication 'To Her Most Sacred Majesty, Victoria'. Rubbing salt into the wound, the Preface clumsily suggests that this selection might assist Wordsworth by winning over readers who, if faced with his poetry *en masse* 'would most probably be repelled . . . altogether', a comment which the poet feared would tend 'to impede the sale of the works in a body'.[49]

Wordsworth has the reputation of being sharp to a fault where his own interests were concerned, but in fact he was often remarkably tolerant. When no fewer than fifty-six of his sonnets appeared without permission in Robert Fletcher Housman's *A Collection of English Sonnets* (1835), Wordsworth did no more than offer the compiler 'a friendly caution' that were he disposed in the future to make collections of this sort, 'it would be better to ask permission of the respective Authors and Proprietors before you proceed to print'.[50] Even now, despite the fact that Gough and

Burns had taken liberties with the text—mutilating *Michael*, for example, by omitting the first thirty-nine lines as extraneous to the narrative proper—Wordsworth was inclined to give them credit for purity of intention at least. But he and Moxon justifiably felt aggrieved. The upshot was that Burns's proposed second edition was quashed and replaced in 1847 by a *Select Pieces*, very similar in format though not identical to the 1843 volume, but this time with Edward Moxon's name firmly on the title-page. Moxon seems also to have made it clear to the now very elderly poet that in future *all* requests for permission to select must be referred to him.

The Burns–Moxon imbroglio had an unfortunate consequence. It may be that, notwithstanding the poet's objections, Moxon and the executors would have wanted to issue a selection after his death while they still enjoyed complete control of copyright. Maybe not. But what Burns had done was rob them of freedom. Forced to respond, Moxon had taken over someone else's selection and there it was, in print, a selection from the official Wordsworth publishing house, representing money already tied up.[51] The so-called *Earlier Poems* in 1857 was not really a selection, rather a reissue of the lyric poetry up to 1815, and so the field remained open. Willmott's very successful illustrated selection and Bennett's almost equally attractive *Our English Lakes, Mountains, and Waterfalls* occupied it.[52]

Moxon's one attempt to reclaim the ground was a failure. As already mentioned, Francis Turner Palgrave's *A Selection from the Works of William Wordsworth* (1865) is a beautiful little book, an object of pride to its designer no doubt, but that is the best that can be said of it. In his prefatory essay, which ranges over the whole canon to touch in the most general terms on Wordsworth's qualities and in particular on his religious tenor, Palgrave makes not the slightest allusion to the fact of *selection*—the need for it, the principles on which it has been made, problems thrown up by Wordsworth's classification of his poems and so on. It is as if selection has meant finding which few of the best-loved lyrics would fit the format of 'Moxon's Miniature Poets'. When Clough's observation that it was to be hoped that posterity 'will have an instinct to cast away the dross and keep the good metal' was repeated by Pater, who called for the winnowing of the 'tedious and prosaic' from the 'energetic and fertile', they were not enunciating a very sophisticated principle of selection, but it was a principle.[53]

Their demand was met by the one selection in the century that really mattered, Matthew Arnold's *Poems of Wordsworth* (1879). Certain that anything Arnold produced on Wordsworth would be good in itself and of immense advertisement value, Macmillan featured his introductory essay in *Macmillan's Magazine* before the selection appeared.[54] Rightly so, for it is Arnold at his most persuasive and a remarkable document. Every other prefatory essay since Wordsworth's death, even W. M. Rossetti's, the most ambitious to date, had followed the same format. A biographical sketch leads to some definition of the poet's characteristics and some assessment of his appeal. Arnold ignores the biographical almost completely. He makes no reference to Wordsworth's special position as the one Romantic poet who had actually lived in revolutionary France, nor to the issue of his political apostasy, nor, save for brief mentions of Coleridge and Scott, to Wordsworth's place in the literary context of his time, nor even of what was biographically significant about the 'great decade', 1798–1808. Arnold attends solely to the poetry as an essence, if not *sub specie aeternitatis*, at least in an overview that reaches back to Dante, and he does so with a particular intent.

His publishers knew exactly what market they served and there is more than a touch of cynicism in Macmillan's remark to Arnold—glancing at his straw man creation in *Friendship's Garland*—that ' "*Bottles*" *touched with emotion* is the sort of audience you seek to reach—and create'.[55] But Arnold took his mission seriously. It was 'to spread the reading of Wordsworth' and to hasten on the time when he would attain the measure of 'glory' due to a poet who ranked with Dante, Shakespeare, Molière, Milton, and Goethe.[56] Achieving it required a strategy. The true Wordsworth, whose poetry 'is inevitable, as inevitable as Nature herself', had to be saved from that other Wordsworth, who loaded his seven volumes with so much 'poetical baggage'. He had to be saved, too, from his admirers, from the 'Wordsworthians', whose judgements being never disinterested are always wrong. Arnold's method of assisting Wordsworth to 'make his way' was selection and his principle was that selection must define the *true* Wordsworth, not present a sample of the characteristic Wordsworth across the whole range of his output. Readers must be dissuaded from looking for the wrong things and reading the wrong poems. They must be freed from guilt if they find much of Wordsworth dull.

With the authority of one who actually knew the poet (as he unassumingly reveals) and is a true devotee, yet who can survey European poetry and Wordsworth's place in it so disinterestedly as to allot him his proper rank, Arnold deploys a series of oppositions to propel the reader to a climax of assent. Lifetime fame against true glory, conscientious laboriousness against Nature's inevitability, the disinterested against the Wordsworthian judgement, articulated morality against poetic truth—choosing between these oppositions Arnold arrives with an air of inevitability at his most important statement, that Wordsworth's 'philosophy' is an 'illusion': 'we cannot do him justice until we dismiss his formal philosophy.'

Even as the Wordsworthian is reeling from the brutality of this thrust, a salve is offered in Arnold's capacious definition of where Wordsworth's true greatness lies:

Wordsworth's poetry is great because of the extraordinary power with which Wordsworth feels the joy offered to us in nature, the joy offered to us in the simple primary affections and duties; and because of the extraordinary power with which, in case after case, he shows us this joy, and renders it so as to make us share it.

And of course the opposition between 'poetry' and 'formal philosophy' is not as simple as it looks—Arnold's oppositions rarely are. The selection that follows, however, adheres to the proposition in its simplest form. The great work over which Wordsworth laboured for years, the corner-stone of his projected poetic edifice *The Recluse*, dematerializes. All that remains of *The Excursion* is Margaret's story, a truncated version of Book I. The full text of *The Prelude* (still in copyright) might as well not have been published, as Arnold only prints excerpts which Wordsworth had himself made. Nothing more is offered to give any sense of Wordsworth's command of large poetic structures or of his philosophical ambition. The Prospectus to *The Recluse* is included—largely, perhaps, because Arnold was attached to the line 'Of joy in widest commonalty spread'—but sandwiched between *The Simplon Pass* and *The Old Cumberland Beggar* it is completely decontextualized to become just one more of Arnold's selection of 'Reflective and Elegiac Poems'. Arnold's Wordsworth is essentially a lyric and narrative poet.

Though graceful and assured, Arnold's essay is slight, but its impact was enormous.[57] It demolished the gigantic monolith that was Wordsworth and constructed from the pieces a new one of manageable size. Lesser fry were grateful. As the compiler of the Wordsworth volume in W. Kent and Co.'s *Miniature Library of the Poets* observed in 1880, with evident relief, 'many of the shorter pieces are of such inferior merit that it is difficult to believe they are written by the same author. This fact has recently been remarked by one of the acutest and most learned critics of the day, Mr. Matthew Arnold, in an admirable preface to a selection edited by him.' Or, as one J. S. Fletcher observed three years later, Arnold's 'prefatory words are worthy to be set in gold'.[58]

V

Marketing the Prose

Wordsworth's executors had published *The Prelude* and incorporated it from 1857 in the collected works; overseen the appearance of the official biography; added some of the Fenwick Notes to the poems and authorized Johnston's and Palgrave's selections. Although aware that one substantial poem, *Home at Grasmere*, remained unpublished, they could be satisfied that they had faithfully carried out their duty. Only one unavoidable task remained, the publication of Wordsworth's prose. Late in life the poet had indicated that he wanted Christopher Wordsworth to do it, and his son-in-law Edward Quillinan also thought that he had been earmarked for the task, but the death of one and the disinclination of the other had prevented anything being done.

There was, moreover, no urgency. The Preface, Appendix, Essay Supplementary, and Postscript to *Lyrical Ballads*, the 1815 *Poems*, and *Yarrow Revisited* were in print and most readers probably thought that quite enough. The editor of the 1865 Nelson volume evidently did when he declared that with the exception of the *Guide to the Lakes*, 'few of [Wordsworth's] prose writings will ever be read again'.[59] Henry Crabb Robinson, however, judged very differently. 'I enjoy these prose writings much', he commented in 1857, adding, 'indeed, I hope one day there will be a collection of his prose compositions'.[60] But Crabb Robinson did more than just hope. At his death in 1867 he left £500 each to William

Wordsworth Jr. and to William and John in the next generation, with the suggestion, 'not meaning to raise a trust, that a portion of the Legacies to the Wordsworths might be well employed by them in defraying the cost of an Edition of the Prose Writings of their Ancestor the great Poet'.[61]

Such a direction from the grave could hardly be more irritating. Crabb Robinson might not have intended to 'raise a trust', but he had certainly created an obligation. It was not one, however, which the Wordsworths rushed to honour, until once again they were pressured from outside their circle. On 18 April 1874 a Mr Grosart intimated to William Wordsworth Jr. that he was at work on an edition of Wordsworth's prose.

Even by Victorian standards the Reverend Alexander Balloch Grosart was an extraordinary man. The energy and obsessive single-mindedness which enabled others to claim vast tracts of the globe for the Queen, he channelled into writing and editing. As a minister of the United Presbyterian Church, Grosart wrote safely improving books with titles such as *The Lambs All Safe; or, The Salvation of Children* or *The Prince of Light and the Prince of Darkness in Conflict*, but it was in editing that he heard the call of the wild. It was as if he wanted to explore not unknown territory but the forgotten, to reclaim it for his age. In what one scholar has called 'almost indecent profusion', Grosart published over 300 volumes during his lifetime (1835–99), 200 of them on seventeenth- and eighteenth-century literature.[62] He generally funded his work by issuing volumes to subscribers only and that was the method he intended to employ in his mission to rescue Wordsworth's prose from oblivion. As he told William Wordsworth Jr., the subscription list was already out and looked promising.

The executors had to act. Grosart was informed that it was the family's intention that the job should be done by William Wordsworth, Principal of Elphinstone College, Bombay, on his return from India. He was warned, furthermore, that the Fenwick Notes to the poems were 'still in copyright & must not be interfered with'.[63] Grosart replied that he would of course proceed no further and that he would write to inform his subscribers. When William of Bombay got back to England, however, he announced that he had changed his mind, leaving William Jr. with no option but to tell Grosart that he could, after all, go ahead. The only stipulations were that the edition was to be handled by the poet's official publishers and that it was to appear as if it had been undertaken by invitation from the executors.

William Jr. had behaved honourably, but in the eyes of at least one troublesome member of his family, not carefully enough. William had not thought to question the Reverend Mr Grosart's cloth, but Charles Wordsworth, the sanctimonious Bishop of St Andrews, did, and on 16 March 1875 he protested that it was a 'scandal', touching 'the honour due to your illustrious Father', that 'a Presbyterian *Dissenter* should be chosen to edit his prose works'. William could only miserably apologize that it just had not crossed his mind that Grosart 'was not a Minister of the Church of England. This fact, since it came to our knowledge, is indeed a great sorrow to us, but . . . it is now too late for us to remedy.'[64]

It certainly was and Grosart wasted no time. The *Prose Works of William Wordsworth*, in three volumes, appeared the following year, issued by Ward, Lock and Tyler, but under the Moxon imprint, with the declaration by the editor, a forgivable white lie, that his work was undertaken 'in response to a request put in the most gratifying way possible of the nearest representatives of WORDSWORTH'.

Grosart's was to remain the standard edition for just under one hundred years, but it was a very strange production. He brought off one undoubted coup in printing—whether from a copy or from the original MS is unclear—*A Letter to the Bishop of Llandaff,* 'by a Republican', which Wordsworth had written at white heat in 1793 but had not published then or later. In his treatment of it, Grosart's 'errors are . . . egregious', as Wordsworth's twentieth-century editors point out, but this is of a piece with the whole edition which is pitted with mistakes.[65] Trawling for material, Grosart had plundered the *Memoirs of William Wordsworth*, plagiarizing directly on occasion, and whenever Christopher Wordsworth blunders, Grosart usually does too.

Grosart's failings, however, were hidden to all but a few. What mattered in 1876 was the overall character of the volumes. Defining 'a prose work' is not easy, as later editors have admitted, but Grosart's definition is so wide that it seems to encompass anything not written in verse. As well as the incontrovertibly separate prose works such as the *Convention of Cintra* and the *Guide to the Lakes,* he includes letters and fragments of letters, under headings such as 'Of the People, their Ways and Needs', or

'Education of Duty'. Interpretative headings of this kind determine how much else is to be read. The 1815 Preface becomes 'Poetry as Study', and the 1835 Postscript, 'Of Legislation for the Poor, the Working Classes, and the Clergy'. Wordsworth's private letter of 1802 to John Wilson is printed as if it had been published as an open letter of the 'To —' variety, under the title 'Of the Principles of Poetry and His Own Poems'.

Even Grosart's most important revelation is subjected to the same interpretative treatment. *A Letter to the Bishop of Llandaff* is an inflammatory document which Christopher Wordsworth— writing the life of Victoria's Poet Laureate—contrived to douse by quoting at length whatever could be found in other letters of roughly the same period to contradict it. Grosart performs the same dousing operation, but in a different way. Emphasizing, both in the running title given it, 'Apology for the French Revolution' and in his prefatory words, that this letter is primarily an expression of 'sympathy with the uprising of France against its tyrants', Grosart brings the youthful, republican Wordsworth into congruity with his later self by emphasizing that what motivated the writer of *A Letter* was what always motivated him—sympathy for 'the oppressed, the suffering, the poor, the silent'. The sentiments take one back to Keble, but he at least was discomfited by the knowledge that Wordsworth had begun life as a radical. Grosart seems to see no problem.

The Prose Works of William Wordsworth are a mish-mash. Public and private utterances, finished works and extracts wrenched from letters hurriedly penned to catch the post, are jumbled together, non-chronologically, under broad classifications for each volume: 'Political and Ethical' (vol. I), 'Aesthetical and Literary' (vol. II), 'Critical and Ethical' (vol. III). What results from such an heterogeneous collection is the impression that what really matters is the sum total of Wordsworth's *opinions*—on whatever subject. The volumes exhibit Wordsworth the Sage. And the third volume reveals clearly that this is the unconscious motive shaping Grosart's whole endeavour. Drawn partly from published sources and partly from material supplied by surviving friends of the poet such as R. P. Graves and Aubrey de Vere, the last section consists of 'Conversations and Personal Reminiscences of Wordsworth'. These pieces cannot possibly claim a place in an edition of Wordsworth's prose works, but they are wholly appropriate in volumes designed to honour Wordsworth the Sage. As Grosart points out, here are preserved 'opinions and sentiments, criticisms and sayings, actually spoken by Wordsworth', and *everything* that can be garnered while witnesses are still alive, must be garnered. Needless to say, there are no dissenting voices. Reminiscences by De Quincey, or Hazlitt, or Landor are not included. A similar justification is made for the inclusion of so many letters. The day will come, Grosart avers, when the name of Wordsworth 'will be the grand name of the 18th–19th century'. How vital it is that his letters 'be put beyond the risks of loss, and given to Literature in entirety and trueness'.

In his other scholarly work Grosart labours over the long dead, aware of the limitations of evidence that has survived by chance. But in this work he has talked to and corresponded with people who actually knew the poet, the last links with the spirit of one whose life was 'so rounded and completed, so august and so genuine' that 'it is a benediction to the race'. What began as a work of editorial scholarship on certain writings becomes an act of recording and preserving the man. It has been, moreover, as the dedication 'To The Queen' implies, a patriotic duty. Thanking Her Majesty for permission to print for the first time a poem of homage, written by Wordsworth in 1846 on the presentation of a copy of his collected works to the Royal Library at Windsor, Grosart declares that her gracious consent is abundant proof of her awareness 'that of the enduring names in the reign of Victoria, Wordsworth's is supreme as Poet and Thinker'.

4

The Poetry of Humble Life

That is what I call democratic art—the revelation of the poetry which lies in common things. And surely all the age is tending in that direction . . . from Crabbe and Burns and Wordsworth to Hood and Dickens, the great tide sets ever onward, outward, towards that which is common to the many, not that which is exclusive to the few . . .[1]

I

'Bozzy's next number'

Early in 1842 Wordsworth was fretting about the prospects for his new volume, *Poems, Chiefly of Early and Late Years*. The world, he sensed, was changing, and not for the better. Dr Arnold of Rugby had recently told him that 'his lads seemed to care for nothing but Bozzy's next No.', and in bewilderment he asked his publisher, 'Can that Man's public and others of the like kind materially affect the Question—I am quite in the dark'.[2] Courteous and encouraging to his great poet as he always was, Moxon knew the answer. Dickens's circulation figures boomed it out: yes.

Worried about his own sales, Wordsworth would probably not have been much comforted if the following Christmas he had come across this passage in Stave Two of *A Christmas Carol*:

The noise in this room was perfectly tumultuous, for there were more children there, than Scrooge in his agitated state of mind could count; and, unlike the celebrated herd in the poem, there were not forty children conducting themselves like one, but every child was conducting itself like forty.

But he should have been if not comforted, at least proud, for the allusion to a little known effusion written forty years earlier— *Written in March, while resting on the Bridge at the foot of*

Brother's Water—signals that Wordsworth was, however slightly, a presence in Dickens's imaginative make-up and that his writing had in part created the conditions in which Dickens 'and others of the like kind' could flourish.

Many factors of course contributed to the ascendancy of the Victorian novel—the sensibility of evangelical Christianity; increased literacy; developments in the technology of printing and distribution; the professionalization of the literary market-place; the Scott phenomenon. The list could readily be extended and scholars understandably give differing emphases to such factors in accounts of the empire of the novel. But what is not in dispute is that in some not easily quantifiable way the poets, essayists, and novelists of the Romantic period played a major part. As Donald Stone puts it, 'For the great Victorian novelists, the literary past was a blessing rather than a burden, and Romanticism was the part of that past that perhaps affected them most strongly.'[3]

Evidence of Wordsworth's contribution to this blessing is not difficult to find. Dickens, for example, recognized in Wordsworth a fellow spirit on topics such as the factory system, the new poor law, and education, but his debt went beyond alignment on specific issues. Behind Oliver and Smike and Little Nell stands the Wordsworthian child—*We Are Seven* is the one Wordsworth poem Dickens is on record as valuing extravagantly.[4] Dickens's wise fools and outcasts are prefigured in Wordsworth's vagrants and old beggars. The humanitarian generosity of Dickens's early stories touched those who were receptive in the way that *Lyrical Ballads* had. Certain that Boz was 'doing a world of good', Caroline Fox observed that 'he forces the sympathies of all into unwonted channels, and teaches us that Punch and Judy men, beggar children, and daft old men are also of our species, and are not, more than ourselves, removed from the sphere of the heroic'.[5] By 1841, when this journal entry was made, it was commonplace to define Wordsworth's beneficial effect in similar terms.

Charles Kingsley, whose tribute to Wordsworth as 'not only poet but preacher and prophet of God's new and divine philosophy—a man raised up as a light in a dark time', has already been mentioned, saluted his democratic tendency in the passage from *Alton Locke* (1850) quoted as epigraph to this chapter.[6] Wordsworth figures briefly in chapter 25 of *The Professor* (1846; published 1857), where Crimsworth 'doses' Frances with his 'deep, serene, and sober mind' to expedite her move away from Byronic tumult. L. J. Swingle has demonstrated that Trollope may be viewed fruitfully in relation to Romanticism, and in particular to Wordsworth, the teller of tales.[7] On one occasion, it seems, Wordsworth even went beyond being a presence in just the limited sense being exemplified here. Late in life Mrs Humphry Ward, who as a child had sat at the feet of Mary Wordsworth in Rydal Mount, actually moved into the poet's old home. There her daughter had a vision of the aged Wordsworth so compelling that Mrs Ward drew it to the attention of the Psychical Society.[8] Wordsworth, as far as I know, did not visit anyone else in this fashion, but for many he was an abiding presence.

Substantial and intricate though the continuity is between Romanticism and Victorian fiction, however, to claim that Wordsworth was a creative force on any of these writers would be foolish special pleading, of a kind to which books such as this are too often prone. Dickens, Kingsley, Charlotte Brontë, Mrs Humphry Ward, and others allude to Wordsworth, use the figure of Wordsworth for local purposes, even acknowledge largely his significance, but Wordsworth does not fundamentally shape their art. This is true of even the other great writer of the century who is popularly conceived as resembling Wordsworth in that he celebrates rural life in one particular region of England—Hardy. Peter Casagrande's very helpful record of 'Hardy's Wordsworth' notes how often Wordsworth is alluded to in the novels and demonstrates that Hardy sought aid in Wordsworth's theoretical writing for the formulation of his own poetics.[9] But Hardy the novelist (the poet is largely outside the chronological limit of this study), did not need Wordsworth to point out to him that 'dramas of a grandeur and unity truly Sophoclean' are enacted in Little Hintock, or to awaken him to contemporary debate about the nature of Nature, or to confirm for him the importance of telling tales. Wordsworth's presence was so widely diffused through Victorian culture that he must feature in any account of Hardy's intellectual development, but Wordsworth did not determine the shape and texture of his novels.[10]

With two major figures from the mid-century, however, a much stronger case can be made. Angus Easson has claimed that '*Silas Marner* could not have been written, certainly not written as it is, without Wordsworth, nor indeed could so much else in Victorian fiction'.[11] The 'so much else' includes the other early work of George Eliot and that of Elizabeth Gaskell. Examining these writers in detail one can pass beyond generalized assertions about Romantic continuities, for their indebtedness to Wordsworth was both great and specific. Wordsworth's achievement served both as a validating authority for their own projects and as a model of artistic possibilities. In their work many of Wordsworth's deepest concerns were explored afresh and the force of his poetic formulations renewed.

II

Elizabeth Gaskell: 'The author of "Mary Barton"'

On 20 July 1849 Elizabeth Gaskell met the poet whose work she had cherished since her youth. She had recently become famous as 'the author of *Mary Barton*', but Wordsworth had come to the end of writing and had tinkered with his collected poetical works for the last time. There had been some earlier contact between Manchester and Rydal Mount. In 1839 William Gaskell had sent Wordsworth a copy of *Temperance Rhymes*, and had received a letter which, praising their intention, if not their poetic achievement, at least indicated that the verses had been read with some care.[12] Throughout the 1840s Elizabeth Gaskell had also been edging closer to the poet through acquaintances who actually knew him.

Foremost early in the period were the indefatigable writers, editors and publishers William and Mary Howitt. They had featured notes she sent them on Cheshire customs in the second edition of *Rural Life* in 1839 and an account of Clopton Hall in *Visits to Remarkable Places* in 1840, but they did not meet until their paths crossed in Heidelberg in 1841.[13] Here Gaskell spent some days with a couple who not only worshipped Wordsworth's poetry, but were proud to be able to claim that they knew the poet's famous home from the inside. For twenty years they had been friends of the Wordsworth family, had entertained them and enjoyed hospitality in return. Professionally the Quaker Howitts worked within the Wordsworthian aura. Personal affection smoothed disagreements over religion and politics, the more easily because of shared commitment. Their goals were his goals—notably the celebration of the lives of the humble and poor—and as they were also Gaskell's, *Howitt's Journal of Literature and Popular Progress* was the appropriate place for the publication in 1847 of the three tales of Manchester life which mark the real beginning of her career.[14]

By that time Gaskell had made other friends who were still nearer to the poet and it was through them that the meeting came about. In the summer of 1849 Elizabeth and William Gaskell stayed at Skelwith in Little Langdale in farmhouse lodgings arranged through the good offices of the Wordsworths and the Arnolds. As Jenny Uglow observes, although the Gaskells 'had escaped the city heat' they did not lack its society, as a 'stream of visitors' from their own circle descended.[15] But they were also in demand by another group, the extraordinary cluster of figures who had gathered around Ambleside. There were the Arnolds at Fox How and W. E. Forster at nearby Fox Ghyll; Sir James and Lady Kay-Shuttleworth at Briery Close, Low Wood on Windermere; Mr and Mrs William Rathbone Greg at Wansfell, Ambleside; Harriet Martineau, also at Ambleside. At Lancrigg, her house in Easedale, just out of Grasmere, lived the elderly Eliza Fletcher and close by was her family—Margaret and husband Dr John Davy, brother of Sir Humphry, and Mary and husband Sir John Richardson, the Arctic explorer. And 'at the fountain-head', as Eliza Fletcher put it, of this 'circle of people singularly free from the frivolities of fashionable life', lived the Sage of Rydal Mount.[16]

Any one of these people could have given Elizabeth Gaskell news of Wordsworth, but Eliza Fletcher was the strongest personal link between the two. As the wife of a Scottish advocate she had known Gaskell's father in Edinburgh at the turn of the century. Well connected and much travelled, Mrs Fletcher had been friendly with Wordsworth since the early 1830s and had called on him for help in arranging the purchase of the house in Easedale in 1840. She had been an intimate of Isabella Fenwick, the beloved companion of Wordsworth's old age, and was on close terms with his wife and daughter. She was already acquainted with Elizabeth Gaskell and now renewed their friendship with gusto, calling on the Gaskells at their farmhouse and entertaining them at Lancrigg.[17]

With Mrs Fletcher Elizabeth Gaskell could talk about Wordsworth with someone who liked him as a man and revered him, to quote from her memorial verses on his death, as a teacher of 'beautiful realities', 'simple but sublime'.[18] And it was in the home of Mrs Fletcher's daughter Mary, Lesketh How, that she encountered the poet at last. The meeting was arranged by his son-in-law Edward Quillinan, who on meeting Gaskell at the Davy's was so delighted with this 'very pleasing interesting person' that he had invited her to tea at his own house and decided that notwithstanding Wordsworth's great age, he and 'the author of *Mary Barton*' should be brought together.[19]

'Mr Wordsworth . . . liked her'. Quillinan's maddeningly brief report seems to be the only surviving record of the meeting and it does not say whether the poet's liking was reciprocated.[20] But the occasion must have been agreeable for before they parted Wordsworth entered in Elizabeth Gaskell's autograph album a quotation from his early poem *Lines Left upon a Seat in a Yew-Tree*:

> He that feels contempt
> For any living Thing hath faculties
> Which he hath never used.[21]

It must have been a very satisfying moment. Here in the form of the 79-year-old poet was the material embodiment of an intellectual relationship Elizabeth Gaskell had valued for many years and what she carried away were words registering with fine appropriateness the particular aspect of Wordsworth's poetry that she endorsed throughout her early career as a writer.

III

'My heart feels so full of him'

In May 1836 the 25-year-old Elizabeth Gaskell was at work on the Romantic poets:

I have brought Coleridge with me, & am *doing* him & Wordsworth—*fit place for the latter*! I sat in a shady corner of a field gay with bright spring flowers—daisies, primroses, wild anenomes, & the 'lesser celandine,' & with lambs all around me—and the air so full of sweet sounds, & wrote my first chapr of W. yesterday in pencil—& today I'm going to finish him—and my heart feels so full of him. . . .

The whole letter, an expression of enraptured contentment, suggests how fully she was Wordsworth's ideal reader. Describing her situation at Sandlebridge, with 'the song of birds, the hum of insects[,] the lowing of cattle the only sounds', Gaskell bursts out that 'one can't think of anything but poetry & happiness'.[22] As she names the 'lesser celandine' the quotation marks merge Wordsworth into her enjoyment and invoke him as the tutelary presence of this idyll. Her heart is 'full' of the Wordsworth who celebrated the remarkable but unremarked of Nature's phenomena and the bonding of Man and Earth in, for example, 'It is the first mild day of March',

> Love, now an universal birth,
> From heart to heart is stealing,
> From earth to man, from man to earth,
> —It is the hour of feeling.

When the young Elizabeth Gaskell responded to the poet who insisted that 'Poetry is passion: it is the history or science of feelings', she did so in the same spirit as John Sterling, who recommended Wordsworth's poetry as an antidote to the 'dry, hard spirit of modern Unitarianism'.[23] When she invoked him two years later, however, it was with a more defined awareness of the social *and* artistic implications of Wordsworthian 'feeling'. At the close of a long letter to Mary Howitt about country customs, Gaskell mentions that her husband has been giving lectures on 'The Poets and Poetry of Humble Life' in the poorest part of Manchester and as she reports how well they have been received she segues into a serious artistic manifesto:

As for the Poetry of Humble Life, that, even in a town, is met with on every hand. We have such a district, and we constantly meet with examples of the beautiful truth in that passage of 'The Cumberland Beggar:

> Man is dear to man: the poorest poor
> Long for some moments in a weary life
> When they can know and feel that they have been,
> Themselves, the fathers and the dealers out
> Of some small blessings; have been kind to such
> As needed kindness, for this simple cause,
> That we have all of us a human heart.

In short, the beauty and poetry of many of the common things and daily events of life in its humblest aspect does not seem to me sufficiently appreciated.

We once thought of *trying* to write sketches among the poor, *rather* in the manner of Crabbe . . . but in a more seeing-beauty spirit; and one—the only one—was published in *Blackwood*, January 1837.[24]

This statement rests solidly on personal experience of life in Manchester—'We have such a district'—but it is also a reprise of Wordsworthian fundamentals. Gaskell was not to know it, but she had chosen the passage of verse which Wordsworth himself chose when trying to convey succinctly what he took to be the essence of his work: 'If my writings are to last, it will I myself believe, be mainly owing to this characteristic. They will please for the single cause, "That we have all of us one human heart!" '.[25] These words, like many of Wordsworth's most characteristic utterances, lie at the division where profundity and platitude become indistinguishable. Feeling an awkwardness that assails most lovers of Wordsworth's poetry, Crabb Robinson confessed that, when reciting the *Ode: Intimations of Immortality* to friends, he usually left out one or two verses 'lest I should be rendered ridiculous, being unable to explain precisely *what* I admired'.[26] Coleridge voiced a similar unease, but took the darker view, when he concluded that a passage from *The Brothers*, 'like some other few of W's *many* striking passages means less than it seems, or rather promises, to mean'.[27] The line from *The Old Cumberland Beggar* might cause similar doubts. Extracted from any context of human experience it can seem just full-phrased emptiness, but within active human situations its simplicity can act as a flash of illumination, the more powerful for being brief, as it does when Gaskell calls on it again in *North and South*, where 'Once brought face to face, man to man, with an individual of the masses around him [Mr Thornton] had begun to recognise that "we have all of us one human heart" '.

The passage quoted in Elizabeth Gaskell's letter also highlights another conviction fundamental to Wordsworth's poetry. 'Low and rustic life was generally chosen, because in that condition, the essential passions of the heart find a better soil in which they can attain their maturity', or, as Wordsworth put it simply, 'men who do not wear fine cloaths can feel deeply'.[28] Wordsworth never reneged on the early attempt made in *Lyrical Ballads* to shift the centre of poetic gravity. When Joseph Hine was compiling *Selections from the Poems of William Wordsworth*, Edward Quillinan intimated that it might be advisable to omit *The Idiot Boy*, no doubt thinking that what Coleridge dubbed Wordsworth's 'daring Humbleness'[29] had always been an easy target for ridicule and that by 1831 the author of *The Excursion* had outgrown it. But Wordsworth had sounded off passionately thirty years before when John Wilson had slighted *The Idiot Boy*, making appreciation of that poem a touchstone of readerly aptitude, and he did so again now. 'It was precisely for his perception of the merit of this Class of Poems', Wordsworth told Moxon, 'that I allowed Mr Hine to make the Selection.'[30] Elizabeth Gaskell read like Mr Hine. *The Old Cumberland Beggar*, like *The Idiot Boy*, focuses on a useless human being in order to bring out both his intrinsic worth and his power as a social agent. Stripped of the Jacobinical charge it carried in the 1790s, Wordsworth's conviction serves again in a changed social and political situation. As the factory system was consolidated in cities that grew uncontrolled, radicalism might take on a new complexion, but one imperative remained, that 'the beauty and poetry of many of the common things and daily events of life in its humblest aspect' be acknowledged.

The artistic ideal outlined to Mary Howitt aligns Elizabeth Gaskell with Wordsworth in a further way. The conviction that beauty and poetry lie hidden in common things and daily events lays on the artist the duty of disclosing them. Whether he or she is seeing 'what is really there', or adding 'the light that never was, on sea or land', is a question with enormous ramifications philosophically, but it is not one Wordsworth wrestled with in any very sophisticated fashion in his early years, nor did it engage Elizabeth Gaskell. Both writers operate on a conviction—it is the faith they live and work by—that what Wordsworth called in the letter to John Wilson the 'strength, disinterestedness, and grandeur of love', is the ultimate reality of life and that its manifestations are everywhere to be found. The 'more seeing-beauty spirit' is what shapes *The Old Cumberland Beggar*, *Simon Lee*, *The Idiot Boy*, and it is what shapes all of Gaskell's early work.

Her one attempt in verse at rendering the poetry of humble life was *Sketches Among the Poor, I*, published in *Blackwood's Edinburgh Monthly Magazine*, 41 (January, 1837), 48–50.[31] In its verse form and structure the poem reflects Crabbe, but its relation to Wordsworth is more one of homage. Echoes of Wordsworth's diction reverberate in such lines as:

> A single, not a lonely woman, sage
> And thoughtful ever, yet most truly kind;

Without the natural ties, she sought to bind
Hearts unto hers, with gentle, useful love,
Prompt at each change of sympathy to move.

'Coronal'd, a memorable word from the *Ode: Intimations of Immortality*, appears, as does the biblical figure of the broken bowl at the fountain, used in the story of the Ruined Cottage in *Excursion*, Book I. And the material of the poem recalls Wordsworth. One exemplary life is singled out, 'prosaic' but 'charmed with daily poesy, | Felt in her every action'. Mary has come to Manchester after childhood in the Lake District. Although she always hopes to return, her escape from the 'weight of smoke' is repeatedly postponed because of the web of obligations she has woven through her concern for the 'woes and pains' of others. Like Wordsworth's Poor Susan in Cheapside—as Uglow observes—Mary's heart flushes at recall of the brook and the gnarled hawthorn-tree of her childhood home, but eventually it is too late for return. Robbed of her senses by old age, Mary is pitied by those she has counselled and loved, but she is beyond their pity. Memory, which has been the vital agent of continuity throughout her years of exile, maintains its power:

                              Fancy wild
Had placed her in her father's house a child;
It was her mother sang her to her rest;
The lark awoke her springing from his nest;
The bees sang cheerily the livelong day,
Lurking 'mid flowers wherever she did play;
The Sabbath bells rang as in years gone by,
Swelling and falling on the soft wind's sigh;
Her little sisters knelt with her in prayer,
And nightly did her father's blessing share;
So, wrapt in glad imaginings, her life
Stole on with all her sweet young memories rife.

Loss and separation; old age and imminent death; compensation and survival; the active power of memory and imagination—both Gaskell and Wordsworth were drawn to these themes and their appearance in *Sketches Among the Poor* link the young novelist to both the young poet of *The Ruined Cottage*, *Old Man Travelling*, and *Michael*, and to the poet in old age, one of whose last pieces was a sketch of how a 'worn-out Labourer', confined to a workhouse, finds 'Some recompense for all that he had lost' ('I known an aged Man . . .'). But there are also affinities between Gaskell and Wordsworth less easily demonstrable by quotation from this or that text, but strong none the less.

Perhaps the most important is simply that both writers fed off stories. Jenny Uglow calls her biography *Elizabeth Gaskell: A Habit of Stories*, to emphasize a point made repeatedly, that 'Stories were intrinsic to her cast of mind'. Uglow observes that her letters are 'studded with swift character sketches and condensed narratives'. She liked gossip, not because of any malicious streak in her make-up, but because in gossip people turn trivia into narratives of how ordinary human beings live and Gaskell was 'always hungry for stories' of this sort.[32] It is revealing that she wanted Trollope to 'go on writing Framley Parsonage for ever'.[33]

Wordsworth's art rested on the same foundations. In its opening lines *Michael* is presented as a reworking of a 'history | Homely and rude' which the poet heard while still a boy and there is no reason to doubt the truth of this. Like Coleridge, Dickens, and many other writers Wordsworth revelled in the *Arabian Nights* and enjoyed action-packed narratives like Smollett's, but he also absorbed tales from the world round about him. As a child he was entertained by Ann Tyson, his surrogate mother, with tales about shepherds and tinkers, vagrants and poor, abandoned women. He was, as one of the most learned of Wordsworth scholars has put it, 'a poet who listened'.[34] And who continued to listen. Many of his poems originated in what he had been told, as numerous acknowledgements testify, such as on *The Female Vagrant*, 'All that relates to her sufferings . . . were faithfully taken from the report made to me of her own case by a friend who had been subjected to the same trials', or on *The Last of the Flock*, 'a friend of mine *did* see this poor man weeping *alone*, with the lamb, the last of his flock, in his arms'.[35] The core of *The Excursion* consists, not of indigestible metaphysical discourse as is popularly supposed, but of stories, designed 'to put the commonplace truths, of human affections especially, in an interesting point of view; and rather to remind men of their knowledge, as it lurks inoperative and unvalued in their own minds, than to attempt to convey recondite or refined truths'.[36] One who knew the vital worth of stories, Elizabeth Gaskell would have instinctively appreciated the weight of this statement.

Gaskell would also have understood one of Wordsworth's odder literary practices, because on one striking occasion she followed it herself. Both writers introduce into their work real people, whose personal story—their real story—is attested by biographical and other historical evidence outside the world of the fiction itself. In *The Excursion*, Book VII, the Wanderer gives a sketch of an obscure parish priest, whose life for so many years exhibited

> a temperance—proof
> Against all trials; industry severe
> And constant as the motion of the day,

that his shepherd parishioners dubbed him 'the Wonderful'. It is one sketch among many and the Wanderer soon moves on to the story of a Dalesman deaf from childhood. In the *River Duddon* sonnet sequence, however, published six years later in 1820, Wordsworth returns to 'the Wonderful', identifies him as the Reverend Robert Walker, curate of Seathwaite, and appends a long memoir of his life. Once extracted from the fiction of *The Excursion*, Walker's life ceased to be, so to speak, under the copyright of Wordsworth's imagination—like Margaret in Book I, for example—and in 1843 Richard Parkinson, a Canon of Manchester, fictionalized Walker's ministry in a story called *The Old Church Clock*, with the avowed intention of bringing before humble readers the inspiring figure of the real-life man.[37]

The fluidity here of the traffic between life and art is paralleled in Gaskell's introduction of a real person into the fictional cast of *Mary Barton*. Esther, Mary's aunt who has become a prostitute, is sent to prison for a month. At the beginning of chapter 14 the narrator reflects on what that length of time can mean and then comments:

'Sick, and in prison, and ye visited me.' Shall you, or I, receive such blessing? I know one who will. An overseer of a foundry, an aged man, with hoary hair, has spent his Sabbaths, for many years, in visiting the prisoners and the afflicted, in Manchester New Bailey; not merely advising, and comforting, but putting means into their power of regaining the virtue and the peace they had lost; becoming himself their guarantee in obtaining employment, and never deserting those who have once asked help from him.*

Esther's term of imprisonment was ended. She received a good character . . .

The asterisk directs the reader to Gaskell's footnote:

*Vide *Manchester Guardian*, of Wednesday March 18, 1846; and also the Reports of Captain Williams, prison inspector.[38]

Thomas Wright is not actually named, but the footnote is sufficient to make identification possible. This is a different order of historical reference from those which establish the context of the novel—reference, for example, to the presentation to Parliament of the People's Charter in 1839 in which the fictional John Barton is supposed to participate. Wright existed and was known within Manchester for his selfless work, but with the publication of *Mary Barton* he became famous. Visitors to Gaskell's home at Plymouth Grove might meet him in the drawing-room, saying 'By Jingo' in a way that delighted William Gaskell.[39] But as the beginning of the second quoted paragraph implies, the reader of *Mary Barton* might also expect to find him on an errand of mercy to the fictional aunt Esther in prison.

In *Mary Barton* Gaskell allows two realms of reality to interact, just as Wordsworth does in *The Excursion* and the *River Duddon*, and for the same reason. Both writers are first and foremost moralists. On the publication of *Mary Barton* Mrs Arnold wrote to Elizabeth Gaskell: 'May the sinful and the sorrowful and the oppressed be taught and cheered and helped by you as they severally need; and may the hard be softened and the careless roused'.[40] Wordsworth received letters in this tenor throughout the second half of his career, as Chapter 1 has demonstrated, letters which evince a moral response to what is perceived as moral, didactic art. There is no philosophical finesse about such a response, but it goes to the heart of what readers, and their writers, took to be the value of *The Excursion* and *Mary Barton*. And neither Wordsworth nor Gaskell draw a demarcation line between life and art. In Walker and Wright they celebrate figures whose lives have the same exemplary force as those represented in the idealizing imaginings of art.

That Gaskell and Wordsworth were drawn to the prison visitor and the lowly curate of Seathwaite points to the strongest affinity between them as artists. Both men exemplify the virtues of self-denial, perseverance in good, and love of fellow human beings. Theirs are heroic lives, but they are heroes of a certain kind of adventure. In his critique of *The Excursion* Francis Jeffrey remarked that, 'Mr Wordsworth delineates only feelings—and all his adventures are of the heart'.[41] Overall the review is notoriously unsympathetic to the poem's aims, but this comment is absolutely right and it confirms that Wordsworth has not deviated from the claim he made in the Preface to *Lyrical Ballads*—which might stand as epigraph to his collected works—that what distinguishes his poems is 'that the feeling therein developed gives importance to the action and situation, and not the action and situation to the feeling'. Both Jeffrey's comment and Wordsworth's embrace Elizabeth Gaskell's work.

Recognition of Gaskell's sensibility has rarely introduced unmixed praise. Taking the opportunity of a review of *Wives and Daughters* to attempt a definition of her genius—and he does not doubt that she has genius—Henry James deploys his favourite opposition, head and heart: 'Were we touching upon her literary character at large, we should say that in her literary career as a whole she displayed, considering her success, a minimum of head.' 'Writing', he further remarks, 'was a matter of pure feeling with her.'[42] William Rathbone Greg had implied as much at the beginning of Gaskell's career, when judgement of this kind was potentially much more damaging. His long and conscientious essay on *Mary Barton* in the *Edinburgh Review* does some justice to the novel in that it takes it seriously, but his burden is that Gaskell's depiction of the lives of the hand-loom weavers never rises to become analysis of their situation because she sees it only in the light of feeling. Had she shone on it the light of political economy, Greg demonstrates with a parade of evidence, the individual cases which prompt her compassion would have taken on their proper proportion.[43]

Gaskell was deeply discomfited by Greg's review and by one with a similar drift from W. E. Forster, not least because both men were respected acquaintances, and, lamenting that 'no one seems to see my idea of a tragic poem', she confessed, 'I . . . mourn over my failure'.[44] In so far as she does defend herself, however, she does so in terms that are both revealingly simple and uncompromising. To her publisher she declared: 'I have faith that what I wrote so earnestly & from the heart must be right', and to a friend, 'I have . . . firm faith that the earnest expression of any one's feeling can only do good in the long run'.[45] She also repeats what the Preface to *Mary Barton* had implied, that in the figure of John Barton she was trying to enter the feelings of 'an ignorant man full of rude, illogical thought, and full also of sympathy for suffering which appealed to him through his senses'.[46] None of these declarations is an answer to Greg or Forster. No answer could be given within the discourse of political economy they both employ. What they do is reaffirm Gaskell's occupation of a particular imaginative standpoint. It was one from which she never moved. All of her finest tales and novels are 'adventures of the heart'.

IV

'The Poetry of Humble Life'

The strength of Elizabeth Gaskell's literary relationship with Wordsworth is not to be measured by the number of times she alludes to his work. Allusions do matter. As Graham Handley and Michael Wheeler among others have observed, Gaskell's realism is a construct in which apparently painstaking verisimilitude functions with, not against, invocation of an overtly literary order of reality.[47] In *The Moorland Cottage*, for example, Frank sees Maggie through a poem:

When he looked at Maggie, and thought of the moorland home from which she had never wandered, the mysteriously beautiful lines of Wordsworth seemed to become sun-clear to him.

> And she shall lean her ear
> In many a secret place
> Where rivulets dance their wayward round,
> And beauty born of murmuring sound
> Shall pass into her face.

This is not artless decoration. What the interpolation of the verse does is emphasize that even here, in matters of the heart, reality is not unmediated. Maggie is not Lucy, but remembering Wordsworth's lines gives Frank the language to formulate for himself how she differs from Erminia: 'The one appeared to him the perfection of elegant art, the other of graceful nature.'[48] As Suzanne Lewis has pointed out, Gaskell alludes to the Lucy poems similarly in *Cousin Phyllis*, *Ruth*, and *Wives and Daughters*,[49] but across the body of her work she also alludes to many other poets—Shakespeare, Herbert, Coleridge, Tennyson, John Wilson, Felicia Hemans, and

Samuel Bamford, to songs and nursery rhymes. What Wordsworth offered Gaskell, and what she took, cannot be established by counting quotations.

Some of the short stories invoke Wordsworth simply because they are set in the region he had claimed imaginatively. Taking its origin, as many of Wordsworth's narratives did, in a real-life tale, *Half A Lifetime Ago* is set in the *Excursion* landscape of Coniston, Oxenfell, Blea Tarn, and Yewdale, widening out to Wordsworth's own special area itself: 'His [Michael Hurst's] father was a wealthy statesman at Wythburne, up beyond Grasmere; . . . and the Dixons went off to the High Beck sheep-shearing, and the Hursts came down by Red Bank and Loughrigg Tarn and across the Oxenfell, when there was the Christmas-tide feasting at Yew Nook.'[50] The names of these places are rolled out with a relish that is still present, ten years after Gaskell had visited them herself for the first time, when she tells Charles Bosanquet exactly where to go and who to meet on his projected Lake District tour.[51] He is to take with him 'a portable "Excursion" ', not least, one may surmise, because that poem records many tales of the region, *Half A Lifetime Ago* might have been included in it. It begins with one of Wordsworth's favourite devices, most memorably instanced in *Michael*. Just as that story evolves from the poet's declaration that he knows the tale behind the 'straggling heap of unhewn stones' up Green-head Ghyll, which the traveller 'Might see and notice not', so *Half A Lifetime Ago* begins with observation of a farmhouse, to which 'a story appertains'. The closeness to *Michael* is also established by Gaskell's exposition to readers of *Household Words* of what it means that William and Margaret Dixon were 'statesmen', an exposition that emphasizes—as Wordsworth did when he extolled the virtues of 'statesmen' to Charles James Fox—how their character was formed by their intense attachment to their land and by the hardship of life among the fells.[52] That there is something unusual about this farm, that there is a story here, is suggested by the fact that the 'statesman' running it half a lifetime ago was a woman.

What Wordsworth recalls in *The Prelude* about the stories told by Ann Tyson is that many dwelt on 'tragedies of former times, | Or hazards and escapes', and that 'images of danger, and distress, | And suffering . . . took deepest hold of [him]'.[53] *The Half-Brothers* is one such tale that would not be out of place in *The*

Excursion or following 'The Matron's Tale' in *The Prelude*, and it almost certainly owes something to Gaskell's response to an actual tragedy, publicized because of the poet's involvement, but recorded not by him but by his sister, Dorothy. In the letter to Bosanquet Gaskell urges him to get Mrs Davy to arrange that he should see 'Miss Wordsworth's account of the two poor Greens who were lost in the snow . . . And then go into Easedale & see the place where the Greens lived'.[54] This injunction comes from Gaskell the teller of tales. Bosanquet is to read the narrative that will pass on the history of the Greens through generations, but he is also to search out the other memorial to the tragedy of fifty years ago, the cottage that time will soon erase.

On 19 March 1808 George and Sarah Green went to Langdale to attend a sale and to see one of their daughters who was in service. Their path home took them straight over familiar fells into Easedale, but they lost their way in the mist and snow as night came on and both died, falling over crags and rolling down the mountainside. Their shouts had been heard, but disregarded as probably coming from drunken men returning from the sale, and, as Dorothy Wordsworth records, 'at the spot where they perished they might have seen lights from the windows of that same house where their cries were actually heard'.[55]

The particular horror of this situation, when trusted landmarks are blotted out and safety, so near at hand, is unreachable, is picked up in *The Half-Brothers*. In its gripping climax a 16-year-old lad is caught by nightfall as he tries to shorten a long journey by cutting off from the road across the fells. Bewildered by the dark and unable to trust the ground beneath his feet because of the even snow, he tires and weakens and to his 'terrible, wild shouts' no answer comes but 'unfeeling echoes'.[56] Just as numbness is overtaking him he is rescued by his slighted half-brother and the family dog, but his life is saved only at the expense of his brother's.

These stories invoke Wordsworth by their subject-matter and setting. *The Sexton's Hero* does so partly in the same way, but more strikingly through its narrative manner, which mirrors that of the most popular book of *The Excursion*, the story of 'The Ruined Cottage' in Book I.[57] *The Sexton's Hero* is a simple framework story.[58] The young narrator and his friend, resting in a churchyard while on a country walk, start to discuss the nature of the 'hero'. Hearing one of them defend martial heroism, the old sexton butts into their conversation and asks indulgence to tell a tale of real heroism. His narrative, which eschews suspense, for he mentions the hero's violent death early on, occupies the rest of the story. The conclusion is a single sentence addition by the narrator.

The story opens with consciously poetic scene-setting.

The afternoon sun shed down his glorious rays on the grassy churchyard, making the shadow, cast by the old yew-tree under which we sat, seem deeper and deeper by contrast. The everlasting hum of myriads of summer insects made luxurious lullaby.

A buried allusion to Wordsworth ('murmuring sound') in the third paragraph suggests one contributor to the literary matrix of this tapestried prose—the beginning of *The Excursion*, Book I:

> 'Twas summer, and the sun had mounted high:
> Southward the landscape indistinctly glared
> Through a pale steam; but all the northern downs,
> In clearest air ascending, showed far off
> A surface dappled o'er with shadows flung
> From many a brooding cloud; far as the sight
> Could reach, those many shadows lay in spots
> Determined and unmoved, with steady beams
> Of bright and pleasant sunshine interposed;

The purpose of both passages is to introduce the narrator and the important facts about his setting. In *The Excursion* the traveller is ill at ease, aware of the beauty and calm of nature but only conscious personally of vexation and discomfort. But his irritated observation, 'Pleasant to him who . . .', is not merely local in its effect, for it sets up the tension between differing responses to the natural scene on which the poem is to build. The emphasis in the passage from *The Sexton's Hero* is rather different, but equally important to the narrative unfolding. The scene is a churchyard where sunlight and the yew-tree's shade make up a highly literary setting that would speak *memento mori* if the young men would listen. But they have been totally absorbed in sensuous appreciation, 'living in sight and murmuring sound', and are not a little pleased with themselves:

It is one of the luxuries of holiday-time that thoughts are not rudely shaken from us by outward violence of hurry and busy impatience, but fall maturely from our lips in the sunny leisure of our days. The stock may be bad, but the fruit is ripe.

As in *The Excursion*, Book I, the narrator's feelings and understanding are changed by the encounter that follows this significant opening. In the poem the narrator meets the pedlar at a ruined cottage. The wise wanderer reveals the human reality behind the broken down walls and does so explicitly to celebrate a human life:

> 'Tis a common tale,
> An ordinary sorrow of man's life,
> A tale of silent suffering . . .

The poet is so moved by the bleakness of the tale of Margaret that the pedlar, secure in his own faith in the power of 'natural wisdom' and 'natural comfort', has to counsel him to deeper insight into the natural scene, and once the actual landscape has been reordered in the pedlar's reconciling interpretation, the more overtly literary tone reappears as the poem draws to its close:

> He ceased. Ere long the sun declining shot
> A slant and mellow radiance, which began
> To fall upon us, while, beneath the trees,
> We sate on that low bench: and now we felt,
> Admonished thus . . .
> .   .   .   .
> Together casting then a farewell look
> Upon those silent walls, we left the shade;
> And ere the stars were visible, had reached
> A village-inn,—our evening resting-place.

Wordsworth invokes Milton in this rather grand close. *The Sexton's Hero* ends more abruptly, but the same sense of literary reassertion is unmistakable: 'He turned to his work; and we, having rested sufficiently, rose up, and came away.'

The structural parallel is not superficial, but leads directly to the heart of Gaskell's story. In *The Excursion*, the pedlar directs the emotion of the poet-narrator and teaches him to see the deeper truth to which he is initially blind. After the encounter the poet is changed, as one draft has it, 'a better and a wiser man'. So it is in *The Sexton's Hero*. The question the two friends are discussing at the beginning of the story is important, but their immaturity is only too apparent. When the sexton breaks in the narrator is impatient at the interruption from someone he had dismissed from his mind 'as though he were as inanimate as one of the moss-covered headstones', and anxious to continue his high-toned discussion. But the old man's wisdom deepens their purely intellectual approach to the question of heroism, because his is the fruit of such a damaging personal experience and long, self-reproaching meditation. He tells the story of a true hero, the Christian Gilbert, who refuses to assert his manliness by fighting, but who sacrifices his life for the woman and the friend he loves. The sexton is like one of his own gravestones, on the borders of life and death. His age and growing blindness suggest that he too will soon rest under the yew-tree, but he has wisdom born of suffering and this he imparts.

Wordsworth is not the only influence on *The Sexton's Hero*. The New Testament is immeasurably more important to this story, as to all of Gaskell's work. But as this exposition of structural parallels between the two narratives has tried to establish, it was Wordsworth's poetry that presented Gaskell with enabling models for a certain kind of moral fable. It did so, clearly, because she found in it congenial expression of her own deepest responses to human life.

For Gaskell, Wordsworth was primarily the poet of human suffering. Many of the lyrical ballads and the stories in *The Excursion* dwell on the pain of loss, the deprivations of age, isolation, and grief. The shepherd, weeping, with the last of the flock in his arms; Simon Lee, too enfeebled to sever a tangled root; the palsied old Cumberland beggar, vainly trying to eat his meal without spilling it; Michael at the unfinished sheepfold; Margaret straining her eyes into the distance for Robert, after all hope has gone—these are all emblems of the human condition. Gaskell's stories similarly venture into the extremities of suffering. In *Libbie Marsh's Three Eras* the sickly and wasted boy, Franky, doomed to an early death, is first seen fretfully moving an arm to and fro as he struggles with continuous pain. The eponymous heroine of *Lizzie Leigh* is restored from her fallen state, but her baby dies and she devotes her life to caring for others, 'a sad, gentle looking woman, who rarely smiles (and when she does, her smile is more sad than other people's tears)'. The heroes of *The Half-Brothers* and *The Sexton's Hero* both sacrifice their lives, leaving those they have saved to a lifetime of self-recrimination.

Human suffering—this is 'the burthen of the mystery',[59] and for it there is only 'one adequate support', the Wanderer declares in *The Excursion*, IV. 8–17:

> one only; an assured belief
> That the procession of our fate, howe'er
> Sad or disturbed, is ordered by a Being
> Of infinite benevolence and power;
> Whose everlasting purposes embrace
> All accidents, converting them to good.

Lines such as these divided Victorian Wordsworthians. What was to Leslie Stephen the corner-stone of Wordsworth's ethical system was to Matthew Arnold only 'abstract verbiage' that lacked 'the characters of *poetic* truth'.[60]

Gaskell read Wordsworth with Leslie Stephen. From religious standpoints that were poles apart, both responded to the *gravitas* of Wordsworth's depiction of human suffering and to the consolation offered in the Wanderer's position in the face of the otherwise inexplicable. It is voiced in *Mary Barton* through the Wordsworthian figure of Alice, who longs to return to her childhood home among the mountains but is never to do so. Constantly helping her neighbours to accept the 'sentness' of human affliction, she declares that our duty is 'to find out what good it were to do'. Gaskell also made the same declaration in her own voice when writing to Mrs Greg about *Mary Barton*. What bewildered men like John Barton need, she asserts, is wise guidance towards 'an acknowledgement of some kind of suffering, and the consequent necessity of its existence for some good end'.[61]

Although the hesitant sentences of this letter betray the difficulty Gaskell felt in formulating her conviction, such a summary dictum cannot but sound bland. Her fictional explorations of the mysterious ways of suffering, however, are anything but, and in them, as Angus Easson has observed, she 'moves into the very territory of Wordsworth'.[62]

In the Preface to *Lyrical Ballads* Wordsworth declared that his purpose was to 'follow the fluxes and refluxes of the mind when agitated by the great and simple affections of our nature'.[63] This grandly confident statement, unembarrassed by the directness of its appeal to fundamentals, might stand as an epigraph for Gaskell's stories. They centre on feelings, the deepest and most instinctual feelings of which we are capable, and they are set amongst the low and insignificant, not because Gaskell is in thrall to Wordsworth's untenable conviction that 'in that condition, the essential passions of the heart find a better soil in which they can attain their maturity',[64] but rather because the 'seeing-beauty spirit' compels her to demonstrate that even here, where the struggle for existence is hardest, human beings can behave nobly.

Libbie Marsh's Three Eras opens with Libbie changing lodgings in Manchester:

Dixon's house was the last on the left-hand side of the court. A high dead brick wall connected it with its opposite neighbour. All the dwellings were of the same monotonous pattern, and one side of the court looked at its exact likeness opposite, as if it were seeing itself in a looking-glass.[65]

Nearly fifty years later Arthur Morrison depicted a similarly functional world, bare of grace or imagination, in his *Tales of Mean Streets*:

[This street] is not pretty to look at. A dingy little brick house twenty feet high, with three square holes to carry the windows, and an oblong hole to carry the door, is not a pleasing object; and each side of this street is formed by two or three score of such houses in a row, with one front wall in common. And the effect is as of stables.[66]

Both writers seize on the numbing dreariness of the typical street of artisan houses, but this narrative starting-point leads them in quite different directions. Morrison reveals a way of life whose most graceful element, it turns out, is the line of the houses in a row. In *Lizerunt*, the triptych that parallels *Libbie Marsh's Three Eras*, for example, Elizabeth Hunt's affections are fought for by two men who savagely beat and kick each other. The winner is soon kicking the pregnant Liza and extorting money from his mother with a punch to the head. Liza 'Unt's third era culminates in her husband pushing her out into the street at night with the command not to return until she has earned some money. Gaskell, on the other hand, while not scanting economic realities—all of Libbie's possessions fit into one box—brings to the fore qualities and human agencies that work against the deadening environment. Libbie's loneliness is lessened by her interest in the ailing boy opposite. A present of flowers and then a canary give him some focus for affection and serve also to bring Libbie and Franky's mother together. Their mutual kindliness awakens sympathy in the neighbours, who had previously shunned Franky's mother as a termagant and on a day's outing to the country it is their attention to the sick boy that adds an extra dimension for everyone to the holiday pleasure. Franky dies, Libbie moves in with his mother, and the young girl, who at the beginning of the story 'moved slowly and heavily along the streets, listless and depressed', ends her third era with 'such peace shining on her countenance, as almost makes it beautiful, as she tenders the services of a daughter to Franky's mother, no longer the desolate lonely orphan, a stranger on the earth'.

Libbie Marsh's Three Eras chart a moral progress. Although Franky dies, and it is made clear that the Dixons are too preoccupied to worry long about his grieving mother, the overall movement of the episodes is from isolation and depression towards community and the purposefulness that comes of having someone to love. *Half A Lifetime Ago*, the most Wordsworthian of Gaskell's tales, explores the similar themes and describes the same trajectory, but is altogether more sombre, for this depiction of the 'great and simple affections of our nature' acknowledges the cost of selfless dedication.

As her mother is dying Susan Dixon makes a covenant that she will always look after her 'idiot boy' brother, Willie. Susan is wooed by Michael Hurst, but he comes to loathe Willie's 'gibbering, his uncouth gestures, his loose shambling gait',[67] and schemes to have him confined in Lancaster asylum. Susan chooses her brother, so Michael leaves, and one scene, as powerful as anything in all of Gaskell's work, brings out just what her choice means for Susan. Returning to the farm she sees Willie,

hanging listlessly on the farm-yard gate to watch for her. When he saw her, he set up one of his strange, inarticulate cries, of which she was now learning the meaning, and came towards her with his loose, galloping run, head and limbs all shaking and wagging with pleasant excitement. Suddenly she turned from him, and burst into tears. She sate down on a stone by the wayside, not a hundred yards from home, and buried her face in her hands, and gave way to a passion of pent-up sorrow; so terrible and full of agony were her low cries, that the idiot stood by her, aghast and silent.

Willie dashes off to find something to comfort her, and returns with a windmill. It is the toy Michael Hurst bought for him in Kendal, the very day he was trying to get him certified:

He leapt before her to think how he had cured all heart-sorrow, buzzing louder than ever. Susan looked up at him, and that glance of her sad eyes sobered him. He began to whimper, he knew not why: and she now, comforter in her turn, tried to soothe him by twirling his windmill. But it was broken; it made no noise; it would not go round. This seemed to afflict Susan more than him. She tried to make it right, although she saw the task was hopeless; and while she did so, the tears rained down unheeded from her bent head on the paper toy.

'It won't do', said she at last. 'It will never do again.'

Willie dies and Susan is left alone, unloved, and worse, 'there was no one left on earth for her to love'. Her desolation is complete when Michael marries someone else and, not yet 30, she turns into an old woman. Michael goes to the bad, drinking and neglecting his farm, and he dies in a snow storm. Susan finds him and suffers a mild stroke when she goes to tell his widow. Nursed back to health, Susan takes Michael's wife and children into her own house to 'fill up the haunted hearth with living forms that should banish the ghosts'.

Half A Lifetime Ago risks sentimentality but avoids it, largely because of the starkness with which it presents what Susan's choice really entails. Defending his *Idiot Boy* Wordsworth invoked 'that sublime expression of scripture that *"their life is hidden with God"* ', challenging his readers to dare to find anything distasteful in a subject sanctified by holy writ.[68] Gaskell, to the contrary, emphasizes how unpleasing Willie becomes as he grows up, large, shambling, uncontrolled, so that Susan's demonstration of the 'strength, disinterestedness, and grandeur of love', is the more striking. But it also highlights both the cost of self-sacrifice and the unfairness of a world in which it is necessary. The figures in the stories discussed have little of the world's goods, and yet they lose either their lives, or the possibility of enriching existence through love and sexual pleasure, marriage and children. Self-sacrifice is an enabling posture before the fact of human affliction, the one sure way open for human beings to convert into a reality the theological assertion of the 'consequent necessity of its existence for some good end'.

V

'such whose lives are tragic poems'

By directing attention to the lowly, Gaskell's short stories share the aim that Wordsworth defined so crisply when he commended

Michael and *The Brothers* to Fox: 'men who do not wear fine cloaths can feel deeply'.[69] Works that challenge the accepted hierarchy of poetic value also, it is claimed, have a social and political significance. They have something important to say to Fox, a statesman involved in the direction of national policy. *Mary Barton* (1848) and *Ruth* (1853) are inspired by similar motivation. Both demand the awakening of sympathy, by bringing into focus the lives of those who might elsewhere appear just as statistics in a report on the problems posed to society by 'the poor' or 'the fallen woman'. In this general way both novels draw on the Wordsworthian inheritance. Hilary Schor is right to observe that 'one cannot overemphasize Wordsworth's importance as a myth-maker who set the project and validated the language of the novel of the self', and her subtle reading of *Ruth* is based on perception of it as Gaskell's 'most Wordsworthian novel'.[70] Donald Stone judges *Mary Barton* superior to other 'Condition-of-England' novels because its aim 'is more than the correction of specific abuses: it is a Wordsworthian expansion of the reader's sympathy'.[71] But if 'Wordsworthian' is to be anything more than a portmanteau term signifying approvingly a broadly humanitarian discourse, it needs to be given sharper definition. The Wordsworth who mattered to Gaskell undoubtedly played a part in shaping these two novels, but which Wordsworth was it, and how big a part did he play?

Gaskell mentions two different genres which model the story of *Mary Barton*. One is Romance. In the Preface to this 'Tale of Manchester Life', she records how a historical tale she had in hand was displaced by one which might embody her realization of 'how deep might be the romance in the lives of some of those who elbowed me daily in the busy streets of the town in which I resided', and later in the novel the point is repeated: '[John Barton] could not, you cannot, read the lot of those who daily pass you by in the street. How do you know the wild romances of their lives . . . ?'[72] The Wordsworthian element in this kind of Romance does not need labouring, particularly because Gaskell herself identified it in the 1838 'Poetry of Humble Life' letter. Wordsworth's reverent disclosure of the worth of the humble, the isolated, the infirm and 'useless', is transposed into the urban setting. In the Preface to *Lyrical Ballads* he had identified the 'encreasing accumulation of men in cities' as one of the chief causes of the degradation of the age. *Mary Barton* demonstrates that even here the Wordsworthian 'seeing-beauty spirit' will find noble acts, alert minds, and feeling hearts.

The 'wild romances' of the streets, however, also include Tragedy. On three occasions immediately after the publication of *Mary Barton* Gaskell acknowledged this as the genre uppermost in her thought as she began writing. The novel was conceived, she told Chapman, as 'a tragic poem'. Insisting that John Barton was the 'hero' of her 'tragic poem', she lamented that 'So many people overlook John B or see him merely to misunderstand him'. To Mrs Greg she made an even stronger avowal: 'Round the character of John Barton all the others formed themselves; he was my hero, *the* person with whom all my sympathies went.'[73] But though Barton is prominent in Gaskell's imagination as a tragic hero, her observation tells her that he is not unique. Among the 'care-worn men' who 'elbowed [her] daily in the busy streets' were many 'whose lives are tragic poems which cannot take formal language', and it is the dreadful fact that John Barton is not a special case that indicates the kind of tragedy he plays in.

It is the tragedy of individuals who are powerless in the face of historical forces they can neither understand nor resist. Wordsworth had responded to the pathos of such victims in many of his poems. The female vagrant in *Lyrical Ballads*, the old shepherd in *Michael*, Margaret in *The Excursion*, Book I, the sailor in *Guilt and Sorrow*—these bewildered figures struggle with the particular sufferings of their own lives, but dimly aware that they are at the pressure point where national events or historically determined economic change render the individual insignificant and dispensable. *Mary Barton* also presents such people and, as the one who cracks under the strain, John Barton is the 'hero'.

By the 1840s an unequal struggle had been going on for decades between the hand-loom weavers and the factories and machines. Slowly the hand-loom weavers, who either worked their own looms in their cottages or worked up material for the mills on hired looms, became more and more impoverished, but for a time they were able to compete with machines by working long hours at very low rates.[74] When their decline was almost complete, a Royal Commission investigated their plight and its report, delivered in 1841, was without hope. Palliative measures—among them emigration and education—are suggested, but the Report's conclusion is that the hand-loom weavers are doomed. John Barton is not a hand-loom weaver, but a steady worker who has always been confident of employment, but his sufferings are indivisible from those of the less skilled, less steady mass below. When Barton's employer fails, the weaver discovers that in a labour market already glutted by impoverished workers, many of them drawn into the mills through the decline of the hand-loom trade, even a steady man is threatened and once out of a job, done for. As he trudges on from mill gate to mill gate looking only for work to support his family, the iron enters John Barton's soul.

Barton's suffering is intensified by two goads. One is his inability to understand what is happening. Sometimes fully employed, sometimes laid off, the weaver perceives that he is a commodity with a varying value, but the smattering of the terms of political economy he can summon up do nothing to feed his children: 'I say, our labour's our capital and we ought to draw interest on that. They get interest on their capital somehow a' this time, while ourn is lying idle, else how could they all live as they do?' 'They' in this sentence is the other goad. Deprivation is not shared equally and for some in the 'hungry-forties' life goes on as usual. Mrs Hunter loads her carriage with food for a party as Barton's son dies for want of proper nourishment. The ladies of the Carson household drive out to an afternoon lecture, while Mrs Davenport shivers in a filthy cellar by the side of her dying husband. Mr Carson may tell George Wilson, 'I shall ha' to retrench, and be very careful in my expenditure during these bad times', but Barton's response to this is unanswerable: 'Han they ever seen a child o' their'n die for want o' food?' The failure of the Chartist petition confirms to him not only that the wealthy do not know, but that they do not want to know, about the lives of working men and all his struggles to make sense of his experience leave him only 'bewildered and lost, unhappy and suffering'.

John Barton is strikingly realized. On the writer of 'The Manufacturing Poor' in *Fraser's Magazine* the 'Wordsworthian extension of the reader's sympathy' acted exactly as intended. Do people want to know 'why working men turn Chartists', he exclaimed, 'Then let them read *Mary Barton*'.[75] Even more guarded reviewers registered the impact of the novel's depiction of the plight of the labouring poor. Many recent critics, however, have expressed unease about what happens to Barton in the second half of the novel. He slips from the foreground and the opening to chapter 15 is an awkward reminder of the fact: 'We must return to John Barton. Poor John! He never got over his disappointing journey to London . . .'. The weaver becomes an assassin, slinks out of the plot, only to return at the end, a broken and contrite man ready to die. Critical formulations differ, but most agree that somewhere in the realization of the character John Barton becomes artistically intractable.

The reason may lie, in part, in Wordsworth's influence on the conception of Barton as 'tragic hero'. One of the epigraphs added to *The White Doe of Rylstone* in 1836 includes the declaration: 'Suffering is permanent, obscure and dark, | And has the nature of infinity'. It could stand at the head of all of Wordsworth's principal poems of suffering. His figures exemplify what he called 'the fortitude of patience',[76] and in so far as the poet situates their distress in a metaphysical context, it is that of the Wanderer's assurance that for the 'calamities of mortal life' only one 'adequate support exists', faith in God's inscrutable purpose for good. Gaskell's letter to Mrs Greg suggests a similar matrix for her conception of the tragic weaver, Such men as John Barton grope 'after the causes of suffering, and the reasons why suffering is sent', and what they need is help to acknowledge the 'universality of suffering, and the consequent necessity of its existence for some good end'.[77] *Mary Barton* repeatedly endorses the belief, chiefly in utterances from old Alice, with her 'wait patiently on the Lord', and from Job Legh, who asserts more positively that sorrow can work for noble ends. John Barton suffers because suffering is man's lot. Heroism consists in enduring with fortitude what God sends.

Such a conception of the tragic hero, however, limits what Gaskell can do with John Barton. As long as he is depicted within the Wordsworthian model, the realization of him as a character, and of his function in the novel, works successfully. Wordsworth's celebration of the virtue of fortitude joins with Gaskell's 'seeing-beauty spirit', to create a figure whose life becomes the more exemplary the more he selflessly endures. But Gaskell's larger purpose of showing how bitterness can erode the soul of even a good man, involves John Barton in action that is not selfless and immediately his usefulness, artistically, is diminished. In the early part of the novel Gaskell is able to demonstrate the 'beautiful truth' that 'we have all of us one human heart', through the scenes in which John Barton's concern for others illuminates the dark world of poverty she wants to expose. After the murder Barton is not susceptible to such fullness of realization. No longer a Wordsworthian 'hero', his moral stature forfeited, Barton fades out and *Mary Barton* ceases to be a 'tragic poem'.

Ruth is also a life-history cast as a tragic poem in the Wordsworthian mould. While the title invokes Crabbe's poem from *Tales of the Hall*, another treatment of the betrayed woman, it also brings to mind *Ruth* from *Lyrical Ballads* and with it many other early Wordsworth poems about innocent women, abandoned and alone—*The Female Vagrant*, *Poor Susan*, *The Affliction of Margaret*, even Margaret of *The Ruined Cottage*. Noting the connection, Schor points out that Wordsworth's 'abandoned-women poems all focus on the difficulty of reading the meaning of the woman', and in her detailed discussion she explores how Gaskell moves beyond the poet's incomprehending awe in the face of suffering in a critique 'enacted through the particular lenses of a Victorian woman trying to write herself into the story'.[78]

Others have dwelt on what can only be called the 'Romantic' realization of Ruth. What differentiates the young seamstress from the other girls is the intensity of her response to natural beauty and the readiness of her tears to flow at the prompting of memory. Whereas Ruth's seducer, Bellingham, is easily bored, she gazes with rapture on the mountains, feeding on every movement of the clouds and rain. Ruth is a Wordsworthian observer, who half-creates and half-perceives, identifying from her own passionate self with Nature's 'beauteous forms'.

If the presence in *Ruth* of the Wordsworth of *Poor Susan* and *Tintern Abbey* has been recognized, however, the importance to the novel of a different Wordsworth seems not to have been acknowledged. Quotations from his poetry appear three times. Two are insubstantial, moments when a line encapsulates for Gaskell the strength of maternal affection she is trying to express, but the third is more weighty—four lines from the *Ode to Duty*.[79] As she accustoms herself to living with the Bensons, Ruth comes to sense an affinity between the peace of her new home and that of her childhood which emanated from her mother:

The gentle, blessed mother, who had made her childhood's home holy ground, was in her very nature so far removed from any of earth's stains and temptations, that she seemed truly one of those

> Who ask not if Thine eye
> Be on them; who, in love and truth,
> Where no misgiving is, rely
> Upon the genial sense of youth.

In the Bensons' house there was the same unconsciousness of individual merit, the same absence of introspection and analysis of motive, as there had been in her mother; but it seemed that their lives were pure and good, not merely from a lovely and beautiful nature, but from some law, the obedience to which was, of itself, harmonious peace, and which governed them almost implicitly, and with as little questioning on their part, as the glorious stars which haste not, rest not, in their eternal obedience.

The gloss on the quotation consists in fact of further reference to Wordsworth's poem. The epigraph to the *Ode to Duty* from Seneca translates: 'Now at last I am not consciously good, but so trained by habit that I not only can act rightly but cannot act otherwise than rightly.' The stars in 'their eternal obedience' have their counterpart in the poet's address to the 'awful Power', Duty:

> Thou dost preserve the stars from wrong;
> And the most ancient heavens through Thee
>   are fresh and strong.

The *Ode to Duty* points to what is at the core of *Ruth*, an unyielding commitment to the 'Stern Lawgiver'. This is a novel about Duty. Occasionally there is humour in the treatment of it. The servant Sally's homily on the genuine Christian life, for example, includes a comic account of how she erred by believing that attention to the needs of the soul entailed neglecting her duty to cook a good pudding and it is a splendid irony that it should be the vacillating Mr Farquhar, of all people, who muses on 'how grand a life might be, whose every action was shaped in obedience to some eternal law'. But overall *Ruth* is uncompromisingly severe.

For modern readers, accustomed essentially to varieties of relativist morality, Ruth Hilton is bound to be seen as a victim. While little more than a girl she is seduced and abandoned and she spends the rest of her life in expiation. The quotation from the *Ode to Duty* gestures towards Gaskell's view. Young though she is, Ruth disregards her conscience when she walks in the country with Bellingham, and Alan Shelston is right to insist that 'if Mrs Gaskell burdens her heroine with guilt it is because she, unlike Hardy, has absolutely no doubt that what she did, whatever the circumstances, was wrong'.[80] Ruth's plight demands compassion from the Christian reader, but compassion is not absolution.

Were Ruth's the only struggle with Duty the novel would have all the appeal of a tract. What saves it, and makes it a novel, is that Gaskell embeds Ruth's story in others which also depict how fallible human beings confront the eternal law. At one extreme is Bellingham, who knows no law but the impulse of the moment and whose idea of Duty is to behave 'handsomely' to Ruth as he deserts her. At the other is Mr Bradshaw—a forerunner of Mr Bulstrode in *Middlemarch*—who is convinced that he knows what Duty demands in all situations, but is broken when forced to recognize how far he has failed in the moral education of his son. The dissenting minister Mr Benson clearly follows Duty when he takes the pregnant Ruth in, but he comes to accept that he erred in not disclosing the truth to his congregation, even though he knows that had he revealed the 'widow' for what she was, a fallen woman, Ruth would never have been allowed the opportunity to demonstrate her virtue. Each of these stories is discomfiting and the degree of our resistance measures the success of Gaskell's intent. The *Ode to Duty* is Wordsworth's most intractable poem. *Ruth* is Gaskell's most intractable novel.

5

Wordsworth at Full-Length: George Eliot

Our dignity and rectitude are proportioned to our sense of relationship with something great, admirable, pregnant with high possibilities, worthy of sacrifice.[1]

I

'Wordsworth at full length'

In June 1841 Isaac Evans of Griff Farm returned from his honeymoon in the Lake District with a gift he knew his sister would prize, 'some rose-leaves from Wordsworth's garden'.[2] Like Elizabeth Barrett, the young Mary Ann Evans now had something that connected her with the Sage of Rydal Mount, something he had looked at, possibly touched. Perhaps the rose-leaves were pressed between the pages of the set of Wordsworth she had acquired in 1839, sign of an affectionate relationship that was to be sustained over her whole life. In her earnestly evangelical phase Mary Ann Evans was inclined to be severe on the poet for his 'satisfaction in terrene objects', wishing for 'a more frequent upturning of the soul's eye', but there was pleasure enough and it lasted. In 1877 George Eliot could say simply to Charlotte Carmichael how delighted she was to find that 'we are agreed in loving our incomparable Wordsworth'.[3]

'Loving'—a strong word, but George Eliot's relationship with Wordsworth was always ardent. By her twentieth birthday in 1839 she had read at least half of his poems and the associated prose and throughout the late 1840s and the 1850s she alluded to them in her letters, reviews, and essays.[4] In January 1858 she and George Henry Lewes were deep in Wordsworth, 'with fresh admiration for his beauties and tolerance for his faults', and a month later they had finished *The Excursion*, 'which repaid us for going to the end by an occasional fine passage even to the last', and started on the other poems.[5] The following year they tackled *The Excursion* again, Lewes reading it aloud over a four-day period. George Eliot knew *The Prelude* equally well. In 1867 Lewes was reading it aloud for the second time.[6] After his death Eliot shared her pleasure in this poem with John Cross, reading from the same volume over July to August 1880, just months before she died. In the last weeks of her life she was reading her friend F. W. H. Myers's *Wordsworth*, just published in the English Men of Letters series. As Thomas Pinney observed when he presented the record of her reading, 'it seems to confirm Cross's remark that George Eliot's early burst of enthusiasm for Wordsworth "entirely expresses the feeling she had to him up to the day of her death".'[7]

George Eliot's pleasure in Wordsworth's poetry remained keen and, what is much more unusual, so did her appetite for it in its entirety. When the 21-year-old confessed that she had been 'so self-indulgent as to possess myself of Wordsworth at full length', she had already worked through the first three volumes of her six-volume set and was looking forward to the rest.[8] She recommended the ode *On the Power of Sound* to Maria Lewis, describing it as 'a short poem', though it consists of 244 lines, and copied out a passage from the stupefyingly dull *Ode: 1815*, which is shorter at 128 lines but feels a lot longer.[9] This is commitment that even the most fervent Wordsworthians did not match. By 1879 most of them agreed with the Master of Balliol that, while reading Wordsworth 'makes you better', the benefit could only be increased by selection and that Arnold's effort was a step in the right direction.[10] George Eliot disagreed. She wanted Wordsworth whole. 'Except for travelling and for popular distribution', she told Frederic Harrison in 1880, 'I prefer Moxon's one-volumed edition of Wordsworth to any selection. No selection gives you the perfect gems to be found in single lines, which are to be found in the "dull" poems.'[11]

In 1878 Lord Acton reported to George Eliot that during a *tête-à-tête* Lewes had said to him that 'both Wordsworth and yourself write in reality for a chosen audience and are shut out from intelligent appreciation by many schools of men'.[12] By 1878 there was certainly nothing inappropriate about claiming equal literary stature for the authors of *Middlemarch* and *The Prelude*, but what is striking about Lewes's remark is that he yokes the novelist and the poet as having a special affinity as artists going much deeper than obvious resemblances. George Eliot had always sensed such an affinity and throughout her life had had a relationship with Wordsworth based on sympathetic identification. When she told Maria Lewis in 1839 that encountering Wordsworth, 'I have never before met with so many of my own feelings, expressed just as I could <wish> like', she showed herself to be Wordsworth's ideal reader.[13] Although she could not have known it, in stressing that Wordsworth seemed to speak to her of what she already knew, George Eliot was using the kind of terms the poet employed when he characterized *The Excursion* as an attempt 'to put the commonplace truths, of the human affections especially, in an interesting point of view; and rather to remind men of their knowledge, as it lurks inoperative and unvalued in their own minds, than to attempt to convey recondite or refined truths'.[14] Wordsworth provides more epigraphs for her novels than anyone except Shakespeare,[15] and the unostentatious allusion to lines and phrases in her letters indicates the easy commerce of her own thoughts with Wordsworth's words, a traffic that was continually reinvigorated by serious rereading. One Sunday in April 1880 an 'At Home' conversation with Frederic Harrison turned inevitably to his endeavours for the Religion of Humanity and his hostess mentioned some passages from *The Prelude* she thought he might find helpful.[16] In Harrison's Monday post came the references and further suggestions. It is a small example, but revealing. Such was George Eliot's inwardness with Wordsworth that from a fourteen-book poem and across the rest of a massive corpus, she could recall and locate at will.

George Eliot was drawn to Wordsworth in part simply by temperamental affinity. The *gravitas* of the poet who arranged his expanding lyric collection so that it should always end with the lines:

> To me the meanest flower that blows can give
> Thoughts that do often lie too deep for tears.

was matched by that of the novelist who acknowledged that it was perhaps rather too much her way 'to <teach> urge the human sanctities through tragedy—through pity and terror as well as admiration and delights'.[17] As a direct result of their unremitting high seriousness, both artists became objects of veneration in their own lifetimes. F. W. H. Myers, who famously thrilled to the 'terrible earnestness' of the woman who turned 'her grave majestic countenance toward [him] like a sibyl's in the gloom', was only one of many who found, as did the pilgrims to Rydal Mount, confirmation in the writer's own being of the tenor of their art.[18] Both George Eliot and Wordsworth had an elevated sense of their vocation, which they were not loth to articulate in the grandest terms. Compare Eliot's,

the only effect I ardently long to produce by my writings is that those who read them should be better able to *imagine* and to *feel* the pains and joys of those who differ from themselves in everything but the broad fact of being struggling erring human creatures.

—written when she had published no fiction other than *Scenes of Clerical Life*—with Wordsworth's,

the Poet, singing a song in which all human beings join with him, rejoices in the presence of truth as our visible friend and hourly companion. Poetry is the breath and finer spirit of all knowledge ... [the poet] is a rock of defence of human nature; an upholder and preserver, carrying every where with him relationship and love.

—written when all he had to his name were two loco-descriptive poems and a small gathering of lyrical ballads.[19]

In one of her notebooks George Eliot copied out these lines from *The Prelude*:

> Nor general Truths, which are themselves a sort
> Of Elements and Agents, Under-powers,
> Subordinate helpers of the living mind.[20]

The entry provides a further clue to the affinity between them. Both Eliot and Wordsworth habitually move from experience towards 'general Truths'. On occasion neither escapes the censure of '*mental bombast*', applied by Coleridge to those moments in even Wordsworth's finest poetry, when 'there is a disproportion of thought to the circumstance and occasion'.[21] But lovers of both Eliot and Wordsworth find such moments rarely, and what remains problematic for other readers constitutes for them a powerful appeal. Regretting that Arnold had omitted from his selection Wordsworth's sonnet, 'I grieved for Buonaparte', George Eliot commended this passage to Frederic Harrison as 'precious':

'Tis not in battles that from youth we train
The governor who must be wise and good,
And temper with the sternness of the brain
Thoughts motherly, and meek as womanhood.
Wisdom doth live with children round her knees.[22]

Arnold almost certainly left the sonnet out because it represented the preacherly Wordsworth he wanted to efface. Eliot values it precisely because it contains a 'precious' truth, of a kind with which her own letters, essays, and novels are studded. Although Lewes and Eliot surreptitiously encouraged Alexander Main in the compilation of *Wise, Witty, and Tender Sayings* culled from her writings, she was discomfited when she realized that one of his prefatory observations might be taken as licensing readers to discriminate between direct and indirect teaching. Protesting that she was always severely watchful 'against anything that could be called preaching', she insisted that her novels must be read 'as wholes', not as 'an assemblage of extracts'.[23] She was incontestably right. But her vehement caution only highlights the truth that the apophthegm is one of the most powerful instruments of her art, as it was of Wordsworth's, and the appearance of four editions of Main's book by 1880 indicates that both her publisher and her readers recognized the fact.

There is a comfort in the strength of love;
'Twill make a thing endurable, which else
Would overset the brain, or break the heart.

The lines are from *Michael*, but they could be inserted with barely a ripple into the texture of *Silas Marner* or *The Mill on the Floss*.

II

'nature's unambitious underwood'

Wordsworth's part in the genesis of *Adam Bede* is signalled on the opening page. George Eliot read in his poetry in two spells in 1858 when the novel was being written, and during the early phase of composition she and Lewes completed *The Excursion*.[24] Using a passage from that poem as epigraph, the title-page to *Adam Bede* announced in 1859 a new work from the author of *Scenes of Clerical Life* and simultaneously placed it in a line of literary descent. In Book VI of *The Excursion*, set in 'The Churchyard among the Mountains', the Pastor recalls members of his little flock, whose lives have served to convince him of 'The native grandeur of the human soul'. In keeping with the spirit of a sacred place, 'where the voice that speaks | In envy or detraction is not heard', he proposes to confine himself to stories that excite 'love, esteem, | And admiration',

> So that ye may have
> Clear images before your gladden'd eyes
> Of nature's unambitious underwood
> And flowers that prosper in the shade. And when
> I speak of such among my flock as swerved
> Or fell, those only shall be singled out
> Upon whose lapse, or error, something more
> Than brotherly forgiveness may attend.[25]

These lines introduce *Adam Bede*.

There is a similarity between the novelist's role and that of Wordsworth's Pastor. In the mountain churchyard the graves are mostly unmarked by memorial stones and inscriptions, because the dalesmen entrust 'The lingering gleam of their departed lives | To oral record'. Acting as the articulate memory of the community, the Pastor, as he tells his stories, restores the virtue of these spent lives as moral agents for the listening Wanderer and Poet. So with her drop of ink the novelist, who opens her scene sixty years earlier in a carpenter's shop. And both Pastor and novelist celebrate 'nature's unambitious underwood' with the affectionate reverence George Eliot identified as the basis of Cowper's power as a moralist: 'that genuine love which cherishes things in proportion to their nearness, and feels its reverence grow in proportion to the intimacy of its knowledge'.[26]

Although Wordsworth was the laureate of a particular region and of its humble inhabitants, however, his example did not of itself determine that George Eliot's early work should centre on a farm, a mill, and a weaver's shop. From the exquisite closing paragraph of the essay on Young by the *Westminster* reviewer, memories stretched back to the childhood of Mary Ann Evans, and a more recent reviewing task had focused ideas on art and rural life. Most of her contemporaries would have found struggling through Riehl's *Die Bürgerliche Gesellschaft* (1851) and *Land und Leute* (1853) a rebarbative exercise, but for George Eliot it was an important moment in her overall intellectual development, and it has long been recognized that her sense of how fascinating *Land und Leute* would be 'as literature, if it were not important for its facts and philosophy', anticipates the direction of her first attempts at fiction.[27] But it might also be noted that her absorption in Wordsworth had in large measure prepared George Eliot for Riehl and that in the Wordsworth she reread while writing *Adam Bede* she found imaginative representation of much that she dwelt on in 'The Natural History of German Life'—that 'peasant conservatism' stems from adherence to 'the old custom of the country'; that the peasant feels intense 'historical piety' to the familiar and what is immediately connected with himself; that manners and customs are 'determined' by physical geography; that 'men's affection, imagination, wit and humour' are bound in 'with the subtle ramifications of historical language'. *Lyrical Ballads* and *The Excursion*, Wordsworth's theoretical prefaces and the notes to the poems on language, customs, and places, provided quite as much reinforcement as Riehl for George Eliot's reverence for the vitality that inheres in the local, the known, 'familiar with forgotten years',[28] and for her conviction that it is the artist's duty to direct 'our sympathy with the perennial joys and struggles, the toil, the tragedy, and the humour in the life of our more heavily-laden fellow-men' towards a true object rather than a false one.

The epigraph to *Adam Bede* aligns George Eliot with Wordsworth. Hayslope and its inhabitants, 'nature's unambitious underwood', their customs, their sense of traditional community and awareness of threats to it, the routines of labour and of life determined by weather and season, even the story of the ruined maid, all place the novel, as has often been noted, in the Wordsworthian line.[29] But the affinity between novelist and poet around the time of *Adam Bede* extends beyond the choice of subject-matter. What is striking is not so much the similarity of subject-matter in itself, but the similarity of the way in which George Eliot and Wordsworth highlight their choice and its significance.

Both announce the beginning of their careers as imaginative artists with imperious manifestos.[30] The 'Advertisement' to the first edition of *Lyrical Ballads* (1798) is short but not modest; the Prefaces to the second (1800) and third (1802) are much longer and more vaunting still. Wordsworth insists against prevailing aesthetic norms that 'Low and rustic life was generally chosen' because here will be found materials for poetry of permanent interest; that this choice and the manner in which the subject is treated constitutes a move towards a more vital and healthy literary production than that which is current; that resistence is to be expected but must be overborne for the sake of nothing less than the nation's well-being. Every innovative writer marks out territory, but these are none the less astonishing claims from a writer who has, as yet, produced very little. George Eliot's pretensions are as massive. She may have been a writer who, as Gordon Haight has influentially argued, shrank from exposure and criticism, but there is nothing shrinking about her aesthetic pronouncements in the late 1850s. Before she had written any fiction herself, George Eliot extracted the 'truth' of *Modern Painters*, '*realism*—the doctrine that all truth and beauty are to be attained by a humble and faithful study of nature', and intensified its moral agency by declaring it sufficient to 'remould our life'.[31] In the same year, 1856, she assaulted the greatest novelist of the day for 'transcendent . . . unreality' in his representation of the deeper aspects of life and dismissed all current painters (identifying Holman Hunt explicitly) for falsehood in their treatment of the peasantry. And in *Adam Bede* she returned to the topic of truth and falsehood at length, not as in many Victorian novels in a Preface, but within the flow of the narrative, requiring the reader to 'pause a little' for reflection on a series of propositions around the declaration that it is the artist's duty 'to give the loving pains of a life to the faithful representing of commonplace things'.[32]

On receiving *Lyrical Ballads* (1800) Charles Lamb shrewdly remarked that while Wordsworth's critical 'dogmas' were 'true and just', they 'associate[d] a *diminishing* idea with the Poems that follow, as having been written for **Experiments** on the public taste, more than having sprung (as they must have done) from living and daily circumstances'.[33] George Eliot courts the same criticism in *Adam Bede*. But Lamb mistook the nature of Wordsworth's creativity. Wordsworth was always a programmatic writer, not, that is, one who worked conscientiously to a programme, but one who was always ready to conceptualize his aims and justify his achievements with reference to a plan. So was George Eliot. Chapter 17 of *Adam Bede* is not a reprise of any Wordsworth utterance—although many of its formulations closely parallel his— but it serves the same function in George Eliot's artistic trajectory as the *Lyrical Ballads* Prefaces did in Wordsworth's. Each writer makes declarations about truth and falsehood in art as if writing *ab initio*, as if previous debate had not existed. Wordsworth, widely read as he was in recent poetry, sweeps the ground clear. What he did in poetry, George Eliot seeks to do sixty years later for the novel. Favourable references in 'The Natural History of German Life' to Scott (a favourite author) and to Kingsley are token gestures. True writing about rural life, her utterances suggest—and for her creative confidence need to suggest—begins here, with her first novel.

For both George Eliot and Wordsworth artistic truthfulness was not just a matter of aesthetics. Rectification of public taste was integral to purification and elevation of social life and discourse. With breath-taking certitude Wordsworth asserts in the *Lyrical Ballads* Preface that causes 'unknown to former times' are producing the 'general evil' of national degradation, a symptom of which is public appetite for 'frantic novels, sickly and stupid German Tragedies, and . . . idle and extravagant stories in verse'.[34] George Eliot's 'Silly Novels by Lady Novelists' is much less strident, but its drift is similar. 'Mind-and-millinery' novels are not harmless. Their effect is incalculably pernicious, in that they weaken their readers' ability to discern the true from the false, and they demean the art they represent. The menace must be exposed.[35]

Underpinning the claims made by both Eliot and Wordsworth is a profound conviction of the 'sacredness of the writer's art'. Wordsworth's profession of his faith in the Preface to *Lyrical Ballads* (1802) is the loftiest in English in the nineteenth century, but George Eliot's comes a close second, and versions of both are repeated whenever the value of humanist education is brought into question. Poetry for Wordsworth is the 'most philosophic of all writing', the 'breath and finer spirit of all knowledge', whose power is that it 'binds together by passion and knowledge the vast empire of human society'.[36] For George Eliot—and the declaration is too familiar to need quotation in full—'Art is the nearest thing to life'. And what points with particular emphasis towards her early fiction is the conviction that, 'sacred' though the task of the artist is at all times, it is all the more so 'when he undertakes to paint the life of the People'.[37]

If the epigraph to *Adam Bede* makes the link between Wordsworth and George Eliot, the novel's opening sentence confirms it,

by pointing up a problematic feature common to the art of both—
the use of the past. *Adam Bede* was published in 1859, but its story
opens in 1799. *Michael*, though published in 1800, is set in the
past, well before the boyhood of the poet. The artistic use of the
past is not in itself the problem. In a still unsurpassed essay, 'The
Authority of the Past in George Eliot's Novels', Thomas Pinney has
demonstrated the various ways in which the past was a rich and
essential resource for Eliot's art and almost all of his observations
can be applied unmodified to Wordsworth.[38] The problem is the
use of the past in a programme that has corrective designs on the
present. As has already been noted, when Wordsworth brought the
tale of *Michael* to the notice of Fox, he presented it as evidence
about a certain class of farmer, to a politician he believed to be
much concerned with contemporary forces bearing on the lives of
such people. Declaring that his poems were 'faithful copies from
nature', the poet hoped that his efforts would co-operate with
Fox's, 'to stem [the] evils with which the country is labouring'.[39] If
such was his aim, was it helpful to send Fox not an account of
contemporary circumstances, but a story that had passed into
legend before the poet was born? The case is similar with *Adam
Bede*. In her review essays from the late 1850s George Eliot focuses
urgently on contemporary needs. To follow Ruskin's prescription
would 'remould our life', *now*; Dickens would render a great
service to 'the awakening of social sympathies' *now* were he to
deploy his art in such and such a way; Holman Hunt's depiction of
the peasantry is false to how they are. The manifesto in *Adam Bede*
likewise addresses the needs of the present. The story she actually
tells, however, concerns landlord and tenant, farming practices,
village education, and religious experience as they were at the end
of the previous century. Of course, as Pinney and many others have
pointed out, the relation between past and present is a dynamic one
in *Adam Bede*, as the narrator continually registers the significance
of historical distance, but it is none the less curious that this novel,
which rests within a matrix of protestations about the need for a
truthful representation of the common people, should present not
rural life in the present—as Kingsley does in *Yeast*—but in the quite
distant past.

Contemporary reviewers betrayed not even a hint of unease as
they joined in chorus to praise not only George Eliot's ability to
make her characters 'realities' (*Saturday Review*), but the accuracy

of her depiction of farm and village life: 'We do not know whether our literature anywhere possesses such a closely true picture of rural life', or, 'the great merit of *Adam Bede* consists in the singular grace and skill with which . . . characteristic details of country life are rendered'.[40] And it is clear why they were able to use the word 'true' with such ease. All of the reviewers have only one template against which to test the truth of George Eliot's depiction of rural life and that is timeless universality. Like Kingsley, George Eliot conscientiously amassed information for her novels, but no one in 1859 suggested that the authenticity of *Adam Bede* had anything to do with fidelity to facts that might be verified from other sources.[41] Critical reference is exclusively to the higher truth of universal art. The author of *Adam Bede* is a genius and not an ordinary mortal, John Chapman averred in the *Westminster Review*, because she has 'the power of seeing realities where the latter see only appearances'.[42] And what constitutes the most important reality was spelled out by E. S. Dallas in *The Times*. It is the 'truism which very few of us comprehend until it has been knocked into us by years of experience—that we are all alike—that the human heart is one'.[43]

Once again the line from *The Old Cumberland Beggar*—'That we have all of us one human heart'—is invoked, and appropriately, for Dallas's half-conscious recollection brings into focus what is most important in the relationship between the George Eliot of *Adam Bede* and Wordsworth. Whenever he defended *Lyrical Ballads*, in the Prefaces, or the 1800 note to *The Thorn*, or in his 1802 letter to John Wilson, Wordsworth stressed his concern with the universal truths of human nature, and in particular the primacy of feeling. Feeling was both subject-matter and aesthetic agent, and rectification of feeling was the goal, to give readers 'new composi tions of feeling, to render their feelings more sane pure and permanent'.[44] Feeling is what binds men together 'in relationship and love', what confirms that 'we have all of us one human heart'. Since her first reading of Wordsworth George Eliot's thought about culture and society, environmental determinism and moral freedom, had developed in directions unbroached by him, but the grand truths Wordsworth had dared to utter still commanded her assent. They helped shape *Adam Bede*.

In chapter 5 Arthur Donnithorne tells Mr Irwine that his 'fellow' in London has sent him a parcel of books including *Lyrical Ballads* (1798). *The Ancient Mariner*, he says, is a 'strange, striking thing', though he cannot 'make head or tail of it', but the rest of the poems Arthur dismisses as 'twaddling stuff' (p. 65).[45] The 'Advertisement' to this anonymous volume urges readers to ask themselves, not whether what they read is 'Poetry', but whether it is 'a natural delineation of human passions, human characters, and human incidents', but Arthur is not won over. To him the mariner's wondrous story is just a striking tale, and the other lyrics, which dwell on states of mind and feeling, are just pointless.

This brief excursus into literary criticism in the Rector of Broxton's parlour is important. In a dryly humorous fashion it signals an indebtedness, but more than this, it marks the axes on which the novel moves. Like *Lyrical Ballads*, *Adam Bede* emphasizes feeling as the fundamental connective between human beings, between themselves and their environment, and between their sense of present and past. Key sequences of the novel recapitulate *Lyrical Ballads* and *The Excursion* on this theme, such as the lengthy expositions in chapter 18, 'Church', for example, which branch out from the narrator's declaration that the 'secret of our emotions never lies in the bare object but in its subtle relations to our past' (p. 199).

But the novel also presents feeling as the most sensitive calibrator of moral discrimination. That a young and vigorous Captain of Militia should be unmoved by *Simon Lee* is hardly culpable but it points to a lack in him, a potential fault-line in his relation to other human beings, especially to women and those beneath him in rank. Similarly, should a 17-year-old milkmaid be blamed for finding the Hall Farm children 'tiresome', or for having so little sense of rootedness that 'Hetty could have cast all her past life behind her and never cared to be reminded of it again' (p. 154)? But the text is as unmisgivingly emphatic that Hetty is deficient as Mrs Poyser, who has 'formed a tolerably fair estimate of what might be expected from Hetty in the way of feeling' (p. 155).

Varying ways of perceiving order in human life are offered in *Adam Bede*. Mr Irwine draws on Greek tragedy as he outlines to Arthur the workings of Nemesis: 'Consequences are unpitying. Our deeds carry their terrible consequences . . : consequences that are hardly ever confined to ourselves' (p. 172). Dinah preaches to the contrary, assuring the villagers on the green that redemption from sin's clutch is possible through the Man of Sorrows. As he trots to Hayslope, ignorant of what has happened to Hetty, Arthur

constructs a moral sequence of his own, in which future amend-
ment shall wipe clean stain in the past. But against these inclusive
schema, the novel repeatedly sets the local test of feeling. Although
he is a Christian priest, Mr Irwine does not waste time expounding
the meaning of the liturgy to the likes of blacksmith Chad Cranage:
'If he had been in the habit of speaking theoretically, he would
perhaps have said that the only healthy form religion could take in
such minds was that of certain dim but strong emotions, suffusing
themselves as a hallowing influence over family affections and
neighbourly duties' (p. 68). Dinah's instinctive response to the news
of Lizbeth Bede's bereavement, 'I must go and see if I can give her
any help' (p. 193), prefigures her reaching out to Hetty in the
condemned cell, both acts of human comfort which, unlike the
preaching on the green, have lasting effect. Adam Bede himself in
old age says most about feeling in fewest words, and what he says
directly parallels Wordsworth's dismissal of systems of moral
philosophy for lacking the power 'to incorporate [themselves] with
the blood and vital juices of our minds'.[46] 'I've been pretty clear,
ever since I was a young 'un', says Adam, 'as religion's something
else besides notions. It isn't notions sets people doing the right
thing—it's feelings' (p. 180). 'Twaddle' or 'truism'? It is a corner-
stone of the greatness of Wordsworth and George Eliot, and
perhaps the strongest link between their art, that they were ready
to deal in truisms, knowing them to be the truths that always need
resaying.

Adam Bede was published in February 1859. George Eliot at
once began work on a new novel and during the early stage of
composition, at the beginning of September, Lewes read *The
Excursion* aloud to her.[47] Too much must not be made of this—
George Eliot was reading much else too—but the fact remains that
during a very stressful year, which saw the death of her sister and
the vexatious controversy over the authorship of *Adam Bede*, Eliot
turned once again to the familiar poetry. Wordsworth was a
presence as work quickened on the first volume of *The Mill on the
Floss*.[48]

It has been termed her 'most Wordsworthian novel', and critics
have noted, for example, the similarity between Mr Tulliver's
attachment to the mill and Michael's to his fields, or that between
the way in which narrator figures are employed. 'In telling Maggie's
story', it has been suggested, 'George Eliot's narrator hopes to

produce the same effect that the Wanderer induces through his tale of Margaret's suffering and death'.[49] But the most important association between Wordsworth and *The Mill on the Floss* is in their use of memory and it is signalled on the first page. When recalling moments of intense experience, the poet characteristically fixes on discrete things—'the single sheep, and the one blasted tree, | And the bleak music of that old stone wall' (*Prelude*, 1850, XII. 319–20). So the narrator of *The Mill on the Floss* fuses the present with the past through memory of specific objects: 'I remember those large dripping willows. I remember the stone bridge' (p. 7). In other passages Wordsworthian acts of memory are paralleled in still more striking fashion, as the narrator dwells on childhood and the value of what is loved and known:

We could never have loved the earth so well if we had had no childhood in it,—if it were not the earth where the same flowers come up again every spring that we used to gather with our tiny fingers as we sat lisping to ourselves on the grass—the same hips and haws on the autumn hedgerows—the same redbreasts that we used to call 'God's birds,' because they did no harm to the precious crops. What novelty is worth that sweet monotony where everything is known, and *loved* because it is known? (p. 36)

Tom's return from school to the 'familiar hearth' prompts a further meditation on the power of objects and surroundings loved in childhood, however commonplace, to retain their grasp on us. Where would we be, the narrator asks, 'if our affections had not a trick of twining round those old inferior things—if the loves and sanctities of our life had not deep immoveable roots in memory' (p. 133).

Writing such as this recalls passage after passage from *The Prelude*, where Wordsworth lingers on incidents from childhood and boyhood, as if unable to stem the flood of memories, until driven to confess how loth he is,

>   to quit
> Those recollected hours that have the charm
> Of visionary things, those lovely forms
> And sweet sensations, that throw back our life,
> And almost make remotest infancy
> A visible scene on which the sun is shining.[50]

And it is impossible not to detect in such language from George

Eliot the yearnings of one whose own journey to adulthood has entailed severance from family and the familiar hearth. But the recollections of childhood are not the whole of *The Prelude* and these passages of nostalgic yearning are not the whole of *The Mill on the Floss*. In its entirety the novel exposes the limitations of the narrator's Wordsworthianism as it engages, in the presentation of given human lives, with the recalcitrant complexities of Wordsworth's apparently simple wish for a continuity of life in which 'affinities [are] preserved | Between all stages of the life of man'.[51]

All of the major figures in *The Mill on the Floss* feed off memories which foster their sense of identity—Mr Tulliver and the mill—or validate action—Tom in his determination to restore his father's honour—or provide solace for life's disappointments—Mrs Tulliver as she dwells on what she once was—but the life-story that engrosses us is Maggie's. In it the actual process is enacted through which experiences become memories, and a past is created and then interpreted. Maggie's tragedy is that eventually she proves to be in thrall to her past. 'I could wish my days to be | Bound each to each by natural piety', is the affirmation Wordsworth draws from his paradox that 'The Child is father of the Man'. Maggie is 'bound', but the bondage that sustains the poet's sense of self denies hers. Wordsworth's major poems propose a model of human development in which the 'glad animal movements' of childhood give way but continue to feed into the 'still sad music' of adulthood. Objects and places loved in childhood continue to be loved and their mysterious power to 'nourish' and 'repair' the mind remains. But Wordsworth's model is not regressive. Nothing can bring back the hour of splendour in the grass. What the poet values in his bond to the past is, as Margaret Homans puts it, 'the wider sense of connectedness and vitality engendered by that bond', and the bond survives even though the poet transcends its originating objects, even 'nature's material presence'.[52] Whatever his awe at the mystery of the past—'Oh! mystery of man, from what a depth | Proceed thy honours' (*Prelude*, 1850, XII. 272–3)—Wordsworth habitually plundered it to minister to his imaginative freedom. At the crucial test of her life, what Maggie lacks is this saving egotism.

The test comes when at last Maggie and Stephen Guest confront one another, their mutual passion no longer a matter of glances and suppressed electric shivers, but out in the open. So overwhelming is the threat to the existing progression of their lives that, whereas other lovers might murmur about lips and eyes, they debate fundamentally the nature of what is happening to them. Claiming that their love is 'natural', Stephen declares that their feelings constitute a 'natural law' that 'surmounts any other' (p. 417). Maggie concedes that 'Love is natural', but having earlier insisted that 'pity and faithfulness and memory are natural too' (p. 395), she eventually poses as a question what is in fact a declaration of principle: 'If the past is not to bind us, where can duty lie?' (p. 417). To Stephen's answering, 'There is nothing in the past that can annul our right to each other', Maggie responds, 'with timid resolution', that such is the hold of 'memories and affections' that, were it possible, she would choose to go back in time and 'to be true to [her] calmer affections and live without the joy of love' (p. 418). Maggie's eventual death in her brother's arms is no more than a recapitulation of what has already taken place in this debate. Maggie cannot grow and, as Margaret Homans has persuasively argued, the bitter irony is that her fatal lack of self-worth is the construct of the past to which she now defers. Clinging to a fixed image of the past as her only resource denies its ability to take on new configurations when recalled from a changing present.

Maggie's attempt to be true to her best self by acknowledging the claims of the past might seem to parallel Wordsworth's exposition in *The Prelude* of how he was enabled to maintain a 'saving intercourse' with his 'true self' at its moment of greatest vulnerability (1850, XI. 341–2). But the two life-stories are crucially different. As Wordsworth presents his history, it becomes clear that what he judges to be his 'true self' has been impaired only momentarily by alien influences—abstract reasoning, sectarian politics—and that in shaking them off the poet not only loses nothing of value, but is able to transform the experience of threat into augmented imaginative strength. Maggie's situation is quite other. Stephen Guest's morality, judgement, even his common sense may be open to question, but when he declares, 'it is the first time we have either of us loved with our whole heart and soul' (p. 418), he recognizes at least the truth that sexual awakening challenges their perception of their own being and of their relation to their past. It will bring pain and rift, but it cannot be wished away. For Maggie, however, who has already deceived herself, and Lucy, and Philip, about her feelings, the dread of undeceiving her brother determines her response: 'To have no cloud between herself and Tom was still a perpetual yearning . . . that had its root deeper than all change' (p. 399). And so, at a crisis which ought to contribute to the continuing unfolding of her newly-recognized adult self, Maggie retreats, being prepared explicitly to 'live without the joy of love'. In clinging to a past that 'binds', Maggie succumbs to a misreading of Wordsworth's myth of childhood.

George Eliot, however, was not Maggie Tulliver (any more than Mary Ann Evans was), and the result of her engagement with the central Wordsworthian themes was an act of new creation, which exploits fruitfully both her debts and her resistance to her Romantic forebear. Critics have differed in their estimate of both. When Basil Willey long ago declared that Eliot's early novels were 'her *Prelude*', he meant it as praise, whereas Donald Stone sees the Wordsworthianism of *The Mill on the Floss* as a 'blight on Eliot's creative imagination'.[53] In the justly praised essay already cited, Margaret Homans offers a more nuanced account of both indebtedness and resistance. But what is generally agreed is that *The Mill on the Floss* embodies a creative encounter with her own past and with Wordsworth, both as part of that past and as a continuing agent for its interpretation.

George Eliot's next novel, *Silas Marner*, was explicitly located by her in the same relation. Deeply stirred memories cut across preparation for *Romola* and from recollection of a figure that is Wordsworthian in its haunting power—'a linen-weaver with a bag on his back'—emerged in a rush of imaginative release the tale of 'The Weaver of Raveloe'. It was not, she admitted to Blackwood, a story she 'believed that any one would have been interested in . . . but myself (since William Wordsworth is dead) . . .'. Eliot was right to invoke Wordsworth as her ideal reader. The sombreness of the opening chapters, which John Blackwood had found 'very sad, almost oppressive', would have appealed to the poet of *Michael* and *The Excursion*. The unfolding of the rest of the story, intended, Eliot said, to set 'in a strong light the remedial influences of pure, natural human relations', would have spoken to the author of *Lyrical Ballads* and *The Prelude*.[54]

To say that *Silas Marner* is profoundly Wordsworthian is not to imply that it is any the less a characteristically Eliot moral fable. The marvellous—Silas's catalepsy, the arrival of Eppie—operates within an otherwise conscientiously realistic story, whose structure rests on the kinds of moral dilemma which recur throughout Eliot's work. Godfrey Cass is allowed a moment when he could acknowledge the baby Silas has found as his, but dazzled by the cluster of possibilities offered by silence, he does not, and in so doing Godfrey prefigures Tito Melema in his moment of choice in *Romola*. Compared with what befalls Mr Bulstrode, Godfrey's Nemesis may be, as George Eliot assured Blackwood, 'a very mild one',[55] but it is a none the less severe demonstration of the truth of Mr Irwine's warning to Arthur Donnithorne about Nemesis: 'Consequences are unpitying . . .'. Eppie's refusal to leave Silas and become a lady, which is fired by a positive preference for 'working-folks, and their victuals, and their ways', and her determination 'to marry a working-man' (p. 168), looks forward to Esther Lyon's similarly motivated rejection of her silken bondage in *Felix Holt*.[56]

The dominant story of *Silas Marner*, however, is that of the weaver himself, and it, more than any other of Eliot's fictions, is so embedded in Wordsworth that, as Robert Dunham has suggested, 'one well acquainted with him almost imagines portions of it dictated to the author by the spirit of the poet'.[57] This fancy is justifiable both locally and overall. The trajectory from trauma and alienation to recovery and integration into domestic and community life parallels the movement of *The Prelude* and it is embodied throughout in Wordsworthian language.[58] Silas is imaged as one whose affections have died under the bruise of the unjust conviction, whose stream of feeling for the past is blocked up, whose memory even of that past grows dim. He is saved from insensibility by the demands of the child, whom Silas appropriates fiercely from the moment he finds her. The 'fibres' of Silas's life 'cling' to Eppie. Like the brawny artificer Wordsworth saw in London, bending over an infant and eying it 'with love unutterable' (*Prelude*, 1850, VII. 618), Silas loves Eppie unconditionally and it is through love that his 'true self' is recovered and released:

By seeking what was needful for Eppie, by sharing the effect that everything produced on her, he had himself come to appropriate the forms of custom and belief which were the mould of Raveloe life; and as, with reawakening sensibilities, memory also reawakened, he had begun to ponder over the elements of his old faith, and blend them with his new impressions, till he recovered a consciousness of unity between his past and present. (p. 138)

This one quotation must stand for many such that are couched not

1. Stopford Augustus Brooke (1832–1916)

2. William Angus Knight (1836–1916)

3. Hardwicke Drummond Rawnsley (1851–1929)

4. Edward Dowden (1843–1913)

only in Wordsworthian language but in Wordsworthian cadence. The last clause is all but blank verse.

If the fable of Silas's redemption parallels the main movement of *The Prelude*, however, other aspects of the story have a different relation to the Wordsworthian narratives they invoke. When she suggested to Blackwood that lines from *Michael* might serve as the motto for *Silas Marner*:

> A child, more than all other gifts
> That earth can offer to declining man,
> Brings hope with it, and forward-looking thoughts

George Eliot asked him, 'Do you think it indicates the story too distinctly?'[59] Her worry is strange, for the motto in fact misleads the first-time reader. It of course anticipates more than one moment in the novel when having a child is said to be a stimulus for hopeful endeavour, and, placed in its fuller context, the passage from *Michael* anticipates the tender humour with which Eppie is depicted as a troublesome and inquisitive infant—like Luke, 'something between a hindrance and a help'. Any reader familiar with Wordsworth's pastoral, however, would read *Silas Marner* expecting the opposite of what does happen. In *Michael* Luke falls into 'ignominy and shame', leaving his father in extreme old age with no alternative but to labour on. Our final image of Michael is of him alone with the elements, unable to complete the sheep-fold that had once been the object of 'hope ... and forward-looking thoughts'. How different this is from the close of *Silas Marner*, as Eppie and Aaron, and Silas and Dolly walk together from the wedding home to the cottage in which the weaver will live a cosseted old age.

When he is at his most isolated, 'so withered and yellow, that, although he was not yet forty, the children always called him "Old Master Marner" ' (p. 19), Silas's locked emotions are released momentarily when he smashes the pot used to fetch water from the well. He picks up the pieces 'with grief in his heart' and sticks them together, propping 'the ruin in its old place for a memorial' (p. 70). This touching incident recalls the best-loved of Wordsworth's narratives—the story of Margaret in Book I of *The Excursion*—in which the Wanderer tells what he knows about the history of the ruined cottage, whose desolation is caught in 'the useless fragment of a wooden bowl' (l. 493). Again the significance of the symbolic materials is reversed. In the story of Margaret the decline of the abandoned woman is signalled by her neglect of her garden and home. Weeds encroach and fruiting bushes are dragged down as her spirit fails. Eventually all that remains is a ruin in a wilderness. In *Silas Marner* the garden serves a similar poetic function, but its tenor is wholly positive. Eppie's desire for a garden is matched by Aaron's eagerness to serve both the woman he loves and her infirm father. The deserted stone-pit, where Dunsey Cass has kept his secret in death for sixteen years, yields up not only Silas's gold, but materials for Eppie's garden walls. At the end of the novel 'flowers shine with answering gladness, as the four united people [come] within sight of them' (p. 176).

This closing scene, the most joyous in her fiction, focuses essentially what George Eliot has made of her Wordsworthian inheritance in *Silas Marner*. Reworking *The Prelude*'s account of crisis and redemption, she emphasizes Silas's reintegration into the world in which he can become once more 'the same Silas Marner who had once loved his fellow with tender love' (p. 84). Whereas the poet is redeemed to a vocation which calls him, a 'prophet of Nature', to speak to men of their 'deliverance, surely yet to come' (*Prelude*, 1850, XIV. 445–6), Silas's vocation, to nurture Eppie, has been his redemption. Eliot's handling of the stories of Michael and Margaret is similar in emphasis. In both poems Wordsworth directs the reader's gaze on from the suffering protagonists to the greater whole in which they have been subsumed. There is no transcendental significance to the end of *Silas Marner*. On the contrary, its focus is on the power of love in very ordinary human beings in this world. But it achieves as successfully as Wordsworth ever did the goal he set himself in the lines prefacing *The Excursion*, that of conveying a vision of paradise as 'A simple produce of the common day'.

III

'Man's unconquerable mind'

After *Silas Marner* Wordsworth's role in George Eliot's creative life diminished. Textually he remained a visible presence. Lines of verse are quoted as mottoes and chapter epigraphs in *Felix Holt*, *Middlemarch*, and *Daniel Deronda* and occasional snatches from favourite poems appear in the flow of the prose. Wordsworthian continuities connect *Middlemarch* and some of *The Impressions of Theophrastus Such* to the earlier novels—notably *Adam Bede*[60]—and the Wordsworthian note of this opening to chapter 3 of *Daniel Deronda* is unmistakable:

A human life, I think, should be well rooted in some spot of a native land, where it may get the love of tender kinship for the face of earth, for the labours men go forth to, for the sounds and accents that haunt it, for whatever will give that early home a familiar unmistakable difference amidst the future widening of knowledge: a spot where the definiteness of early memories may be inwrought with affection, and kindly acquaintance with all neighbours, even to the dogs and donkeys, may spread not by sentimental effort and reflection, but as a sweet habit of the blood.

After Lewes's death in 1878 she even amended the manuscript of his *Problems of Life and Mind* to include a passage from *The Excursion* she thought apposite.[61] But, visibility notwithstanding, there is no strong case for arguing that Wordsworth's poetry was an active, shaping agent in the later direction of George Eliot's art as it was in the earlier.

It was not, however, discarded, or placed on the shelf with other former favourites, to be recalled with nostalgic tenderness and gratitude. George Eliot went on reading Wordsworth's poetry until the end of her life and was able to find sustenance in it because it was capacious and flexible enough to allow her to construct a Wordsworth she could continue to value. When the 20-year-old evangelical Mary Ann Evans wished for 'a more frequent upturning of the soul's eye' in Wordsworth's 1836–7 volumes, she was one of a numerous company. Ironically, however, just as the Christian reading of Wordsworth was gaining ground, she shed her evangelicalism, with the result that her later reading distanced her from what was becoming the received view of the poet. After the publication of Wordsworth's 1845 collection, with the explicitly Christian revision to important texts, and the appearance six years later of Christopher Wordsworth's portrait of his uncle as a devout High Anglican, Christian readers of most colours were able to feel comfortable with Wordsworth's soul's eye. During her early years as a novelist George Eliot diverged from this gathering consensus, as she incorporated the humanist Wordsworth of *Lyrical Ballads* into her own depictions of nature's unambitious underwood, and it was this Wordsworth, interpreted ever more loftily as humanist, who retained her allegiance to the end of her life.

The allegiance is attested, for example, by the entry into one of her notebooks of two lines from Wordsworth's *Ode: 1815*, 'Commemoration holy that unites | The living generations with the dead', or by the fact that in what must have been a very high-toned conversation, she quoted to Jowett Wordsworth's lines, 'For every gift of noble origin | Is breathed upon by hope's perpetual breath'.[62] But it is most fully and forcefully acknowledged in the letter already touched on to Frederic Harrison of 19 April 1880. Commending certain passages of Wordsworth to him, she begins with a passage from the book of *The Prelude* which was entitled in 1850, 'Retrospect: Love of Nature leading to Love of Man', in which the poet defines the 'human nature' to which he pays homage as 'a spirit | Diffused through time and space' (VIII. 608–15). Next comes the ringing statement, also from *The Prelude*, (XI. 393–5):

> There is
> One great society alone on Earth:
> The noble Living and the noble Dead.

The third passage recommended consists of the 'precious lines' already quoted from 'I griev'd for Buonaparte'. Finally George Eliot cites the 'magnificent sonnet on Toussaint l'Ouverture', declaring, 'I don't know where there is anything finer than the last eight lines of it.' They are:

> Yet die not; do thou
> Wear rather in thy bonds a cheerful brow:
> Though fallen thyself, never to rise again,
> Live, and take comfort. Thou hast left behind
> Powers that will work for thee; air, earth, and skies;
> There's not a breathing of the common wind
> That will forget thee; thou hast great allies;
> Thy friends are exultations, agonies,
> And love, and man's unconquerable mind.

The mosaic constructed from these Wordsworthian fragments offers a vision of the human potential for greatness and of the immortality of the noble dead, conferred by the admiration and aspiration of the noble living, and there can be little doubt that the ardour of the letter is fuelled by Eliot's undiminished sense of loss at Lewes's premature death in November 1878. But the vision itself was one she had long nurtured and it had inspired her own attempt at a Wordsworthian ode over twenty years before. In '*O May I Join*

The Choir Invisible' Eliot had hymned the 'immortal dead who live again | In minds made better by their presence', and, envisioning the individual's part in the growing good of the world, had ended with a prayer that she might reach,

> That purest heaven, be to other souls
> The cup of strength in some great agony,
> Enkindle generous ardour, feed pure love,
> Beget the smiles that have no cruelty—
> Be the sweet presence of a good diffused,
> And in diffusion ever more intense.
> So shall I join the choir invisible
> Whose music is the gladness of the world.[63]

Despite echoes and glimpses, however, '*O May I Join*' is not the *Ode: Intimations of Immortality*. Reflecting all too obviously as it does Eliot's appetite for the exhortatory Wordsworth, the language of the poem is dead and no amount of exegesis can make it live.[64] The contrast could not be more marked with the beautiful, unlaboured declarations that arise spontaneously throughout her later letters, such as,

The inspiring principle which alone gives me courage to write is, that of so presenting our human life as to help my readers in getting a clearer conception and a more active admiration of those vital elements which bind men together and give a higher worthiness to their existence.

Unlike Eliot's verse, passages such as this live in the memory. They testify to the continuance of her faith, whose keystone is identified in the letter to Harrison. In them George Eliot is most magnificently herself and the most eloquent meditator of the humanist vision inherent in all of Wordsworth.

6

The Active Universe:
Arnold and Tennyson

Emphatically such a Being lives,
Frail creature as he is, helpless as frail,
An inmate of this active universe.[1]

I

'the old raptures about mountains'

A few weeks after the death of their mother in 1873 Matthew
Arnold wrote to his sister Frances, who had returned to the family
home near Ambleside:

And so you are again at Fox How. That is well, if you are able to bear it. It
will be a long time before you feel of your grief, as you look out on the hills
and the fern and the trees and the waters,

It seems an idle thing, which could not live
Where meditation was—

and yet that is undoubtedly the right thing to feel, and that the thought of
dearest mamma should be simply a happy memory and not a gnawing
regret.[2]

Like many another Victorian who looked to Wordsworth's
poetry for succour at a time of grief, Arnold summons a passage
which registers fully the ineluctability of loss while offering a
consolatory vision that transcends it. Strength might be found in a
declaration of fortitude, such as 'Not without hope we suffer and
we mourn', from *Elegiac Stanzas . . . Peele Castle*, but Arnold
reaches elsewhere, to the more familiar Wordsworth, the poet of
lonely tarns and misty peaks. Imagining how his sister will feel as
she gazes desolately over Loughrigg or Wansfell, Arnold directs her
to lines that might help her eventually to look differently upon the

'hills and the fern and the trees'. In Book I of *The Excursion*, when the Wanderer has concluded his tale of Margaret's decline and death, he admonishes the Poet-listener not to 'read | The forms of things with an unworthy eye', but to see the deeper truth in them:

> I well remember that those very plumes,
> Those weeds, and the high spear-grass on that wall,
> By mist and silent rain-drops silvered o'er,
> As once I passed, did to my heart convey
> So still an image of tranquillity,
> So calm and still, and looked so beautiful
> Amid the uneasy thoughts which filled my mind,
> That what we feel of sorrow and despair
> From ruin and from change, and all the grief
> The passing shows of Being leave behind,
> Appeared an idle dream, that could not live
> Where meditation was.[3]

The Wanderer's words are striking, but they are not transparent and other passages of Wordsworth's quasi-philosophical verse would have to be summoned to answer the question, 'What do they mean?' They might be glossed, for example, by reference to *Tintern Abbey*. By applying the words of poetry to his sister's real-life situation, however, Arnold moves the Wanderer's words of wisdom out of the domain where self-referential explication suffices, and implicitly raises another question, 'Are they *true*?'[4] Piling up further quotations from Wordsworth's *œuvre* cannot furnish an answer.

Whether what Wordsworth had to say about Man and Nature is true or not is a question few modern critics would feel happy with, and little philosophical rigour is required to deconstruct it, but, in various formulations, it was a question Victorian readers asked themselves. In his review of Arnold's selection of Wordsworth, for example, John Addington Symonds sets out his critical premises with the caution of a man who knows he is walking through a theoretical minefield, but his starting-point is clear: 'Though style is an indispensable condition of success in poetry, it is by matter, and not form, that a poet has to take his final rank.'[5] If the question was routinely asked of literature in general, however, it was posed with more than usual force to Wordsworth simply because so much of Wordsworth insistently makes it unavoidable. Unlike any other of the widely read Romantics—Blake being excluded as not widely read in the Victorian period—Wordsworth continuously offers formulations which observe what Arnold referred to as the 'conditions immutably fixed by the laws of poetic beauty and poetic truth', but which do not disguise their pretension as utterances of truth in the common meaning of the word. In Book IX of *The Excursion*, for example, the 'venerable Sage' delivers his culminating discourse, which opens with the declaration that 'An *active* Principle . . . subsists | In all things . . .'. One of the few passages of *The Prelude* Wordsworth printed in his lifetime hymns the activity of the 'Wisdom and Spirit of the Universe' in purifying and elevating his youthful soul.[6] In *Tintern Abbey* the poet, inspired by his communion with the 'sense sublime | Of something far more deeply interfused', declares himself content to rest on 'nature and the language of the sense' for the very basis of his 'moral being'. Hundreds of lines throughout *The Prelude* could be assembled and placed alongside the 'Prospectus' to *The Recluse* to establish the fundamentals of Wordsworth's beliefs about the relationship of Nature and Man. None of these utterances is hedged about with a disclaimer that it is to be read only as a poetic fiction.

Faced with poetry of such palpable design readers adopted (and still adopt) various strategies. One was to dwell on those aspects of the philosophical poetry which serve to celebrate humble life, the primary affections of our nature, and man's unconquerable mind— essentially the strategy of the novelists already discussed. Another was to confront the philosophical pretension head on—and to dismiss or contain it. Jeffrey characterized *The Excursion* 'as a tissue of moral and devotional ravings', expressed in the 'mystical verbiage of the methodist pulpit'. So, thought Macaulay, was *The Prelude*: 'The story is the old story. There are the old raptures about mountains and cataracts; the old flimsy philosophy about the effect of scenery on the mind; the old crazy metaphysics . . .'. In the Introduction to Macmillan's new edition of Wordsworth in 1888 John Morley was more delicate, but his message was the same. Wordsworth's notions about impulses from a vernal wood must be seen as half-playful fancies, charmingly poetic and no more. And when Wordsworth does point to 'a set of philosophic ideas, more or less complete', it has to be said that they are nonsense:

It is a beggarly conception, no doubt, to judge as if poetry should always be capable of a prose rendering; but it is at least fatal to the philosophic pretension of a line or a stanza if, when it is fairly reduced to prose, the prose discloses that it is nonsense, and there is at least one stanza of the great *Ode* that this doom would assuredly await.

And, of course, when he insisted that it is 'best to be entirely sceptical as to the existence of system and ordered philosophy in Wordsworth', the rationalist, agnostic former editor of the *Fortnightly Review* was doing no more than follow Arnold, who—his letter to his sister notwithstanding—was prepared by 1879 to declare that 'we cannot do [Wordsworth] justice until we dismiss his formal philosophy'.[7]

There were other strategies. The poetry could be historicized, acknowledged as having value as a truthful record of a particular moment in intellectual and cultural history. J. A. Froude, for example, warmly acknowledged his pleasure in Wordsworth, but what he seems to have valued most are the poems 'which describe the character of a period', *The Excursion* in particular, 'a precious picture of English country life and thought at the period of the French Revolution'.[8] In *The Lucid Veil* W. David Shaw has indicated the various, more sophisticated ways in which Wordsworth was placed by thinkers who recognized his historical position in the development of nineteenth-century philosophy.[9]

As this book's opening chapters have already indicated, however, the commonest way of dealing with the direct pretensions of Wordsworth's philosophic utterances was to interpret them in the light of revealed religion, to gather him within the Christian fold of whatever denomination. That as late as 1970 Professor Basil Willey, a devout Christian and in his own words 'devout Wordsworthian', could avow simply that Wordsworth had given him his continuing 'belief in the holiness of Nature', is a testimony to the longevity of this approach and a reminder that the reverential reading of Wordsworth did not die out with the First World War or the publication of Aldous Huxley's 'Wordsworth in the Tropics'.[10]

For most readers accommodating the Wordsworthian creed meant absorbing it somehow into the matrix of beliefs and conceptions which regulated the course of their lives. At the very least it was possible to extract propositions about Nature as scenery which could be embraced whole-heartedly—that mountains and waterfalls could relieve for a while the cares of a world of getting and spending, that fresh air and exercise were beneficial, that beautiful and wild places ought to be preserved for future generations, and, at a stretch, even that 'if you appreciated nature it made you better able to do your duty'.[11] Of those who gave time and money to help preserve the Lake District, few could have explicated the theology of *Tintern Abbey*, but all those who believed it did you good to walk in mountains and to contemplate beautiful landscape in quiet, were heirs of the poet who declared that 'Nature never did betray | The heart that loved her'.

On this axis of accommodation no one was duty bound to take a firm stance, except perhaps clergymen and philosophers. Poets certainly were not. Explicit statements, however, of belief (faith, profession—a less dogmatic term is required) are so integral to Wordsworth's finest poems, to those aspects of his art most likely to nourish the art of others, that even poets were nudged into taking a position on what more there was to salute in Wordsworth once his imaginative and verbal power had been acknowledged.

While being highly responsive to Wordsworth's force as a writer, Swinburne was unequivocally hostile to the reverence still accorded to Wordsworthianism. As poet, Wordsworth's 'concentration, his majesty, his pathos have no parallel', but as seer Wordsworth peddled illusion, not a saving illusion but one which robbed Man of the strength that comes from knowing and facing the truth: 'Man's welfare' is 'not the aim of nature'.[12] To Peter Bell a primrose by a river's brim is just a yellow primrose—and so it was to Swinburne, whose own sense of the primrose's meaning was fully sufficient to resist the Wordsworthian conversion that 'saves' Peter Bell the potter.

Hopkins was as unequivocal in the opposite direction. His reservations about Wordsworth's 'lovely gift of verse' were considerable, summed up in the remark to Canon Dixon that 'in his work there is *beaucoup à redire*', but he had no misgivings about the genuineness of Wordsworth's '*charisma*, as theologians say', or about the value of continuing to mediate it to the later time. Lord Selborne's presidential address to the final meeting of the Wordsworth Society may not have inspired Hopkins by its intellectual brilliance, but he referred to it and to Wordsworthians with respect. When Dixon, on the other hand, astonished him by belittling the *Ode: Intimations of Immortality*, Hopkins was provoked to one of the century's most eloquent essays in Wordsworth criticism. The *Ode* is a work of 'extreme value', because it meets art's highest demand that execution match the 'interest and matter of the subject', and in the *Ode* both are 'of the highest'. Musical interlacing of rhymes, happy succession of rhythms, diction charged and steeped in beauty and yearning, all serve a historically momentous utterance. Hopkins's *confessio fidei* deserves quotation at length:

> There have been in all history a few, a very few men, whom common repute, even where it did not trust them, has treated as having had something happen to them that does not happen to other men, as having *seen something*, whatever that really was. Plato is the most famous of these . . . human nature in these men saw something; wavers in opinion, looking back, whether there was anything in it or no; but is in a tremble ever since. Now what Wordsworthians mean is, what would seem to be the growing mind of the English speaking world and may perhaps come to be that of the world at large is that in Wordsworth when he wrote that ode human nature got another of those shocks, and the tremble from it is spreading. This opinion I do strongly share; I am, ever since I knew the ode, in that tremble.

In his earlier letter Hopkins had likened Wordsworth's charisma, 'his spiritual insight into nature', to that of Plato, and demanded who else had been granted it 'in equal measure'. Drawing the analogy with Plato for a second time, Hopkins could hardly have pitched his claim higher and his last words to Dixon were as unrestrained. This, addressed to an Anglican clergyman by a Catholic priest working in Dublin: 'For my part I shd. think that St. George and St. Thomas of Canterbury wore roses in heaven for England's sake on the day that ode, not without their intercession, was penned.'[13]

For both Swinburne and Hopkins, Wordsworth as philosopher-poet was indubitably a presence (as he simply was not, for example, to Dante Gabriel Rossetti), to be confronted in opposition or embraced. For the two poets who are the focus of this chapter Wordsworth was also a massive presence, but it was one they had to put by. Both Arnold and Tennyson, for differing reasons, felt the urgency of the matters addressed in Wordsworth's philosophic poetry, but for the establishment of their own poetic voices both had to be free of the colossus who felt able to apostrophize the 'Wisdom and Spirit of the Universe'. Tennyson managed it; Arnold never quite did.

II

Matthew Arnold

'*Those who cannot read Greek should read nothing but Milton and parts of Wordsworth: the state should see to it*'[14]

When he was a schoolboy Matthew Arnold built himself a fort on the slopes of Loughrigg Fell, the hill range that rises behind Fox How. Playing there one day he was surprised by the arrival of Wordsworth, who had sought him out in his 'Strong hold'.[15] It would be pleasing to know that the old man had entered into the spirit of a boyish adventure, stealthily creeping up on the young sentinel, but even if it were merely a chance encounter, this incident is an apt emblem of Arnold's lifelong relationship with the great poet. Wordsworth was always coming upon him in his stronghold.

Arnold is the one major Victorian writer of whom it can be said without metaphor that he was nurtured in the Wordsworthian presence. Over the turn of the year 1831/2 the Arnolds enjoyed 'five weeks of almost awful happiness' in a house just below Wordsworth's at Rydal and for Thomas Arnold 'intercourse with the Wordsworths was one of the brightest spots of all'.[16] One evening they heard at Rydal Mount 'Mr Wordsworth and Dora read to us much of his unpublished poetry'.[17] Smitten by the Lakes—'I could still rave about Rydal' Dr Arnold exclaimed in the letter just quoted—the family went north whenever possible and the presence of the poet there—disagreements about the Reform Bill notwithstanding—was a powerful lure. For a while they actually retraced his steps, for when they had to find a house in Grasmere, they settled not on any property but on Allan Bank, the house in which Wordsworth had lived from 1808 to 1811. Here in the house in which much of *The Excursion* had been composed and Coleridge had struggled with *The Friend*, every room had some association with Wordsworth, his wife and sister, with De Quincey who stayed there, and with Coleridge and Sara Hutchinson. That summer as before the two families saw a good deal of each other. On one occasion Dora Wordsworth presided over a picnic for the Arnold children on the island in Rydal lake, at which her father 'stretched on the grass' while her mother read out some of his unpublished poetry.[18] And it was Wordsworth who helped Dr and Mrs Arnold realize their dream of living where they already entertained 'a home-like feeling'—in the valley of the Rothay.[19] He acted as intermediary in the purchase of the estate of Fox How and advised on the building of the house. When Wordsworth later celebrated the view from Fox How in the sonnet, 'Wansfell, this Household has a favoured lot', it was with the complacence that had had a hand in establishing its occupants in such a favoured spot.

Only a short and beautiful walk separates Fox How from Rydal Mount across the valley of the Rothay, and the young Matthew Arnold made it frequently. The 'dear, dear Sister' of *Tintern Abbey* was by now a sad figure, and Hartley Coleridge, though great fun, was a pathetic reminder of *Frost at Midnight* and hopes unfulfilled, but the poet himself was still hale and he often crossed the valley to Fox How, to sit 'on Mrs Arnold's stool at the fire'. There the fledgeling poet would draw the old one out 'on Coleridge and Italian poetry'.[20] No doubt Wordsworth talked about much else too, about his own poetic career certainly. In the introduction to his Wordsworth selection, Arnold was to remark, 'I have myself heard him declare that, for he knew not how many years, his poetry had never brought him in enough to buy his shoe-strings.'

As a family friend, and especially as an intellectual sparring-partner of his father, Wordsworth the man was such a large presence in Arnold's youth that it would be quite understandable had he resisted it by ignoring Wordsworth the writer. Obviously this was not the case, and the evidence of Arnold's reading in what he termed 'the most important work done in verse, in our language, during the present nineteenth century', is too familiar from his essays to need reiteration.[21] Some observations, however, might be made about the nature of Arnold's reading. The first is that it prospected adventurously. In 1848, for example, Arnold capped his remarks to Clough about events in France and the nature of 'progress' with the comment, 'If you remember it is exactly Wordsworth's account of the matter in his letter in the "friend" . . .'.[22] Did Clough remember? Wordsworth's declaration that the 'progress of the species . . . may be more justly compared to that of a river . . .', comes in his 'Reply to "Mathetes" ', and that in 1848 remained buried in *The Friend*. It is not a Wordsworth text—then or now—that falls open to any but the most zealous reader.

The second observation is that, in today's academic jargon, Arnold 'kept up' with Wordsworth scholarship. In a letter to his mother about *Thyrsis* Arnold commented that 'the images are all from actual observation, on which point there is an excellent remark in Wordsworth's notes, collected by Miss Fenwick'.[23] What this passing remark indicates is that Arnold had been struck by Wordsworth's note to *An Evening Walk*. He might have found it in Christopher Wordsworth's 1851 *Memoirs of William Wordsworth* (I. 67–8), or in the 1857 edition of Wordsworth's poems, in which the Fenwick Notes were printed *in extenso* for the first time. The fact that Arnold used this edition, with others, in the preparation of his 1879 selection adds weight to this latter conjecture. By the time he was editing Wordsworth himself, Arnold could also read the Fenwick Notes in Grosart's 1876 compilation of Wordsworth's prose and his notebooks furnish evidence that, sapped as he was by ill health and the harassments of his time-consuming profession, Arnold did take the trouble to find out what was new in Grosart's pioneering volumes. In 1881 he read Myers's *Wordsworth*, the first serious critical biography for thirty years, and, perhaps prompted by it, reread the early books of *The Prelude*.[24] Arnold, in short, did not rest on the Wordsworth, or on the Wordsworth editions, he had absorbed when he was young, but continued to follow both the critical debate and the progress of scholarship.

The wording of Arnold's commendation, 'there is an excellent remark in Wordsworth's notes collected by Miss Fenwick', raises a further question about his knowledge of Wordsworth's writings. Had Arnold been allowed to study the Fenwick Notes in manuscript? The 1857 edition, in which they were first printed with the poems to which they referred, identified the notes only as 'dictated by the Author at the request of a dear friend of his, by whom they were written down' (vol. I, p. v). This disclosure was not even as forthcoming as Christopher Wordsworth's, who had identified the 'dear friend' in the *Memoirs* as the 'I.F.' of two of Wordsworth's sonnets (I. 21). But Isabella Fenwick was a loved figure in the Fox How–Rydal Mount circle and Arnold's comment to his mother is only an indication that both of them knew how the notes had come into being. Further evidence, however, suggests a little more. In his life of Arnold, Park Honan points to the close similarity between Arnold's diatribe to Clough about how 'deeply *unpoetical* the age & all one's surroundings are', and Wordsworth's 1843 Fenwick Note to *Love Lies Bleeding*, which laments that the English, now driven by 'Trade, commerce, and manufactures', are 'now the most unpoetical nation in Europe'.[25] The parallel is strong, but it cannot be confirmed on the grounds Honan proposes. Wordsworth's note was not printed in 1845, as he avers, but in 1851 in Christopher Wordsworth's *Memoirs of William Wordsworth*, some time after Arnold's apparent allusion to it in his letter to Clough, the dating of which seems secure. If Arnold was influenced by the language of Wordsworth's diagnosis of England as unpoetical, it can only have been because as a young man he was included amongst those 'nearest friends' of the poet who were—as the 1857 volumes reveal—permitted to 'peruse' Miss Fenwick's manuscript.[26] It is a small point, but revealing in its implications. In his formative years Arnold not only knew Wordsworth personally and knew his writings, but it may be that he was embraced into the small group who were allowed to be intimate with the poet's unpublished reflections on his life's work. In 1879 the one time Professor of Poetry at Oxford admitted, 'I am a Wordsworthian'. He had been practically ever since he was known as 'Crabby' and was surprised in his fort on Loughrigg.

III

On publication of his *Poems of Wordsworth* Arnold sent a copy with his 'compliments and regards' to Wordsworth's biographer, Christopher Wordsworth, Bishop of Lincoln. The Bishop was moved to verse himself and wrote in the book these lines, dated 8 October 1879:

> Down from Parnassus flow'd Castalia's Fount
> To Delphi; there in a cool grot to dwell,
> So, in the book, pure streams from Rydal Mount
> Find in Fox How beneath, a crystal well.[27]

As a flight of fancy this was appropriate in one sense—Arnold had a passion for clear water—but as an image of the relationship between the two poets of Rydal Mount and Fox How it was quite inadequate. In Christopher Wordsworth's eyes Arnold, eminent, perhaps pre-eminent Wordsworthian, was the crystal well into which the pure stream of Wordsworth's creative genius had flowed, to be drawn on for the refreshment of future generations. But it must be surmised that the Bishop had not troubled himself over-much with Arnold's poetry, for it records a much more uneasy relationship. Arnold was steeped in Wordsworth. In his critical writings he quoted from him, alluded to him, used him as a touchstone, and repeatedly affirmed his high estimate of Wordsworth's permanent stature. But before he had attained the security of judgement he displayed in *On Translating Homer: Last Words* (1862) or *Essays in Criticism* (1865), Arnold's relationship with Wordsworth had been one of not quite clearly defined struggle. Wordsworth's presence had been the creative stimulus for some of Arnold's finest poems, but what each one revealed in differing ways was that, even as Arnold positioned himself towards his acknowledgedly greater predecessor, the gulf between them opened up.

When Arnold acceded to Edward Quillinan's request in April 1850 that he mark Wordsworth's passing, he might tactfully have 'dirged W.W. *in the grand style*' with no very specific definition of what his achievement amounted to.[28] An elegy in the *Spectator* for 25 May did just that, gracefully weaving together quotation and allusion in celebration of Wordsworth's 'deep human sympathies'.[29] Arnold's *Memorial Verses* is more ambitious, and like all of his finest poetry, it attempts to characterize the ailing present by evocation of a different past. The poet stands 'by Wordsworth's tomb', but his concern—inevitably with Arnold—is the needs of the present.

From its opening words, 'Goethe in Weimar sleeps', the poem places Wordsworth historically.[30] Goethe, the 'Physician of the iron age' has 'done his pilgrimage', and Byron's 'Titanic strife' is long since stilled. Only Wordsworth remained of comparable stature, living on in 'a wintry clime', but now he too is gone, the 'last poetic voice is dumb'. What this historical placing suggests, however, is not just that Wordsworth ranks with the greatest, but that he belonged to a specific generation which he has outlived. Byron died in 1824 fighting for Greek independence. Goethe died in 1832, having looked on 'Europe's dying hour'. Wordsworth came of age at a time of European convulsion, but lingered into a different age, an 'iron time | Of doubts, disputes, distractions, fears'. His death is only now mourned, but Wordsworth has long been a figure from the past.

The note of historical lament becomes more insistent still in the second part of the poem. Wordsworth once released souls bound by the age's 'benumbing round'; he restored us, as in the *Ode: Intimations*, to sunlit fields where 'Our youth returned'; he shed

> On spirits that had long been dead,
> Spirits dried up and closely furled,
> The freshness of the early world.[31]

All the past tenses proclaim a power that worked, but is gone. Time may restore 'Goethe's sage mind and Byron's force', and others unnamed may strengthen us to bear, but where can be found again 'Wordsworth's healing power'?

Versions of the exclamation, 'ah! who will make us feel', reverberate throughout Arnold's poetry—in this he was Wordsworth's heir. Both poets were possessed by the conviction that their age was inimical to true feeling, that new forces ('unknown to former times', claims the Preface to *Lyrical Ballads*), were at work to coarsen or deaden feeling, but whereas Wordsworth gestured outwards, diagnosing causes and effects from a secure centre, in his poetry Arnold invariably included himself within the diagnosis. His possessive, as in 'Our souls . . .', always reveals his sense that in him personally, as much as in other men, the disease is far advanced. It is the disease of the age. The Scholar Gypsy is exhorted to flee 'our feverish contact', for strong is 'the infection of our mental strife, | Which, though it gives no bliss, yet spoils for rest'. In his notebook for June 1849/50 Arnold formulated it: 'The misery of the present age is not in the intensity of men's suffering—but in their incapacity to suffer, enjoy, feel at all, wholly & profoundly . . .'.[32] It is also, simply the disease of life. A late poem, *Growing Old*, asks, 'What is it to grow old' and gives the answer:

> It is to spend long days
> And not once feel that we were ever young;
> It is to add, immured
> In the hot prison of the present, month
> To month with weary pain.
>
> It is to suffer this,
> And feel but half, and feebly, what we feel.

The image from the *Ode: Intimations* of life as a prison-house, whose shades close around the growing boy and go on closing, haunts Arnold's poetry, but it never appears more dreadfully than here.

There are questions to be asked about *Memorial Verses*—Arnold might be pressed, for example, on the meaning of 'make us feel'—

but the poem does not allow them to materialize to the point of discomfort. It is sufficient for the remit of elegy that Wordsworth's particular virtue be established in loosely suggestive terms and then be compressed into one memorable phrase, 'healing power'. But however warmly the poem celebrates Wordsworth, the yearnings of its conclusion cast the celebration into shadow. The value of his healing power is magnified by the intensity of Arnold's conviction that the age needs it, but *Memorial Verses* blanks off any consolatory suggestion that it is easy of access.

Within two years Arnold returned to Grasmere's poet lying dead in the shadow of Fairfield in *The Youth of Nature*, whose reflections constitute a second, more wide-ranging elegy. It begins, so to speak, where *Michael* ends. Wordsworth's poem closes with all that remains as memorial to the shepherd's labours:

> the Oak is left
> That grew beside their Door; and the remains
> Of the unfinished Sheep-fold may be seen
> Beside the boisterous brook of Green-head Gill.

So, all around Wordsworth's last resting place, 'The spots which recall him survive', and Arnold lists them, tying together the real places—Fairfield, Rydal, Pillar, Ennerdale, Egremont, Grasmere—whose existence was 'lent a new life' in Wordsworth's writing. 'These survive', the poet exclaims, as he rests in his silent boat, raising the dripping oars as if in salute to the young oarsman of the *The Prelude*. These survive, but 'their poet is gone'.

As in *Memorial Verse* Arnold projects Wordsworth as one who 'grew old in an age he condemned', but whereas he was later to censure Wordsworth for voluntary withdrawal 'from the modern spirit',[33] here he likens him to the 'Theban seer' who 'died in his enemies' day'. Thebes was not to see such a prophet again and nor will we. Wordsworth was 'a priest to us all | Of the wonder and bloom of the world', but he is dead 'and the fruit-bearing day | Of his race is past on earth'.

Thus far *The Youth of Nature* is little more than a reprise of *Memorial Verses*. From the sixth strophe, however, the poem changes, as a series of exclamations and apostrophes raises questions prompted by Arnold's love of a particular place and of the poetry that claimed it as its own domain. Do the mountains 'fill us with joy, | Or the poet who sings you so well?' Can all share

Nature's message or is it 'Too deep for most to discern?' Nature's answer makes up the rest of the poem. 'Loveliness, magic, and grace' exist. Not even the greatest poet has known or sung them to the full. Men have believed they have captured Nature's secret, but 'They are dust, they are changed, they are gone! | I remain'.

That exegesis of *The Youth of Nature* has dwindled into paraphrase is itself a comment on the structure and texture of the poem. Its latter part is couched in language dense with paraphrasable content but nothing more. And what these declamatory strophes generate is a sense of the separation of Man, who questions, and Nature, which responds. It is the most striking thing about the poem. In *The Prelude* (1850, I. 586–8), Wordsworth declares that 'The earth | And common face of Nature spake to me | Rememberable things', but throughout that poem what Nature speaks is inseparable from how she speaks it. The child holds 'unconscious intercourse | With the eternal beauty, drinking in | A pure organic pleasure from the silver wreaths | Of curling mist'; the wind blows through his ears and far into his heart carries the voice of mountain torrents. The 'Wisdom and Spirit of the Universe' intertwines the human soul with enduring things. Arnold's Nature, utterly unlike Wordsworth's, exhorts. There is not a line or an image in *The Youth of Nature* that enacts, or even speaks of fusion or combination between the mind and the natural world. The poet questions across a gulf and answers return. But the gulf remains and it is in the existence of the gulf that Arnold finds the only kind of consolation possible. Nature is ultimately unknowable, but the mystery survives. Fairfield, on a moon-drenched night, still looks down on Grasmere and Rydal.

A similar consolation had been entertained in the earlier poem *Resignation*—written 1843–8—which does not mention Wordsworth, but which quite clearly confronts him and in one of his most assured utterances.[34] As U. C. Knoepflmacher has pointed out, 'the core of the poem is Wordsworthian: the setting is the Lake County of the Romantics; the situation, a return to the earlier associations of the scene by a matured poet and his sister; the import, a creed handed down by the poet to his listener'.[35]

Arnold, like Wordsworth, drew creatively on revisitings. The latter went back, for example, in middle-age to the Swiss landscape he had walked in youth and was not satisfied until he had located the very path he and his companion had taken as they began their crossing of the Simplon Pass. As an old man he returned to the Quantocks, the prompt, as the Fenwick Notes begun shortly afterwards testify, for memories of Coleridge and the heady days of *Lyrical Ballads* to flood back. Wordsworth visited the Yarrow, and later revisited both the river and his poem on first seeing it.[36] Arnold was subject to the same compulsion. *The Terrace at Berne*, for example, strikingly recalls *Tintern Abbey* in its opening particularity of time and place: 'Ten years! and to my waking eye | Once more . . .'. *Obermann Once More* revisits not so much Senancour as *Stanzas in Memory of the Author of 'Obermann'*: 'Glion?—Ah, twenty years . . .'. After Clough's death Arnold returned to *The Scholar Gypsy* for the creation of *Thyrsis*, but also, literally, to 'the Cumner hills where we have so often rambled'.[37] For both poets revisitings were an opportunity consciously to gauge feelings against earlier feelings, to assess continuities and dislocations, to register the workings of what Hardy was to call in another fine revisiting poem, *At Castle Boterel*, 'Time's mindless rote'.

The revisiting that is the scene of *Resignation* was certain to be charged with emotion, for it focused not only memories of his own youth, but thoughts about his father and most loved sister. Ten years earlier Dr Arnold, 'our leader', had led 'his motley bands' on an arduous walk over Wythburn Fells, which ended at nightfall, to the 'speechless glee' of his children, at the shore of 'the wide-glimmering sea'. Now Arnold and Fausta—Jane Arnold—tread the 'self-same road', but they are 'ghosts of that boisterous company'. Death has snatched their father in his prime; disappointment has marred Fausta's youth. The Fells have not changed. 'Once more', 'again' 'the self-same', 'familiar'—in such words the poet insists that all is the same. Even the stones on the path 'Lie strewn, it seems, where then they lay'. But can it be true, as Fausta says, that the human beings 'Are scarce more changed, in truth, than they'?

In *Tintern Abbey* a similar situation and the pressure of the same implied question propel a series of affirmations which intensify in energy and profundity as the poet surveys past and present and projects into the future. Immediate joy at beholding once more the scene which has acted in memory as an agent of continuity over five years, recalls earlier joys, of childhood and boyhood and is the basis for the conviction that it is to 'These forms of beauty' that the poet owes his experience of 'that blessed mood' in which 'We see into the life of things'. Time has not changed Nature, it has tempered the observer, but the loss of youthful sight is amply recompensed by access of mature joy, 'a sense sublime | Of something far more deeply interfused . . .'. Dorothy Wordsworth is the poet's second self, her 'wild ecstasies' not yet 'matured | Into a sober pleasure', but the certainty that they will be is embraced, in the knowledge that it is Nature's privilege 'Through all the years of this our life, to lead | From joy to joy'.

At the climax of *Tintern Abbey* Wordsworth affirms the unity of sun, air, ocean, animate and inanimate, and the mind of man, in lines that enact in their own unexcerptable unity the wholeness they declare. Lines 144–98 of *Resignation* also evoke the whole, as the poet gazes on Man and Nature. What moves him to tears, however, is the thought of the majestic impersonality of it all. The 'dumb wish' of the 'general life' is fulfilled 'If birth proceeds, if things subsist; | The life of plants, and stones, and rain'. The words 'things' and 'life' recall 'see into the life of things', but Arnold's 'things subsist' is, unmetaphorically, a universe away from Wordsworth's 'active principle'. Wordsworth—'laid asleep | In body and become a living soul'—penetrates; by contrast in *Resignation* the poet's adequacy to the scene as life unrolls is measured by the degree of his detachment. Whereas Dorothy Wordsworth is already one with her brother as a 'worshipper of Nature', Fausta, 'Time's chafing prisoner' is exhorted to 'set free' her soul by recognizing the truth her brother expounds.

The poet must cultivate 'His sad lucidity of soul'. Such language warns Fausta, and the reader, not to look for joy, and there is none in this poem. But from his sense of separation from Nature Arnold does wrest a certain consolation, mutedly pronounced rather than proclaimed as conclusion to the most passionate lines of the poem:

> The world in which we live and move
> Outlasts aversion, outlasts love,
> Outlasts each effort, interest, hope,
> Remorse, grief, joy; and were the scope
> Of these affections wider made,
> Man still would see, and see dismayed,
> Beyond his passion's widest range,
> Far regions of eternal change.
>
> . . . .
>
> This world in which we draw our breath,
> In some sense, Fausta, outlasts death.

This crescendo of negatives, in which the worst always comes first—aversion/love, effort/hope, remorse/joy—and which ends with death, prefigures the even more desolate climax to *Dover Beach*. A lover's pledge of undying love is usually uttered in the extremity of joy that transfigures the world, but here it breaks from the anguish of knowing that

> the world, which seems
> To lie before us like a land of dreams,
> So various, so beautiful, so new,
> Hath really neither joy, nor love, nor light,
> Nor certitude, nor peace, nor help for pain.

Both passages point to the essential differences between Arnold and Wordsworth as poets.

The fundamental difference is that Arnold could not draw on the sense of connectedness which charges all of Wordsworth's finest poetry. Rapturous lines in *The Excursion*, I. 197–218, depict the Wanderer reading 'Unutterable love' in the 'silent faces' of the clouds, as 'sensation, soul, and form | All melted into him'. The conclusion of the passage expounds the relationship between this physical rapture and faith. In the mountains,

> All things, responsive to the writing, there
> Breathed immortality, revolving life,
> And greatness still revolving; infinite:
> There littleness was not; the least of things
> Seemed infinite; and there his spirit shaped
> Her prospects, nor did he believe,—he *saw*.

Commenting on affirmations such as this, Stephen Prickett has sensibly observed that they left Victorian readers generous room for interpretation. The relationship between Naturalism and Platonism in Wordsworth was always, he suggests, one of 'tantalising ambiguity'.[38] Arnold's controversial prose demonstrates that he was not impervious to the attractions of tantalizing ambiguity, but ambiguity had to straddle real possibilities. For Arnold, Wordsworth's confident absorption of believing in seeing was, as David Riede observes, 'simply impossible'. Arnold 'could not accept the logo-centric romantic epistemology that fused perception and object in language'.[39] Nature could not speak 'rememberable things', for she could not speak. The only voice to be heard in the 'strange-scrawled rocks, the lonely sky' in *Resignation* is that which the poet 'might lend' them.

An aspect of this primary difference between the two poets is their representation of being alone. 'I was taught to feel, perhaps too much, | The self-sufficing power of Solitude' (*Prelude*, 1850, II. 76–7). The 'perhaps' counts for little. There are figures in Wordsworth's poetry corroded by solitude—the Solitary of *The Excursion*, for example, or the disappointed man of the *Yew-Tree Lines*—but usually solitude is either the ground of an assured sense of identity, or the prerequisite for experience that nurtures spiritual growth, or both. In all moments of heightened experience in *The Prelude* the poet is alone, or, as in the crossing of the Simplon Pass and the climbing of Snowdon, is rapt away from companions into alone-ness. In every case solitude grants access to 'the sentiment of Being spread | O'er all that moves and all that seemeth still' (*Prelude*, 1850, II. 401–2).

For Arnold solitude heightens awareness of the human condition—isolation—his sense of which was profound and ever-present. In *Isolation: To Marguerite* and *To Marguerite—Continued* the lover's disappointment not surprisingly brings the pain of loneliness, but both poems go beyond the specific occasion of a love poem to image human life as a general yearning for connectedness that is denied. Other lovers may be happier,

> for they, at least,
> Have *dreamed* two human hearts might blend
> In one, and were through faith released
> From isolation without end
> Prolonged.

But the happiness of this dream, the poet concludes, only disguises 'their loneliness'. In *Self-Dependence* the poet braces himself to a better life by reading a lesson in the stars, the inhuman, distant, unknowable other. Senancour haunts Arnold because he embraced isolation, but even as the poet reluctantly turns back to life in *Stanzas in Memory of the Author of 'Obermann'*, he images it in *Human Life* as being a fate-driven voyage in which all men leave behind,

> As, chartered by some unknown Powers,
> We stem across the sea of life by night,
> The joys which were not for our use designed;

The friends to whom we had no natural right,
The homes that were not destined to be ours.

The inaccessibility to Arnold of Wordsworth's vital connectedness enhanced his sense of isolation and, in addition, denied him Wordsworth's recuperative strategy before the fact of loss. *Tintern Abbey* presents a model for understanding the progress of a life, which recognizes continuity and growth not in despite of loss but with loss as a beneficial agent. The 'aching joys' and 'dizzy raptures' of youth pass, but for such loss, the poet asserts, he has been granted the 'abundant recompence' of a fully matured vision of Nature. This is only the most memorable expression of a kind of affirmation, loss into gain, found throughout his poetry. It structures the presentation of small things, such as his lack of application at Cambridge, which is glossed as allowing the development of powers that academic study would have stultified, and of great, such as the ascents of the Simplon Pass and of Snowdon, where on both occasions the poet does not see what he went for, but experiences something much richer, a revelation of the profundity of the human mind and its relation to the divine. Wordsworth's finest poetry treats of suffering and death, and it acknowledges loss and change as ineluctable facts of human life, but countering all these is the pressure towards an inclusive vision that subsumes loss in joy. Joy is the principle of the universe.

A quite different vision of life's shaping was offered in an early poem of Arnold's that challenged Wordsworth directly—and again Wordsworth at his strongest—by inviting comparison with the *Ode: Intimations of Immortality from Recollections of Early Childhood*. In *To a Gipsy Child by the Sea-shore* the poet is transfixed by the steady gaze of a child, whose 'soul-searching vision' prompts him to reflect on its state and future. The child says nothing and does nothing—'drugging pain by patience'—it just exists. Arnold's construction of meaning around the figure counters Wordsworth in detail. The child of the *Ode* luxuriates 'among his new-born blisses', 'Fretted by sallies of his Mother's kisses'; the gipsy child knows not 'superfluity of joy' and is 'half averse | From thine own mother's breast, that knows not thee'. Far from 'trailing clouds of glory', the gipsy child's brow is massed round with 'clouds of doom'. In the *Ode* the infant is apostrophized as 'Mighty Prophet' because it is still bathed in the glory of its heavenly origins;

the gipsy child is wise too: 'Thou hast foreknown the vanity of hope, | Foreseen thy harvest, yet proceed'st to live'.

In *Tristam and Iseult* life is imaged as a 'gradual furnace',

> In whose hot air our spirits are upcurled
> Until they crumble, or else grow like steel—
> Which kills in us the bloom, the youth, the spring—
> Which leaves the fierce necessity to feel,
> But takes away the power . . .

So the world will treat the gipsy child, who may none the less succeed in life, gleaning 'what strenuous gleaners may, | In the thronged fields where winning comes by strife'. But not for this child Wordsworth's glimpses of past glory that irradiate adult life. Its moment of insight will be to realize that its 'success' is its 'chain', and at that moment the adult will become the child, 'And wear this majesty of grief again'.

Few of Arnold's poems are as bleak as this, but many entertain the same idea of life as a steady continuum, in which there is no consolation for pain other than recognizing it as a fact of the human condition. Even the poem titled *Consolation* offers only the minimal, intellectual consolation that distress here is matched by happiness there. The bareness of its diction and the tightly constrained stanza form indicate the paucity of the consolation:

> Time, so complained of,
> Who to no one man
> Shows partiality,
> Brings round to all men
> Some undimmed hours.

At the end of the *Ode* Wordsworth declares that though the radiance that was once so bright is gone for ever, a more habitual delight has taken its place, and that, thanks to it, 'To me the meanest flower that blows can give | Thoughts that do often lie too deep for tears'. The statement is grounded on naturalist and supernaturalist underpinnings closed off to Arnold. The 'After-thought' to Wordsworth's *River Duddon* sonnet sequence finds a chaste joy in the knowledge that even though we perish, 'as tow'rd the silent tomb we go, | Thro' love, thro' hope, and faith's transcendent dower, | We feel that we are greater than we know'. The speaker of *The Buried Life* feels that we are greater than we know, but the feeling perplexes and disquiets with yearnings towards the better, the nobler, the clearer, that are never realized.

More than twenty-five years after writing *The Buried Life* Macmillan's desire to publish a Wordsworth selection finally gave Arnold the opportunity, and the prompt, to deliver a considered judgement on the poet he had repeatedly touched on in his critical and polemical writings. When the necessary reservations about the scope of Wordsworth's genius have been made; when the inflated claims for his philosophy advanced by Wordsworthian devotees have been punctured; even when much of the poetry has been assayed as dross, Wordsworth must be ranked as the greatest English poet after Shakespeare and Milton. Why? Arnold's answer is commanding:

> Wordsworth's poetry is great because of the extraordinary power with which Wordsworth feels the joy offered to us in nature, the joy offered to us in the simple primary affections and duties . . . The source of joy from which he thus draws is the truest and most unfailing source of joy accessible to man. It is also accessible universally . . . Here is an immense advantage for a poet. Wordsworth tells of what all seek, and tells of it at its truest and best source, and yet a source where all may go and draw for it.[40]

This would have been a generous tribute coming from any one of Arnold's contemporaries. Coming from him it is also very poignant. 'Here is an immense advantage for a poet'. Arnold's own poetry had not had it. For all his striving after classical repose, the success of Arnold's poetry, like Wordsworth's, lies in its power to unlock feeling. What it articulates most characteristically, however, is not the joy 'all men seek', but what all men feel, pain and longing for serenity that is something more than just freedom from agitation.

IV

Alfred Tennyson

'*Come, brother bard*'

Both Laureates chosen by Victoria were a little vain. Wordsworth was proud of his height, Tennyson of his legs, but neither appeared before the Queen in dress that showed them to advantage. In 1845 Wordsworth kneeled before her in court dress borrowed from Samuel Rogers, as anxious about its seams as about his old knees.[41] Six years later, Tennyson—taller and heavier than Rogers and

Wordsworth—was presented at the Queen's levee in the same costume. It was with relief that he reported to his wife, 'the inexpressibles were not hopelessly tight'.[42]

The symbolism of the presentations is almost too apt. Tennyson succeeded as Laureate a poet whom he came to regard as one of 'the three immortals' of the English tradition.[43] Wordsworth would undoubtedly have approved the choice of 'decidedly the first of our living Poets' as his successor, and many factors other than mutual esteem ought to have brought the two men close.[44] They both had a warm relationship with the same publisher, Edward Moxon, and their circle of acquaintance overlapped considerably. But Tennyson's relationship with Wordsworth was never quite comfortable.

Had the two poets met when they ought to have done, location and biography would have made it one of the most fitting encounters of Victorian literary history. Late in 1830 Wordsworth paid a long visit to Cambridge, staying with his brother in the Master's lodgings at Trinity, and was entertained one evening by the undergraduate James Spedding. Wordsworth had been close to his father at Hawkshead School, and now, forty years later, Tennyson was as intimate with the son and his presence in Spedding's rooms would have dovetailed the line of poetic succession. At the end of his Cambridge career Wordsworth had published his first substantial poems; the Chancellor's prize-winning undergraduate Tennyson had just published his, *Poems, Chiefly Lyrical*. But Tennyson was not amongst the young men who lionized 'the Great Poet', as Spedding called him, he having left for Somersby the previous day. Wordsworth clearly heard about him, however, for he reported with an air of collegiate pride, 'We have a respectable show of blossom in poetry. Two brothers of the name of Tennyson in particular are not a little promising.'[45]

Five years later, because of Spedding, Tennyson ventured on Wordsworth's home ground. After a stay at Mirehouse, the Spedding family home on Bassenthwaite, Tennyson, Edward FitzGerald, and Spedding moved to the Salutation Inn at Ambleside, less than a mile along the road from Rydal Mount. FitzGerald was no Worthsworthian, but he was devoted to Tennyson and here he bought him a copy of the newly published *Yarrow Revisited*, to add to the 1827 five-volume *Poetical Works of William Wordsworth* Tennyson had possessed since Cambridge days. The title poem remained a favourite to the end of his life.[46] Rowing, fishing, drinking gin with Hartley Coleridge took up their time, but eventually Tennyson and Spedding called on Wordsworth at Rydal Mount.

It was clearly a non-event. Not quite such a non-event as Spedding, FitzGerald, and latterly Hallam Tennyson made out, all of whom declared that 'sulky' Tennyson would not pay a call, even though the Rydal Mount Visitors Book records that he and Spedding did. Robert Martin conjectures that the two waited until FitzGerald had left for London before walking to Rydal Mount and that they kept the visit from him 'for fear of hurting his feelings'.[47] But whereas practically all other visitors of note left some account in letters, diaries, or published works, of their pilgrimage to the Wordsworth shrine, no record of Tennyson's has come to light.

In 1845, three years after Wordsworth had closed his career with a final new volume and Tennyson had established his with his first uncontestably great collection, the two poets at last met properly in London. The intermediary was the poet-struck Aubrey de Vere.

Invited by Hallam Tennyson to reminisce for the *Memoir* many years later, De Vere was not a wholly reliable witness. It does not matter that he confused dates, recalling the meeting as in 1842 not 1845, but it does matter that he shaped his memories just a little to please the families of both the poets he reverenced. One would like to be certain, for example, that in the spring of 1845 De Vere really did read out to Wordsworth Tennyson's 'You ask me, why, though ill at ease' and 'Of old sat Freedom on the heights' and that the sceptical poet listed 'with a gradually deepening attention', until he said, 'I must acknowledge that these two poems are very solid and noble in thought. Their diction also seems singularly stately.'[48]

According to this narrative, Wordsworth in extreme old age was still generous enough to recognize poetic genius in the young. What De Vere also wanted to recall, and so did recall, was that Tennyson was no less generous in his attitude to Wordsworth before he had even met him. 'He was always glad to show his reverence to the "Old Poet",' De Vere declared, in the same *Memoir* reminiscence. ' "Wordsworth," he said to me one day, "is staying at Hampstead . . . I must go and see him." ' De Vere's diary for 4 May 1845, however, tells a different and more credible story: 'Brought Alfred Tennyson, murmuring sore, to Hampstead, to see Mr. Wordsworth,' and even De Vere's later memory does not conceal the truth that this first encounter was spiky.[49] Tennyson, he recalls, tried to 'stimulate some latent ardours' in Wordsworth by telling him about a tropical island where the trees came into leaf 'the colour of blood', but the old poet was unstirred.[50] But it may be that it was on this occasion that Tennyson mentioned his idea that balloons could 'perhaps be fixed at the bottom of high mountains so as to take people to the top to see the views', and if so Wordsworth's coldness becomes more intelligible.[51] No conversational gambit was less likely to fire the poet who had recently attracted much criticism by his *Kendal and Windermere Railway* argument against the kind of day-tripper who wanted 'to see the views' in the Lake District without exertion.

At a later dinner party on 6 May, however, each man made the effort needed to please the other. It seems unlikely that on this or any other occasion Wordsworth said, 'Mr Tennyson, I have been endeavouring all my life to write a pastoral like your "Dora" and have not succeeded,' as one of Hallam Tennyson's correspondents avers. The old Wordsworth was capable of magnanimity, but not of foolish magnanimity. As Christopher Ricks has observed, the *Memoir*'s report is 'without plausibility'.[52] But what each poet did say to the other is recorded in Tennyson's own contemporaneous account to Aubrey de Vere and can be trusted. As they went into dinner at Moxon's house, Wordsworth took Tennyson's arm, saying, 'Come, brother bard, to dinner', and afterwards Tennyson, 'had at last, in the dark, said something about the pleasure he had had from Mr. Wordsworth's writings'.[53] They were sufficient gestures. De Vere noted that 'Tennyson was evidently much pleased with the old man'. Wordsworth was equally pleased with the young one: 'I saw Tennyson when I was in London, several times. He is decidedly the first of our living Poets ... he expressed in the strongest terms his gratitude to my writings. To this I was far from indifferent.' Even as he handed on his own laurels, however, Wordsworth could not refrain from observing how little sympathy he thought Tennyson had with 'what I should myself most value in my attempts, viz the spirituality with which I have endeavoured to invest the material Universe, and the moral relation under which I have wished to exhibit its most ordinary appearances'.[54] Did Tennyson mention, one wonders, what Wordsworth had driven him to a few years earlier? In 1841, his 'imagination inflamed' by a note to *The White Doe of Rylstone*, Tennyson had paced alongside the river Wharfe at Bolton Abbey and had remarked with self-mocking astonishment how potent must be the combination of Wordsworth and Nature that 'could get nine miles out of legs (*at present*) more familiar with armchair and settle than rock and greensward'.[55] It is to be hoped so, for Wordsworth had a soft spot for *The White Doe*. What is certain is that Wordsworth would have taken pleasure in hearing in 1846, a year after the meeting in London, that lines of his were inflaming Tennyson's imagination in anticipation of experience in the Alps. Over half a century before Wordsworth had crossed the Simplon Pass and been awe-stricken by Nature's tumultuous workings as he descended with the stream. It was not until 1845, however, that he released the marvellous lines on the 'gloomy Pass' that had lain in manuscript for forty years, and when he did Moxon was quick to draw them to the attention of his travelling companion just before they set off for Switzerland. 'We shall often think of you', he wrote to Wordsworth, 'especially when we come to the Simplon Pass, your fine lines of which have made a great impression on Tennyson.'[56] The same lines were to rise up again in Tennyson many years later when he and Hallam were in Switzerland. On 5 September 1873 Hallam noted in his journal that his father was 'full of the description in Wordsworth's *Prelude*'. A few days before a particularly striking configuration of thunderous noise, blue sky, and sunlight piercing a 'lacework of leaves' had moved the poet to declaim 'in a voice which sounded very awful . . . Wordsworth's sonnet *Two Voices are there, etc.*'.[57]

Alluding gracefully to Wordsworth's *A Poet's Epitaph*, Tennyson remarked to Frederick Locker-Lampson in 1869: 'Byron's merits are on the surface. You must love Wordsworth ere he will seem worthy of your love.'[58] By the time Tennyson was declaiming Wordsworth in the Alps the process of loving in order to love was complete and Tennyson's attitude to his great predecessor had settled into one of high and frequently expressed regard. His 'hearty admiration', according to his son, was founded on reverence for the 'purity and nobility of his teaching'. The line from *Tintern Abbey*, 'Whose dwelling is the light of setting suns', he thought 'almost the grandest in the English language, giving the sense of the abiding in the transient'. Wordsworth's blank verse at its best was 'the finest since Milton', and his sonnets ranked him as one of 'the three immortals' with Shakespeare and Milton.[59]

That these tributes follow familiar contours is not important. Hallam Tennyson was reporting what he and others had heard Tennyson say at one time or another, not quoting from a full-dress critical appraisal, and it was not to be expected that Tennyson would strike on original formulations for his overall appraisal of Wordsworth's stature. Cutting sharply athwart these tributes, however, are Tennyson's equally often expressed reservations about Wordsworth's poetic craft. Palgrave, who as editor of *The Golden Treasury* had relied on Tennyson's discernment and knew better than anyone his estimate of Wordsworth, recalled that though Tennyson revered Wordsworth as a poet of 'supreme dignity', he thought he too often attempted subjects 'which more or less defied successful treatment'. In such attempts Wordsworth struck him as '*thick-ankled*'.[60]

'His ancles they are swoln and thick'. Wordsworth mentions the old man's ankles in *Simon Lee* again:

> Few months of life has he in store,
> As he to you will tell,
> For still, the more he works, the more
> His poor old ancles swell

and one can gauge Tennyson's response to such ponderous metrical jocosity by his choice of '*thick-ankled*' to skewer an aspect of Wordsworth that always discomfits. What is revealing about the comment, though, is Tennyson's distinction—if it is his and not Palgrave's—between 'subject' and 'treatment', since it points up an important difference between the two poets. In his most innovative period Wordsworth did not admit that any subject could defy successful treatment, 'The objects of the Poet's thoughts are every where,' he declared in the Preface to *Lyrical Ballads*, and the spade of a friend is as good a subject as any. When Sara Hutchinson criticized the first version of *Resolution and Independence* Wordsworth's instinctive and characteristic response was not to defend the quality of his treatment of the leech-gatherer, but to point to the inherent quality of the figure himself—to the subject as subject. The old man 'presented in the most naked simplicity possible' is already poetic in the richest sense of the word.[61]

A quite different attitude to subject and treatment, sensibly untheorized and not broadcast in manifesto, underpinned Tennyson's extraordinarily varied output. Notionally he subscribed as whole-heartedly as Wordsworth to the belief that the objects of the Poet's thoughts are everywhere, but in practice he dealt only with subjects that could be worked to the full with his particular powers. Many criticisms might be levelled at Tennyson, but no one ever called him thick-ankled. Wordsworth's obdurate attempts at subjects that were not susceptible to treatment—or not susceptible to his characteristic treatment—demonstrated a 'want of literary instinct', a lack that betrayed him, in Tennyson's opinion, into frequent clumsiness and into publishing too much.[62]

Familiar charges also, but what is surprising is that Tennyson detected the thick-ankled even in Wordsworth at his finest. What seems to have grated especially is what he saw as Wordsworth's diffuseness, the result of his characteristic repetition of key words. In conversation with Locker-Lampson Tennyson deplored the fact that 'the word "again" occurs four times in the first fourteen lines' of *Tintern Abbey* and observed that,

> lofty cliffs
> Which on a wild secluded scene impress
> Thoughts of more deep seclusion

'might have been more terse'. Taking up his copy of Wordsworth, Tennyson, according to Locker-Lampson, 'made these emendations, for his amusement & mine', the diffuse lines shrinking to:

> That makes a lone place lonelier.[63]

The poem's first great mystical profession also struck Tennyson as too wordy. The repetition of 'that blessed mood . . . that serene and blessed mood' was 'ridiculous' and was deleted in Tennyson's revision, as were the lines,

> While with an eye made quiet by the power
> Of harmony, and the deep power of joy . . .

Tennyson prefers to heighten the spirituality of the experience being evoked by passing directly from the 'living soul' to its power of seeing 'into the life of things'.[64]

Tennyson's rewriting of *Tintern Abbey* must be one of the most audacious assaults ever by one great poet on another and it would not be difficult to deflect it. A Wordsworthian might affrontedly observe that terseness is not one of Tennyson's characteristic virtues, nor is it clear that the repetition of 'lone . . . lonelier' or of 'woods decay' at the opening of *Tithonus* is less injurious than repetition in *Tintern Abbey*. But exactly what Tennyson did to *Tintern Abbey* is not what matters here. The significance of the revisions to this, one of Wordsworth's most important and admired poems, is that Tennyson was ready to make them at all. In a sense Tennyson lived with Wordsworth. His carved head looked out from the fireplace at Aldworth, alongside Homer, Dante, Chaucer, Spenser, and Milton, and a half-life-size bust of Wordsworth stood in the drawing-room at Farringford.[65] Late in Tennyson's life Palgrave noted in his journal that 'He emphatically repeated to me his constant estimate of Wordsworth as the greatest of our poets in this century'.[66] But Tennyson's was not a disabling reverence. Seeing the thick ankles enabled him to know the more confidently his own place as Wordsworth's proper successor as great poet, as Poet Laureate, and as Victorian cultural icon.

V

'The abiding in the transient'

Tennyson said of *Tears, idle tears*: 'This song came to me on the yellowing autumn-tide at Tintern Abbey, full for me of its bygone memories. It is the sense of the abiding in the transient.'[67] Tennyson's emotion at the apprehension of what is passing and what abides has its counterpart in Wordsworth's vision of the river Duddon: 'I see what was, and is, and will abide; | Still glides the Stream, and shall for ever glide; | The Form remains, the Function never dies'.[68] But Tennyson's intimation was associated by him more closely with another Wordsworth poem. Tintern Abbey, brushed with thoughts of Arthur Hallam's last resting-place, was also *Tintern Abbey* and the glorious line already quoted, which Tennyson singled out as capturing 'the permanent in the transitory'.[69]

For many of Tennyson's early readers his quest for a hold upon the permanent in the transitory, for uneroding truth, was what gave his poetry its intellectual and moral claim. As one of a generation which had found 'the lights all drifting, the compasses all awry, and nothing left to steer by except the stars', Froude recalled how,

the best and bravest of my own contemporaries determined to have done
with insincerity, to find ground under their feet, to let the uncertain remain
uncertain, but to learn how much and what we could honestly regard as
true, and believe that and live by it. Tennyson became the voice of this
feeling in poetry; Carlyle in what was called prose . . . Tennyson's poems,
the group of poems which closed with 'In Memoriam,' became to many of
us what the 'Christian Year' was to orthodox Churchmen.[70]

From *Supposed Confessions of a Second-Rate Sensitive Mind Not
in Unity with Itself* in 1830 to *In Memoriam* in 1850, Tennyson's
was the voice, Froude avers, which spoke to those determined to
enquire without 'a preconceived resolution that the orthodox
conclusion must come out true'.

Froude's recollection is sensitive to its historical position,
conscious of how quaintly distant the agonizings of his generation
must seem to the 'present generation which has grown up in an
open spiritual ocean . . . and has learned to swim for itself'. But
there is a further historical placing to be made, which gestures
towards the ironies of literary history. By 1884 Froude's young,
courageous questioner had become the Sage of Farringford, a
source of spiritual comfort to his monarch and a great many of her
subjects. The author of *The Higher Pantheism* was a founder
member of the Metaphysical Society and, as many earnest passages
in the *Memoir* testify, his views on God and Nature, Death and the
After-Life, weighed with friends across the whole spectrum of late
Victorian belief and scepticism. Tennyson might grumble about
being taken as a philosopher, but he was powerless to prevent the
construction of *In Memoriam* as the triumphant Christian poem for
the post-evolutionary decades of accommodation between science
and religion, nor could he avoid the veneration that was its
corollary. In the years to which Froude refers, 1830–50, the same
kind of construction of Wordsworth had taken place. The challenge
of his poetry of humanitarian sensibility had been taken up.
Whatever was conservative in his radical-conservatism was stressed.
Above all, Wordsworth's spiritual utterances were absorbed not as
a challenge but as a buttress to most structures of religious belief.
For a poet who was to speak to a generation determined 'to learn
how much and what we could honestly regard as true', this
Wordsworth was a presence as much to be resisted as embraced.
The overlap between the two men biographically, where it
mattered most to them as poets, was considerable. Wordsworth's

Arthur Hallam was his brother John. Both Hallam and John Wordsworth died suddenly, far away, and the news of their deaths brought not just grief but the obliteration of large hopes. At John's death he was embarked as captain of the *Earl of Abergavenny* on the voyage that was expected to make his fortune, enabling him on return to join the family circle in Grasmere and perhaps even eventually to marry Sara Hutchinson. Arthur Hallam was in love with Tennyson's sister, Emily, and as for his future, all of his friends, many themselves destined for eminence, were certain that Hallam would be the pre-eminent figure of their generation. For both poets natural bewilderment at such untimely and unnatural deaths was intensified by the recognition that the projected shape of their own lives had crumpled.

In one respect both poets' response as writers to their loss was similar. *In Memoriam* occupied Tennyson for the next seventeen years. During this period he wrote and published much else in various kinds, but what was also driving him, as only his closest friends knew, was the composition of elegies, whose slight form individually and exquisite finish belied the emotional and intellectual energy that furnished their making. Wordsworth, too, laboured long over his great poem. Given that what was to become Book I of *The Excursion* was conceived in 1797 but not published until 1814, it is tempting to observe that both poets spent seventeen years on the construction of a single work, during which period they published other poems that made their name. But this would be forcing the parallel. Although *The Excursion* as part of the projected *Recluse* had long figured in Wordsworth's vision of his poetic destiny, it did not begin to take coherent shape until a decade after his ambitions for a great philosophical poem had been announced.[71]

What emerged as Wordsworth revised existing materials in the light of the larger and more complex structure now being conceived, was a poem no less dominated by loss than *In Memoriam*, and lacerating grief at the deaths of two of his children within months of each other in 1812 served to darken still more deeply the poem's colouration. *The Excursion* has barely opened before the Wanderer exclaims to the Poet, 'Oh, Sir! the good die first', as he enters on the story of Margaret's suffering and death.[72] Four ruined walls are her memorial and they prefigure the other memorials whose meanings are to be expounded in the course of the poem. In Book II the old man and the poet encounter a funeral procession as they make their way to the home of the Solitary, a man in retreat from a life distorted by the pressure of loss. Every book of *The Excursion* does not need to be analysed to make the point—the only part of the philosophic poem to be completed rests in its entirety on stories about loss and on questions about what appropriate and efficacious response bewildered human beings can make to it. Many readers, such as those mentioned in the early chapters of this book, were drawn to *The Excursion* because in their own grief or depression they found there moving witness that loss and grief are universal.

'That loss is common would not make | My own less bitter, rather more' (VI).[73] *The Excursion* did not, of course, speak to such as Sir William Maynard Gomm just because it reminded him that 'Loss is common to the race', but because it explored the grounds for resilience and eventual joy. Since they are the inevitable questions *The Excursion*, like *In Memoriam*, asks them all—what kind of divine order permits suffering and untimely loss; why such waste of human potential; is anything permanent; is death the end?—and they are not canvassed in any perfunctory or complacent manner, but with the recognition that human pain remains human pain whatever the answers. The trajectory of the poem is none the less positive. Through the interplay of the damaged and mis-anthropic Solitary, the sage Wanderer, the devout but not blinkered Pastor, and the questioning Poet, the poem touches on the various ways in which human beings have constructed intellectual and emotional defences against loss and death and in the Wanderer's great declarations on the 'active principle', on admiration and love, and on duty, it eloquently affirms not so much the necessity of belief in the God-given order of things, but the irresistibility of such belief.

Tennyson's comment on *In Memoriam*, 'It's too hopeful . . . more than I am myself', indicates the strength in him of resistance, but in at least one all-important conviction *In Memoriam* aligns itself four-square with *The Excursion*. Neither poem is permitted to entertain with due openness the hypothesis that death is the end. In Book V, surrounded by churchyard memorials, the Pastor discourses on what binds the living and the dead and on Life as 'energy of love | Divine or human' (1012–13), and as a note to this discourse Wordsworth appends in full his own first *Essay upon Epitaphs*. Its

opening is a passionate declaration of faith, a 'plain avowal', that
the 'sense of immortality' *must* be anterior to all else, and that only
under its countenance are 'the human affections . . . gradually
formed and opened out':

I confess, with me the conviction is absolute, that, if the impression and
sense of death were not thus counterbalanced, such a hollowness would
pervade the whole system of things, such a want of correspondence and
consistency, a disproportion so astounding betwixt means and ends, that
there could be no repose, no joy. Were we to grow up unfostered by this
genial warmth, a frost would chill the spirit, so penetrating and powerful,
that there could be no motions of the life of love. . . .[74]

Sections XXXIV and XXXV of *In Memoriam* confront the
blankness with the same appalled sense that only one possibility is
supportable:

> My own dim life should teach me this,
>   That life shall live for evermore,
>   Else earth is darkness at the core,
> And dust and ashes all that is;

'*Else* earth is darkness', and as Wordsworth had declared:

>   If Death were seen
>   At first as Death, Love had not been,
>   Or been in narrowest working shut,
>
> Mere fellowship of sluggish moods,
>   Or in his coarsest Satyr-shape
>   Had bruised the herb and crushed the grape,
> And basked and battened in the woods.

Earlier poems had deployed traditional responses to death. In the
companion pieces *Nothing Will Die* and *All Things Must Die* the
natural cycle is interpreted both as evidence of ceaseless renewal
and as a demonstration of the ceaseless decay man cannot but
acknowledge his part in, as cheeks pale and limbs stiffen. The
beautiful *On a Mourner*, written immediately after Tennyson heard
of Hallam's death, listens to Nature's 'kind words', 'Thy friend is
mute: his brows are low: | But I am with thee till thy death', but
recognizes that, though 'the woods and ways are pleasant', Nature
can offer no adequate consolation:

> Yet is she mortal even as I,
> Or as that friend I loved in vain:
> She only whispering low or high,
> Through this vast cloud of grief and pain
> I had not found my peace again.[75]

In the stanzas from *In Memorian*, however, a particular compound of grief and fear breaks out, which the familiar consolatory formulations have no power to soothe. In the *Supposed Confessions* it is a sign of the speaker's disunity of mind when he contrasts the happy state of the lamb, who rejoices in life unconscious of what awaits it, with that of man who cannot:

> Shall man live thus, in joy and hope
> As a young lamb, who cannot dream
> Living, but that he shall live on?

But *In Memorian*, XXXV, entertains the thought again with new intensity and draws out its chilling implications, just as Wordsworth does in the *Essay upon Epitaphs*. The fear is not simply that there is nothing after death, but that, were this to be so, our three score years and ten would be emptied of what most gives human life its value. 'Love had not been' and 'dust and ashes all that is'. Neither proposition follows necessarily from the belief that no part of us is imperishable, but they are irresistible inferences to Wordsworth and Tennyson, and insupportable.

At this fundamental level the two poets unite in a conviction that is independent of historical change. In most other respects, however, comparison of *In Memoriam* with *The Excursion* indicates divergence that highlights their historical positioning. It was with a sense that Tennyson's was a contemporary voice, whereas Wordsworth's had to be recovered by intellectual archaeology, that Laurie Magnus observed in 1897 in *A Primer of Wordsworth*: 'if every other record of our times were to perish, except the poems of Wordsworth and Tennyson, history would still be able to draw conclusions as to our intellectual and moral development by no means remote from the truth.'[76] The word 'development' itself suggests how Magnus perceives his century's cultural history. Wordsworth's greatest poetry pre-dates the impact of science on religion and philosophy; Tennyson's registers it. Such was the view also of a much greater figure, Henry Sidgwick, Cambridge philosopher and follow member with Tennyson of the

Metaphysical Society, who told Hallam Tennyson that he agreed with a note in *Nature* to the effect that his father was 'preeminently the Poet of Science', and commented:

I have always felt this characteristic important in estimating his effect on his generation. Wordsworth's attitude towards Nature was one that, so to say, left Science unregarded: the Nature for which Wordsworth stirred our feelings was Nature as known by simple observation and interpreted by religious and sympathetic intuition. But for your father the physical world is always the world as known to us through physical science: the scientific view of it dominates his thoughts about it; and his general acceptance of this view is real and sincere, even when he utters the intensest feeling of its inadequacy to satisfy our deepest needs.[77]

Sidgwick differentiates between the two poets by employing oppositions that now seem less clear-cut than they did. The distinction between religion on the one hand and science on the other has blurred in recent intellectual history, not least through recognition of the variety of positions that made up Sidgwick's 'scientific view of [Nature]', and acknowledgement that, for example, even such a conservative cleric as Bishop Wilberforce was not hostile to science as such, only to science he regarded as flawed in method, or as making claims it could not support.[78] Nor will it do to oppose—however sympathetically—the ignorance of one period with the enlightenment of the next. That Tennyson was profoundly affected by reading Lyell and Chambers is well established, but geological science did not begin in 1833 with *Principles of Geology*. The contention between competing, often overlapping theories about the history of the world's formation had been given a new vigour by scientifically rigorous research in the latter part of the eighteenth and early nineteenth centuries and, as John Wyatt has recently demonstrated in an important study, Wordsworth was familiar with them.[79] Amongst his friends and acquaintances were some of the leading geologists of the day and they respected him as a poet whose imaginative celebration of mountains was based on an increasingly well-informed understanding of the history inscribed in boulder and scree.

What distinguishes Tennyson from Wordsworth is not that the former knew about science and the latter did not. It is rather the different degrees of intellectual turbulence their knowledge caused in their confrontation, as artists, with the greatest mysteries of life—change, loss, and death. As Wyatt has argued, Wordsworth's work accommodates his growing awareness of contemporary geological research without evident strain. In 1842 Adam Sedgwick—as has already been mentioned in Chapter 2—honoured a promise twenty years old by contributing a series of letters on the geology of the Lake District for an enlarged edition of Wordsworth's *Guide*.[80] There is no suggestion that the man of science is either updating the poet or offering an empirical as opposed to a visionary account of the region. The poet's prose can be complemented by that of the Woodwardian Professor of Geology at Cambridge because nothing in Wordsworth's understanding of nature as rocks and stones and trees has been unsettled by Sedgwick's research. More importantly, geology—especially that practised by a Reverend Professor—does not at all unsettle the sense of Nature as 'eternal nature . . . the great moving spirit of things', which has been the religious underpinning of Wordsworth's greatest work.[81] It is not quite, as Sidgwick suggests, that Wordsworth's poetic exploration of loss and grief leaves 'Science unregarded', but that for him Science neither sharpens the questioning nor indicates, if not answers, at least the terrain in which answers might be sought.

For the younger poet the situation was very different. Though he was unmoved by niceties of theology, Tennyson craved assurance on fundamental religious issues, but all that he read in the 1830s and 1840s, prompted only in part by the death of Arthur Hallam, served to agitate his hair-trigger scepticism.[82] Voting 'No' to the question put before the Cambridge Apostles in 1829, 'Whether the existence of an intelligent First Cause is deducible from the phenomena of the universe', had required no more than participation in a debate whose parameters and possible outcomes were well rehearsed.[83] What Lyell and Chambers did for Tennyson—not for everyone—was to confirm the nullity of the argument from design, while pointing up questions about the phenomenal world which eliminated the possibility of salvaging any part of it. Much of the power of *In Memoriam* is generated by the earnestness with which the poet parades the questions, only to recognize that one after another answers are either inadequate or unavailable. The transformation of the earth over aeons demonstrates instability and change as principles of the universe. Can the individual survive in any form when Nature is so profligate and uncaring? Is waste, too, a principle, or can science support the hypothesis that in some sense 'then were nothing lost to man' (XLIII)? Are God and Nature 'at strife' (LV)? Can the reasonings of the heart consort with those of science, or must religious faith insist on the separateness of its own domain?

To Tennyson, as he explored these issues throughout the long composition of *In Memoriam*, the great religious poet of the previous generation presented himself as a model of high seriousness, but not as a nourishing source. Tennyson returned repeatedly to *Tintern Abbey*—'the abiding in the transient'—but almost all of the declarations that make up the affirmatory movement of that poem voice a confident faith that Tennyson could not share. *Tintern Abbey* hymns the reciprocity between Man and Nature in which the 'blessed mood' engendered by Nature and Memory enables penetration 'into the life of things'. The presence of the power 'Whose dwelling is the light of setting suns', validates the 'Therefore' of the poet's argument that 'Therefore am I still | A lover of the meadows and the woods'. Gathering all the affirmations into an inclusive credo, the poet declares his trust,

> In nature and the language of the sense,
> The anchor of my purest thoughts, the nurse,
> The guide, the guardian of my heart, and soul
> Of all my moral being.

And underpinning the whole is the assertion that through a providential economy of loss and gain, for whatever the poet has lost he has been granted 'Abundant recompence'.

The exploratory forays of *In Memoriam* probe all of these declarations, but the poem cannot rest on them. In the *Prelude*'s climactic hymn to the Imagination Wordsworth characterizes the power with which creative minds 'deal | With the whole compass of the universe' (1850, XIV. 91–2). The poet of *In Memoriam*, to the contrary, knows no such astonishing confidence, being acutely aware of his inadequacy to deal with the whole compass of the universe. Vulnerable, hesitant, and doubting, the speaker registers through much of the poem the fragility of his sense of self, in contrast to the imperious egotism of *Tintern Abbey*.[84] It is also the case that for him, as Joanna Rapf has remarked, there can be 'no foundation for his moral being in the fabric of the universe'.[85] Kerry McSweeney is certainly right to argue that sources of consolation in Nature emerge strongly in the poem,[86] but nothing in *In Memoriam* approaches either Wordsworth's whole-hearted commitment in *Tintern Abbey* to Nature as guardian and guide, or his profoundly mysterious faith that 'Nature never did betray | The heart that loved her'.

Nor, finally, does *In Memoriam* endorse Wordsworth's perception of the workings of providential economy. Its trajectory is positive. Repetition of motifs such as the 'dark house' in VII and CXIX, and the Christmases, mark the speaker's progress towards a calm utterly unlike the 'calm despair' of XI. Strengthened by the certainty briefly but powerfully vouchsafed in XCV, the poet can eventually (CXV) image even his grief in terms of the natural cycle of renewal:

> and in my breast
> Spring wakens too; and my regret
> Becomes an April violet,
> And buds and blossoms like the rest.

And as Tess Cosslett has observed, the 'acceptance and celebration' manifested in the latter part of the poem 'involves the perception of ordered law, patterned interconnection, and organic process, giving structure and stability to the changes of a mutable and transient universe'.[87] But though this comment is just, the note of *In Memoriam* is not that of *Tintern Abbey*. What emerges most strongly is a sense that consolation has been wrested from loss, not, as in *Tintern Abbey*, that loss is fundamental to growth and to Nature's power 'Through all the years of this our life, to lead | From joy to joy'.

As was noted at the beginning of this chapter, Wordsworth's overtly philosophical poems are rich in statements such as this and they command assent by an authority whose ground is an inextricable fusion of content and form. Assent to confident affirmations is won through blank verse whose rhythm, syntax, line-endings, and sound drive the reader through sweeps of argumentative and hortatory verse. If it is the blank verse that makes the argument compelling, however, it might be as true to say that the argument demands blank verse. Wordsworth's determination to present professions of faith as if they are logically constructed propositions, with sinews of 'Yet', 'Therefore', 'If', requires a verse form flexible enough to sweep, pause, and turn. Whichever one chooses to emphasize, content or form, in Wordsworth at his most persuasive they interact inseparably and the result is authority. And it is the same authority whether the poet speaks as himself or as a dramatic figure. Hazlitt was right to be impatient with the supposedly dramatic structure of *The Excursion*—the authority figures in the poem, the Wanderer and the Pastor, do sound alike.[88] Whatever their differences of faith, they speak with the authority that derives from their command of blank verse.

Tennyson could write good blank verse that was not Wordsworth's—no small achievement—but for *In Memoriam* blank verse, Wordsworth's or not, was exactly the form he could not use. The structure of the poem is pinned by the Prologue and Epilogue, but within these two formulations of faith, far from aspiring to authority, the poem eschews it:

> Behold, we know not anything;
> I can but trust that good shall fall
> At last—far off—at last, to all,
> And every winter change to spring. (LIV)

The poet enquires but questions the grounds of his enquiry. He outlines hypotheses but remains tentative about conclusions. Incompatible speculations are entertained, but a firm resting-place is not achieved by endorsing any one of them. *In Memoriam* is a provisional poem and, as Ricks has finely said, its form in little encapsulates the larger provisionality: 'The *In Memoriam* stanza, though it permits convergence, does so on the strict condition that it be temporary—that it not be, in the strictest sense, final.'[89]

When Sidgwick contrasted Wordsworth and Tennyson he did so by dwelling on their differing response to Science. He developed the point, however, by introducing the question of authority. Tennyson's has been the identifying voice for the age, he suggests, because he knows the limits of what the poet can properly utter. Tennyson's defiance of 'the atheistic tendencies of modern Science' has been the stronger for his circumspect recognition of how far the claims of 'an Intuitive Faculty of theological knowledge' can be advanced against 'the results laboriously reached by empirical science'.[90] Wordsworth recognizes no limits to poetic authority. Though he too was to be revered eventually as Poet-Sage, Tennyson was always more guarded. That Wordsworth's claims for poetic authority were so massive is one reason why, though Tennyson might be the identifying voice of the age, Wordsworth remained for so long another, a continuing resource for Victorian readers who wanted poetry that could teach and guide.

7

The Wordsworth Renaissance

Some people would like to know whence the poet whose philosophy in these days is deemed as profound and trustworthy as his song is breezy and pure, gets his authority for speaking of 'Nature's holy plan'.[1]

I

Wordsworth's Posthumous Reputation

When Hardy slipped this mordant observation into *Tess of the D'Urbervilles* in 1891 he had good reason for feeling that it was about time somebody made it. For two decades articles and books had been honouring either Wordsworth's 'song' or his 'philosophy' and often both. A society of notable people had been formed to promote the Wordsworthian message. In the same year as *Tess* was issued in book form *The Wordsworth Dictionary* also appeared and the poet's home in Grasmere was bought by a group of devotees as a shrine for posterity.[2] Memorials were being erected. At the unveiling of a Wordsworth Fountain in Cockermouth the testimony of the Grand Old Man set the tone:

I revered his genius and delighted in his kindness and in the grave and stately but not austere dignity of his manners. But apart from all personal impressions, and from all the prerogatives of genius as such, we owe him a debt of gratitude for having done so much for our literature in the capital points of purity and elevation.[3]

Wordsworth was once more in various forms a living cultural force, after a long period during which, even though he was being energetically marketed, his visibility as an intellectual presence had faded.

During these years of diminishment articles and books continued to appear, of course, none more striking than John Wright's *The*

Genius of Wordsworth Harmonized With the Wisdom and Integrity of His Reviewers (1853).[4] This is the work of someone who knew Wordsworth very well indeed and who *hated* him. 'Nature designed not the late Poet Laureate for the purpose of song: but he had a morbid ambition to be thought a poet, and no man to whom enthusiasm has been denied, ever toiled so long and so patiently after such distinction,' Wright declares, as he draws on detailed knowledge of the poetry and of the life depicted in the *Memoirs*, to attack every aspect of Wordsworth with obsessional zeal.

Wright's book would not be worth bothering with, save as a source of comically self-regarding quotations, were it not for the fact that its scorching anger has another target than simply 'the greatest literary impostor of his time'. Wright attacks those who have constructed Wordsworth and his reputation. He has looked carefully at the poetry and sees that there is nothing there, and yet people are still taken in. Necessarily he believes in a conspiracy. This, he asserts, is a new age of general illiteracy and at a time when standards are being debased by national education, cheap printing, and the spread of journals designed by comparatively illiterate editors to meet the demands of 'an inferior class', Wordsworth has been 'a veritable god-send' with his puerile, bogus profundity. His reputation rests not on intrinsic merit, but on the needs of a shoddy age.

Iconoclasm, however, was not the order of the day after the death of the Poet Laureate. In his *Memoirs of William Wordsworth* (1852), George Searle Phillips, under the pseudonym 'January Searle', attacked Christopher Wordsworth for his 'studied exclusiveness' in omitting mention of such friends of the poet as John Wilson and De Quincey, and promised a juster treatment, 'compiled from authentic sources', but since Searle was wholly dependent on published material, he in fact could do little more than pad out his text with such rhapsodies as this one, which declares that like all true poets Wordsworth was 'an expounder of the hidden truths of the universe . . . an oracle of the Infinite . . . [who] stands in our presence like the Hebrew *law-giver*, covered with the golden glory and lightning of the Highest, whom he has *seen* upon the summits of Sinai'.[5]

Some Victorians could go on like this for hours—Dickens's Mr Chadband, for example, or the real-life Edwin Paxton Hood, whose *William Wordsworth: A Biography*, was published in 1856. All that needs to be said about this book is contained in the opening sentence of Richard Holt Hutton's review: 'Mr. Hood's life of Wordsworth is written with a violent desire to be transcendental.'[6] Most commentators, however, were content to make gentler music on familiar themes.

One old favourite was the Sage of Rydal Mount. In 1862, for example, Alexander Patterson fantasized in his *Poets and Preachers of the Nineteenth Century*:

His lovely little home was the seat of calm, domestic affections; and *he*, its honoured head, was the some-what stately, but, notwithstanding, mild and meek-eyed shepherd of the flock. Tranquil, and almost passionless, he sometimes might appear. But sedate solemnity of manner is quite compatible with yearning earnestness of heart; and those who knew him best aver that, when his words were few and his countenance was calm, his inward being overflowed with deep, though noiseless tenderness.[7]

To some extent Wordsworth was responsible for the special veneration his disciples accorded the composite of poet-in-his-home. All collected editions since 1815 had carried a dedicatory letter to Sir George Beaumont which closed with the poet's address, and the engraved title-page to the popular one-volume editions of 1845, 1847, and 1849 had depicted it.[8] Every reader knew that he lived in a handsome house nestling beneath a mountain, Nab Scar, and could glean some idea of how he lived from the Westall engraving for which he had willingly posed.[9] First-hand accounts, such as William Howitt's in *Homes and Haunts of the Most Eminent British Poets*, helped fill out the picture.[10] Even Christopher Wordsworth's *Memoirs of William Wordsworth* fed the interest by opening, not with Cockermouth, where the poet was born, but with an atmospheric evocation of Rydal Mount and its setting, as if Wordsworth were an emanation of the spirit of the place.[11]

As Patterson's rhapsody suggests, however, Wordsworth at Rydal Mount survived as an idea for loving contemplation because it accommodated the poet in the developing cult of hearth and home. Earlier in the century both Coleridge and Keats had seen it as a fault that Wordsworth was content to ease himself into domesticity. Lording it over his 'fireside Divan' was, they feared, incompatible with the masculine energy and independence of mind needed for poetry.[12] The generation of Dickens, Tennyson, and Ruskin, Augustus Egg, and Birket Foster, however, saw things very differently. Now it was deemed one of Wordsworth's most admirable qualities that he had drawn such strength from domestic life and that he had maintained a household of women in one beloved home for so many years. Patterson's 'meek-eyed shepherd of the flock' merges a Sunday-school print with the Westall engraving, simultaneously spiritualizing and domesticating the poet of *Michael*.

Another familiar *topos* was Wordsworth tested and triumphant. Treatment of this theme inevitably followed *The Prelude* and Christopher Wordsworth's *Memoirs*. In John Campbell Colquhoun's *Scattered Leaves of Biography* (1864), the issue of Wordsworth's radical politics is dealt with in a way that reveals how smooth the rough edges of Wordsworth's career had become through frequent handling:

Wordsworth was led by his sincere sympathy with humanity, and his intense love for the humbler classes of mankind, to regard the French Revolution as the advent of a new era, which would scatter countless blessings on the poor . . . But the excesses, into which the Revolution soon passed, and by which his own friends were destroyed, dispelled these visions; and after this time, chastened by experience, Wordsworth reverted to his natural habits, and resumed the retired pursuits and thoughts which had occupied his youth.

Colquhoun is evidently blind to alternative interpretations of his words. Wordsworth, it seems, ventured into the world briefly, had visions dispelled, and so reverted to retirement and to thoughts which had occupied him before this damaging brush with reality. This is a picture more of an ineffectual angel than an apostate. But Colquhoun registers not a hint of unease, or any sense that he has considered what it might mean to have visions dispelled, for to him Wordsworth's value is precisely that he is non-worldly: 'he lifts us, with a gentle pressure, from the earth, on which we are so apt to grovel, to heaven and its enduring rest.'[13]

What is so dreary about writing such as this is not the grandiloquence or its opposite, the flatness, but the absence of any thought. Throughout the 1850s and 1860s received ideas about Wordsworth were promulgated, a particular slant being given by the writer's opinions, but there was little probing or questioning.

Only in a few articles was there any sign of either a considered review of the grounds for asserting Wordsworth's continuing importance, or dissent from the consensus judgement which could provoke debate.

The most thoughtful piece of the whole period was Richard Holt Hutton's reassessment of Wordsworth's achievement in the *National Review*, occasioned by the appearance of Hood's biography.[14] After an attempt to define the 'essential simplicity', which he declares 'the most striking characteristic of Wordsworth's mind and poetry', Hutton proceeds to examine his imaginative processes before considering the question of the value of Wordsworth's poetic achievement as a whole.

It is a long and difficult essay, notable for arresting quotation, subtle distinctions, and sentences which have (to borrow a characteristic Hutton phrase), 'an exactness as well as a fullness of meaning'. As Hutton's best commentator has said, the essay 'provided a vocabulary for discussing Wordsworth's idealism which directly and explicitly affected the reading of Wordsworth for the rest of the century'.[15] But equally important was the example it offered as to method. The article is not an exercise in revaluation. No startling claims are made for this or that neglected poem. Nor is it an attempt to shift the Wordsworthian centre of gravity, by arguing, for example, that his genius is best represented in the dramatic or narrative modes. The essay, in fact, addressed familiar topics. What was so valuable was that it addressed them as if for the first time and as if they were so complex that the bases even for discussion needed to be established afresh.

No other essay of the period matched it, but some marked out lines for future debate. In 1864 the high-toned *National Review* carried two articles by Walter Bagehot and Matthew Arnold, whose essential concern is the present state of culture.[16] 'We live in the realm of the *half* educated. The number of readers grows daily, but the quality of readers does not improve rapidly'—not Arnold, but Bagehot, who sees current neglect of Wordsworth's 'pure art' as a symptom of cultural *malaise*. Arthur Hugh Clough disagreed. In a rather cross-grained contribution to the *North American Review* in 1865 he suggested that Wordsworth's virtues had been taken on trust too long: 'To live in a quiet village, out of the road of all trouble and temptation, in a pure, elevated, high, moral sort of manner, is after all no such very great feat.' Wordsworth withdrew from the world of 'life and business, action and fact', and, preaching his gospel of nature, had persuaded too many a reader 'that it was his business to walk about this world of life and action, and, avoiding life and action, have his gentle thoughts excited by flowers, and running waters, and shadows on mountain-sides'.[17] Swinburne's comment on 'that great poet, perverse theorist, and incomplete man' was tarter still. Wordsworth, he wrote, used nature 'as a vegetable fit to shred into his pot and pare down like the outer leaves of a lettuce for didactic and culinary purposes.'[18]

Each of these essays, however, reads like a contribution to a debate which is not quite taking place. When they appeared there was no context of controversy in which they could matter. Nothing was happening either in textual or biographical scholarship, or in criticism, to stimulate reassessment. The devout Wordsworthian John Campbell Shairp rightly observed in 1864 that the poet's reputation was 'at the ebb'.[19]

When the tide did turn it flowed strongly, gathering force throughout the 1870s and 1880s. The publication in 1873 and 1881 of Mill's *Autobiography* and *The Autobiography of Mark Rutherford* were important events, but they served more to recall what Wordsworth had meant earlier in the century than to define his continuing force. This was the issue of the moment and it was one on which an astonishing number of critics and lecturers, reviewers and scholars felt they had something to say. Editors made claims—though disagreeing with one another—certain that the one thing needful was accurate texts accompanied by every scrap of scholarly information that could be gleaned. Reviewers and essayists debated—often on the occasion of a new edition—the nature of Wordsworth's art and its value. The Wordsworth Society was founded in 1880 in response to current perceptions of the poet and its proceedings were an organized attempt to remould them, which in turn prompted further comment. And in each field of activity debate took place generally at a high level, exemplifying both in its energy and *gravitas* the strength of the intellectual élite whose vitality is one of the distinctive features of High Victorian culture.[20]

Detailed exposition of this mass of writing is unnecessary, but one aspect of it is worth touching on—the significance of the timing of this renewed bustle around a poet who had been dead for twenty or more years and whose finest work dated back into the previous century.

Equally concerned to establish afresh both the characteristics of the authentic Wordsworth and the grounds for his continuing importance, major figures in the 1870s and early 1880s conducted an antiphonal debate about both, as an outline chronology demonstrates. In 1871 Hutton's 1857 essay was reprinted as 'Wordsworth and His Genius' in his *Essays, Theological and Literary*. Three years later Walter Pater's 'On Wordsworth' appeared in the *Fortnightly Review*, in the same year as Stopford A. Brooke's famous lectures were published as *Theology in the English Poets*. In 1876 Leslie Stephen explicated 'Wordsworth's Ethics' in the *Cornhill Magazine*. He was answered by Matthew Arnold's essay in *Macmillan's Magazine* in 1879, which provoked many replies, notably by Edward Caird in *Fraser's Magazine* the year following and by Aubrey de Vere. With titles such as 'The Genius and Passion of Wordsworth' and 'The Wisdom and Truth of Wordsworth's Poetry', De Vere left no room for doubt that his were to be full-blooded defences of the poet he all but worshipped. In 1880 the Wordsworth Society was founded and began its programme of publication and into the next decade the high-priests of the religion of Wordsworth such as 'Principal' Shairp continued to intone.[21]

These writers plot out strikingly divergent ways of arriving at an assessment of the greatness of Wordsworth's achievement—a greatness on which they all agree.[22] On the one hand there is the line of Hutton, Brooke, Stephen, Caird, Shairp, De Vere. Differing in their religious persuasion, from the devoutly Roman Catholic Aubrey de Vere to the godless Leslie Stephen, they are united in the conviction that the closing lines of *The Prelude* point to the heart of Wordsworth's achievement. His poetry warrants and will bear elucidation because Wordsworth had truths to utter about the greatest mysteries of life. Stopford Brooke, combining sermon and lecture from the pulpit of his London chapel, expounds at great length the 'theological idea [which] is at the basis of Wordsworth's representation of Nature'. Leslie Stephen, who had renounced his orders in the Church of England but not the seriousness of the ideal clergyman, presents Wordsworth as a poet of earnest intellectual endeavour, whose ethics are capable of 'systematic exposition'. For Edward Caird, Professor of Moral Philosophy at Glasgow and later

Master of Balliol, immersion in Wordsworth is 'a kind of religious retreat', beneficial to those who can stand being shocked by the reversal of normal expectations. All of these writers find Wordsworth a very present help in Man's search for, in Stephen's words, 'some profounder solution for the dark riddle of life'.[23]

Pater and Arnold, on the other hand, without dissenting at all from the consensus about Wordsworth's stature, approach it in a very different spirit. 'What [Wordsworth] values most is the almost elementary expression of elementary feelings,' Pater declares, 'And so he has much for those who value highly the concentrated expression of passion, who appraise men and women by their susceptibility to it, and art and poetry as they afford the spectacle of it.' Pater extols Wordsworth's 'mobile' sensibility and the 'sensuousness' of his perceptions, but his philosophy, he intimates, is unsystematic and even inconsistent, a view put forward still more directly in Arnold's notorious assertion that 'in Wordsworth's case ... we cannot do him justice until we dismiss his formal philosophy'. Dismiss this obfuscatory cladding and Wordsworth's real profundity stands out clear: 'the extraordinary power with which [he] feels the joy offered to us in nature, the joy offered to us in the simple primary affections and duties; and ... the extraordinary power with which, in case after case, he shows us this joy and renders it so as to make us share it'. Not one of what Arnold witheringly terms Wordsworth's 'small band of devoted followers' would have disagreed, but for Hutton, Stephen, and Caird, Arnold's proposition would have been the germ of an expository discourse, not its end.

Gathered together in an anthology of Wordsworth criticism these essays would have a certain coherence and historical interest. Two or three are of abiding value. Read in their original context, however, they take on a richer significance.

In 1868 Pater had smuggled into the *Westminster Review* under the guise of an unsigned notice of 'Poems by William Morris' his credo that the 'service of philosophy, and of religion and culture as well, to the human spirit, is to startle it into a sharp and eager observation'. 'Not the fruit of experience but experience itself is the end,' Pater declares, defining experience as sensuous intensity, as burning with a 'hard gem-like flame', as catching 'at any exquisite passion' and as resisting any 'facile orthodoxy'.[24] Robert Buchanan was pretty sure he knew where this kind of thing led—to the

subversive unhealthiness of Swinburne and Rossetti, the protagonists of 'The Fleshly School of Poetry', who were leagued together 'to
aver that poetic expression is greater than poetic thought, and by
inference that the body is greater than the soul, and sound superior
to sense'.[25]

When Pater reissued the 'gem-like flame' passage as the
'Conclusion' to *Studies in the History of the Renaissance* in 1873,
one of Wordsworth's descendants decided that now Pater had
publicly acknowledged authorship a stand for morality had to be
made. The Reverend John Wordsworth, grand-nephew of the poet
and a colleague of Pater at Brasenose College, protested at the
doctrine, implied throughout the *Studies* and encapsulated in the
'Conclusion', that 'no fixed principles either of religion or morality
can be regarded as certain, that the only thing worth living for is
momentary enjoyment and that probably or certainly the soul
dissolves at death into elements which are destined never to
unite'.[26]

Did John Wordsworth read Pater's article on his illustrious
forebear the following year? If he did he cannot have been
reassured. Throughout it the keywords resonate—'passion',
'sensuousness', 'intense', 'spectacle'—as Pater reveals that the
Wordsworth he values has nothing to say worth noting on the
topics deemed important by the future Bishop of Salisbury. If there
is a 'lesson' to be learnt from Wordsworth, Pater suggests, it is the
'supreme importance of contemplation in the conduct of life'. And
as if this were not enough Pater throws down his final gage. The
'principle of all the higher morality', he pronounces, is that 'the end
of life is not action but contemplation'; Wordsworth is a true
master of 'this art of impassioned contemplation'; this is what is
'powerful and original' in Wordsworth, not 'those weaker elements
. . . which for some minds determine their entire character'; and,
finally, Wordsworth's is a type of the truest and most valuable art.

Ever since Swinburne's *Poems and Ballads* (1866) a suspiciously
French contagion had been around and what Pater did was to
contaminate Wordsworth with it. Leslie Stephen and Edward Caird
recognized the danger and fought it, on behalf both of Wordsworth
specifically and more generally in defence of literature and
humanist values. In an essay for the *Cornhill Magazine* in 1875
entitled 'Art and Morality' Stephen attempted to demolish a fallacy
which he admitted was nowhere fully articulated but which was

'pervading a good deal of contemporary writing', namely, that 'art and morality are two different things',[27] and a year later he focused on Wordsworth to demonstrate that the opposite is true in art of the highest quality.

Stephen's personal investment in this position was considerable. After the death of his first wife in 1875 when he was only 43, Stephen confided to Charles Eliot Norton what reading Wordsworth had meant to him: 'I used not to care for him especially; but now I love him. He is so thoroughly manly & tender & honest as far as his lights go, that he seems to me to be the only consoler. I despise most of your religious people, who cultivate their maudlin humours, & despise even more your sentimentalist of the atheist kind; but old W.W. is a genuine human being, whom I respect.'[28] Although he recognized that 'people generally think me a fool about poetry', Stephen courageously spelt out in 'Wordsworth's Ethics' the grounds for finding Wordsworth 'the only consoler', burying the autobiographical origins of the essay in the remark that 'Wordsworth is the only poet who will bear reading in times of distress'. For Stephen 'that man is the greatest poet whose imagination is most transfused with reason; who has the deepest truths to proclaim as well as the strongest feelings to utter'— Wordsworth was such a man. Compared with the 'sickly school' of Byron and Shelley—and the echo of Buchanan's 'Fleshly School' summons Rossetti—Wordsworth was adult enough to deal with the realities of life and 'to supply an answer [to its riddle] worthy not only of a poet, but a man'. Wordsworth's ethics are capable of 'systematic exposition' not because he was a professional philosopher, but because he was both a true man and a true poet, whose poetry 'derives its power from the same source as his philosophy. It speaks to our strongest feelings because his speculation rests upon our deepest thoughts.'

'Wordsworth's Ethics' is one of Stephen's finest essays, but it is more than an essay about Wordsworth. In his exposition of Wordsworth's value Stephen implicitly attacks what he sees as a contemporary tendency to divorce art from morality, matter from form, and artist from man. Edward Caird's 1880 article in *Fraser's Magazine*, prompted by Arnold's attack on Stephen and the 'Wordsworthians', is more explicit. Contrasting Wordsworth's sublime conception of the poet's role to William Morris's depiction of himself in the 'Apology' to *The Earthly Paradise* as the 'idle singer of an empty day', Caird denies that to such can be given 'the name of sacred poet'. Yes, form is uppermost in poetry, but above that the issue is truth. This is not the view of 'some critics at the present day who tell us that . . . poetry has nothing to do with the teaching of truth, or with truth in any shape. Some go so far as to say, that what we have to regard in a poet is not what he has said, but simply how he has said it.' Wordsworth demonstrates how false this is. With him we have to ask 'what are the main ideas by which he is guided and inspired, or, in other words, what is the *content* of his poetry', and by this route alone, as with all valuable poets, can we have access to his virtue.[29]

Stephen and Caird, flanked by the less subtle cohort of Brooke, Shairp, and De Vere, present a Wordsworth who matters in contemporary culture, not only because he has a message which can instruct, sustain, and console, but also because his poetry demonstrates, against the aesthetic tendencies of the day, that this is poetry's true office.

After so much earnest apologetic, what need of more? That was the question posed by William Knight in 1878, as he surveyed a critical succession which began with Coleridge and had reached its apogee in 'above all . . . Mr. Stopford Brooke, and the present Professor of Poetry at Oxford [John Campbell Shairp]'.[30] But the question was merely a rhetorical flourish introducing yet another lecture, for 'there is no possibility of exhausting Wordsworth any more than of exhausting Plato'.[31] The hyperbole of this and the absurdity of Knight's 'above all' typify the worst of the inbred Wordsworthianism of the 1870s and it was bound to provoke a reaction stronger than Henry James's mild rebuke to Stopford Brooke that 'there are reasons in the nature of things why a prolonged commentary on the author of the *Prelude* and the *Excursion* should have the air of superfluity'.[32]

Ruskin was incapable of such suavity. For him *The Excursion* had been, next to the Bible, the Book of Life, and there was no hyperbole in his declaration in 1880 that he had 'used Wordsworth as a daily text-book from youth to age, and [had] lived, moreover, in all essential points according to the tenor of his teaching'.[33] With advancing age, however, Ruskin was reassessing all intellectual commitments and in *Fiction, Fair and Foul*, acknowledgement of lifelong indebtedness notwithstanding, he made deep thrusts at 'the gentle minstrel of the meres . . . the hermit of Rydal Mount'.[34] But these essays sweep across so many topics—Scott, Byron, style, dialect, Wordsworth, Burns, Southey—and blast off in so many directions that it is not easy to see what the target is. In an attack on Wordsworth's sonnet about Frederick Barbarossa before Pope Alexander III, an attack which takes the form of a passionate history lesson, Ruskin does pillory Wordsworth directly for 'having no shadow of doubt of the complete wisdom of every idea that comes into his own head', and elsewhere he points to the limitations of the 'pitying and tender imagination' that arrived 'in lacustrine seclusion at many valuable principles of philosophy' while Europe burned.

What makes Ruskin splenetic, however, is not so much Wordsworth himself as the 'affection of his disciples', who elevate him in all respects above Byron, who refuse to recognize that their 'excellent master often wrote verses that were not musical, and sometimes expressed opinions that were not profound' (p. 350), and who profess to be 'Wordsworthian' when, in Ruskin's experience, 'these sentimental students . . . are seldom inclined to put in practice a single syllable of the advice tendered them by their model poet' (p. 349).

In the second of his papers Ruskin mentions his 'extreme pleasure' in Arnold's 1879 *Poems of Wordsworth*, but observes that 'though it is very proper that Silver How should clearly understand and brightly praise its fraternal Rydal Mount, we must not forget that, over yonder, are the Andes, all the while' (p. 318). This comment—ironically only fully intelligible to those sufficiently inward with Wordsworthian matters to know where the Arnold family home stood in relation to Wordsworth's—wings Arnold twice, by suggesting both that he is essentially within the Wordsworthian charmed circle, whatever he may claim, and that his high estimate of Wordsworth shares its subject's limitation of vision. Silver How is not the Andes. But when Arnold offended again the following year he provoked much stronger comment than this.

In March 1881 *Macmillan's Magazine* carried what was to be the Preface to Arnold's selection of the *Poetry of Byron* issued later in the year.[35] Its conclusion is that 'Wordsworth and Byron stand out by themselves. When the year 1900 is turned, and our nation comes to recount her poetic glories in the century which has then just ended, the first names with her will be these' (p. 237), an affirmation which might not have upset anyone too much were it not for what had preceded it. In the body of the essay Arnold praises Byron for waging war 'with such splendid and imperishable excellence of sincerity and strength' against the cynicism of the Barbarians and the 'impregnable Philistinism' of the middle class, but he also judges him wanting in the 'true artist's fine passion for the correct use and consummate management of words'. Byron stands, none the less, well above Keats, Coleridge, 'poet and philosopher wrecked in a mist of opium', and Shelley, 'beautiful and ineffectual angel, beating in the void his luminous wings in vain'—and this is to stand very high. But it is not quite as high as Wordsworth, Arnold asserts, when final discriminations are made, for Wordsworth reaches profundity in his criticism of life beyond Byron. Wordsworth is not in the same order as Homer, Dante, or Shakespeare, but he is close, and to buttress this estimate Arnold repeats, in part verbatim, the climax of his 1879 essay in which he identifies Wordsworth's power as that which feels and renders 'the resources of joy offered to us in nature'. An essay supposedly about Byron becomes a reprise of all that Arnold has said about Wordsworth's superiority, with a casual demolition of Coleridge and Shelley thrown in.

This is Arnold at his most maddening. All his favoured devices are deployed with the usual grace—touchstones, quotation in three or four languages, comparative discussion of an Italian poet, a touch of historical scholarship for gravity's sake, repetition of key phrases, self-quotation, ranking according to criteria gestured at rather than defined—and, as usual, Arnold goaded others into intemperate response. Needled by 'that air of tranquil and well-bred triumph of which Mr. Arnold is so consummate a master', the future Poet Laureate, Alfred Austin, tried to overturn Arnold's ranking of Byron and Wordsworth, by denying the latter's achievement almost entirely.[36] Playing Arnold at his own game of repetition, Austin invokes Arnold's 'distinterested lovers of poetry' again and again, to ask what is there of poetical merit in most of Wordsworth's lyrics and narratives. Only 103 of Arnold's 317 pages in the selected Wordsworth are worth preserving 'on a liberal estimate', and even they do not add up to much as Wordsworth does not treat Great Material and he totally lacks Character, Action, Invention and Situation.

Austin's target is Arnold and the Wordsworthians and the need to demonstrate that his standards of judgement are ludicrous and their devotion utterly misplaced requires Austin to prove that Wordsworth is barely a poet at all. Two years later Swinburne attacked Arnold too, with still keener anger, but his critical aim is quite different from Austin's. Swinburne denigrates Byron in order to elevate Coleridge and Shelley. With his 'malevolent and cowardly self-conceit . . . ever shuffling and swaggering and cringing and backbiting in a breath' Byron, Swinburne declares, is 'as fit to be considered the rival of Coleridge and Shelley as Offenbach to be considered a competitor with Handel and Beethoven'.[37]

For much of the essay Swinburne exploits his considerable resources of invective to confirm this judgement and his equally rich resources of rhapsody to affirm that Coleridge and Shelley are the 'two coequal kings of English lyric poetry', but his argument is not germane here. Nor does much need to be said about Swinburne's actual assessment of Wordsworth, save to note that criticism which extols the *Ode to Duty* and *Song at the Feast of Brougham Castle* above the *Ode: Intimations of Immortality*, singles out *Tribute to the Memory of a Dog* as an indication of 'that very sublimity of tenderness which [is] Wordsworth's distinctive and crowning quality', which deems *Margaret* [*The Ruined Cottage*] 'a failure', and which asserts that there is 'hardly in any literature a poem of more perfect power, more awful and triumphant beauty, than *The Affliction of Margaret*', at least has the virtue of being unusual.

What is of greater interest is Swinburne's protest at most Wordsworthian criticism of the previous two decades. In order to assign Wordsworth to his proper place—which is almost in the highest order of poets, Swinburne acknowledges—the current consensus has to be prised apart. Why is it that most critical writing on Wordsworth, whatever its local ingenuities, examines the same material in the same way and arrives at roughly the same result? It is because critics of 'this great and misappreciated poet' are generally 'disciples' misled 'by their more or less practical consent to accept Wordsworth's own point of view as the one and only proper or adequate outlook from which to contemplate the genius and the work, the aim and the accomplishment of Wordsworth. Not that he did wrong to think himself a great teacher: he was a teacher no less beneficent than great: but he was wrong in thinking himself a poet because he was a teacher, whereas in fact he was a teacher because he was a poet.' As Swinburne notes approvingly, Arnold had said something like this in 1879. But Swinburne's is the more considered and critically useful formulation, in that it identifies the problem which writers on Wordsworth still struggle with, that of escaping from the poet's well-nigh irresistible self-representation.

Each of these essays was a counter-blast to orthodoxy, but they were individually so odd that they served as spectacles of critical pyrotechnics rather than foundation stones on which others could build. *Fiction, Fair and Foul*, impassioned, learned, dauntingly allusive and bewilderingly wayward, surely the most extraordinary series of papers ever to appear in the *Nineteenth Century* or any other comparable periodical, indicated only that the aged Ruskin was reassessing Wordsworth, as everything else, driven by the 'profound conviction' now mastering him 'that about ninety-nine hundreths of whatever at present is, is wrong'. A severe and not unjustified rebuke was administered by Hutton in the *Spectator*, who accused Ruskin of scoring cheap points, writing as if he were not one of the most sensitive critics of the age but a 'mere man of the world'.[38] Austin's piece was simply hopelessly belated. Dusting off Jeffrey's critical armoury Austin found still serviceable weapons, but to mount a frontal attack with them on Wordsworth in 1882 was foolhardy. Maybe elevation of Byron required some chipping away at Wordsworth, but to attempt to demolish the whole edifice was neither necessary, nor likely to succeed—at least not as made by the rather ponderous Austin. Compared with him Swinburne is fire and air and his essay remains a pleasure to read. It is magnificently intemperate and his judgements are arrestingly unexpected, but comprehensive revaluation of Wordsworth's stature is not Swinburne's goal. For all his *ad hominem* impudence to Arnold—a great critic, but one, he insinuates, exhibiting alarming signs of softening of the brain—the essay confirms Arnold's judgement on Wordsworth, even as it assaults his judgement on every other Romantic poet.

By the mid-1880s, when Swinburne's essay appeared, the most energetic phase of critical activity was closing. Until the end of the century lakes of printer's ink were to be consumed in Wordsworth's service, but not by major critics. Now it was the turn of the editors, who took Wordsworth's stature for granted. But even as they pursued what they believed to be a truly disinterested endeavour, they too, in fact, were constructing a Wordsworth, as they pored over textual revisions, recovered manuscripts, suppressed poems, letters, diaries, and all the other *disjecta membra* which scholars love.

II

Wordsworth's Editors

All of Wordsworth's work was to come out of copyright in 1892 and as the 1870s passed the executors were uneasily aware that more than half of their allotted span of freedom had elapsed. But they were not prepared for the bombshell that exploded amongst them in 1879. In August of the previous year William Knight approached them for permission to include some copyright material in his little book *The English Lake District as Interpreted in the Poems of Wordsworth*. When the volume appeared the executors were once again dismayed by how much Knight had appropriated, especially from *The Prelude*, though they were mollified by the highly respectful tone in which their courtesy was acknowledged. But Knight had bigger ambitions, and, having gained a bridgehead with the Lake District book, he next stunned William Jr. with a request on 26 March 1879 which went straight to the point. Asserting that earlier kindness 'encourages me to ask a further favour at your hands', he went on:

I propose editing a complete edition of the Poet's Works, inserting all my topographical notes, & giving *all* the variations in the text in successive editions, as well as writing a biography, & a critical or expository essay. May I, in this edition which will extend to, (probably) 8 vols. insert the I.F. 'Notes and illustrations' of the Poems?

I infer from passages in the 'Memoir' by the Bishop of Lincoln that there are fragments of 'the Recluse' still unpublished. If this be so, will you permit me to publish these fragments . . .?

I think the time has come for the preparation of a complete library edition of the Poet's works, which will be the best memorial of him. I am anxious to make my edition complete . . .

This was just what the Wordsworths had been dreading. With sales of the Complete Works dwindling to vanishing point, the family had for some time been toying with the idea of a new, big edition.[39] Charles Wordsworth, the Bishop of St Andrews, had raised their hopes that John Campbell Shairp would undertake it, but when Shairp said he was too busy, the Bishop had indicated that he would do it himself, rather than have the project collapse 'for want of an editor' (15 December 1877), and family negotiations about timing, remuneration, and even the publisher, were still in progress when Knight's request arrived. William recognized the urgency of the situation, for Knight's letter, though respectful, had overtones of reproach and even threat. He could not just be fobbed off—he was too substantial a scholar for that—but he had to be stopped, otherwise, William Jr. foresaw, there would be no end to his 'ravenous requests' (27 March 1879). The answer was to assure him that the family was well aware of its duty and had the matter in hand. But the Bishop's plan was never more than the pipe-dream of someone who had not the faintest idea of what the editorial task would entail, and eventually Knight won the day.[40]

He triumphed partly through perseverance and courteous assiduity and partly because he won the support of the next Wordsworth generation. Just as the family was constructing a front against Knight, William Wordsworth, son of John Wordsworth, blew it apart. In a letter of 14 December 1879, written from Bombay where he was Principal of Elphinstone College, this William staggered his seniors by announcing that he had never thought Charles Wordsworth's editorial scheme would come to anything; that he was in contact with Professor Knight and intended to assist him; and that he hoped the family would do everything possible to facilitate his proposed edition.[41] Bishop Charles was clearly hurt and retired, just commenting to William Wordsworth of Bombay: 'I dare say the arrangement is the best possible *under all* the circumstances . . . and I sincerely hope that no occasion will be given for subsequent regret.'

Knight won, however, also simply because he had a weapon the Wordsworths could not resist. As he hinted more than once, in a few years time he would be free, as others would, to do as he liked. Sensing that they needed Knight almost as much as he needed them, the Wordsworths capitulated, sold *The Prelude* rights for £100 to Knight's Edinburgh publisher, Paterson, and co-operated in the production of the first ever fully edited Wordsworth through 1882 to 1889. They oversaw, in other words, the transference of and care for Wordsworth's text, and for the reputation of the family, into academic control.

Knight was a zealot for Wordsworth, but he was not alone in that, and other zealots viewed his progress with dismay. Without any open declaration of war, for the combatants were gentlemen as well as academics, battle was joined and for the next twenty years it was waged through prodigious feats of publishing, whose embodiment remains many feet of uniform bindings on library shelves. Knight issued eight volumes of *The Poetical Works of William Wordsworth* between 1882 and 1886 and complemented them with a three-volume *Life of William Wordsworth* in 1889. Knight's edition was challenged by Edward Dowden's in seven volumes. Dowden, a professor at Trinity College, Dublin, had been at work since the late 1870s on collation and annotation for an edition based on principles opposed to Knight's, but an earlier project foundered and it was not until 1892–3 that his Aldine edition appeared.[42] Dowden's mantle passed to his colleague Thomas Hutchinson, whose edition for Oxford University Press in 1895 is still, astonishingly, the basis for Oxford's standard one-volume Wordsworth. The heroic phase of editorial warfare came to an end in 1896 when Knight returned to the fray with a further eight volumes, published by Macmillan.[43]

In this period of editorial fervour there were other players. A comically manic scheme, for example, was floated by J. H. Shorthouse, author of *John Inglesant*, whose passion for Wordsworth, *The Excursion* in particular, led him to approach Macmillan to see if he would '*publish an edition of the "Excursion" with a very large proportion of the other poems, interleaved, as it were, with the poem*' (his italics). There were problems, Shorthouse conceded, not the least being 'the mass of matter to be introduced. I do not suppose it could be done under three moderate-sized octavo volumes; but I feel certain that, were the plan successfully carried out, *no other edition of Wordsworth would ever be read in the future*' (his italics).[44] One might suspect that the unexpected success of *John Inglesant* had gone to Shorthouse's head, but it is more likely that, with out-of-copyright Wordsworth still in the ascendant, Knight's monumental edition indicated, to someone unversed in the commercial realities of publishing, that anything was possible. But George Macmillan, not surprisingly, demurred, and Shorthouse had to leave the field to Knight and Dowden.

As befitted combat between gentlemen their warfare was conducted in public with due regard to chivalry. Dowden, for example, probed Knight's weakest point with exquisite periphrasis: 'I desire to speak with great gratitude of Professor Knight's labours ... But his collation in the earlier volumes of his edition, where collation was most important, is of a kind which cannot be called final.'[45] Knight played the game with only slightly less finesse. 'I have the greatest admiration for the work which Professor Dowden has done', is the preface to the assertion that his rival's edition demands such trouble to use that he 'greatly doubt[s] if many who have read and profited—for they could not but profit—by a perusal of Professor Dowden's work, *have* taken that trouble, or that future readers of the Aldine edition will take it'.[46]

In private, however, the knives were out. Dowden, Hutchinson, the Revd Thomas Hutchinson, nephew of Mary Wordsworth, and John Ramsden Tutin of Hull, Wordsworthian extraordinary, formed an epistolary alliance and as they swapped information, announced discoveries, and lent one another early editions of Wordsworth to assist collation, they spiced their letters more often than not with ridicule of Knight's many blunders.[47] But though Pope's line, '*Art* after *Art* goes out, and all is Night', has occurred to most Wordsworth scholars at one time or another when tracing the progress of an error through Knight's voluminous output, he was not one of the Dunces. As Wordsworthian discoverer, enabler, and publicist he towered above contemporaries and neither public correction nor private sniggers could diminish his stature. He was first in the field and continued to labour longer than anyone else. He amassed information which others plundered, sometimes without scruple or acknowledgement.[48] He was magnanimous and genuinely concerned for Wordsworth rather than his own standing, as the dignity of his behaviour demonstrated when Macmillan stunned him in 1888 by issuing *The Recluse*, Wordsworth's one major poem yet unpublished, even though the firm knew that Knight was planning to print it in its proper place in the chronological sequence of his edition.[49] Perhaps most important of all, Knight made what he had learned as editor accessible to the non-specialist in a massively documented *Life*.

In his 1880 essay in *Fraser's Magazine* Edward Caird remarked that though 'Wordsworth cannot be made popular', more might be done to make him accessible: 'his poems might be re-arranged in chronological order, and each of them might be accompanied with an explanation of the circumstances of its composition'. Then follows an observation so timely that one wonders whether Caird had been prompted: 'We hope that, before long, Professor Knight, or someone equally competent, if such can be found, may be induced to undertake the labour of such an edition.'[50] Knight needed little urging and his achievement is impressive. His eight-volume *Wordsworth's Poetical Works*, and the three-volume *Life of William Wordsworth*, which was issued in matching format, are astonishing feats of labour in an age before photocopying machines, research grants, graduate assistants, and all the other aids to twentieth-century scholarship, and they fully justify the self-confidence of his initial approach to William Wordsworth junior. Presenting every scrap of information he could glean, Knight laboured to establish the chronology of Wordsworth's life and writings. Chronology above all was his obsession. But he wanted also to compile a full bibliography of the published works, to annotate the poems as densely as possible and to record their textual evolution. Comprehensiveness was the goal, yet so great was the mass of information that Knight elicited or uncovered himself that as it proceeded the great edition took on the air more of a work in progress than a final monument. The editor excitedly records the acquisition of new facts ascertained 'within the last few days' (I, p. x) or 'since the foregoing sheets had gone to press' (V. 434), and is compelled to reissue the chronological table printed in the first volume, not because it was slovenly but simply to take account of what has been recently discovered.[51] The *Life* was similarly presented as primarily a record of facts. Disclaiming an overall interpretative scheme, Knight promises to present information and so great has been the flow, he explains to his readers, that a modest one-volume project has grown into three.[52]

The *Poetical Works* demonstrate Knight's eagerness to be faithful custodian of an ever-growing mass of material, but there was nothing self-effacing about them. Knight's stated intention was to inaugurate a new approach to the study of Wordsworth. Anxious to shape an edition capable of 'giving a genetic view of the poet's mind and of the development of his genius' (I, p. xx), Knight broke with the poet's own arrangement and classification of his work—honoured in all authorized and derivative complete editions to date—in favour of a chronological presentation in order of composition.[53] As far as the text was concerned he drew back from radical measures and observed the poet's wishes—after some consideration of alternatives—by printing the poems in their latest revised state. But the order of the poems had to be, wherever practicable, chronological.[54] What the poet had with deliberation tried to prevent, the chronological reading of his *œuvre*, Knight was determined to facilitate.

Imperious though Knight's editorial decision was, it was motivated by profound reverence for Wordsworth as teacher. Only by tracing the unfolding of his power could one could best profit, Knight believed, from the work which was a continuing embodiment of the man. But the same reverence also led to inconsistency and suppression clearly at odds with the main thrust of Knight's policy. Despite the intention of providing the materials for study 'of the development of his genius' (I, p. xx), Knight declined to print Wordsworth's first published poem, the sonnet *On Seeing Miss Helen Maria Williams Weep At A Tale Of Distress*, though he announced its discovery, and he judged it 'neither necessary nor expedient' (I, p. xxxvii) to reproduce *The Convict*.[55] The first version of *Descriptive Sketches*, published in 1793, Knight judged so bad 'that its reproduction (except in the form of footnotes) would be an injustice to Wordsworth' (I, p. xxv). And Knight's sense of justice took him further. Unable to resist telling the world about an unpublished poem from Wordsworth's Alfoxden period, *A Somersetshire Tragedy*, Knight declared it 'the chronicle of a revolting crime, with nothing in the poem to merit its being rescued from oblivion. The only curious thing about it is that Wordsworth could have written it' (I, p. xxxvii), and he seems to have done what he could to ensure that no one else could rescue it from oblivion either. Believing, rightly, that the Wordsworth family would concur, Knight 'burned a copy of that poem, sent to me by one to whom it had been confided'.[56]

Acting as editorial custodian of Wordworth's reputation Knight declared himself able to 'rejoice' over the destruction of *A Somersetshire Tragedy*, but as biographer he went further in suppressing—this time unannounced—the disturbing and unpalatable. His prefatory remarks to the *Life of William Wordsworth* promise fair dealing, in implied contrast to Christopher Wordsworth's *Memoirs*. The weaknesses of the subject must not be glossed over, for 'to conceal them is to be unfaithful to posterity' (I,

p. vi). Only a few pages later, however, Knight introduces an almost infinitely flexible get-out clause. Declaring that the lives of all great teachers are instructive, Knight justifies the nature of his approach to biography through a factual narrative: 'what the many mostly need is the careful collection of all relevant data regarding the chief teachers of the world . . . and the suppression of all that is irrelevant' (I, p. x).

Only two areas of Wordsworth's private life really trouble biographers. Controversial aspects of his public life—his behaviour in the 1818 election or his hostility to electoral reform, for example—had been live issues from the moment he began to achieve fame. Whether or not Wordsworth was a political apostate was a question which contemporaries tussled with just as unsatisfactorily as twentieth-century biographers. Certain troubling aspects of Wordsworth's more private life had likewise been matters of concern (and gossip) for a long time—the quarrel with Coleridge, for example, or the irrevocable break with De Quincey, one-time darling of the Wordsworth household. But two elements in Wordsworth's most private life had remained private—the intensity of his relationship with his sister and the fact that as a young man he had fathered a child with a French woman. Knight learned about them both.

Knight's greatest scholarly breakthrough came early in his work when William Wordsworth Jr. trusted him with the manuscripts of his aunt Dorothy's journals.[57] The evidence suggests that he was both enthralled and discomfited by what he read. On the one hand here was more information about the interweaving of domestic and poetic life than existed for any other writer of Wordsworth's stature, a biographer's and editor's god-send. On the other hand, here too was one artless disclosure after another, in journal entries which continue to put all Wordsworthians on the defensive,[58] that the brother–sister relationship of William and Dorothy Wordsworth was very like that of lovers.

With the straightforward material Knight clearly had no difficulty—he simply let Dorothy speak, quoting copiously in sequential extracts. Despite the appearance of openness, however, and the protestation of his preface, Knight silences Dorothy whenever he deems it prudent. On 31 January 1802, for example, Wordsworth had a headache and Dorothy 'petted him on the carpet'.[59] Knight quotes almost all of this longish entry, but not this detail. On 4

March 1802 Dorothy entered her thoughts about how she was going to cope with a short absence of her brother: 'I *will* be busy, I *will* look well & be well when he comes back to me. O the Darling! here is one of his bitten apples! I can hardly find [*sic*] in my heart to throw it into the fire.' Knight omits the whole entry. He also excises revelations about how physically close brother and sister were. 'After dinner we made a pillow of my shoulder, I read to him & my Beloved slept' (17 March 1802), is omitted, as is this description of the two crossing Stanemoor on the coach when rain came on: 'we buttoned ourselves up, both together in the Guard's coat & we liked the hills & the Rain the better for bringing [us] so close to one another—I never rode more snugly' (14 July 1802).

It is in his treatment of Wordsworth's wedding-day and his marriage, however, that Knight's discomfiture is most apparent, as well it might be, given that what Dorothy records and the way in which she records it are astonishing.

As the narrative approaches October 1802 Knight shifts from narrative to commentary. 'Readers of the Journal that follows in this chapter may be surprised at the way the marriage at Brompton is recorded, and still more at what followed it;—the poet, his wife, and sister, all starting together in a post-chaise for Westmoreland!' (I. 339), he observes. Clearly Knight thought such behaviour only explicable from the poet's lack of interest in sex. Wordsworth's 'austerity', he comments, meant that he was blind to 'one side of our complex human life . . . (I grant it to be a lower side) . . .' (I. 339). Eulogy of Mary Hutchinson, who in his view behaved better on the wedding-day than either William or Dorothy, leads to comment on Dorothy which is designed to explain why 'her brother was the very light of her eyes', but which Knight recognizes fast becomes 'criticism, from which I return with speed to the narrative' (I. 339–40). But he cannot quite let the subject rest. Before actually quoting from Dorothy's journal Knight discourses on the fact that Wordsworth's marriage was *not* very important to him, but that judging by 'any ordinary standard' would be inappropriate for one who 'went on, in his own intense way of visionary musing, though at times of painful self-involvement, profound yet *solitary*, wrapt in contemplation of ideal visions' (I. 341).

By focusing the reader's attention on Wordsworth's marriage in this paragraph—whose uncharacteristically soupy prose suggests how uneasy he is with this material—Knight diverts it from what is most fascinating about Dorothy's journal entries at this period, namely the insight they give into the feelings of brother and sister for one another. And as if recognizing his feint, Knight does return again now to the issue of Dorothy's importance to William, repeating what *The Prelude* says about her redemptive role before summarizing in a question which is also a challenge: 'Was it strange that one who had been thus identified with him, in the one great crisis of his life, should remain to the end, a part of his very being?' (I. 342).

Having provided both a diversionary and an anodyne gloss on the journal entries, Knight at last presents them, but the most remarkable detail of all he omits. The wedding-day entry reads:

On Monday 4th October 1802, my Brother William was married to Mary Hutchinson. I slept a good deal of the night & rose fresh & well in the morning—at a little after 8 o clock I saw them go down the avenue towards the Church. William had parted from me up stairs. *I gave him the wedding ring—with how deep a blessing! I took it from my forefinger where I had worn it the whole of the night before—he slipped it again onto my finger and blessed me fervently.* When they were absent my dear little Sara prepared the breakfast. . . .

Knight omits, without indication, everything in italics. In the manuscript of the Grasmere journal the italicized words are inked out, but as their most recent editor observes, 'under a bright light, they can be read with the naked eye' and Helen Darbishire managed to recover them without sophisticated aids in 1958.[60] Given that the nature of Knight's elision here is consistent with all of his others it seems unlikely that the omission has anything to do with his eyesight.

Presenting Dorothy Wordsworth's journals in the edition and the *Life* Knight suppressed whatever might have given rise to inappropriate conjecture about the lifelong devotion of brother and sister and he continued to do so almost as totally when he edited the journals as a separate publication in 1897.[61] It is not difficult to imagine his justification. In the *Life* Knight had repeated what *The Prelude* had affirmed about Dorothy's importance to Wordsworth *as a poet*. Nothing else, it could be argued, was relevant.

As he began his work on Wordsworth Knight already knew that Wordsworth reverenced his sister. This much was obvious to anyone familar with the poetry and so when he studied the manuscript journals Knight was already aware in part of what he would find. The intensity of the relationship was a revelation, but not the existence of a close bond in itself. The uncovering of Wordsworth's illegitimate daughter, by contrast, issued from scholarly detection applied to a variety of documents, whose result Knight could not have anticipated. As he edited the poetry and gathered materials for his biography of Wordsworth, the Professor of Moral Philosophy was piecing together the puzzle of what had become, posthumously, the secret of the poet's life.[62]

In the 1802 sonnet 'It is a beauteous evening, calm and free' Wordsworth addressed someone as 'Dear Child! dear Girl!'. Who was she? Annotating the poem for the second volume of the *Poetical Works*, published in 1882, Knight identified her as Dorothy Wordsworth. Given the nature of Wordsworth's address to his sister in *Tintern Abbey* it is a just possible suggestion, although calling a woman 'Dear Child!' when she was 30 years old and your intellectual equal might have seemed a little strange. But the address is not the only odd thing about this poem. The sonnet commemorates a walk along the sea-shore at Calais. What was Wordsworth doing there at all? He was about to get married to Mary Hutchinson and in July had travelled to her home in the north-east to make arrangements. Now, at the very first opportunity to travel to France since 1793 offered by the Peace of Amiens, Wordsworth and Dorothy made the long journey from Gallow Hill to Calais. Not Paris, like so many others swarming to see Napoleon's spoils, but Calais, where Wordsworth seems to have been so little in the mood for a foreign holiday that he thought longingly about cricket, Englishness, and home. As soon as the French visit was over Wordsworth returned north and got married. Why did he make this inexplicable trip at all, and why *now*?

What faced Knight as he transcribed Dorothy's journals was the answer to the first of these questions and material for inferences towards an answer to the second. He learned from numerous entries in 1801 and 1802 that the household at Dove Cottage received letters from 'Annette' and 'Caroline' in France, to which they replied, and that on 22 March 1802 Dorothy and William 'resolved to see Annette, & that Wm should go to Mary'. Four days later Wordsworth wrote to Annette and a little over four months later he and Dorothy were knocking on the door of the lodgings of 'Annette & C' in Calais. The weather was hot and 'We walked by the sea-shore almost every Evening with Annette and Caroline or Wm & I alone'.

Knight knew now why Wordsworth had gone to Calais. But who were Annette and Caroline? A journal entry for 3 July 1802 records delivery of a letter from Annette sent from Blois. Wordsworth stayed in Blois in 1792, so at the very least Knight might have deduced that Wordsworth had then formed a friendship which had lasted through nine years of war, which Dorothy knew about, and which was of such importance that once opportunity offered itself they 'resolved to see Annette', despite the travelling and the expense involved.

It is impossible to know what Knight thought about this evidence as he first encountered it around 1882, but what is clear is that by the time he wrote the *Life of William Wordsworth* he had decided to suppress almost all of it and to give no prompt to conjecture. 'We do not know much of how Wordsworth spent his time at Blois' (IX. 64), Knight observes, even more tight-lipped than Christopher Wordsworth had been, and then ensures that no reader can make any connection later by suppressing altogether Dorothy's journal entry for 3 July 1802 with its reference to a letter from Blois. The omission is clearly deliberate. Chapter 15 of the biography consists largely of extracts from the Grasmere journal and the entries for 2 and 4 July are reproduced in part. But receipt of Annette's letter is not reproduced, nor the entry for 5 July in which Dorothy noted that she sent letters to various friends including Annette. Dorothy entered: 'Wrote to Annette Mrs Clarkson, MH, & Coleridge'. Knight prints this sentence minus 'Annette'.

Knight does reproduce Dorothy's Calais journal account of how she and William found Annette and Caroline and walked often with them by the sea-shore. But its significance is greatly reduced, partly because he has excised all mention of the correspondence with Annette and thus veiled the reason for the visit to France, and partly because Knight does not speculate at all about why Wordsworth might have made this strangely timed journey. A biographer who trumpeted his faith in fact and chronology ought at the least to have given the evidence that the mysterious Annette and Caroline were not just chance acquaintances.

Had Knight drawn the right conclusion? Almost certainly, yes. In the prefatory account of his sources for the *Poetical Works* Knight says that he has looked at Henry Crabb Robinson's diaries and in the *Life* he notes that he has examined them afresh and gained enormously from them. Here Knight would have found plenty of astonishing material—evidence that the Wordsworths spent time with Annette, Caroline, and her husband in Paris in 1820 and that Caroline adressed the visiting Englishman as 'father'; that in 1834–5 Crabb Robinson was negotiating on Wordsworth's behalf about regular payments of money to a 'Mons. Baudouin' in Paris; and that after the poet's death Crabb Robinson was involved with the same person over money when threats seem to have been in the air.[63] Blackmail? And the truth was there too. Under 28 September 1820 Crabb Robinson refers to 'conversation with Miss Baudouin, whose brother married a natural child of Wordsworth'. This and other snippets of information are locked away in a shorthand-longhand combination of the diarist's own devising. Did Knight unlock it? It would be very surprising if he did not try. To any biographer code, especially in a diary, is like the X on a map of buried treasure.

Another fragment of evidence would have helped tie together Wordsworth and the French family. In 1817 Wordsworth wrote to his old friend Daniel Stuart, who had been helping him transfer money to France, to ask what sum exactly 'Mr Baudouin' had recently received.[64] The first paragraph of the letter is all about money, the second longer one about politics. This document was much reprinted. It appeared in Knight's biography, in *Letters from the Lake Poets . . . to Daniel Stuart* (1889), and in Knight's later *Letters of the Wordsworth Family* (1907).[65] In every case the first paragraph is omitted. There is no doubt that by the time he was completing work on the family letters in 1906 Knight knew what was in this one and that, as other letters confirmed the conjecture he had offered Gordon Wordsworth around 1895, he wanted now to print the text in full.[66] But did he know the full contents of the letter to Stuart when he was writing the biography? In his preface he thanks Miss Stuart 'for use of the letters' sent to her father. Did she send the importunate professor the original, or only a censored copy?

Whether or not Knight knew the full text of the letter to Stuart, by the time he was writing the biography he had seen sufficient evidence to understand the origin and nature of Wordsworth's dealings with Annette, Caroline, and 'Mons. Baudouin'. Such knowledge placed him in a very tight position. It may be that free from any external pressure Knight would still have judged that there was no call for revelation of Wordsworth's early sexual experience. A case could plausibly be made, after all, that it had not greatly influenced his growth *as a poet*. But Knight was not free from pressing considerations. Good relations with William Wordsworth Jr. and the rest of the family had only been established with some difficulty and it was vital that they be maintained. But it was evident from the open manner with which he had lent out his aunt Dorothy's journals that the head of the family had no idea of the secret they contained. Was Knight to be the one who told the son what his father had withheld from him? Knight was, moreover, the prime mover in the Wordsworth Society, a body of august persons whose image of the poet certainly did not include the possibility of an illegitimate child. What an irony if the result of his call for members to amass every scrap of information about Wordsworth and his family were to be the disclosure that his conduct had not always been above reproach.

Knight opted for suppression and the next scholarly biographer, George McLean Harper, suggested that he did so in collusion with the Wordsworth family. Commenting on Christopher Wordsworth's scanty treatment of the poet's residence in France, he acknowledged that there had been legitimate 'theological, political, and domestic reasons' for reticence. 'Unfortunately', Harper continues, 'Professor Knight, in his voluminous "Life," was affected by the same restrictions . . .'.[67] But soft though this impeachment is, it is unfair. It was not until around 1895 that Knight told Gordon Graham Wordsworth—now head of the family following the death of his father in 1883—of his surmise about Annette and Caroline and the response he received was dismissive. Ironically, Gordon Wordsworth scouted the story as 'idle gossip' because he doubted the scholarship of the messenger. 'Careful weighing of evidence', he observed, 'was not [Knight's] strongest point.'[68] All that Knight could do was to declare in his 1896 edition of Wordsworth's poems that a new biography was one of the desiderata of Wordsworth scholarship, a remark that must have struck many of the unknowing public as odd, coming from a scholar whose massive *Life of William Wordsworth* was not yet ten years old.

Knight's scholarly peers would have understood its meaning. At the turn of the century, as James Butler has established, Dowden,

Hutchinson, Legouis, were all in possession of most of the facts. But they did not publish them and it was Knight's editorial and biographical work that determined the image of Wordsworth current until Harper's revelations in 1916. Knight's many volumes had amassed what was surely almost all of the available evidence about the poet and it confirmed that he was the only one of the Romantics whose *life* was as exemplary as his *work*. The private lives of Coleridge, Shelley, and Byron hardly bore inspection, and even Keats's was not, it seemed, free from unwholesomeness.[69] Wordsworth alone was, as Mrs Humphry Ward thankfully observed, 'a *respectable* genius'.[70]

8

The Last Decade: From Wordsworth Society to National Trust

His daily teachers had been woods and rills,
The silence that is in the starry sky,
The sleep that is among the lonely hills.[1]

I

The Wordsworth Society

Engrossed by his passion for Wordsworth and Wordsworthiana William Knight did what all men with a hobby do—he joined, or rather founded, a club. In Grasmere on 29 September 1880 the Wordsworth Society was established, at a meeting which elected Charles Wordsworth, Bishop of St Andrews, as President, George Wilson as Treasurer, and Knight himself as Secretary. The Constitution adopted—which adhered closely to proposals made privately to Knight by Edward Dowden[2]—declared that the organization was to act primarily as 'a bond of union amongst those who are in sympathy with the general teaching and spirit of Wordsworth', but it also listed specific scholarly aims. 'to carry on the literary work which remains to be done in connection with the text and chronology of the poems . . . to collect for preservation, and, if thought desirable, for publication, original letters and unpublished reminiscences of the poet . . . to prepare a record of opinion, with reference to Wordsworth, from 1793 to the present time . . .'.[3] It was also proposed, though not made an article of the Constitution, that the 'Society might, by-and-by, issue a selection of Wordsworth's poems bearing upon the Lake District of England'.[4]

It is no surprise that these objectives are identical to Knight's own. According to the official version, put out by the Bishop in his presidential address and repeated by Knight after the Society's demise, the Society had grown out of the idea, which 'sprang up amongst a few friends in 1879', of forming a semi-private club to make an annual poetry study excursion to the Lakes.[5] If the idea did just 'spring up', there can be no doubt who planted and watered it, for Knight had in fact been sounding out influential people about the desirability of a club with specific aims throughout 1880.

Although Matthew Arnold was to tell Knight in 1881 that life was too short for him to join 'your Wordsworth club',[6] the earlier auguries had been good. The Chancellor, Lord Selborne (Roundell Palmer), for one, shared the professor's enthusiasm for a club.[7] Ruskin's approval was welcome and his name could be used in the recruitment drive, even if his actual response to Knight's approach did dismiss out of hand the two topics nearest to the latter's heart:

What the text of Wordsworth is is of no consequence—and the localities of less:—one bit of rock or moor is as good as another—and one can gather leeches in any pool, and break stones on any road. But his general temper, teaching, and view of life are of much consequence, and if you set yourselves to illustrate those—you may do endless good, and I shall be honoured in any help you think me able to give you.[8]

Ruskin joined. Leslie Stephen joined and nominated James Russell Lowell, a future President of the Society. Professor Edward Dowden in Dublin sent Knight a list of the great and the good who ought to be approached and soon His Grace the Archbishop of Dublin became a member,[9] as did the Reverend E. H. Cradock, Principal of Brasenose College, Oxford, Professor Edward Caird, the Reverend Stopford Brooke, Dorothea Beale and Frances Buss, the great movers in the education of women, Lord Coleridge, Robert Browning, W. E. Forster, Secretary of State for Ireland, F. J. Furnivall, the Reverend Alexander Grosart, the Principal of Owens College, Manchester, Professor David Masson, Lord Houghton, the Honourable Roden Noel, Principal Shairp, John Shorthouse, author of *John Inglesant*, Aubrey de Vere, and Ellis Yarnall from Philadelphia. Wordsworths and Arnolds of course joined—even Matthew Arnold himself, who could hardly not join when the members of the Society elected him their President.[10]

The 1884 membership list printed as an appendix below indicates the complexion of the Society—middle and upper class and predominantly mainstream Anglican—and its proceedings reflect the august membership. After two meetings in Grasmere all pretence that this was any sort of Lake District reading party was dropped and the Society thereafter convened in London, rising from the Freemasons' Tavern in 1882, with Robert Browning in the chair, to the Jerusalem Chamber, Westminster Abbey, in 1886. Once the administrative items were completed and the Secretary had reported on the year's activities, the members listened to the presidential address and long papers which were not at all light after-dinner speeches—'Wordsworths's Modernisations from Chaucer' (Dowden), 'The Early and Late Styles of Wordsworth' (Hutton), 'On the Poetic Interpretation of Nature' (Roden Noel), 'The Theism of Wordsworth' (Veitch). Other papers were published in the *Transactions of the Wordsworth Society*.

As a formal record of proceedings the *Transactions* give little idea of what the meetings were actually like. Did anyone nod off on 3 May 1882 during Knight's reading of Dowden's paper on Wordsworth's Chaucer? Did the little spat between Lord Houghton and R. H. Hutton over Wordsworth's supposed lack of humour raise the temperature on 8 July 1885? Did anyone feel it indecorous that on the same occasion Lord Houghton—a very minor poet even though he was a Lord—should have claimed poetic kin by reminding the members that he had himself written a sonnet countering the poet's own on the incursion of the railways into the Lake District?[11] The *Transactions* do not say. The Secretary reports; the President addresses; a vote of thanks is moved; a motion is proposed and seconded. Only towards the end of the series is there a discordant note when Knight, feeling the exasperation known to anyone who has ever been the secretary of a society, reports on 8 July 1885 that a meeting of the executive committee did not take place the day before as, 'although the day was specially chosen to suit the convenience of members, only one of them besides myself could find it possible to attend', and that of the thirty members he had approached for papers, only two had promised to submit one—'a pretty clear indication', Knight remarks, 'that the Society ought to conclude its work without delay'.

Perhaps the poor turn-out was not simply the result of slackening zeal. Many of the Society's eminent members were elderly and their awareness of this fact emerges from the pages of the *Transactions* in a discernible odour of belatedness. The atmosphere of the meeting on 2 May 1883 is caught in Matthew Arnold's comment to his wife: 'The grave would have been cheerful compared to the view

presented by the Westminster Chamber and the assembled Wordsworth Society . . . the Society is not composed of people of a festive
type.'[12] But it has to be said that the President did little to raise their
spirits, when he introduced himself as one who, having in view life's
'inevitable close' and tired of 'life's business . . . its labour and
contention', really wanted to enter a monastery. Of course it was a
pose, one Arnold had been adopting for years, but its current
aptness was reflected in what he went on to say, which was nothing
more than a tired restatement of earlier utterances. Lord Houghton
in the presidential chair on 8 July 1885 reminisced over his youthful
enthusiasm of the 1830s and before the next meeting he was dead.
Similarly James Russell Lowell on 10 May 1884 observed that he
had already had his say over twenty years ago and that it was 'as
wearisome to repeat one's-self as it is to repeat others'. Aubrey de
Vere's memories reached back to the 1830s, as did those of Lord
Selborne, who in a long and rather moving presidential address to
the concluding meeting on 7 July 1886 recalled the beginning of a
lifetime's worship 'at the innermost shrine of Wordsworth', during
his undergraduate days at Oxford.

If these luminaries were weary with age, however, William
Knight was not. From the start he had concurred with Dowden's
notion that the Society should be a working group, pledged to
dissolve itself once the limited, practical aims defined in its
constitution, were achieved, and in pursuit of those aims he was
indefatigable. Adept at corralling others, but in fact doing most of
the work himself as part of his ongoing labours as editor and
biographer, Knight issued a series of papers which made the
Transactions a primary scholarly resource. He published bibliographies of Wordsworth's publications and a list of the poems in
chronological order; bibliographies of periodical criticism and of
Wordsworth's influence in America; a bibliography of letters in the
Dyce and Forster collections in the South Kensington Museum and
of the known portraits of the poet; a great many previously
unpublished letters and a reproduction of the Rydal Mount library
sale catalogue.

Substantial though these achievements were, two projects dear to
Knight remained unfulfilled when the Society was dissolved in
1886. The first was the idea floated at the inaugural meeting that
the Society should issue its own selection from Wordsworth's
poems. Although it was not enshrined in the constitution as one of

the Society's objects, Knight always treated the project as if it were. In 1884 he indicated that the selection was to be made by a committee of twelve or so members, and when he came to edit the *Transactions* he was able to report 'definite progress', even though from his actual words at the final meeting in 1886 it is clear that little had been done. In fact it was 1888 before *Selections From Wordsworth*, by William Knight and Other Members of the Wordsworth Society was published by Kegan Paul, Trench and Co..

It is not difficult to imagine why there was such a delay. Canvassed for his opinion in 1880 on the choice of text Lord Selborne observed: 'I should at once say, Take—not the earliest text, nor the latest,—but the *best* text, if it were not for the inevitable differences of opinion, as to which *is* the best.'[13] This was obliging but no more helpful than Ruskin's flat, 'What the text of Wordsworth is is of no consequence', and had Knight continued to try to edit by committee it is unlikely that the book would ever have appeared. Eventually he recognized that he had to lead from the front and as usual he did so with gusto. By 1886—the year of 'definite progress'—he was firing off letters to the informal committee parcelling out responsibility and suggesting choices. Dictating would perhaps be the more accurate word. In a letter to Charles Wordsworth, Bishop of St Andrews, for example, Knight wooingly asserted that nothing could be more appropriate than that the Bishop should make the selection from the *Ecclesiastical Sonnets*, but then he went on to detail exactly the number of sonnets to be included, the selection he proposed, and even the principle of selection, namely, that 'the literary intent & excellence must guide us, in *this* Selection, more than the ecclesiastical or doctrinal'.[14] The Bishop made his suggestions in annotation to Knight's letter, but not one of them was adopted. The selection from the *Ecclesiastical Sonnets* appeared exactly as Knight had proposed.

The *Selections* is fuller than Arnold's competitor volume and the poems are more sensibly presented, in chronological order of composition across Wordsworth's whole career from 1786 to 1846. But they do not represent the whole of Wordsworth. No attempt is made to portray the complexion of his lifetime's endeavour. This is a winnowed offering of 'the best'. The poet's radical years are not represented, as they might have been from excerpts from *Guilt and Sorrow* or *The Borderers*. Also absent is the philosophical Wordsworth. The surprising omission of *The Ruined Cottage* and all of the meditative verse of *The Excursion* means that Wordsworth's long struggle with what Coleridge hoped would be 'the first genuine philosophic poem' is erased. The subtle self-interrogator of *The Prelude* does not appear, save in the discrete extracts Wordsworth chose to publish in his lifetime.[15] And Wordsworth the narrative poet hardly figures, *Peter Bell* and *The White Doe of Rylstone* being severely curtailed. However much the members of the Wordsworth Society may have relished papers on 'Wordsworth's Position as an Ethical Teacher' or 'The Theism of Wordsworth', the selection issued in their name is one which tacitly accepts Arnold's contention that 'Wordsworth's poetry is the reality, his philosophy . . . the illusion'.

When first issued the *Selections* was another example of handsome Victorian typography and binding. In the more expensive of its two formats, decorated full vellum binding cased high-quality deckle-edged paper, which lent the book as an object an air of antiquity and vaguely ecclesiastical significance. It sold at twelve shillings in cloth and fifteen shillings in vellum. These details would not be worth mention outside a Wordsworth bibliography, were it not that they point up a rift between the book and Knight's perception of its purpose. No artisan was likely to buy this volume, but it was the artisan masses who most needed its contents. In his 1879 Preface Arnold had sought to identify the nature of Wordsworth's greatness, to make more readily discernible what he had to offer of enduring value. Knight's Preface strikes the same note, but whereas Arnold seems to be addressing the issue of Wordsworth's value *sub specie aeternitatis*, Knight approaches it with the contemporary world oppressively in mind.

In his presidential address to the Wordsworth Society on 7 July 1886 Lord Selborne attempted to sum up what he had learnt from Wordsworth about Man and Nature. Wordsworth's special quality, he suggests, is that he feels sympathy for 'Man everywhere, man in all conditions . . . common men, men in every condition of life', that the poet saw 'that which was great, that which was divine, that which was beautiful pervading them all, in every condition'. Such sympathy is 'a great thing', he continued, 'because there is in the world in which we live a wonderful amount of distracting force in the glory and glitter of worldly success, worldly ambition, and in the miserable inequality of ranks'. To which he added: 'I do not say this in any socialistic sense, but I say it in the sense of a man sympathising with his fellow-men.'[16]

Disquisitions on Wordsworth's 'sympathy' are so commonplace in Victorian tributes that one would not expect anyone to be ruffled by yet another, so why did the elderly President of the Wordsworth Society on this occasion feel constrained to limit possible interpretation of his words and pointedly to disallow the 'socialistic'? Wordsworth had declared that 'We have all of us one human heart', and in the 1880s there were those who were translating this truth into threatening political action. In a period of renewed trade depression, when striking miners and cotton workers focused attention on the poverty of those in work and newspaper articles and books daily illuminated the degradation of those who were not, everyone hearing Lord Selborne's words could have joined with him in deploring 'the miserable inequality of ranks'. But Socialism was quite another matter and it seemed to be making headway. The Socialist League was numerically small, but it received a lot of notice, not least because its leading member, William Morris, repeatedly appeared in court on public order charges. In 1884 H. M. Hyndman's Democratic Federation changed its name to the Social Democratic Federation and members of it had been to the fore when a rally of the unemployed in 1886 rampaged through St James's, smashing the windows of the Pall Mall clubs. The following year saw much more serious disturbance in Trafalgar Square, when on 'Bloody Sunday', 13 November, leaders of the SDF were arrested and subsequently imprisoned. Only a week later Alfred Linnell was killed by mounted police near the same spot and William Morris spoke at his grave of the 'holy war' in which Socialists were engaged.[17] With the creation of the first Socialist martyr, Hyndman's scheduled date of 1889 for the British Revolution seemed a shade less unlikely.

It is explicitly as a counter to the spirit of these events that Knight presents the *Selections*. There is no need to praise Wordsworth—it would be an impertinence he avers—nor need of more book-making. But there is an urgent need that Wordsworth should reach the masses. Knight observes that in a period of national crisis the poet had called on the shade of Milton: 'Milton, thou should'st be living at this hour, | England hath need of thee'. These words must now be applied to Wordsworth himself:

We do not wish him back amongst us, but we desire that his influence should increase, for nothing is more needed in our time than the elevating and tranquilising influence of poetry of the first magnitude,—such poetry as lifts us above ourselves to what is great, elemental, and enduring. The publication, in a convenient form, of the best things that Wordsworth has given us—issued with the sanction of representative members of a Society founded to promote the study of his works, and edited by several of them in concert—should help towards this end.[18]

In the same year William Watson's elegiac poem, *Wordsworth's Grave*, presented a similar nostrum. His Wordsworth offers what men *now* most crave, 'Peace—peace—and rest!' In the first decade of the century Francis Jeffrey and others had detected in Wordsworth's poetry sedition, a maverick spirit at odds with the norms of society. At the beginning of the last Watson sees in it the norm from which a disordered age has strayed. And here in Watson's leaden verses one strand of the Victorian construction of Wordsworth is finally played out. The Wordsworth who saluted the imprisoned Toussaint L'Ouverture with a paean to 'Man's unconquerable mind' could always be recruited to oppose evident tyranny. Stopford Brooke was to do so in 1897 when he issued *Poems Dedicated to National Independence and Liberty*, 'Reprinted on behalf of the Greek Struggle for the Independence of Crete', and of course it was this Wordsworth who was summoned during the Great War.[19] To those suffering at home, however, what Wordsworth can most valuably offer is an antidote to 'socialistic' fretting and unrest—contemplation of the enduring and 'Rest! . . . and peace! . . . shade . . . for spirits fevered with sun'.[20]

Playing, as does Arnold's poem *The Youth of Nature*, with the place-names Wordsworth had made known throughout the English-speaking world—Rydal, Helm Crag, Silver How—Watson's poem merges the power of the poetry with the beauty and serenity of one place and leads the seeker to a shrine at the heart of it—Wordsworth's grave in Grasmere churchyard. William Knight would have approved. The author of *The English Lake District As Interpreted in the Poems of Wordsworth* (1878) was obsessed with amassing all that could be known about the Lake District of Wordsworth's poems and with ensuring that what evidence remained of Wordsworth's actual life there should be preserved. The establishment of a suitable Wordsworth memorial was the second project outstanding on Knight's agenda when the Wordsworth Society was dissolved.

From a number of acts of local piety projected or carried through—such as the screwing of a glass plate over the desk in Hawkshead School on which Wordsworth had carved his name—one achievement could be pointed to with justifiable satisfaction. On 29 September 1800 William and Dorothy Wordsworth accompanied their brother John to the point at Grisedale Tarn where the path drops towards Patterdale. As they 'stood still till [they] could see him no longer, watching him as he *hurried* down the stony mountain', they did not know they would never see him again. Five years later Wordsworth stood on the same spot, blinded by tears for his drowned brother, and extemporized a memorial poem.[21] For Wordsworthians this parting and the poems commemorating it hallow an austerely beautiful place and by the second meeting of the Wordsworth Society in Grasmere in 1881 it had been decided that some of Wordsworth's elegiac lines should be carved in the rock at the parting place, so as to bring together for hikers passing by the biographical fact, Wordsworth's poetry, and the mountain landscape itself.

The prime mover in the creation of the memorial was the Reverend Hardwicke Drummond Rawnsley, a man of extraordinary energy and pertinacity. Initiated early into Wordsworth by his headmaster at Uppingham School, Edward Thring, Rawnsley fell under Ruskin's spell while at Oxford[22] and Wordsworth and Ruskin remained the shapers of his life, second only to Christianity. It was inevitable that as a young Christian idealist Rawnsley should have sought to serve humanity on the edge of the abyss in London and Bristol, but his health gave way and it is impossible to know what might have become of him had his life not changed dramatically in 1877, when the offer came of a living in the gift of his cousins at Low Wray, a small community on north-western Windermere. With Ruskin nearby at Brantwood on Coniston and Grasmere only a few miles away Rawnsley was where he belonged and for the rest of his life he served the Lake District as a vigorously practical priest, first at Wray and then at Crosthwaite, and as an activist against destructive incursions, who became skilled at pulling the levers of local power. He was also a prolific writer and in a series of books about the Lake District he performed a valuable service by recording a great deal about the region's customs and literary associations. Fittingly the last three years of his life were passed in Allan Bank, the Grasmere house Wordsworth had lived in a little over a century before.

As the Wordsworth Society was dissolving both Knight and Rawnsley were keenly aware that now was the time, or probably never, to harness the energies of Wordsworthians met in fellowship towards a grander project, which should act both as a memorial to Wordsworth and as an agent continuing the Society's educative goal to 'promote and extend the study of the poet's works' (article two of the constitution). At the final meeting Knight suggested the possibility of purchasing Dove Cottage. Rawnsley had a more inclusive vision of a memorial building to Southey, Coleridge, and Wordsworth, 'such a building to be a kind of Valhalla for their works and portraits, busts, and any MSS and objects of interest that belonged to them, and to be placed in Keswick, as being the home of Southey and Coleridge, and in the county which gave Wordsworth his birth'.[23] Inevitably a committee was set up.

Although the outcome of these visions was eventually the securing of Dove Cottage and the foundation of what is now the Wordsworth Trust, some time elapsed before anything was done. Rawnsley's scheme foundered and Knight was preoccupied with completing his massive edition and biography. What was needed was the fresh energies of a committed Wordsworthian with access to persons of influence outside the Lake District.

Such was the Reverend Stopford A. Brooke and it was he who pushed through the Dove Cottage project. Brooke is a fascinating figure, whose life opens windows on to many aspects of the Victorian religious culture with which twentieth-century historians are still uneasy. Although he was ordained into the Church of England in 1857, Brooke was the epitome of the clergyman totally devoted to the idea of God, but unsatisfied with dogma of all varieties, and when he began to pack St James's Chapel from 1866 it was clear that his move away from the Church was already under way. The tenor of his *Life of F. W. Robertson* (1865) aroused the suspicion of evangelicals and his odd position as incumbent of a 'proprietary chapel' put him askew of the Anglican establishment, but his intelligent oratory, his determination to preach on social as well as metaphysical topics, and above all the latitudinarianism of his theology won him a devoted following. When the lease on his chapel expired in 1876 his admirers bought for him Bedford Chapel, Bloomsbury, and here, having at last seceded from the Church of England in 1880, he continued to preach until 1895.

An energetic, passionate man, Brooke sought 'to reconcile the two currents of his being in a deep synthesis of Art and Religion, of Nature and Spirit',[24] and not surprisingly in this struggle Wordsworth was an effectual aid. All over Brooke's copy of *The Prelude* marginal notes and extended commentary dating from 1857 testify to a painstaking attempt to understand the full import of every phrase—particularly in Book VIII, 'Love of Nature Leading to Love of Man'—and his explication of such passages as 'Wisdom and Spirit of the Universe' in his sermon-lectures, *Theology in the English Poets*, indicate how closely in spirit the Victorian clergyman felt identified with the Romantic poet of natural theology. Brooke's love of Wordsworth was of course inseparable from love of the Lake District. His biographer declares simply that Grasmere was the place 'which of all places in England he loved the most'.[25]

Brooke's special virtue in 1890, however, was not just that he was a Wordsworthian mystic—a not inconsiderable band—but that he was also a man of the world, with powerful friends. A sometime chaplain to the Queen, with whom he had often dined, and an intimate friend of the Earl and Countess of Carlisle, Brooke numbered amongst his disciples and acquaintances many of London's intellectuals, artists, and earnest seekers-after-truth. His congregation was a subscription list waiting to be opened.

In May 1890 he issued a fund-raising booklet in which it was claimed that the idea of buying Dove Cottage had occurred to his brother William and himself only the year before on a particularly delightful visit to Grasmere: ' "Why should we not try and secure it, as Shakespeare's birthplace is secured, for the eternal possession of those who love English poetry all over the world?" And we agreed to try, and as we walked back to the inn drew up the scheme . . .'.[26] Brooke succeeded, not least because he was businesslike. He made practical and attainable proposals. He had contacted the owner of Dove Cottage—one Edmund Lee of Bradford—had agreed a price at £650, had devised a management structure, and worked out the long-term viability of the undertaking, based on an assessment of the likely number of visitors. At a meeting in London on 30 June 1890 an Executive Committee, consisting of Mr W. G. Brooke, Revd Canon Ainger, Mr C. E. Mathews, Mr James Bryce, MP, Revd H. D. Rawnsley, Revd Stopford A. Brooke, Professor Knight, and Mr George Lillie Craik, was established to buy Dove Cottage. Its money-raising activities were greatly helped by the grandeur of the so-called Provisional Committee, whose names were emblazoned across an early fund-raising leaflet. The list began with Lord Tennyson, the Duke of Argyll, the Earl of Selborne and graduated down through knights, bishops, deans, principals, professors and MPs to such eminent esquires as Edward Burne-Jones, G. F. Watts, Alfred Austin, Aubrey de Vere, and F. W. H. Myers. More than enough money was soon raised to complete the purchase on 9 October 1890, to provide a sweetener to the outgoing tenant, one C. Walmsley, and to pay local handymen to put the building and garden in good order. On 30 June 1891 an account of the year's activities was presented to subscribers, together with a subscription list. The largest sum of £50 was given by 'A Disciple of the Poet who gave us "The Prelude" ', the smallest by 'A Working Woman'—one shilling. A body of trustees was elected and Dove Cottage opened to the public on 27 July 1891.[27]

The early meetings of the trustees continued the institutionalizing of Wordsworth, trammelling poet and poetry with agendas, minutes, and date of next meeting, but they also represented a significant moment in the mediation of Wordsworth into the outside world, the world beyond literary journals, competing editions, academic reputations, and boards of trustees. By raising the money to buy Dove Cottage so that it could be maintained and opened to the public, the trustees identified the heart, so to speak, of Wordsworth. The poems might be read from Calcutta to San Francisco, a source of delight independent of time or place, but their genesis had been here, in a humble cottage in the English Lake District and it had to be preserved, as Brooke's fund-raising appeal put it, 'for the pleasure and good of the English race'.[28]

II

Wordsworth and the Preservation Movement

The saving of Dove Cottage was a practical triumph, but it was also a symbolic gesture, an indication of a wider commitment by Wordsworthians to preservation. At the fourth meeting of the Wordsworth Society on 2 May 1883 William Knight had read out a letter from Ruskin in which he declared that the 'grand function' of the members must be 'to preserve as far as possible in England the conditions of rural life which made Wordsworth himself possible:

and which if destroyed would leave his verse vainer than the Hymns of Orpheus'.[29] Perhaps few of those present would have shared Ruskin's typically all-or-nothing proposition, but none would have demurred from the underlying claim that questions of meaning and value in Wordsworth involved realities beyond the purely literary. He was not the first to image the Lake District as an English *locus amoenus*, nor was he its only poet, but he was its best-known interpreter and his work gave access not only to a landscape of the mind but also to what was really there. Treated as an imaginative source book, Wordsworth's poetry could lead to enjoyment outside the study, which in reciprocation enhanced enjoyment of the poetry. One did not have to pant up Greenhead Ghyll towards Fairfield to appreciate *Michael*, but no Wordsworthian doubted that to do so enriched the poem even as the poem enriched the walk. Of no other poet in the language could this claim seriously be made. Extension of knowledge of Wordsworth was a duty enshrined in the constitution of the Wordsworth Society: preservation of the Lake District was not. It was a duty none the less.

The terms in which the case for conservation might be made had been established by Wordsworth himself much earlier. Obsessed as he was by the need to preserve the moral virtue of 'rural life'—the impetus behind the foundation of the Guild of St George—Ruskin valued poems such as *Michael* which most forcefully displayed it, but those who wanted to argue simply for the preservation of the Lake District as a landscape of particular value found more assistance in Wordsworth's prose than in his verse. For well before conservation was a pressing issue, Wordsworth had defined what was special about the region and later, when threat did loom, he had restated the argument in terms which armed later conservationists with vocabulary and concepts, but which also exposed the difficulties inherent in making the case.

Wordsworth's most sustained hymn to the Lake District—from its earliest form as the letterpress to a volume of *Select Views* in 1810 to its later incarnation as *A Guide Through the District of the Lakes in the North of England*, 1835—is relatively uncontroversial once it is accepted that the audience addressed is 'persons of taste'.[30] In his account of the landscape Wordsworth repeatedly draws attention to unobtrusive beauties of colour, light, and sound, and to the effects of mass and shape that will become apparent with 'exact and considerate observation' to minds 'at once attentive and active' (pp. 171, 211). Some recent developments are deplored, such as the planting of larches, the use of whitewash, and the incursion of inharmonious gentry houses, and there is an elegiac wistfulness on occasion as Wordsworth declares what was 'Till within the last sixty years . . .', but overall the *Guide* is neither defensive nor elegiac.[31] It is a marvellously subtle and eloquent advertisement for the refined pleasures available in this favoured place.

Only in the final paragraph is there a warning note:

> . . . it is probable, that in a few years the country on the margin of the Lakes will fall almost entirely into the possession of gentry, either strangers or natives. It is then much to be wished, that a better taste should prevail among these new proprietors; and, as they cannot be expected to leave things to themselves, that skill and knowledge should prevent unnecessary deviations from that path of simplicity and beauty along which, without design and unconsciously, their humble predecessors have moved. In this wish the author will be joined by persons of pure taste throughout the whole island, who, by their visits (often repeated) to the Lakes in the North of England, testify that they deem the district a sort of national property, in which every man has a right and interest who has an eye to perceive and a heart to enjoy. (pp. 224–5)

The new inhabitants, and by implication the next generation of tourists, need to be worthy of the place.

Ten years after the 1835 *Guide* Wordsworth once again addressed 'all persons of taste', but now he was on the defensive. It was proposed to drive a railway through Kendal on to Windermere, and the clear threat of the first plan for a terminus at Low Wood, actually by the lake shore, was that in the future the line might penetrate the vale of Grasmere and beyond. Wordsworth protested in two letters to the *Morning Post*, not against railways in themselves, but against the extension of existing lines into the heart of the Lake District. What would be the result of facilitating tourists to this extent but 'a destruction of the beauty of the country, which the parties are come in search of? Would not this be pretty much like the child's cutting up his drum to learn where the sound came from?' (p. 346).[32] The railway, it is also argued, is bound to unsettle a way of life that is good in itself. Sheer numbers of people would constitute an invasion the tiny region could not cope with.

There are other points too, but all of these are subsidiary to the main argument which concerns how the Lakes can be 'profitably enjoyed'. Sustaining the proposition implicit throughout the *Guide*, Wordsworth insists that the particular virtue of the area only offers itself to those who are receptive to it, readied either by 'processes of culture or opportunities of observation in some degree habitual' (p. 343). Anyone with 'a mind disposed to peace' (p. 345) will not begrudge the time taken to make a slow entrance to the Lake District from the railhead outside Kendal. Pandering to those who demand speedy access to the choicest beauty spots will not give them profitable pleasure, but it will certainly destroy a wholeness that is fragile, of long evolution, and irreplaceably fine. In a concluding sonnet Wordsworth imagines the mountains echoing to the whistle of the 'long-linked Train' and declares:

> Weighing the mischief with the promised gain,
> Mountains, and Vales, and Floods, I call on you
> To share the passion of a just disdain.

The *Kendal and Windermere Railway* letters and the responses they provoked parade all of the points and the counter-charges that still characterize the conservation debate today. Is Wordsworth's concern for Lake District peace anything more than the selfish alarm of someone who does not want *his* peace disturbed—'not in my backyard'?[33] Why should one sort of pleasure be deemed more 'profitable' than another? Surely the rights of the mass outweigh those of the few? Isn't Mr Wordsworth guilty of condescension to the artisan? Is he opposed to progress? And the campaign was lost: the railway came to Windermere. But Wordsworth had eloquently made the conservationist case and later in the century, when threats to the Lake District multiplied, it was inevitable that those in the forefront of resistance should redeploy his arguments and invoke him as the tutelary spirit of the region.

In 1876 what Wordsworth had feared thirty years earlier rematerialized—the threat to extend the Windermere railway line northwards, along the lake shore to Ambleside, Grasmere, and beyond. Opposition to the scheme was started by a Windermere resident, Robert Somervell, in *A Protest Against the Extension of Railways in the Lake District*, but the pamphlet might not have attracted much attention had Somervell not been able to involve Ruskin.[34] Somervell was an active Companion of the Guild of St George and Ruskin willingly came to the aid of a fellow spirit. He not only urged all those in sympathy with his work to circulate the pamphlet, with its attached petition form, but he also announced in *Fors Clavigera*, Letter 66 (June 1876), that he would receive signed petitions at Brantwood.[35] Ruskin assumed a larger role still by writing a preface to Somervell's *Protest* when it was reissued as a substantial pamphlet with national distribution.[36]

The *Protest* was originally Ruskinian and with the preface it became more emphatically so. Both master and disciple placed the battle against this particular scheme in the wider perspective of Ruskin's campaign against the despoliation of 'the sweet landscapes of England', those 'sacred sibylline books', against the application of utilitarian tests to all questions, against the degradation of the environment in which artisans had to live and work, and against the economic forces accelerating the moral decline of the urban masses. Ruskin is magnificently intemperate and direct throughout the preface, never more so than when he focuses on the future of the one place identified world-wide with Wordsworth—Grasmere. Dismissing the contention that swift transit is necessary to bring workers where they can enjoy scenery, he declares:

all that your railroad company can do for them is only to open taverns and skittle grounds round Grasmere, which will soon, then, be nothing but a pool of drainage, with a beach of broken gingerbeer bottles; and their minds will be no more improved by contemplating the scenery of such a lake than of Blackpool.[37]

Somervell's language is more restrained, proposition rather than assertion:

If we are ever to raise men to communion with the powers of nature,—to develope [*sic*] in them the 'wise passiveness' of the 'heart that watches and receives' her lore—it will not be merely by giving them occasional and hurried glimpses of strange beauty, but by dignifying the labour and adorning the surroundings of their daily life.

But both agree that the real issue is not what might benefit operatives on an occasional holiday excursion, but 'the necessity for a change in the conditions of labour'.[38]

What is striking about Somervell's *Protest* is that in so far as it focuses directly on the local threat to the Lake District he has nothing to add to what Wordsworth had already written. In the quotation above it is Wordsworth's formulations that define the soul of the person receptive to Nature's ministrations, and it is

Wordsworth who provides the bulk of Somervell's environmentalist case. The pamphlet opens with the anti-railway sonnet, 'Is then no nook of English ground secure . . .', and proceeds first to paraphrase and then to quotation pages long from Wordsworth's letters to the *Morning Post*. When the *Daily News* pronounced on the issue it too rested on Wordsworth, not just in a general way to support its judgement that the Lake District should be left inviolate, but also with comical specificity. The projectors of the railway claim that minerals await exploitation. Is this true? The *Daily News* declares it not so, citing the poet's negative of thirty years earlier as if he were a respected mining engineer. In this early stage of the late century assault on the Lake District it is recognized that the Wordsworth of the *Guide* and the *Kendal and Windermere Railway* letters has already articulated the case for the region's defence.

The railway continued to terminate at Windermere (as it still does), but not at bottom because of Wordsworth or Ruskin. The projectors of the extension calculated that it would not pay. Barely had this threat dwindled, however, when another loomed. Manchester needed more water and by 1877 it was determined to get it from the Lake District. As befitted Cottonopolis rampant, its proposal was not modest. In the opinion of the London-based engineer John Frederic Bateman, it would be feasible to enlarge Thirlmere massively and by tunnelling through the hills to bring millions of gallons daily to the thirsty city. With modern technology nothing was impossible. Man would mould Nature to his wishes. But even supporters of the scheme had to concede that one of the Lake District's most beautiful sites was about to suffer more change in a few years than it had undergone since the rocks cooled at its original creation.[39]

Substantial opposition was rapidly mobilized once Manchester's predatory intent became known in late 1877. Somervell, who had learnt what a small pamphlet could do if circulated strategically, was an early mover with *The Manchester and Thirlmere Scheme: An Appeal to the Public on the Facts of the Case*. Ruskin joined in and others nationwide leagued together to form the Thirlmere Defence Association, whose *Statement of the Case* pamphlet is buttressed by a membership list that includes two earls, a bishop, four professors, the head of an Oxford college, and many notable figures from the Lake District.[40] Adverse comment in Hutton's

Spectator (8 Sept. 1877) and a passionate letter to *The Times* (20 Oct.) from the Bishop of Carlisle opened up the debate in the national press. The Thirlmere cause attracted the support of other interest groups, such as the Commons Preservation Society, brought onside by the devout Ruskinian, Octavia Hill.[41] When the Manchester bill was introduced early in 1878 the opposition had managed to spotlight it as a matter of national, not just local concern.

The terms of engagement for the conflict were clearer than they had been in 1876. Opponents of the railway had been vulnerable to the charge that they were trying to exclude the toiling masses from a source of enjoyment and, however disingenuously, the railway projectors played on it. In the case of the Thirlmere scheme the issue was much simpler—had natural beauty any rights? 'I hold the hills and vales of my native land to be the true temples of God,' Ruskin thundered in *Fors*, 'and their waves and clouds holier than the dew of the baptistery, and the incense of the altar.'[42] No one else pitched their opposition at quite this level, but Ruskin's restatement of the elements of Wordsworth's Natural Religion was timely and appropriate. Was the Lake District an unquantifiable good, to be cherished as a 'sort of national property', or was it just another natural resource to be exploited?[43]

Somervell's *Appeal to the Public* presented the opposition case in essence. Letters and articles in the press debated particulars— whether alternative water supplies existed, whether by preventing piecemeal development the Manchester scheme might actually preserve the Thirlmere area, and so on—but his argument was the Thirlmere Defence Association's creed:

. . . we have to consider, not ourselves only, but the interests of those who will come after us. The sentiment of beauty in Nature, and the love of mountain scenery, have been much developed of late years, and are likely to increase in power and importance. Much that is hurtful and destructive has been done, both to Nature and Art, in the hurry and excitement of this age of mechanical enterprise; and the cheering revival of some consideration for the beautiful—though too often misdirected—makes it certain that such scenes of natural grandeur or loveliness as are still unspoiled will be doubly dear to the next generation. . . . when we remember that the possibilities of enjoying natural scenery are being every year curtailed; we must surely feel that nothing short of a cogent and inevitable necessity must exist, before the people of this country suffer the spoiling of their free and birthright inheritance in the loveliness of this Cumberland valley.[44]

And this was the line taken by no less a figure than the member for Bradford, W. E. Forster, when the bill had its second reading on 12 February 1878. Urging MPs to acknowledge that 'the scenery of the Lakes is a public interest' and that 'the object of the House of Commons' must be to preserve 'some of the most beautiful scenery in the world', Forster managed to have the bill remitted a Select Committee, charged with scrutinizing it in its widest aspects and not just 'on those narrow and technical grounds to which . . . Committees are accustomed to confine their attention in dealing with ordinary private Bills'.[45]

Manchester's case rested on impressive sounding figures—inflow, outflow, holding capacity, measured in millions of gallons daily. Whatever its opponents could put up was bound to be disparaged as 'sentimental'. The power of this charge could be lessened by subtle argument—one MP claimed, with some justification, that the opponents had a profounder understanding of Utility than the proponents—but the label stuck. And it was the case that for many Wordsworthians there was a strong element of sentiment in their dismay at one consequence of what was proposed for Thirlmere.

There are many natural shrines in the Lake District special to lovers of Wordsworth's poetry because they were special to the poet himself. These are not the spurious inventions of heritage-mongers, but places mentioned in the poems as wells of particularly intense emotion. 'John's Grove' is one such. The parting place at Grisedale Tarn is another. But none is richer in association than the 'Rock of Names', by the side of the road that skirted the shore of Thirlmere. 'William accompanied Coleridge to the foot of the Rays,' Dorothy Wordsworth noted in her journal for 6 December 1800. 'Sara and I accompanied him half way to Keswick. Thirlemere was very beautiful.' There were many such walks between Dove Cottage and Greta Hall in Keswick in 1800, when it seemed that the Wordsworths and Coleridge might re-establish the intimacy they had enjoyed in Somerset in the *annus mirabilis* 1797–8 and in the course of one of them Wordsworth carved his initials on a rock face. Underneath the others followed suit—Mary Hutchinson, Dorothy Wordsworth, Coleridge, John Wordsworth, Sara Hutchinson—and the rock, half-way between the two homes, became a sacred place: 'We parted from Coleridge at Sara's crag, after having looked at the letters whch C. carved in the morning. I kissed them all. William deepened the T. with C's pen-knife.'[46] In

FIG. 6. The 'Rock of Names'

1836 Wordsworth printed as a note to *The Waggoner* an apostrophe to the rock which has held through so many years its 'memorial-trust' of expressing Love:

> Long as for us a genial feeling
> Survives, or one in need of healing,
> The power, dear Rock, around thee cast,
> Thy momumental power, shall last
> For me and mine! . . .
> .   .   .   .
> And fail not Thou, loved Rock! to keep
> Thy charge when we are laid asleep.[47]

When Wordsworth published these lines what the rock had once drawn together had long since been sundered. John Wordsworth, Sara Hutchinson, and Coleridge were dead and Dorothy Wordsworth was unrecognizable as the young woman who had walked the miles with Coleridge to Wythburn. But the memorial remained—that is, it had remained until until 1877 when it became clear that it was doomed to be submerged beneath Manchester's new reservoir.

To the unidentified author of *The New 'Paradise Lost'. A Poem. Addressed to the People of England and Inscribed to the Thirlmere Defence Association* the threat to the 'Rock of Names' signalled the nature of this conflict. The spirit of place and poetic feeling faced the hard facts brigade, composed of people without historical awareness, or sentiment, or a sense of fitness:

> Then shall the Rock upon the western shore
> Pass from its office at untimely hour,
> And speak no more its single-lettered lore.
> Say now, O Tempter, wilt thou thus deflower
> A monumental pile of mystic power?
> '*Bah! who was Wordsworth that he thus should drag*
> *His "W.W." into all this stour?*
> *If need exists for some such empty brag*
> *We'll make another Rock,—and call it "Batemans's Crag!"*'[48]

To William Knight the threat made the duty of all Wordsworthians even more pressing. His *The English Lake District As Interpreted in the Poems of Wordsworth*, which appeared in the same year as Manchester's bill was debated in the House of Commons, was more than a guidebook. It was an act of historical salvage, a record of places 'undergoing change, and becoming more difficult to identify every year. Such a memorial, for example, as "the Rock of Names," on the shore of Thirlmere, is threatened with immersion fathoms deep below the waters of a Manchester reservoir.'[49] Nine years later, by which time the navvies were hard at work by Thirlmere, Knight again drew attention to the 'Rock of Names', this time complementing his text with a full-page drawing by Harry Goodwin.[50]

To no avail: the 'Rock of Names' was destroyed. The Select Committee imposed certain stipulations, but gave the go-ahead for Manchester to reintroduce its bill. When it did so in 1879 the Thirlmere Defence Association, weakened by internal strife, had spent its force and the Thirlmere proposal was approved all but unopposed.[51] In due course Hardwicke Drummond Rawnsley collected the fragments of the rock and had them built into a cairn, but the other landmarks on Benjamin the waggoner's tipsy journey disappeared forever.[52]

No one took the Thirlmere defeat more to heart than Rawnsley, but unlike Ruskin and many others in the campaign he was still vigorous enough in his early thirties to learn from it, and to retain his optimism that in the conflict between Utility and Beauty it was not inevitable that Beauty should lose. The struggle against Manchester demonstrated the power of an energetically conducted public relations campaign. Big names carried weight. Letters to the press kept the issues in public view. Repeated rebuttals of the opposition's claims, together with reiteration of the main arguments, promoted the impression that the Defence Association had a strong case. The proceedings in the House of Commons possibly indicated a shift in national mood. The preservationist cause had certainly had a more sympathetic hearing that it might have expected twenty years earlier. Manchester had won the day, but not before it had been acknowledged in the legislature that the natural beauty of the Lake District had to be taken into account when weighing the merits of the city's case. Rawnsley learned, too, something about the nature of politics. It was evident that to wield national influence one needed a secure footing in local society and having accepted defeat, he was astute enough to realize that pressure could only be brought to bear on Manchester now by working with the operation and not against it. When the Thirlmere works were formally opened on 12 October 1894 it was Rawnsley who led the prayers, delivered an address, and celebrated the occasion in verse. This was not the action of a turncoat, but of someone who had rightly gauged the realities of local politics.

By this time Rawnsley had become a substantial figure in local and national conservation movements—his dreadful sonnets notwithstanding. In 1883 he led the opposition to the proposal to push a railway line from Braithwaite, near Keswick, into the heart of Lakeland at Buttermere, largely for the benefit of quarry owners. Once again a press campaign and energetic lobbying privately of influential people turned a local issue into a national one, which played some part—though not as large a part as Rawnsley liked to believe—in influencing the line's proposers to withdraw. Almost at once another proposal surfaced, for a line to the head of Ennerdale Water, and once again Rawnsley and his allies had to mobilize local and national opinion.

What had come into being was a *de facto* Lake District Defence Committee, quite distinct from the Lake District Association, from which Rawnsley seceded and ever after anathematized as a treacherous body, no more than a cloak for self-interested promoters of tourism. But it was clear that, faced with Hydra-headed threats, the Lake District needed a disinterested, standing organization, charged with raising funds and mobilizing opinion for the defence of the region whenever threats materialized. In Rawnsley's view it could most appropriately muster under the banner of Wordworth.

On 2 May 1883 at the fourth meeting of the Wordsworth Society Rawnsley recapped recent events to explain the origins of the proposal for a Permanent Lake District Defence Society. Members had just listened to a paper on Wordsworth's *Guide to the Lakes* from Stopford Brooke, a cue for Rawnsley to remind them of its contemporary relevance. The Braithwaite and Buttermere campaign had been hard fought and, Rawnsley declared, 'to Wordsworth is owed all thanks for the winning of it'.[53] Listing the Wordsworthian heroes of the battle—Professor Knight, 'a sheet-anchor of hope and encouragement', Principal Shairp, Professor Blackie, Professor Campbell Fraser, Professor Veitch, Professor Caird, Frederic Harrison, J. H. Shorthouse, Professor Dowden, and others— Rawnsley conjured up the image of an army of doughty warriors, needing only a commander and a general staff to weld them into a still more effective force. The Lake District Defence Society was coming into being and Rawnsley suggested, 'as many members of the Wordsworth Society have already shown their zeal in the cause, it would be a gracious act to the memory of the great poet, if, as a body, they elected to co-operate [with it]'. Rawnsley was to be the society's secretary and his ardour carried the day. In the surviving list of members the whole of the Wordsworth Society is entered as a single item, '*per* Professor Knight'.[54]

Rawnsley's address to the Wordsworth Society is one of the more important documents in the history of conservation in Great Britain because it brought together three ideas—not new or originating in him—which mark the advance of the cause into a new phase. The first is one that Rawnsley had expounded in a private letter on the Braithwaite and Buttermere railway: 'We feel that each year England's pleasure grounds are diminished, that these are not only *pleasure* grounds but *thinking* grounds, & capable of enriching the nation with high thoughts & so are part of the nation's wealth.'[55] To the Wordsworth Society Rawnsley optimistically observed that 'England is beginning to become a nation that believes in education', and he quoted Professor Campbell Fraser's 'wise words' that 'At least the vales of Cumberland and Westmoreland, charged with the spirit of Wordsworth, must be left . . . as Nature's own English University in the age of great cities'. Elementary education had only recently been made compulsory, but few from the great cities would go futher. Here in the mountains, however, was a college open to all. Beauty is not just a national resource for pleasure and refreshment: it serves a higher and vital purpose.[56]

The second proposition was that defenders of the Lake District ought to join forces with other associations. Rawnsley was a lifelong friend of Octavia Hill, to whom he had been introduced by Ruskin, and so it was on the basis of friendship as well as of the history of its notable triumphs against enclosures of common land in the environs of London, that he should mention the Commons Preservation Society, and Hill's Kyrle Society, dedicated to bringing beauty into poor people's lives through a variety of local initiatives.[57] Rawnsley also mentions 'the Ruskin Society'. The following year he joined the Guild of St George, a further recognition that the living sage played as great a part in Rawnsley's spritual development as the dead poet.[58] At this stage Rawnsley talks only of co-operation between groups with 'kindred aims', but his vision is clearly of a national effort in which defence of the Lake District would only be a part.

The third proposition is no more than a hint, but it is the boldest of the three. At one point in his address Rawnsley remarks: 'Some time hence, who knows, a wise Government may enable the Lake District to have a special Act to protect it from railroad outrage for the people, as has been done in the Yosemite Valley of America (though there the State not only provided an Act, but first bought it up for the people's use)'. Similarly far-sighted action in the Adirondacks is also noted.

The comparison with America caught on. Here perhaps was a model, a society recognizing the value of its wild places before it was too late. In 1887 even a provincial journal such as the *Lancaster Observer* could observe that the Lake District ought to be acquired as a 'National Treasure', like the Yellowstone National Park, and its suggestion prompted a letter from Ruskin, glad to 'concur with you in the recommendation that the whole Lake District should be bought by the nation for itself'.[59] The optimism about America was based on very partial information. Neither Rawnsley nor Ruskin knew much if anything about the vicious lobbying, the deals and chicanery, which characterized the politics of the establishment of America's national parks. Nor was the analogy apt. Unlike Yosemite or Yellowstone, the Lake District was not wilderness, but land largely in private ownership, where every dry-stone wall signalled somebody's proprietorial rights.[60] But the idea of a *national* effort at preservation had emerged.

Critical mass had been achieved. A large number of people, many of them distinguished in public life, were now paid up members of this or that preservation society. A small number had emerged as leaders, activists, and gifted publicists. And causes were not wanting. In 1893, agitated by yet another threat to the northern Lake District, Rawnsley sought help from the Commons Preservation Society and Octavia Hill. She approached the Duke of Westminster, while her ally, the lawyer Robert Hunter, set to work drafting proposals. The result was the formation of the National Trust for Places of Historic Interest or Natural Beauty, formally inaugurated on 12 January 1895.

What was the origin of this body that has had an incalculable influence not just on the environment but on the psyche of twentieth-century Britain? John K. Walton has argued that 'it would be difficult to imagine the National Trust emerging if Ruskin had not provided ways of looking at the world which helped to make it thinkable, providing its founders with, in the loosest sense, language and a discourse', and he is clearly right. Ruskin was a living presence, not just for Octavia Hill and Rawnsley but for many other lesser figures who joined the Trust's Council or advanced its work in practical ways.[61] But Wordsworth's had been the originating 'language and discourse' and it is in the *Guide to the Lakes* that one finds the germ of the National Trust's long gestation. Perhaps one ought rather to say that the germ was 'Wordsworth', what he stood for and what his disciples made of him.

The search for origins—let alone an origin—always involves the disentangling of complex webs of indebtednesses, allegiances, and pure happenstance. It is impossible to isolate one originating moment in any intellectual and cultural development, or, when primacy is the issue, to assess justly the interrelation of major figures. And it is quite as difficult to weigh fairly the contribution of minor players. In the line that leads from Wordsworth to the National Trust, how much honour, for example, is due to Edward Thring, Headmaster of Uppingham School, who first introduced his favoured pupil Hardwicke Rawnsley to the Lake District on a pilgrimage to the poet's grave? None the less, while recognizing the danger of making exaggerated claims, what can be said with certainty is that without the drive of Wordsworthians the National Trust of 1895 would not have come into being.[62] Possibly a similar organization would have evolved, resting on a different set of personal alliances—it is impossible to know. But this one emerged after twenty years of agitation in which a key part was played by those who acknowledged their allegiance either to Wordsworth, or to the Lake District inseparably associated with his work, or to both. In the *Guide to the Lakes* the poet had spoken of the Lake District as 'a sort of national property in which every man has a right and interest, who has an eye to perceive and a heart to enjoy'. That hundreds of thousands of people every year walk over unenclosed hills, or enjoy access to lake shores, is his greatest, and most fitting memorial.

Appendix
The Membership of The Wordsworth
Society in 1884

ABRAM, J. C., Esq., Lake Row, Keswick.
AGLEN, Revd A. S., MA, The Parsonage, Alyth, NB.
AINGER, Revd ALFRED, MA, Temple Church, 2 Upper Terrace, Hampstead, London, N.
ALBRIGHT, Miss R. A., Mariemount, Birmingham.
ALLISON, R. A., Esq., Scaleby Hall, Carlisle.
ANDERSON, Miss CHARLOTTE, Fettykil, Leslie, Fifeshire.
ARNOLD, Miss FRANCES, Fox How, Ambleside.
ARNOLD, Miss LUCY A., Winstanley, Great Malvern.
ARNOLD, MATTHEW, Esq., MA, DCL, The Athenæum Club, Pall Mall, London, SW.
ATKINS, HENRY, Esq., Surgeon-Major, Bombay Army, ATKINS, Mrs, ATKINS, Miss, 3 Priory Street, Cheltenham.
BALLINGAL, Revd JAMES, MA, Rhynd Manse, Perth.
BARLOW, Miss ALICE, Greenthorn, Bolton.
BAYNE, THOMAS, Esq., MA, Larchfield Academy, Helensburgh.
BAYNE, Mrs, 40 York Terrace, Regent's Park, London, NW.
BAYNES, Professor T. SPENCER, LL D, St Andrews, NB.
BEALE, Miss DOROTHEA, The Ladies' College, Cheltenham.
BELCHER, Miss, The Ladies' College, Cheltenham.
BELL, Revd CANON, MA, The Vicarage, Cheltenham.
BELL, ROBERT, Esq., Seafield, Broughty-Ferry resigned.
BENSON, LOUIS F., Esq., 715 Walnut Street, Philadelphia, USA.
BIRD, Miss ALICE L., 49 Welbeck Street, Cavendish Square, London, W.
BRADLEY, The Very Revd Dean, The Deanery, Westminster, London, SW.
BRADSHAW, JAMES D., Esq., 30 George Street, Hanover Square, London.
BRADY, Professor GEORGE S., MD, Sunderland.
BROADBENT, CHARLES, Esq., The Hollies, Latchford, Warrington.
BROOKE, Revd STOPFORD, MA, LL D, 1 Manchester Square, London, WC.
BROOKES, WILLIAM MURRAY, Esq., 21 Manor Place, Undercliffe, Bradford.
BROWN BORTHWICK, Revd R., MA, All Saints' Vicarage, Scarborough.
BROWNING, ROBERT, Esq., LL D, DCL, 19 Warwick Crescent, London, W.
BRUNSKILL, Revd J., MA, Threlkeld Vicarage, Keswick.

BURNE-JONES, PHILIP, Esq., The Grange, North End Road, West Kensington, London, W.

BURNET, Miss MARY, 2 St James's Place, Glasgow.

BURT, THOMAS, Esq., MP, Loraine Terrace, Newcastle-upon-Tyne.

BUSS, Miss, 89 King Henry's Road, Regent's Park, London.

CAIRD, Professor EDWARD, MA, LL D, CAIRD, Mrs, 1 The College, Glasgow.

CAMERON, JOHN, Esq., Lindores, by Newburgh—*resigned.*

CARPENTER, Professor J. ESTLIN, MA, CARPENTER, Mrs, Leathes House, Fitz John's Avenue, London, NW.

CARR, FRANK, Esq., The Willows, Walker-on-Tyne.

COLERIDGE, The Right Hon. Lord, DCL, 1 Sussex Square, London, W.

COLERIDGE, Miss EDITH, Eldon Lodge, Tor, Torquay.

CONGREVE, Dr, 84 Palace Gardens Terrace, Kensington, London, W.

CONGREVE, Miss JULIA, 12 Ladbroke Road, Notting Hill, London, W.

CONSTABLE, ARCHIBALD, Esq., 11 Thistle Street, Edinburgh.

COTTERILL, C. C., Esq., MA, Glencorse House, Fettes College, Edinburgh.

COUSANS, Miss, The Ladies' College, Cheltenham.

CRADOCK, Revd Principal E. H., MA, DD, Brasenose College, Oxford.

CRAIK, GEORGE L., Esq., 30 Bedford Street, Covent Garden, London, WC.

DANIELL, C. B., Esq., Lightburne House, Ulverston, Lancashire.

DAWSON, Revd A. P., MA, Clarendon Park Road, Leicester.

DENNIS, JOHN, Esq., The Garrick Club, London.

DENTON, Revd W. D., MA, 22 Westbourne Square, London, W.

DESCOURS, PAUL J., Esq., 49 Alderney Street, Pimlico, London, SW.

DEVAS, Mrs, The Quarry, Colwall, West Malvern.

DOVE, Miss, St Leonards, St Andrews, NB.

DOWDEN, Professor EDWARD, MA, LL D, Trinity College, Dublin.

DOWDEN, Revd JOHN, MA, The Cathedral, Edinburgh.

DRAPER, Miss, The Ladies' College, Cheltenham.

DUBLIN, His Grace the Lord Archbishop of, DD, Dublin.

EALES, Miss, The Ladies' College, Cheltenham.

ELLIS, Mrs E. VINER, Sherborne House, Gloucester.

EMLY, The Right Hon. Lord, Tervoe, Limerick.

FIFE, Miss LOUISA, Westoe, South Shields.

FITCH, J. G., Esq., MA, 5 Lancaster Terrace, Regent's Park, London, NW.

FLETCHER, Mrs, The Croft, Ambleside.

FORSTER, The Right Hon. W. E., MP, FORSTER, Mrs, 80 Eccleston Square, London, SW.

FRANKS, WILLIAM EVAN, Esq., 8 Thurlow Place, Lower Norwood, Surrey.

FRASER, Professor CAMPBELL, MA, LL D, FRASER, Mrs, FRASER, Miss, 20 Chester Street, Edinburgh.

FRY, THEODORE, Esq., FRY, Mrs THEODORE, Woodburn, Darlington; and 22 Queen Anne's Gate, London, SW.

FURNIVALL, F. J., Esq., MA, 3 St George's Square, Primrose Hill, London, NW.

GARTHORP, Miss, Victoria House, Leamington.

GARWOOD, EDMUND JOHNSTONE, Esq., GARWOOD, Miss MARGARET ANN, Westoe, South Shields.

GEFFREYS, Mrs GWYN, Ware Priory, Herts—*dead.*

GILLIES, Miss MARGARET, 25 Church Row, Hampstead, London, N.

GOODRICH, LIONEL, Esq., 11 King's Bench Walk, Temple, London, EC.

GRAVES, Revd ROBERT PERCEVAL, MA, 1 Winton Road, Leeson Park, Dublin.

GREENWOOD, Principal, LL D, Owens College, Manchester.

GRETIN, Miss, The Ladies' College, Cheltenham.

GRINDROD, CHARLES, Esq., LRCP (Ed.), Wyche-side, The Wyche, Malvern.

GROSART, Revd ALEXANDER B., DD, Brooklyn House, Blackburn, Lancashire.

HAGUE, EDWIN, Esq., Orange Street, Halifax.

HARRISON, Revd W.A., MA, The Vicarage, St Anns, South Lambeth, London.

HART, Professor CHARLES F., Rutger's College, New Brunswick, New Jersey, USA.

HARVEY, Miss CLARA J., Latchford, Warrington.

HEARD, W. A., Esq., MA, Carrington House, Fettes College, Edinburgh.

HEATON, Miss, 6 Woodhouse Square, Leeds.

HICKEY, Miss E. H., Clifton House, Pond Street, Hampstead, London, NW.

HIGGINS, Miss, 25 Lansdowne Crescent, Cheltenham.

HILLS, WILLIAM HENRY, Esq., The Knoll, Ambleside.

HODGSON, WILLIAM, Esq., The Fifeshire Journal Office, Cupar, Fife.

HOLIDAY, HENRY O., Esq., HOLIDAY, Mrs, Oaktree House, Branch Hill, Hampstead, London, N.

HOUGHTON, The Right Hon. Lord, DCL, Fryston Hall, Ferrybridge, Yorkshire.

HUNT, ALFRED, Esq., MA, HUNT, Mrs, 1 Tor Villas, Campden Hill, London, W.

HUTCHINSON, Miss ELIZABETH, Rock Villa, West Malvern.

HUTCHINSON, Revd THOMAS, MA, Kimbolton, Leominster, Hereford.

HUTTON, RICHARD H., Esq., MA, LL D, The Spectator Office, 1 Wellington Street, Strand, London, WC.

INCHBOLD, J. W., Esq., 32 Grosvenor Street, London, W.

INNES, Miss, The Ladies' College, Cheltenham.

JEBB, Professor R. C., MA, LL D, The College, Glasgow.

JONES, Revd R. CROMPTON, BA, 37 Broadwater Down, Tunbridge Wells.

KENDALL, Revd H. BICKERSTAFFE, 87 Grange Road, Middlesborough.

KINGSLEY, Mrs HENRY, East Liss, Hants.

KNIGHT, Professor WILLIAM, LL D, KNIGHT, Mrs, Edgecliffe, St Andrews, NB.

LAING, ALEXANDER, Esq., LL D, Newburgh, Fifeshire.

LANE, Miss, LANE, Miss LAURA, Vernon Mount, Cork.

LATHBURY, Mrs B. PENROSE, 1 Oxford and Cambridge Mansions, Marylebone Road, London.

LEE, Miss JANE, 64 Merrion Square South, Dublin.

LIDBETTER, R. M., Esq., 20 Molesworth Street, Dublin.

LITTLEDALE, HAROLD, Esq., The High School, Baroda, Bombay.

LOWELL, His Excellency J. RUSSELL, MA, LL D, 37 Lowndes Street, London, SW, and Legation of the United States, London.

LYNDALL, WM. WORDSWORTH, Esq., 27 Leadenhall Street, London, EC.

LYTTELTON, The Hon. and Revd CANNON, MA, Hagley Rectory, Stourbridge.

M'EWEN, ALEXANDER, Esq., Mottingham Lodge, Eltham, Kent.

MACFARREN, Miss, The Ladies' College, Cheltenham.

MACKAY, ALEXANDER, Esq., MACKAY, Mrs, Trowbridge, Wiltshire.

M'LEAN, Miss MARY M., The Bank, Donne, Perthshire.

M'LEANE, Miss, The Ladies' College, Cheltenham.

M'MILLAN, Revd ARCHIBALD DOUGLAS, MA, Marskaig, Charles Road, St Leonard's-on-Sea.

M'WHIRTER, JOHN, Esq., ARA, 6 Marlborough Road, St John's Wood, London, NW.

MAIN, DAVID M., Esq., 18 Exchange Square, Glasgow.

MAITLAND, J., Esq., 10 Chester Place, Hyde Park Square, London, W.

MARSTON, Revd HERBERT, MA, Durham College for the Blind, Worcester.

MASSON, Professor DAVID, MA, LL D, 58 Great King Street, Edinburgh.

MEIKLEJOHN, Professor, MA, Castle Gate, St Andrews.

MENZIES, Revd ALLAN, MA, BD, Abernyte Manse, Inchture, NB.

MENZIES, Mrs P. S., 9 Seton Place, Edinburgh.

MERZ, J. THEODORE, Esq., Ph.D., MERZ, Mrs, The Quarries, Newcastle-on-Tyne.

MILLSON, ALVAN, Esq., MA, Brackenbed Grange, Halifax.

MISSIE, J. Esq., Sussex House, Leam Terrace, Leamington.

MOBERLY, Revd C., MA, Coln Roger Rectory, North Leach, Gloucestershire.

MOFFETT, T. W., Esq., MA, LL D, President, Queen's College, Galway, Ireland.

MOON, Miss, 37 Norwich Gardens, Kensington, London, W.

MUDIE, ANDREW, Esq., Citizen Office, Glasgow.

MUNBY, ARTHUR J., Esq., 8 Fig Tree Court, Temple, London, EC.

NICHOL, Professor JOHN, MA, LL D, 14 Montgomerie Crescent, Kelvinside, Glasgow.

NICHOLS, Revd WM. L., MA, FSA, Woodlands House, Bridgewater.

NICHOLSON, CORNELIUS, Esq., Ashleigh, Ventnor, Isle of Wight.

NICOL, ANDREW L., Esq., 28 North Castle Street, Banff.

NIXON, Miss, The Ladies' College, Cheltenham.

NOBLE, B., Esq., Gloucester House, Newcastle-on-Tyne.

NOEL, The Hon. RODEN, 57 Annerly Park, London, SE.

OGILVY, LADY GRISELDA, 47 Lower Grosvenor Street, London, SW.

OHRLY, FRANK H., Esq., OHRLY, HENRY G., Esq., Ridgley Oak, Reigate.

OLIVIER, Revd ALFRED, MA, Derby.

OSBORNE, CHARLES G., Esq., 5 Castlewood Avenue, Rathmines, Dublin.

OWEN, Mrs. J. A., The Beeches, Suffolk Square, Cheltenham.

PALMER, Professor G. H., MA, Harvard University, USA.

PATERSON, Mrs, Maybank, The Island, Inverness.

PEARSON, The Revd HUGH, MA, Canon of Windsor, The Cloisters, Windsor Castle—*dead*.

PFEIFFER, Mrs EMILY, Mayfield, Westhill, Putney, London, SW.

PONSONBY, Revd S. G., MA, St Ninians, Moffat.

POOLE, Revd WILLIAM, MA, Hentland, Herefordshire.

POTTS, R. A., Esq., 26 South Audley Street, London, W.

PRICE, Professor BONAMY, MA, LL D, Oxford.

RAPER, R. W., Esq., MA, BCL, Trinity College, Oxford, and Hoe Court, Colwall, Malvern.

RAWNSLEY, Revd H. DRUMMOND, B.A., RAWNSLEY, Mrs, Wray Vicarage, Westmoreland.

RAWSON, Miss ISABEL, 5 Lanesfield, Clifton, Bristol.

REED, HENRY, Esq., 400 Chestnut Street, Philadelphia, USA.

RICE, Mrs L. Y., Grove Hill, Bentham, near Lancaster.

RICHARDSON, LADY, Lancrigg, Grasmere—*dead*.

RICHARDSON, Miss AMY C., South Ashfield, Newcastle-on-Tyne.

RICHARDSON, Miss CAROLINE, Heugh Folds, Grasmere.

RICHARDSON, Mrs JAMES, South Ashfield, Newcastle-on-Tyne.

RICHARDSON, Miss SARAH A., 4 Summerhill Grove, Newcastle-onTyne.

RICHMOND, Revd T. K., MA, Crosthwaite Vicarage, Keswick.

RIX, HERBERT, Esq., BA, 155 Isledon Road, London, W.; and Science Club, 4 Savile Row, London, W.

ROOTES, Miss, 70 Priory Street, Cheltenham.

ROSS, J. CALLENDER, Esq., 46 Holland Street, Campden Hill, London, W.

ROSS, JOHN M., Esq., LL D, 30 Great King Street, Edinburgh—*dead*.

ROWLEY, Professor J., Ardmore, Leigh Woods, Clifton, Bristol.

RUSKIN, JOHN, Esq., MA, LL D, Brantwood, Coniston, Lancashire.

RUSSELL, Revd CHARLES DICKENSON, MA, 4 Lower Ely Place, Dublin.

SALISBURY, The Very Revd The Dean of, MA, The Deanery, Salisbury.

SALMOND, Revd Professor, MA, DD, Queen's Road, Aberdeen.

SAUNDERS, Mrs, 21 Elvaston Place, Queen's Gate, London, SW.

SAUNDERS, T. B., Esq., University College, Oxford.

SAWYER, Miss, The Ladies College, Cheltenham.

SELBORNE, The Right Hon. The Earl, DCL, SELBORNE, The Right Hon. The Countess, 30 Portland Place, London, W.

SELLARS, Miss, St Andrews School for Girls, St Andrews.

SHAIRP, Principal, MA, LL D, St Andrews, NB.

SHELDON, EDWARD W., Esq., The Benedick, Washington Square East, New York City, USA.

SHEPHERD, RICHARD HERNE, Esq., 5 Bramerton Street, King's Road, Chelsea, London, SW.

SHORTHOUSE, J. HENRY, Esq., SHORTHOUSE, Mrs, Lansdowne, Edgbaston, Birmingham.

SLATER, WALTER B., Esq., 264 Camden Road, London, NW.

SOMERS-COCKS, Mrs, SOMERS-COCKS, Miss, 8 Ashburn Place, Cromwell Road, London, W.

SOMERVELL, GORDON, Esq., Hazelthwaite, Windermere.

STANGER, Mrs, Fieldside, Keswick, Cumberland.

STEPHEN, LESLIE, Esq., MA, 13 Hyde Park Gate, South, London, SW.

STEVENSON, JOHN J., Esq., STEVENSON, Mrs, The Red House, Bayswater Hill, London, W.

STEVENSON, Miss LOUISA, STEVENSON, Miss FLORA C., 13 Randolph Crescent, Edinburgh.

STEVENSON, Miss MARGARET, Westoe, South Shields.

STOCK, Mrs VAUGHAN, Holyrood House, Twickenham.

STOKES, Revd H. P., MA, St James' Vicarage, Wolverhampton.

STOKES, Revd LEWIS, MA, 3 Park Hill, Richmond, SW.

STURGE, Mrs JANE, Charlbury, Oxon.

SWAN, ROBERT, Esq., 2 Belsize Terrace, South Hampstead, London, NW.

SWANWICK, Miss ANNA, 23 Cumberland Terrace, Regent's Park, London, NW.

TABOR, Miss MARY C., Richmond Road, Malvern Link, Worcestershire.

TARBUTT, Revd A. B., MA, Brantfield, Bowness.

TAYLOR, Miss HELEN, 8 Albert Mansions, Victoria Street, London, SW.

TAYLOR, JOHN, Esq., Bristol Museum and Library, Queen's Road, Bristol.

TAYLOR, Miss MARY GRACE, Whitethorn, Acton, London, W.

TEAL, J., Esq., 16 Southgate, Halifax.

TEMPLE, Miss ELIZABETH, Grecian Cottage, Crown Hill, Upper Norwood, London, SE.

THACKWRAY, GEORGE BAYNE, Esq., Alma Square, Scarborough.

THOMSON, Revd JOHN DAY, 35 Croft Terrace, Jarrow-on-Tyne.

TOLLEMACHE, The Hon. Mrs, Tatton Park, Knutsford.

TROUTBECK, Revd J., DD, Canon of Westminster, London, SW.
TULLOCH, The Very Revd Principal, DD, LL D, St Andrews, NB.
TUTIN, JOHN R., Esq., 55B Savile Street, Hull.
URWICK, WILLIAM HENRY, Esq., Clapham Common, London, SW.
VEITCH, Professor JOHN, MA, LL D, The College, Glasgow.
VERE, AUBREY DE, Esq., MA, Curragh Chase, Adare, Ireland; and Athenæum Club, Pall Mall, London, W.
WAGSTAFF, Revd CHARLES, Studham, Dunstable.
WALKER, A., Esq., 59 Park Road, Bradford, Yorks.
WALKER, ROBERT, Esq., Glasgow Institute of Fine Arts, Sauchiehall Street, Glasgow.
WATSON, ROBERT SPENCE, Esq., WATSON, Mrs, Bensham Grove, Gateshead-on-Tyne.
WEBSTER, Mrs AUGUSTA, J. WEBSTER, ESQ., 43 Lincoln's Inn Fields, London, WC.
WENT, Revd JAMES, MA Headmaster, The Schools, Leicester.
WEST, Miss ELIZABETH DICKENSON, The Deanery, St Patrick's, Dublin.
WEST, JOHN R., Esq., MB, M.Ch., 11 Upper Pembroke Street, Dublin.
WEST, W. J., Esq., Great Malvern.
WHITE, W. HALE, Esq., Park Hill, Carshalton, Surrey.
WIGHAM, H. M., Esq., WIGHAM, Mrs, Killiney, Ireland.
WILLIAMS, Revd J. D., MA, Bottisham Vicarage, Cambridge.
WILLIAMSON, JOHN, Esq., WILLIAMSON, Mrs, Westoe, South Shields.
WILSON, GEORGE, Esq., MA, WILSON, Miss, WILSON, Miss LINDSAY H., Murrayfield House, Midlothian.
WILSON, Miss, 27 St Mary's Terrace, Paddington, London, W.
WORDSWORTH, CHARLES, The Right Revd Bishop, MA, DCL, Bishopshall, St Andrews.
WORDSWORTH, CHRISTOPHER, The Right Revd The Lord Bishop of Lincoln, DD, DCL, Riseholme, Lincoln.
WORDSWORTH, GORDON, Esq., The Stepping Stones, Ambleside.
WORDSWORTH, Revd J., MA, Gosforth Rectory, by Carnforth, Cumberland.
WORDSWORTH, WILLIAM, Esq., The Stepping-Stones, Ambleside—*dead*.
WORDSWORTH, WILLIAM, Esq., Principal, Elphinstone College, Bombay.
WORDSWORTH, WILLIAM B., Esq., Lichfield.
YARNALL, ELLIS, Esq., 105 South Front Street, Philadelphia, USA.
YARNALL, F. C., Esq., Wyndown, Overbrook, Montgomery Co., Pa., USA.

Notes

INTRODUCTION

1. Abraham Stansfield, 'Rambles in the West Riding (With a Glance at the Flora), II', *Manchester Quarterly*, 3 (1884), 163. In the first of his two articles in the previous issue, 2 (1883), 64–83, Stansfield had declared *The White Doe of Rylstone* 'one of the noblest poems in the English language' which 'celebrates and *consecrates*' the countryside around Bolton Abbey (64–5). I owe this reference to Ms Jane Brownlow.
2. William Wordsworth, *The White Doe of Rylstone; or, The Fate of the Nortons*, designed by Birket Foster and H[enry] N[oel] Humphreys, engraved by Henry N. Woods (London, 1859). Reissued in smaller format in 1867 by Bell and Daldy. The poem was also edited in 1891 by William Knight for a Clarendon Press series of school texts. Inchbold's painting is now in Leeds City Art Gallery.
3. James Pycroft, *A Course of Reading, Adapted to Every Taste and Capacity: With Anecdotes of Men of Genius* (London, 1844), 307. I am grateful to Michael Jaye for drawing my attention to this book.
4. *Selections from Wordsworth*, by William Knight and Other Members of the Wordsworth Society. With Preface and Notes (London, 1888).
5. *Early Poems of William Wordsworth*, ed. J[ohn] R[amsden] Tutin (London, 1889).
6. Henry N. Hudson, *Studies in Wordsworth* (Boston, 1884), 8. James Russell Lowell, *Among My Books: Second Series* (London, 1876), 246.
7. After publication of my biography of Wordsworth I received a great many letters from readers who wanted to tell me what his poetry had meant to them during troubled periods of their lives. One American reader wrote that reacquaintance with Wordsworth had prompted him to give *The Prelude* to a nephew suffering from depression, in the belief that it would help him. In the 1830s and 1840s these letters would have been addressed to the poet himself.
8. In *The Young Darwin and His Cultural Circle* (Dordrecht, 1978) and 'From Wordsworth to Darwin: "On to the Fields of Praise" ', *Wordsworth Circle*, 10 (1979), 33–48, Edward Manier and Marilyn Gaull have discussed, with differing conclusions, the relationship of Wordsworth and Charles Darwin. In 'The Darwin Reading Notebooks (1838–60)', *Journal of the History of Biology*, 10 (1977), 107–53, Peter J. Vorzimmer presents the evidence that Darwin read Wordsworth over 1841–2, but he does not identify which Wordsworth is in question. By chance I was privileged to be allowed to see the set Darwin owned—the six-volume collection of 1840—when it surfaced briefly in 1996. It contains numerous marginal marks and notes. A particularly poignant mark is that against 'Surprised by joy', Wordsworth's sonnet about his dead daughter, Catherine, which indicates that the poem is to be copied out. Darwin grieved intensely for the loss in

1851 of his daughter, Annie. The set has now been sold to a private collector in America.

9. William Allingham, *A Diary*, ed. H. Allingham and D. Radford (London, 1907); Penguin edn. (Harmondsworth, 1985), 53. Adrian Desmond notes in *Huxley: The Devil's Disciple* (London, 1994), 372, that *Nature* opened with quotations from Goethe, but does not mention Wordsworth. Given that he was a known friend to science, Goethe's presence is, in fact, less surprising than Wordsworth's, whose theism was at some remove from Huxley's agnosticism. The quotation is 'To the solid ground | Of Nature trusts the Mind that builds for aye', from the sonnet 'A volant Tribe of Bards on earth are found'.

10. Charles Dickens to W. H. Wills, 27 July 1853. *The Letters of Charles Dickens*, ed. Madeline House, Graham Storey, Kathleen Tillotson (8 vols. continuing; Oxford, 1965–), VII. 121. E. B. Ramsay, *Two Lectures on the Genius of Handel* (Edinburgh, 1862), 72–3.

11. I owe the Burne-Jones reference to Peter Conrad, *The Victorian Treasure-House* (London, 1973), 190. Florence Emily Hardy, *The Life of Thomas Hardy* (2 vols.; London, 1933), I. 151.

12. Katherine Mary Peek, *Wordsworth in England: Studies in the History of His Fame* (Bryn Mawr, Pa., 1943).

13. Christopher Ricks, *Essays in Appreciation* (Oxford, 1996), 339.

14. Andrew Elfenbein, *Byron and the Victorians* (Cambridge, 1996).

15. Norman White, *Hopkins: A Literary Biography* (Oxford, 1992), 89–90.

16. *The Correspondence of Gerard Manley Hopkins and Richard Watson Dixon*, ed. Claude Colleer Abbott (London, 1935; 2nd rev. edn. 1955), 141–42.

17. Quoted Cecil Woodham Smith, *Queen Victoria: Her Life and Times* (2 vols.; London, 1972), I. 276.

18. Fred Kaplan, *Sacred Tears: Sentimentality in Victorian Literature* (Princeton, 1987), 41.

19. W to Hugh James Rose [late Jan. 1829]. *WL*, V. 20.

20. D. J. Palmer, *The Rise of English Studies* (London, 1965) and Chris Baldick, *The Social Mission of English Criticism 1848–1932* (Oxford, 1983).

21. Gauri Viswanathan, *Masks of Conquest: Literary Studies and English Rule in India* (New York, 1989). In his fascinating *The Autobiography of an Unknown Indian* (London, 1951), Nirad C. Chaudhuri recalls reading as a schoolboy in the early years of this century 'the usual things, Wordsworth's "Lucy Gray", "We Are Seven", and "Daffodils", for example. We liked them, but were too young to understand their subtlety. The poem by Wordsworth which me moved me most strongly at the time was "Upon Westminster Bridge" ' (p. 114).

22. Linden Peach, *British Influence on the Birth of American Literature* (London, 1982), has a useful chapter on 'Man, Nature and Wordsworth: American Versions'.

I. FAME

1. Epigraph: W to Lady Beaumont, 21 May 1807. *WL*, II. 150. Elizabeth Barrett to H. S. Boyd, 7 July 1842. *Elizabeth Barrett to Mr Boyd*, ed. Barbara P. McCarthy (London, 1955), 247. John Kenyon (1784–1856)

was a close friend of Elizabeth Barrett and of Wordsworth, whom he had known since 1819. Independently wealthy, he published two volumes of poetry in 1833 and 1838. Elizabeth Barrett publicly declared her reverence for Wordsworth in the *Athenaeum*, 774 (27 Aug. 1842), 757–9, where she moved from a review of his recent volume to focus on his life: 'It is well and full of Exultation to remember *now* what a silent, blameless, heroic life of poetic duty, this man has lived' (p. 759).

2. Edward Quillinan, diary entry, 1 Sept. 1836. WL. Amongst the very many poems sent to Wordsworth now at WL is one by Anne Richler called *On a laurel leaf gathered in Wordsworth's garden at Rydal Mount, 1848*. The tradition continues. One lady caught in the 1980s with trowel and polythene bag at the ready, admitted to the staff at Dove Cottage that she regularly took plants, as she was recreating Wordsworth's garden in her own.

3. Mrs Bourne, *Northern Reminiscences* (Whitehaven, 1832), 25. I owe this reference to the kindness of Nicholas Roe.

4. Illustrated in Frances Blanshard, *Portraits of Wordsworth* (London, 1959), plate 21, discussed 87–8, 166. Future citation to *Portraits*.

5. Quoted from Tim Hilton, *John Ruskin: The Early Years 1819–1859* (New Haven, 1985), 19.

6. *The Life of Thomas Cooper: Written by Himself* (1872), ed. John Saville (Leicester, 1971), 287–95. The 'Venerated Sir' letter, in which Cooper describes himself as a 'dust-covered pilgrim' is 2 Nov. 1847, now at WL.

7. Christopher Wordsworth, *Memoirs of William Wordsworth* (2 vols.; London, 1851), II. 483–6. Future citation to *Memoirs*.

8. William (later Sir William) Boxall to W, 29 Aug. 1836. WL.

9. Wright Wilson, *The Life of George Dawson* (Birmingham, 1905), 80.

10. The pioneering study on this topic is Alan G. Hill, 'Wordsworth and his American Friends', *Bulletin of Research in the Humanities*, 81 (1978), 146–60. See also John Beer, 'William Ellery Channing Visits the Lake Poets', *Review of English Studies*, NS 42 (1991), 212–26.

11. Orville Dewey, *The Old World and the New* (2 vols.; New York, 1836), I. 105–12.

12. Ralph Waldo Emerson, *English Traits* (Boston, 1856). *Essays and Lectures*, ed. Joel Porte [The Library of America] (New York, 1983), 775–8.

13. Charles Sumner to George S. Hillard, 8 Sept. 1838. *Memoir and Letters of Charles Sumner*, ed. Edward L. Pierce (4 vols.; London, 1878–93), I. 355–6.

14. T. Fitzjames Price to W, 28 Mar. 1836. WL.

15. Letters in WL, also a printed sonnet 'On my first and only visit to the Poet Wordsworth, shortly previous to his death, when he regardfully presented me with a walking-stick, which had been an old and much-used favourite'. The mawkish sonnet ends with the poet's 'staff' described as 'the glory of my home'.

16. John Simon to W, 2 July 1841. WL.

17. Thomas Powell to W, 10 Oct. 1836. WL. Powell (1809–87) was a shady literary adventurer, and also a writer, who had contacts with Leigh Hunt, Elizabeth Barrett, R. H. Horne, and other leading figures. Wordsworth contributed to his *The Poems of Geoffrey Chaucer, Modernized* (London, 1841). He eventually had to flee to America.

18. Elizabeth Frances Ogle to Wordsworth, [?5] May 1840. WL. It is astonishing how often the more rhapsodic of Wordsworth's commentators compared his work to the Bible. In *Sketches of the Poetical Literature of the Past Half-Century* (Edinburgh, 1851), for example, D. M. Moir wrote: 'Approximating to the Holy Scriptures themselves, his writings have a simplicity of thought, and a singleness of purpose, which we vainly look for elsewhere' (pp. 80–81). Similar observations by Henry N. Hudson and James Russell Lowell have already been quoted in the introduction.

19. W to Elizabeth Frances Ogle, 20 May 1840. *WL*, VII. 73–5.

20. For publishing details see W. J. B. Owen, 'Costs, Sales, and Profits of Longman's Editions of Wordsworth', *Library*, 5th ser. 12 (1957), 93–107, and Lee Erickson, 'The Egoism of Authorship: Wordsworth's Poetic Career', *JEGP*, 89 (1990), 37–50.

21. See Ian Jack, *The Poet and His Audience* (Cambridge, 1984), 77.

22. Thomas Noon Talfourd, 'An Attempt to Estimate the Poetical Talent of the Present Age', *Pamphleteer*, 5 (Feb. 1815), 462.

23. *Edinburgh Review*, 37 (Nov. 1822), 449.

24. *Edinburgh Review*, 24 (Nov. 1814), 1–31; *Edinburgh Review*, 25 (Oct. 1815), 355–63.

25. The most important of De Quincey's 'Lake Reminiscences: From 1807 to 1830' appeared in *Tait's Edinburgh Magazine*, 6 (Jan., Feb., Apr. 1839), 1–12, 90–103, 246–54.

26. See Henry Taylor, *Autobiography* (2 vols.; London, 1885) and *Correspondence of Henry Taylor*, ed. Edward Dowden (London, 1888).

27. Felicia Hemans to R. P. Graves, May 1834. Archive of Alexandra College, Dublin.

28. Brian W. Martin, *John Keble: Priest, Professor and Poet* (London, 1976), 80.

29. *The Oxford Diaries of Arthur Hugh Clough*, ed. Anthony Kenny (Oxford, 1990), 116. John Peace was also present. He was convinced that the thunderous applause was not mere uproariousness, but that it 'had a beautiful tone about it; just such as one would expect to characterize or burst from the central heart of the best men of England at the best period of their lives'. Letter 12 Aug. 1839. *WL*, VI. 722.

30. *Critical Review*, 3rd ser., 11 (Aug. 1807), 403; *Annual Review*, 6 (1808), 529.

31. *Edinburgh Review*, 11 (Oct. 1807), 218.

32. *Edinburgh Review*, 24 (Nov. 1814), 4.

33. *Edinburgh Review*, 11 (Oct. 1807), 231.

34. 6 Apr. 1842. *Hansard*, 3rd ser., 61. 1347–403.

35. 'Reply to "Mathetes" ', *Prose*, II. 15.

36. William Whewell, *The Elements of Morality, including Polity*, (2 vols.; London, 1845).

37. W to William Whewell, 12 May 1845. *WL*, VII. 673.

38. Gideon Mantell, *The Wonders of Geology* (2 vols.; London, 1838), II. 679–80. In the 1839 revised edn. the pages are II. 792–3.

39. James F. White, *The Cambridge Movement: The Ecclesiologists and the Gothic Revival* (Cambridge, 1962), 28, quoting from the *Ecclesiologist*, 4 (1845), 26.

40. Letter 19 Sept. 1845. WL. Tremenheere was following up conversation he had had with W on 23 Aug. 1845. W's reply, 16 Dec. 1845, is splendid.

While acknowledging all the good work of the Committee of the Privy Council on Education, he suggests that too little value is being placed on children's outdoor play, and says: 'Excuse this disagreement in opinion, as coming from one who spent half of his boyhood in running wild among the Mountains.' He also worries that the inspectors are not paying sufficient attention 'to books of imagination which are eminently useful in calling forth intellectual power. We must not only have Knowledge but the means of wielding it, and that is done infinitely more thro' the imaginative faculty assisting both in the collection and application of facts than is generally believed.' *WL*, VII. 733–4.

41. For information on Tremenheere's astonishingly active public life, see *I was There: The Memoirs of H. S. Tremenheere*, ed. E. L. and O. P. Edmonds (Eton, 1965).
42. W to Charles James Fox, 14 Jan. 1801. *WL*, I. 312–15.
43. Sir Henry Edward Bunbury to W, 8 June 1838. WL.
44. 'Postscript' to *Yarrow Revisited* (1835). *Prose*, III. 246.
45. Keble's tribute appeared in the dedication to his *De Poeticae Vi Medica: Praelectiones Academicae Oxonii Habitae* (2 vols.; Oxford, 1844); trans. E. K. Francis as *Keble's Lectures on Poetry* (2 vols.; Oxford, 1912).
46. *Prose*, III. 241, 246, 261.
47. 'Prelude' to *Poems, Chiefly of Early and Late Years* (London, 1842), p. xi.
48. George Brimley, 'Wordsworth', *Fraser's Magazine*, 44 (June–July, 1851), 104–5.
49. George Dawson, 'The Poetry of Wordsworth', *Biographical Lectures*, ed. George St Clair (London, 1886), 262. Henry Crabb Robinson noted of Dawson: 'He is a popular preacher at Birmingham. There is a dash of radicalism about him which enhances the value of his just estimation of Wordsworth. He will make converts where they are most wanted.' *HCR: Books*, II. 659. Once again it is notable that the language of the mission field is used. Robinson values Dawson as a missionary, making converts in far-flung places—such as industrial Birmingham—where the Wordsworthian gospel might not otherwise penetrate.
50. Vernon Lushington to John Campbell Shairp, undated, quoted in William Knight, *Principal Shairp and His Friends* (London, 1888), 229.
51. The letters, including Kenyon's dated 29 March 1843, are in WL. Relevant excerpts are printed in *WL*, VII. 421–5.
52. Two thousand copies of *The Prelude* were printed and a second edition was called for in 1851. *In Memoriam* sold five thousand copies in the year of publication and went through five editions by the end of 1851. Herbert Lindenberger, 'The Reception of *The Prelude*', *Bulletin of the New York Public Library*, 64 (1960), 196–208, remains an important study, but its findings are based on incomplete evidence. For fuller listing of reviews see N. S. Bauer, *William Wordsworth: A Reference Guide to British Criticism, 1793–1899* (Boston, 1978).
53. Macaulay to Lord Mahon, 2 Aug. 1850. *The Letters of Thomas Babington Macaulay*, ed. Thomas Pinney (6 vols.; Cambridge, 1974–81), V. 118. Journal entry 28 July 1850 in George Otto Trevelyan, *The Life and Letters of Lord Macaulay* (2 vols.; London, 1876), II. 279.
54. *Examiner*, 2217 (27 July 1850), 478–9. *Fraser's Magazine*, 42 (1850), 129; *British Quarterly Review*, 12 (1850), 579; *Prospective Review*, 7 (1851), 130; *North American Review*, 73 (1851), 476.

55. 'On Wordsworth's Poetry', *Tait's Edinburgh Magazine*, NS 12 (Sept. 1845), 545–54. Repr. in *De Quincey as Critic*, ed. John E. Jordan (London, 1973), 397–424.

56. See n. 45. Just as Keble was about to dedicate *Praelectiones* he began to have doubts, which he speedily suppressed, 'on account of his [Wordsworth] having begun life as a Radical'. See Martin, *John Keble*, 81.

57. In *Poems, Chiefly of Early and Late Years*, Wordsworth had presented texts of *Guilt and Sorrow; or, Incidents on Salisbury Plain* and *The Borderers*. But he did not reveal that he had recently revised both poems substantially, in the case of *Guilt and Sorrow* dulling altogether the radical point of the 1795 *Adventures on Salisbury Plain*. For text and discussion see *The Salisbury Plain Poems of William Wordsworth*, ed. Stephen Gill (Ithaca, NY, 1975) and *The Borderers*, ed. Robert Osborn (Ithaca, NY, 1982).

58. For very revealing information about the genesis of the biography and the response of the family and circle to it, see Appendix in *WL*, VIII. 278–92.

59. Information had accumulated over the years through (1) memoirs such as *Biographia Literaria* (2 vols.; London, 1817), Joseph Cottle's *Early Recollections, Chiefly Relating to the Late Samuel Taylor Coleridge* (2 vols.; London, 1837) and De Quincey's articles; (2) the notes and dates Wordsworth appended to his poems; (3) snippets from the poet's conversation, used to good effect, for example, by William Howitt in *Homes and Haunts of the Most Eminent British Poets* (2 vols.; London, 1847), II. 257–91. See Walter E. Swayze, 'Early Wordsworthian Biography: Books and Articles Containing Material on the Life and Character of William Wordsworth that Appeared before the Publication of the Official *Memoirs*, by Christopher Wordsworth, in 1851', *Bulletin of the New York Public Library*, 64 (1960), 169–95.

60. Diary of Edward Quillinan, 11 July 1850. WL.

61. *Memoirs*, I. 4–5.

62. Ibid. I. 89.

63. Quillinan's comments are quoted more fully in Appendix III, *WL*, VIII. 290–1.

64. For an account of the Church of England's turmoil over the Gorham case and 'Papal Aggression' see Owen Chadwick, *The Victorian Church*, Part One: *1829–1859* (London, 1966; 3rd edn. 1971), 250–309.

65. See *HCR: Corr.*, II. 744. Crabb Robinson's letters are a fascinating insight into the anxieties the writing of the *Memoirs* generated in the Wordsworth family.

66. *HCR: Books*, II. 703. Entry 17 August 1850.

67. Letter 21 Mar. 1851. WL.

68. *HCR: Corr.*, II. 744.

69. William Strickland Cookson to Henry Crabb Robinson, 31 Aug. 1850. Ibid., II. 756–7.

70. *Memoirs*, I. 4–5.

71. *Memoirs*, I. 74–5. Crabb Robinson saw the danger in conjecture: 'Wordsworth showed me the proof sheets of the *Life*, in which I am sorry to see a canting commonplace remark on the perils to which Wordsworth was exposed in his youth at Paris, which might make one utterly ignorant of Wordsworth's personal character imagine he had been guilty of some

immorality!' *HCR: Books*, II. 708. Did he fear that the passage might be interpreted as meaning that the poet frequented prostitutes?

72. See letter from Sir William Boxall to Henry Crabb Robinson, 24 Sept. 1851. *HCR: Corr.*, II. 782. Dr. John Davy, brother of Sir Humphry Davy, was the son-in-law of the redoubtable Mrs Elizabeth Fletcher of Lancrigg, Grasmere.

73. 'To the Memory of William Wordsworth a True Philosopher and Poet who, by the Special Gift and Calling of Almighty God whether he discoursed on Man or Nature failed not to lift up the Heart to Holy Things Tired not of Maintaining the Cause of the Poor and Simple: and so, in Perilous Times was raised up to be a Chief Minister, not only of Noblest Poesy, but of High and Sacred Truth.' Quoted and discussed *Portraits*, 103–4; 180–1; plate 36c.

74. Alfred Tennyson to Thomas Woolner, 10 Mar. [1851]. *The Letters of Alfred Lord Tennyson*, ed. Cecil Y. Lang and Edgar F. Shannon, Jr. (3 vols.; Oxford, 1982–90), II. 10.

75. Reed broadcast information about the memorial project in a long letter to the *Literary World*, 25 June 1853, in which he quoted from letters from eminent Americans who had already sent him contributions.

76. Memorial windows to other members of the Wordsworth family were dedicated in due course. In 1863 the residue of the money was put towards the erection of the 'Wordsworth Library' next to the Ambleside school-room. It still stands and is passed every year by thousands of walkers making for Loughrigg Fell, the eminence from which the schoolboy Wordsworth first saw Grasmere.

77. Quotation from the catalogue to the Royal Academy Exhibition, 1852, cited, together with illustration of the design, *Portraits*, 180–1. In 1883 Edmund Gosse reopened the quarrel over the outcome of the competition in an article which attacked Thrupp's 'feeble and ugly work' and called for the rescue of Woolner's 'appropriate and seemly tribute' by 'some wealthy body of devout Wordsworthians' (*Century Magazine*, 26 (1883), 169–70). Perhaps it was in response to Gosse that William Knight contacted Woolner (now a highly successful sculptor back in England) and included a photograph of the centre-piece of Woolner's model as frontispiece to *Wordsworthiana: A Selection From Papers Read to the Wordsworth Society* (London, 1889). Blanshard records that the poet's grandson, Gordon Graham Wordsworth, acquired the centre-piece from Woolner's daughter (regarding the rest as 'distasteful and discordant') and presented it to the Trustees of Dove Cottage.

78. For a beautifully illustrated account of Haydon's role in transmitting an image of the poet, see David Blayney Brown, Robert Woof, and Stephen Hebron, *Benjamin Robert Haydon 1786–1846* (Grasmere, 1996). For Thrupp's indebtedness, see p. 54.

79. 'Character of Mr. Wordsworth's New Poem, The Excursion', *Examiner*, 21 Aug. 1814. *The Complete Works of William Hazlitt*, ed. P. P. Howe (21 vols.; London, 1930–4), XIX. 11. Thrupp used Haydon's life-mask of Wordsworth (1815), the *ne plus ultra* image of him in repose, and explained that of the four models he submitted, the one chosen 'was preferred as giving his [Wordsworth's] contemplative character'. *Portraits*, 178.

80. 'My First Acquaintance with Poets'. Howe, *Complete Works of William Hazlitt*, XVII. 118. Beerbohm's splendidly irreverent cartoon, *William Wordsworth in the Lake District, at Cross Purposes*, in *The Poets' Corner* (London, 1904), depicts something which all of the formal portraits miss. The elderly poet has buttonholed some poor child, as if to extract from her material for a poem such as *We Are Seven*. The perplexity of both—the 'Cross Purposes' of the title—captures the origin of many of Wordsworth's poems, that is, in a human encounter rather than in self-communion.

2. ENGLAND'S SAMUEL: WORDSWORTH AS SPIRITUAL POWER

1. Epigraph: W to John Wilson, 7 June 1802. *WL*, I. 355. *The Poetical Works of Thomas Pringle*, With a Sketch of His Life, by Leitch Ritchie (London, 1839), 186.

2. The tone of John Campbell Shairp's essay on 'Wordsworth: The Man and the Poet', in the *North British Review*, 41 (1864), 1–54, is determined by his perception that W's reputation was slumping rapidly.

3. William Charles Macready, *Macready's Reminiscences, and Selections from his Diaries and Letters*, ed. Sir Frederick Pollock, Bart. (2 vols.; London, 1875), I. 157. The end of *The Ancient Mariner* also seemed apposite to William Ellery Channing when he wrote to W from Boston, 4 Mar. 1835, to acknowledge 'how much I am indebted to you for the pure & quickening influence of your writings on my mind & heart. I think myself a wiser & better man for your poetry. It has been to me for years a familiar friend, & I hope I may say, a fountain of spiritual life.' WL.

4. Sir William Maynard Gomm to W, 24 Feb. 1835. WL.

5. *Letters and Journals of Field-Marshal Sir William Maynard Gomm* . . . *1799–1815*, ed. Francis Culling Carr-Gomm (London, 1881), 376.

6. *The Excursion*, IV. 694–5; 857–60; 1207. PW, V. 130; 136; 148. Since no textual issue is involved, the text of 1849–50 is cited here and in all similar problem-free cases for ease of reference.

7. Against IV. 858–60 in his copy, now in Cornell University Library, Haydon wrote: 'Poor Keats used always to prefer this passage to all others.'

8. *Eclectic Review*, 2nd Ser, 3 (Jan. 1815), 13–39.

9. *Lines written a few miles above Tintern Abbey*, 96–8.

10. John Stuart Mill, *Autobiography and Literary Essays*, ed. John M. Robson and Jack Stillinger (Toronto, 1981), 44. Throughout this discussion of Mill, quotations from the *Autobiography*, unless otherwise noted, are from the 'Early Draft', and page references will be given in the text. The comment on W comes from Mill's lecture 'Wordsworth and Byron', p. 440. Full citation n. 13.

11. Affinities have been noted by John N. Morris in *Versions of the Self: Studies in English Autobiography from John Bunyan to John Stuart Mill* (New York, 1966).

12. See A. W. Levi, 'The "Mental Crisis" of John Stuart Mill', *Psychoanalytic Review*, 32 (1945), 86–101; Janice Carlisle, 'J. S. Mill's *Autobiography*: The Life of a "Bookish Man" ', *Victorian Studies*, 33 (1989), 125–48; William Thomas, 'John Stuart Mill and the Crisis of Benthamism', *The*

Philosophic Radicals: Nine Studies in Theory and Practice 1817–1841 (Oxford, 1979), 147–205. The best biography remains *The Life of John Stuart Mill* by Michael St John Packe (London, 1954), but it is notable that it pays no attention to the *Autobiography* as a literary document. For a wide-ranging account which touches at many points on Mill's self-representation, see Robert Denoon Cumming, *Human Nature and History: A Study of the Development of Liberal Political Thought* (2 vols.; Chicago, 1969), II. 275–449.

13. *The Earlier Letters of John Stuart Mill 1812–1848*, ed. Francis E. Mineka (2 vols.; Toronto, 1963), I. 74–89. The text of the speech, 'Wordsworth and Byron', will be found in John Stuart Mill, *Journals and Debating Speeches*, ed. John M. Robson (2 vols., Toronto, 1988), 434–42. Vols. 26 and 27 (paginated as one vol.) of the *Collected Works of John Stuart Mill*. Page references to the speech will be given in the text. Mill first met W at Sir Henry Taylor's house early in 1831. He visited him on home ground during a tour of 8 July to 8 August 1831. His journal 'Walking Tour of Yorkshire and the Lake District' is printed in *Journals and Debating Speeches*, 501–56. The journal, now in the Bodleian Library, alludes to Wordsworth poems throughout and ends with a fine Wordsworthian flourish, which echoes both *The Solitary Reaper* and 'I wandered lonely as a cloud': 'the image of the lake & mountains remained impressed upon the internal eye, long after the physical organs could see them no more.'

14. Preface to *Lyrical Ballads. Prose*, I. 128.

15. *Autobiography*, 'Early Draft', p. 152.

16. Catherine Macdonald Maclean, *Mark Rutherford: A Biography of William Hale White* (London, 1955), 80.

17. From the autobiographical recollections published posthumously as *The Early Life of Mark Rutherford (W. Hale White)*, By Himself (London, 1913), 62.

18. *The Autobiography of Mark Rutherford, Dissenting Minister*, Edited by His Friend, Reuben Shapcott (London, 1881), 23–4.

19. Hale White, *Early Life*, 61–3.

20. Mark Rutherford, 'Extracts From A Diary on the Quantocks', *More Pages From a Journal* (London, 1910), 196–7.

21. *Autobiography*, 18. For an informed, and highly readable account of the Calvinist milieu of White's upbringing, see ch. 10 of Valentine Cunningham, *Everywhere Spoken Against: Dissent in the Victorian Novel* (Oxford, 1975).

22. Quotation from the *The Tables Turned, Expostulation and Reply*, and *Lines* ('It is the first mild day of March'), all in *Lyrical Ballads* (1798).

23. Mark Rutherford, 'September 1798. "The Lyrical Ballads" ', *Pages From a Journal* (London, 1900), 108.

24. For a good discussion of how Spinoza melded with the other elements in Hale White's theology see ch. 6 of Roger Ebbatson, *Lawrence and the Nature Tradition: A Theme in English Fiction 1859–1914* (Brighton, 1980).

25. In *Mark Rutherford's Deliverance: Being the Second Part of his Autobiography* (London, 1885), 6–7, Rutherford declares that while long poems about nature might have a value in 'keeping alive in the hearts of men a determination to preserve air, earth, and water from pollution', they can only depress those whose lives must be passed in the city. I am not sure,

however, what weight should be placed on this as evidence as to Hale White's own views. Although the 'Mark Rutherford' persona is transparent, Hale White did as a novelist attempt to give the Rutherford character a consistency, with characteristics and views which were not simply his creator's.

26. William Hale White, *An Examination of the Charge of Apostasy Against Wordsworth* (London, 1898), 63.
27. Dorothy V. White, *The Groombridge Diary* (London, 1924), 28.
28. Mark Rutherford, *More Pages From a Journal*, 204.
29. *Macready's Reminiscences*, 157.
30. William Whewell, *The Elements of Morality, including Polity* (2 vols; London, 1845). For a good account of Whewell's importance, accessible to the non-scientist, see ch. 2, 'Natural Theology: Whewell and Darwin', in George Levine, *Darwin and the Novelists: Patterns of Science in Victorian Fiction* (Cambridge, Mass., 1988), and John Wyatt, *Wordsworth and the Geologists* (Cambridge, 1995).
31. See letter of 21 May 1822 cited in Mrs Stair Douglas, *The Life and Selections from the Correspondence of William Whewell, D.D.* (London, 1881), 77. This is a notably early example of the term 'Wordsworthian' used non-opprobriously.
32. 14 Oct. 1841. WL. Printed in part *WL*, VII. 251–2.
33. It is typical of Hare that he should have responded with Charles Kingsley to the events of April 1848, by trying to reach the Chartists and their sympathizers through the broadsheet *Politics for the People*. Whewell dedicated his *On the Foundation of Morals* (London, 1837) to Hare.
34. 11 April 1849. WL.
35. J. B. Schneewind, *Sidgwick's Ethics and Victorian Moral Philosophy* (Oxford, 1977), 89.
36. 4 June 1834. WL.
37. *Westminster and Foreign Quarterly Review*, 58 (Oct. 1852), 349–85. John Stuart Mill, 'Whewell on Moral Philosophy', *Essays on Ethics, Religion and Society*, ed. J. M. Robson (Toronto, 1969), 164–201.
38. Matthew Arnold, *Culture and Anarchy*, ed. R. H. Super (Ann Arbor, 1965), 164 and important note p. 436.
39. As an undergraduate at Brasenose College, Robertson was present in the Sheldonian Theatre when Wordsworth received his honorary degree in 1839.
40. Stopford A. Brooke, *Life and Letters of Frederick W. Robertson, M.A.* (2 vols.; London, 1865), I. 110–23.
41. Ibid., I. 112.
42. Henry Crabb Robinson met Robertson during this period at Heidelberg and was impressed by him. They almost certainly discussed W, for a year later Robertson wrote for advice as to critical reading he might do on the poetry. They became friends when Robinson visited Brighton in 1850 and he wrote an obituary notice of Robertson in 1853. See Edith J. Morley, *The Life and Times of Henry Crabb Robinson* (London, 1935), 174–5 and *HCR: Corr.*, II. 641–2.
43. F. W. Robertson, 'Lecture on Wordsworth, delivered to the Members of the Brighton Athenaeum, on February 10th, 1853', *Lectures and Addresses on Literary and Social Topics* (London, 1858), 204.
44. Brooke, *Life*, I. 140. Amongst Robertson's detractors there may have those

who recalled Richard Price's scandalous *A Discourse on the Love of our Country* in 1789, which uttered Nunc Dimittis at the events in France and called down the wrath of Burke and *Reflections on the Revolution in France.*

45. Ibid., I. 141.
46. Ibid., I. 150.
47. First quotation from Kingsley's 1872 address to the Chester Natural Science Society in the 2nd., 1890, revised edition of the work cited next, II. 286. Second quotation from letter of 21 April 1844. *Charles Kingsley: His Letters and Memories of His Life,* edited by His Wife (2 vols.; London, 1877), I. 120–1.
48. Ibid. I. 121.
49. One of the most remarkable passages in the lecture is where Robertson declares the need for a new poetry in the new age: 'the Poetry of the coming age must come from the Working Classes. In the upper ranks, Poetry, so far at least as it represents their life, has long been worn out, sickly, and sentimental. Its manhood is effete . . . But tenderness, and heroism, and endurance still want their voice, and it must come from the classes whose observation is at first hand, and who speak fresh from nature's heart. What has Poetry to do with the Working Classes? Men of work! we want our Poetry from you.' 'The Influence of Poetry on the Working Classes', *Lectures and Addresses,* 164.
50. Robertson, 'Lecture on Wordsworth', 229.
51. The passage, which deals with the Wanderer's experiences as a boy, describes his intense response to a dawn, and concludes:

> Rapt into still communion that transcends
> The imperfect offices of prayer and praise,
> His mind was a thanksgiving to the power
> That made him: it was blessedness and love.

Later in the lecture, in a not very cogent attempt to address the question of Pantheism, Robertson contrasts it with High Church attitudes. Predictably he was denounced in the press, partly because of his definition of the latter, but most vehemently because he was thought to favour Pantheism. In truth Robertson was vulnerable on this issue. Four years earlier he had had to defend himself, when remarks of his about the democratic availability of experience of the divine were taken (quite rightly) to commend religious experience of the kind described in Wordsworth's lines. See Brooke, *Life,* I. 153–8 and II. 178–86.
52. Robertson, 'Lecture on Wordsworth', 249.
53. Macready's words, see n. 2. Second quotation from Wordsworth's eloquent description of the power of poetry in the Preface to *Lyrical Ballads.* The poet 'is the rock of defence of human nature; an upholder and preserver, carrying every where with him relationship and love'. *Prose,* I. 141.
54. Letter 12 Aug. 1839. Quoted *WL,* VI. 722.
55. John Henry Newman, *A Letter Addressed to the Rev. R. W. Jelf, D.D.* (Oxford, 1841), 27.
56. *HCR: Books,* II. 641, quoting from a Southey letter of 1807.
57. Katherine Mary Peek, *Wordsworth in England: Studies in the History of His Fame* (Bryn Mawr, Pa., 1943), 101.

58. Mary Moorman drew attention to this work in *William Wordsworth: A Biography. The Later Years 1803–1850* (Oxford, 1965), 480. A copy, which belonged to the Archdeacon Edward Churton, survives in the pamphlet collection of Pusey House library, Oxford.
59. Owen Chadwick, *The Victorian Church*, Part One: *1829–59* (London, 1966; 3rd edn. 1971), 183.
60. 'Prospectus' to *The Recluse*, 58–62:

> by words
> Which speak of nothing more than what we are,
> Would I arouse the sensual from their sleep
> Of Death, and win the vacant and the vain
> To noble raptures . . .

61. As will be discussed in more detail below, the note was actually written by Frederick Faber.
62. Wordsworth approved these remarks. See *WL*, VII. 370. In editorial comment on the letter, Alan G. Hill suggests that Wilkinson and the poet are thinking of the treatment of Isaac Williams in the contest for the Professorship of Poetry at Oxford, but it seems likely that both also have in mind the more general harassment of the Tractarians following the publication of *Tract No. 90* in February 1841. For an account of this fevered period see Ian Ker, *John Henry Newman: A Biography* (Oxford, 1988), 216–56.
63. Letter 21 Sept. [1842]. *WL*, VII. 370–1. See also pp. 353–4; 375.
64. *HCR: Corr.*, I. 472.
65. *HCR: Books*, II. 481; I. 158.
66. In 1840 Wordsworth made his own defence in a letter to Henry Alford, later Dean of Canterbury: 'I have been averse to frequent mention of the mysteries of Christian faith; not from a want of a due sense of their momentous nature, but the contrary. I felt it far too deeply to venture on handling the subject as familiarly as many scruple not to do.' *WL*, VII. 23.
67. 'Sacred Poetry', *The Recreations of Christopher North* (3 vols.; Edinburgh, 1842), II. 345, 348, 350. Wilson's strictures first appeared in *Blackwood's Magazine*, 24 (1828), 917–38. They are quoted at greater length in Jonathan Wordsworth, *The Music of Humanity* (London, 1969), 26.
68. Alexander Patterson, *Poets and Preachers of the Nineteenth-Century* (Glasgow, 1862), 36. The book consists of lectures delivered to a young men's 'Association for Mutual Improvement'. [John Campbell Shairp], 'Wordsworth: The Man and the Poet', *North British Review*, 41 (1864), 1–54; revised and expanded for *Studies in Poetry and Philosophy* (Edinburgh, 1868). As William Knight's *Principal Shairp and His Friends* (London, 1888), reveals, Shairp, who was a Presbyterian, was an intense Wordsworthian from youth on.
69. Perhaps because no certainty on such a matter could ever be attained, the question, 'Was Wordsworth a Pantheist?', remained a troubling one for Wordsworthians. In 1853, for example, Professor Adam Sedgwick emphasizes the contrast between 'men who, after a long poetical communion with the outer world, have learned, at length, to be idolators of Nature to the verge of Pantheism' and Wordsworth, 'a man of firm religious convictions', who remained pure 'from the influence of a

principle that soared above any motives which he drew from his communion with Nature'. Quoted Robert Woof, *The Lake District Discovered 1810–1850: The Artists, The Tourists, and Wordsworth* (Grasmere, 1983), 16–17. At the final meeting of the Wordsworth Society in 1886 Lord Selborne used the authority of the presidential address to affirm that the poet was not guilty of what he termed 'Technical Pantheism', but the inordinate length he devotes to his discriminations indicates how important the matter still seemed. *Transactions of the Wordsworth Society*, VIII. 14–24.

70. Robert Perceval Graves, *Recollections of Wordsworth and the Lake Country* (Dublin, 1869), 39–43. Using *The Prelude* to support his case about the consistency of W's beliefs, Graves, of course, refers to the 1850 text, citing in particular lines from Book V, 220–2 which he would have found markedly less helpful had he known them in their 1805 version.

71. Aubrey de Vere, 'The Wisdom and Truth of Wordsworth's Poetry', *Essays Chiefly on Poetry* (2 vols.; London, 1887), 263. Aubrey de Vere first met W in 1841 and retained such devotion to him that he continued to visit his grave annually until late in life. Comparison of his early letters with the *Essays* indicates that De Vere's views on W did not change over more than forty years and that his move to Roman Catholicism in 1851 did not affect his veneration for the spiritual poet. In a letter of 1874, however, he reveals that he used to wonder why 'Wordsworth had not made a more distinct confession of Christianity' in *The Excursion*, but that he had come to think that W was always more Christian than he knew and that his poetry is 'all the clearer proof that a genuine Theism is but the first rehearsal of Christianity'. Wilfrid Ward, *Aubrey de Vere: A Memoir* (London, 1904), 319–21.

72. William Howitt, *Homes and Haunts of the Most Eminent British Poets* (2 vols.; London, 1847), II. 275–9.

73. *The Eclectic Review*, NS 12 (July–Dec. 1842), 579. The *Eclectic* also sniffed out the other problem about W's religious utterance, namely that he often 'expresses himself in a manner which, to all but a pantheist, must be considered altogether inexplicable' (p. 572).

74. *Dublin Review*, 31 (Dec. 1851), 361.

75. Nicholas Wiseman, *On the Perception of Natural Beauty by the Ancients and the Moderns*. Lecture delivered 10 Dec. 1855 (London, 1856), 14, 24.

76. *The Dublin Review*, 40 (June 1856), 343, 346, 362.

77. 17 Apr. 1839. WL.

78. Faber tutored Matthew, son of Mr Benson Harrison, who had married Dorothy Wordsworth, daughter of Robinson Wordsworth, the poet's cousin.

79. 18 Feb. 1848. Letter in WL.

80. *HCR: Books*, II. 628.

81. There is evidence that W was ready to hear anything to Faber's discredit once he had converted. In September 1846 Faber moved to Cotton Hall, Cheadle, in Staffordshire, under the patronage of the Earl of Shrewsbury, and, renaming the house St Wilfrid's, founded a religious community. A series of letters to Wordsworth, now in WL, from a neighbouring Anglican clergyman, the Revd Mr Bill, gleefully relate tales about Faber and his 'monkies'.

82. See Geoffrey Faber, *Oxford Apostles: A Character Study of the Oxford Movement* (London, 1933; 2nd rev. edn. 1936), 229–30.
83. See *HCR: Corr.*, I. 473, and *HCR: Books*, II. 605. Matthew Arnold felt a similar attraction-repulsion to Faber. In a letter of 8 Jan. 1843 to John Duke Coleridge he reported: 'Faber is up here & is just going away: he is still very clever, very amiable, and very absurd. His farewell sermon tonight was absolutely shocking from the Egotism that ran through every line of it even when discussing the most sacred subjects'. *The Letters of Matthew Arnold*, ed. Cecil Y. Lang (1 vol. continuing; Charlottesville, Va., 1996), 51.
84. Letters in WL.
85. De Vere, *Essays Chiefly on Poetry*, II. 278. For Faber's sacramental vision, see G. B. Tennyson, 'The Sacramental Imagination', in *Nature and the Victorian Imagination*, ed. U. C. Knoepflmacher and G. B. Tennyson (Berkeley and Los Angeles, 1977), 370–90.
86. Lawrence Poston gives an account and a good critical assessment of Faber in ' "Worlds Not Realised": Wordsworthian Poetry in the 1830s', *Texas Studies in Literature and Language*, 28 (1986), 51–80. See also G. B. Tennyson, *Victorian Devotional Poetry: The Tractarian Mode* (Cambridge, Mass., 1981).
87. Faber to J. B. Morris, 19 Dec. 1833. *Faber Poet and Priest: Selected Letters by Frederick William Faber from 1833–1863*, ed. Raleigh Addington (Cowbridge, 1974), 46. Future citation to *Faber: Letters.*
88. Faber to J. B. Morris, 31 Jan. 1843. *Faber: Letters*, 95.
89. B. W. Martin, 'Wordsworth, Faber, and Keble: Commentary on a Triangular Relationship', *Review of English Studies*, NS 26 (1975), 436–42.
90. *HCR: Books*, II. 628.
91. Frederick William Faber, *Sights and Thoughts in Foreign Churches and Among Foreign Peoples* (London, 1842).
92. *Musings Near Aquapendente*, 325–30. PW, III. 211.
93. W acknowledged that this note was Faber's in the Fenwick Note (unpublished in his lifetime) to *Stanzas Suggested . . . off Saint Bees' Head*. PW, III. 493. It is interesting that Faber dates *Musings* in 1837, when it was actually composed in 1841. Perhaps he did not know the correct date, but it is at least as likely that Faber was continuing Wilkinson's strategy in the *Contributions* of lengthening as far as possible the period in which W could be seen to have been influenced by Catholic Truth.
94. Keble's Assize Sermon, *National Apostasy*, was preached on 14 July 1833. 'I have ever considered and kept the day, as the start of the religious movement of 1833.' John Henry Newman, *Apologia Pro Vita Sua*, ed. Martin J. Svaglic (Oxford, 1967), 43.
95. *Lives of the English Saints* [ed. J.H. Newman] (4 vols.; London, 1844), II. 181–2. The multi-faceted significance of *Stanzas . . . Saint Bees's Heads* has been brilliantly illuminated by Peter J. Manning, in 'Wordsworth at St. Bees: Scandals, Sisterhoods, and Wordsworth's Later Poetry', *Reading Romantics: Text and Context* (New York, 1990), 273–99.
96. Faber to J. H. Newman, 12 Aug. 1844. *Faber: Letters*, 117.
97. Moorman, *Wordsworth: A Biography*, 401.
98. See letter to Henry Reed, 1 Mar. 1842. WL, VII. 296–8.

99. Martin, 'Wordsworth, Faber, and Keble', 436.
100. W to Samuel Wilkinson, 21 Sept. [1842]. *WL*, VII, 370–2.
101. Faber to John Keble, 12 Nov. 1842. Martin, 'Wordsworth, Faber, and Keble', 436.
102. Maurice Kelley 'The Recovery, Printing, and Reception of Milton's *Christian Doctrine*', *Huntington Library Quarterly*, 31 (1967), 35–41. Only discovered in 1823, *De Doctrina Christiana* was published in 1825, translated by Charles Richard Sumner. Milton's new work excited great interest and it was widely reviewed. 'All but the Unitarians deplored his [Milton's] Arian bias,' Kelley observes, noting too that the Unitarians wanted the anti-Trinitarian parts of the work reprinted cheaply for wide circulation (p. 38). For the quotation from Froude see *Remains of the Late Reverend Richard Hurrell Froude, M.A.* (2 pts., each 2 vols; London, 1838–9), I (i). 188.
103. Anthony Kenny, *God and Two Poets* (London, 1988), 113.
104. Faber to Francis A. Faber, 18 Aug. 1843. John Edward Bowden, *The Life and Letters of Frederick William Faber* (London, 1869), 206. Quoted in part by Poston, ' "Worlds Not Realised" ', 78, n. 16.
105. Martin, 'Wordsworth, Faber, and Keble', 436.
106. Bowden, Life and Letters of Faber, 207.
107. For evidence see Stephen Gill, 'Wordsworth's Poems: The Question of Text', *Review of English Studies*, NS 34 (1983), 172–90.
108. Letter to Sara Coleridge, 12 Feb, 1846. Ward, *Aubrey de Vere*, 105.
109. Martin, 'Wordsworth, Faber, and Keble', 436.
110. *The Ruined Cottage and The Pedlar*, ed. James Butler (Ithaca, NY, 1979), 75. Lines 508–24 of MS D.
111. In 'Sacred Poetry', Wilson had declared that the 'utter absence of Revealed Religion, where it ought to have been all-in-all' in Book I of *The Excursion* promotes 'an unhappy suspicion of hollowness and insincerity in that poetical religion, which at the best is a sorry substitute indeed for the light that is from heaven'. *The Recreations of Christopher North*, II. 350. Wordsworth had long thought Wilson unbalanced and it is doubtful whether the republication of his views had any effect on him, even supposing that he knew about it, which is uncertain.
112. Faber's letters to J. B. Morris, 11 Aug. 1843 and 25 Nov. 1842. *Faber: Letters*, 109 and 92.
113. For details of the sometimes violent response to the appearance of altar crosses see S. L. Ollard, *A Short History of the Oxford Movement* (London, 1915; 2nd rev. edn. 1932), 'The Revival of Ceremonial', 152–203, especially pp. 156–71 on the Cross, and Owen Chadwick, *The Victorian Church*, pt. 1, 212–21, 'The Development of Ritual'.
114. Diary entry, 19 Dec. 1845. *HCR: Books*, II. 655.
115. The comment on Christopher Wordsworth's *Memoirs of William Wordsworth* comes from Bagehot's essay on Hartley Coleridge, *Prospective Review*, 8 (1852), 514–44; repr. *The Collected Works of Walter Bagehot: The Literary Essays*, ed. Norman St John Stevas (2 vols.; London, 1965), I. 166.

3. 'FIT AUDIENCE':
THE MARKETING OF WORDSWORTH

1. Wordsworth's executors were his son William (1810–83) and a distant relative, William Strickland Cookson of Lincoln's Inn. It was a source of great bitterness to John Wordsworth (1803–75) that his father had not named him as an executor.
2. Edward Moxon died in 1858 and control of the firm passed to his wife, Emma. For the next few years a Mr Jones conducted business correspondence with the Wordsworths, until a new partner, J. B. Payne, took over in 1864. Moxon's son Arthur entered partnership in 1869. Ward, Lock and Tyler took over the firm in 1871, but continued to use the Moxon imprint. On 1 September 1877 Edward Moxon, Son and Co. disappeared into Ward, Lock and Co. See Harold G. Merriam, *Edward Moxon: Publisher of Poets* (New York, 1939), Edward Liveing, *Adventure in Publishing: The House of Ward, Lock 1854–1954* (London, 1954), and Patricia Anderson and Jonathan Rose, *British Literary Publishing Houses, 1820–1965* (2 vols.; Detroit, 1991).
3. All quotations from correspondence between the publishers and the Wordsworth family are from documents in WL, unless otherwise noted.
4. A detailed account of the correspondence is given in my 'Copyright and the Publishing of Wordsworth 1850–1900', in *Literature in the Marketplace: Nineteenth-century British Publishing and Reading Practices*, ed. John O. Jordan and Robert L. Patten (Cambridge, 1995), 74–92.
5. W. S. Cookson to William Wordsworth, Jr., 4 Sept. 1855. WL. For some account of Routledge and of his methods and reputation see F. A. Mumby, *The House of Routledge 1834–1934* (London, 1934).
6. Jared R. Curtis, 'The Making of a Reputation: John Carter's Corrections to the Proofs of Wordsworth's *Poetical Works (1857)*', *Texte*, 7 (1988), 61–80.
7. *The Poetical Works of William Wordsworth* (6 vols.; 1857), I. pp. v–vi.
8. Curtis, 'The Making of a Reputation', 77.
9. So called because they were dictated for Wordsworth's friend, Isabella Fenwick, in 1843. Jared Curtis discusses the recension of the notes in his edition *The Fenwick Notes of William Wordsworth* (London, 1993). The selling power of the notes was valued highly—almost certainly too highly—by executors and publishers alike. In February 1870, for example, Moxon and Co. had to reassure the executors that including Wordsworth in *Moxon's Popular Poets* would not interfere with sales of the copyright complete edition: 'Without the Notes this edition can never be more than an *avant courrier* & advertisement to the complete book' (24 Feb.). Four years later, however, it was the turn of the publishers to warn William Wordsworth not to allow Alexander Grosart to print the notes in a proposed collection of Wordsworth's prose, on the surprising ground that 'the value attached' to the complete works now 'lies entirely in the notes' (2 Nov. 1874).
10. *Poetical Works of William Wordsworth* (11 vols.; Edinburgh, 1882–9). The last three volumes are the *Life of William Wordsworth*, the first genuinely scholarly biography.

11. These figures are very rough. They have been arrived at through examination of the most obvious library holdings and of four important private collections. The full extent of Wordsworth publishing even in Great Britain is not represented in the copyright libraries and will only become known on the publication of Mark L. Reed's forthcoming comprehensive bibliography. The figures also do not convey any sense of the *volume* of publication. Many titles—Warne's 'Chandos Poets', for example—remained in print over decades and were issued regularly in two-thousand-copy printings. Until Reed's work is available, George Harris Healey, *The Cornell Wordsworth Collection* (Ithaca, 1957) remains the nearest thing to a Wordsworth bibliography, but it should be noted that it is a catalogue of a specific collection, not a full bibliography.

12. Ian Michael, *The Teaching of English: From the Sixteenth Century to 1870* (Cambridge, 1987), 262.

13. Robinson was Principal of the York Diocesan Training College. My comment on the utilitarian ugliness of his book does not preclude recognition of his importance. His article, 'On the Use of English Classical Literature in the Work of Education', *Macmillan's Magazine*, 2 (Oct. 1860), 425–34, is an eloquent statement of the educational potential of English literature, especially poetry. In his paean to poetry—'it pours into the soul, with the profoundest truths of divine philosophy itself. It is the expression of the purest and most generous emotions of the deep heart of man' (p. 429)—Robinson echoes the Preface to *Lyrical Ballads*.

14. This volume is singled out in Carl Woodring, 'Wordsworth and the Victorians', *The Age of William Wordsworth: Critical Essays on the Romantic Tradition*, ed. Kenneth R. Johnston and Gene W. Ruoff (New Brunswick, 1987), 261–75, but the information given is incorrect. The first edition of Willmott was 1859, not 1866, and it drew on Foster's designs for the 1858 one-volume Routledge edition of Wordsworth. Further details from the Routledge archives are given in Douglas Ball, *Victorian Publishers' Bindings* (London, 1985), 68, and Paul Goldman, *Victorian Illustrated Books 1850–1870: The Heyday of Wood-Engraving* (London, 1994), 65–6.

15. The fag-end of the gift-book line is represented by simultaneous issues in 1884 of a *Wordsworth Birthday Book* by Kegan Paul, Trench, and by Hamilton Adams, the latter compiled and edited by J. R. Tutin and fulsomely dedicated to William Knight.

16. Ball, *Victorian Publishers' Bindings*, 56, mentions the 'malachite' *White Doe* under 'Unusual cover materials'. An example is illustrated in Ruari McLean, *Victorian Publishers' Book-Bindings in Cloth and Leather* (London, 1974), 106.

17. *Our English Lakes, Mountains, and Waterfalls. As seen by William Wordsworth.* Photographically illustrated (London, 1864). The photographs are by T. Ogle. The book is arranged in sections called 'Langdale', 'Rydale', 'Grasmere', and so on, with others called 'Descriptions of Scenery', 'Poems on Flowers', 'Poems on Birds'. It ends with the 'Ode: Intimations of Immortality'.

18. William Wordsworth, Jr., to W. S. Cookson, 1 Dec. 1864. WL. Next quotation from the same letter.

19. The first three editions of *Our English Lakes, Mountains, and Waterfalls,*

1864, 1866, 1868, appeared under the imprint of Bennett himself, but the fourth in 1870 issued from Provost and Co.

20. J. B. Payne for Moxon and Co. to William Wordsworth, Jr., 17 Apr. 1868.

21. Quotation from a letter from J. Payne, Moxon and Co., to William Wordsworth, Jr., 11 July 1865. WL. The volume was reissued in a much plainer format in 1885.

22. W. M. Rossetti became general editor of the 'Moxon's Popular Poets' series and produced a great many such 'Critical Memoirs'.

23. Cookson pointed out to William, Jr., 1 February 1871, that as Moxon had acted on a permission given in a letter of 12 April 1870, it was now out of the question to demand 'the entire suppression of Rossetti's preface'. Corrections in future editions could, of course, be insisted on. After a visit from the Bishop of St Andrews, however, Cookson caved in and in a letter to William of 11 February he agreed that the executors ought to aim for suppression.

24. The Edwin Edwards edition is to be found with both versions of the Preface. Moxon reissued the revised Preface in a simpler and cheaper one-volume for the 'Moxon's Popular Poets' series, 'Edited, With A Critical Memoir, By William Michael Rossetti', illustrated by Henry Dell, an edition which was also issued without the Preface, where the claim is simply that Rossetti is editor.

25. Moxon's *Tennyson* and Routledge's *Poets of the Nineteenth Century*, both 1857, marked the beginning of an era of exceptionally high standards in illustrated books. Gleeson White, *English Illustration: 'The Sixties' 1855–70* (London, 1897) and Forrest Reid, *Illustrators of the Sixties* (London, 1928), remain indispensable studies, complemented by Paul Goldman, *Victorian Illustration* (Aldershot, 1996). For detailed information about illustrators see Simon Houfe, *The Dictionary of British Book Illustrators and Caricaturists, 1800–1914* (London, 1978; 3rd rev. edn. 1996), Rodney K. Engen, *Dictionary of Victorian Wood Engravers* (Cambridge, 1985). Further information about illustrators and publishing practice is also to be found in Ball, *Victorian Publishers' Bindings* and Ruari McLean's *Victorian Book Design and Colour Printing* (London, 1963; 2nd edn. 1972), and *Victorian Publishers's Book-Bindings*.

26. A full account of the Rossetti edition alone, of the kind to be provided by Reed's forthcoming bibliography, would occupy several pages and be inappropriate for this book. One of the many curiosities about its history is that later editions, still issued as 'Moxon's Popular Poets' by Ward, Lock, declared on the title-page that illustrations were by Henry Dell, even though in fact Dell's designs had been replaced by a *mélange* of illustrations, including one by Birket Foster, which have no aesthetic coherence whatsoever.

27. Identifiable artists are W. H. Boot, P. Skelton, J. Cooper, and M. E. Edwards. Many of these plates appeared also in the later issues of the 'Moxon's Popular Poets' volume discussed in the previous note.

28. Controversy over the state of Wordsworth's text continues. Following an article in which I raised some questions about editorial practice, Jack Stillinger and Stephen Parrish have revivified the debate which engaged scholars a century ago. See Stephen Gill, 'Wordsworth's Poems: The Question of Text', *Review of English Studies*, NS 34 (1983), 172–90;

revised for *Romantic Revisions*, ed. Robert Brinkley and Keith Hanley (Cambridge, 1992), 43–63; S. M. Parrish, 'The Whig Interpretation of Literature', *Text*, 4 (1988), 343–50; Jack Stillinger, 'Textual Primitivism and the Editing of Wordsworth', *Studies in Romanticism*, 28 (1989), 3–28, and *Multiple Authorship and the Myth of Solitary Genius* (New York, 1991), 69–95. For an anlysis in a wider context of the varying positions, see Zachary Leader, *Revision and Romantic Authorship* (Oxford, 1996).

29. Quotation from the 'Publisher's Advertisement', dated April 1858, prefacing *The Poetical Works of William Wordsworth, With Illustrations by Birket Foster* (London, n.d.).

30. I am indebted to Mark Reed for pointing this out to me.

31. *The Poetical Works of William Wordsworth* (London, 1885).

32. Arnold to Macmillan, 16 Apr. [1879]. William E. Buckler, *Matthew Arnold's Books: Toward a Publishing Diary* (Geneva, 1958), 136. For an account of the creation of the selection, whose details give a glimpse of the complexity of Wordsworth's bibliography, see Jared Curtis, 'Matthew Arnold's Wordsworth: The Tinker Tinkered', *The Mind In Creation: Essays on English Romantic Literature in Honour of Ross G. Woodman*, ed. J. Douglas Kneale (Montreal, 1992), 44–57; *The Complete Prose Works of Matthew Arnold*, ed. R. H. Super (11 vols.; Ann Arbor, 1960–77), IX. 336–40; and S. O. A. Ullmann, 'A "New" Version of Arnold's Essay on Wordsworth', *Notes and Queries*, 200 [NS 2] (Dec. 1955), 543–4). See also Leon Gottfried, *Matthew Arnold and the Romantics* (London, 1963), 60–74.

33. *The Poetical Works of William Wordsworth* (Edinburgh and London, n.d. [1858]), 332.

34. *The Deserted Cottage* actually consists of the first two books of *The Excursion*.

35. Mark Rutherford, 'Extracts from a Diary on the Quantocks', *More Pages From a Journal* (London, 1910), 196–7.

36. Richard Batt, *Gleanings in Poetry, with Notes and Illustrations* (London, 1836). In his preface Batt argues not only that poetry can awaken the imagination but also that through it pupils can assimilate facts in a much more palatable fashion than Mr Gradgrind's. In the index to subjects in the poems and copious notes, for example, there is an entry 'Banana, the', which leads one to Bishop Heber's poem 'An Evening Walk in Bengal'.

37. Michael, *The Teaching of English*, 223. As the Michael Jaye collection of anthologies containing Wordsworth—including many not noted in Ian Michael's survey—reveals, many of these titles were reissued often in different formats. My dates simply indicate the first publication. The Jaye collection is now in the library of the University of North Carolina at Chapel Hill.

38. This is not to say that they are not important to the study of the teaching of English. As Alan Richardson has pointed out, *Literature, Education, and Romanticism: Reading as Social Practice 1780–1832* (Cambridge, 1994), Wordsworth was himself very conscious that a poet becomes a 'great Power' through the agency of all kinds of dissemination in print (p. 265). Richardson's work, and that of Gauri Viswanathan, *Masks of Conquest: Literary Study and British Rule in India* (New York, 1989), indicate the desirability of detailed studies of actual classroom practice in the teaching of English literature in the empire.

39. Palgrave's note June 1861, quoted in *The Golden Treasury of the Best*

Songs and Lyrical Poems in the English Language, ed. Christopher Ricks (London, 1991), 441. Ricks's splendid scholarly edition gives a full account of the making of *The Golden Treasury*, and of revisions to it. Until the Second World War 10,000 copies of the anthology were sold annually.

40. Palgrave, *Golden Treasury*, ed. Ricks, 432.
41. Ibid. 7.
42. Letter 20 July 1861. WL. Quoted Robert Woof, *Tennyson 1809–1892: A Centenary Celebration* (Grasmere, 1992), 43–4. Had the *Golden Treasury* been compiled under the direction of the later Tennyson it might have been still stricter. William Allingham records this exchange between the Poet Laureate and Aubrey de Vere in 1880: 'T. "His small things are the best. Even his *Tintern Abbey*, fine as it is, should have been much compressed".' 'De V. "But if it pleased the artistic sense more, might it not appeal less to the sympathies?" ' 'T. "A great deal might be left out".' William Allingham, *A Diary*, ed. H. Allingham and D. Radford (London, 1907), 293–4.
43. See Palgrave, *Golden Treasury*, ed. Ricks, 507. Palgrave unaccountably altered the title to *Nature and the Poet*, which obliged him to write a note explaining the origins of this obviously specifically occasional poem.
44. *Eclectic Review*, 2nd ser., 12 (July 1819), 74.
45. W to Allan Cunningham, 9 Jan. 1828. WL, IV. 568.
46. W employs the architectural figure in the Preface to *The Excursion* (1814).
47. 'Mr Quillinan talks of omitting the Idiot Boy—it was precisely for his perception of the merit of this Class of Poems that I allowed Mr Hine to make the Selection.' W to Edward Moxon, 13 June 1831. WL, V, 401. Hine submitted his preface to Wordsworth for approval. See Paul M. Zall, 'Wordsworth Edits His Editor', *Bulletin of the New York Public Library*, 66 (1962), 93–6.
48. W to Edward Moxon, 4 Dec. 1843. WL, VII. 504. The quoted words are W's understanding of what Gough proposed.
49. W to Edward Moxon, 20 Dec. 1843. WL, VII. 510. For a full account and bibliographical description see Mark L. Reed, 'Wordsworth's Surprisingly Pictured Page: *Select Pieces*', *Book Collector*, 46 (1997), 69–92.
50. W to Robert Fletcher Housman [15 Jan. 1836]. WL, VI. 222.
51. Henry Crabb Robinson noted on 19 June 1854: 'Richard Hutton . . . He wished to prepare a selection of Wordsworth's poems, and I am to introduce him to Moxon.' HCR: *Books*, II. 740. I do not know anything more about this project, but it seems likely that Hutton would have been told that the firm had already invested in a selection currently in print.
52. The word selection is obviously a slightly slippery one. *Wordsworth's Poems for the Young*, or *Wordsworth's Pastoral Poems*, or the separate issues of *The Deserted Cottage* or *The White Doe of Rylstone* are in some sense selections, but they do not, of course, attempt to represent the range of the poetry. Conversely, Milner and Sowerby's *Select Poems of Wordsworth* is not a *selection*, but an attempt, which honours the poet's classfication of his poems, to get as many poems from as many classes as possible into one medium-sized volume.
53. 'Lecture on Wordsworth'. *Selected Prose Works of Arthur Hugh Clough*, ed. Buckner B. Trawick (Tuscaloosa, Ala., 1964), 116. Walter Pater, 'On Wordsworth', *Fortnightly Review*, NS 15 (1874), 455.
54. *Macmillan's Magazine*, 40 (July 1879), 193–204.
55. Macmillan to Arnold, 22 Jan. 1877. Buckler, *Matthew Arnold's Books*,

n. 32, p. 133. 'Bottles' in *Friendship's Garland* is Arnold's representative, self-made, wealthy, no-nonsense, upwardly mobile, middle-class Englishman, who, as Park Honan neatly puts it, 'rides the Reigate train while dreaming of marrying his dead wife's sister'. *Matthew Arnold: A Life* (London, 1981), 342. The rest of Macmillan's allusion is to Arnold's notorious definition in *Literature and Dogma* (1873) of religion as '*morality touched with emotion*'.

56. Arnold to Mark Pattison, [July] 1879. Quoted by Curtis, 'Matthew Arnold's Wordsworth', n. 32. 'glory' is the term used in the Preface to *Poems of Wordsworth*, chosen and edited by Matthew Arnold (London, 1879). All future brief quotations from the Preface will not be separately noted.

57. Arnold's selection was reprinted more than forty times in 110 years. An energetic publisher of educational material, Macmillan later issued Richard Wilson, *Helps to the Study of Arnold's Wordsworth* (London, 1897), a school certificate study aid.

58. *Selections From Wordsworth*, ed. with an introductory memoir by J. S. Fletcher (London, 1883), 36. Ten years after Arnold's selection J. R. Tutin, introducing *Early Poems of William Wordsworth* for Routledge's 'Pocket Library' series, declared it to be 'the general opinion that Wordsworth's early work is his best'. As he makes clear, 'early' means 1798–1808, the years of Arnold's Great Decade, not, as it would to most academics nowadays, the years before *Lyrical Ballads* (1798).

59. *Poetical Works of Willian Wordsworth*. With a Life of the Author (London, 1865), p. xiii.

60. Henry Crabb Robinson to James Mottram, 12 Sept. 1857. *HCR: Corr.*, II. 819.

61. Extract from Henry Crabb Robinson's will made by William Wordsworth, Jr. WL.

62. John Delafons, 'A. B. Grosart, "A Prince of Editors": Tribute to a Victorian Scholar', *Bulletin of the New York Public Library*, 60 (1956), 444–54.

63. William Wordsworth, Jr., to A.B. Grosart, 8 Oct. 1874. WL.

64. Charles to William Wordsworth, Jr., 16 March 1875. Reply, undated draft. WL. As his letter reveals, Charles Wordsworth was moved by a sense of solidarity with William West, Incumbent of St Columba's, Nairn, whose edition of the works of Archbishop Leighton had been subjected to the most savage drubbing imaginable by Grosart in the *British Quarterly Review*, 52 (Oct. 1870), 352–85. Grosart's demonstration of scholarly incompetence and stupidity was, Charles thought, 'disreputable', but what seems to have irked him most was that it should have been made by a dissenter on a fellow clergyman, whom he describes as 'a good Christian, & a competent Judge'.

65. *Prose*, I. 28.

4. THE POETRY OF HUMBLE LIFE

1. Charles Kingsley, *Alton Locke, Tailor and Poet: An Autobiography* (1850); quoted from the World's Classics edition by Elizabeth Cripps (Oxford, 1983), 98, currently the most scholarly edition.

2. W to Edward Moxon, 1 Apr. 1842. *WL*, VII. 314.
3. Donald D. Stone, *The Romantic Impulse in Victorian Fiction* (Cambridge, Mass., 1980), 2.
4. Dickens's comment is found in *The Letters of Charles Dickens*, ed. Madeline House, Graham Storey, and Kathleen Tillotson (8 vols. continuing; Oxford, 1965–), III. 57 n. 7; cited in Carl Dawson, *Victorian Noon: English Literature in 1850* (Baltimore, 1979), 131, in a suggestive chapter on some of the ways in which Dickens is heir to Wordsworth. See also U. C. Knoepflmacher, 'Mutations of the Wordsworthian Child of Nature', in *Nature and the Victorian Imagination*, ed. U. C. Knoepflmacher and G. B. Tennyson (Berkeley and Los Angeles, 1977), 391–425, for a wide-ranging survey of the Wordsworthian child.
5. *Memories of Old Friends: Being Extracts from the Journals and Letters of Caroline Fox from 1835 to 1871*, ed. Horace N. Pym (London, 1882), 117.
6. *Charles Kingsley: His Letters and Memories of His Life*, Edited by His Wife (2 vols.; London, 1877), I. 120.
7. L. J. Swingle, *Romanticism and Anthony Trollope: A Study in the Continuities of Nineteenth-Century Literary Thought* (Ann Arbor, 1990).
8. I am indebted to Knoepflmacher, 'Mutations of the Wordsworthian Child of Nature', 391–4, for this story.
9. Peter J. Casagrande, 'Hardy's Wordsworth: A Record and a Commentary', *English Literature in Transition*, 20 (1977), 210–37.
10. Hardy of course uses Wordsworth locally throughout his fiction. Peter J. Casagrande has demonstrated, for example, the part played by allusion to Wordsworth in *Far from the Madding Crowd* in 'A New View of Bathsheba Everdene', in *Critical Approaches to the Fiction of Thomas Hardy*, ed. Dale Kramer (London, 1979), 50–73. For an account of the poetic relationship see Dennis Taylor, 'Hardy and Wordsworth', *Victorian Poetry*, 24 (1986), 441–54.
11. Angus Easson, 'Statesman, Dwarf and Weaver', *The Nineteenth-Century British Novel*, ed. Jeremy Hawthorn (London, 1986), 29.
12. W to William Gaskell, 22 July 1840. *WL*, VII. 94. A copy of *Yarrow Revisited*, 2nd edn. (1836), now in the Beinecke Library, Yale, presented to a Mrs Gaskell at Rydal Mount, 20 July 1839, might seem to indicate a meeting between poet and novelist ten years earlier. I am grateful to Professor J. A. V. Chapple for evidence that the volume belonged to the Milnes Gaskell family and was almost certainly presented to Mrs Gaskell of Thornes House, Wakefield, not to the author of *Mary Barton*.
13. Jenny Uglow, *Elizabeth Gaskell: A Habit of Stories* (London, 1993), 142–3. For a full account of the Howitts, see Carl Ray Woodring, *Victorian Samplers: William and Mary Howitt* (Lawrence, Kan., 1952).
14. *Libbie Marsh's Three Eras* by 'Cotton Mather Mills, Esq.', appeared in *Howitt's Journal of Literature and Popular Progress*, I (1847), 310–13; 334–36; 345–7.
15. Uglow, *Elizabeth Gaskell*, 232.
16. *The Autobiography of Mrs. Fletcher*, Edited by The Survivor of Her Family [Lady Richardson] (Edinburgh, 1875), 254. This book was first issued for private circulation only in 1874.
17. Uglow, *Elizabeth Gaskell*, 232, describes Eliza Fletcher (erroneously called Mary) as a 'new friend'. This is questionable from the evidence of Mrs

Fletcher's autobiography, where she notes her meeting with Gaskell
through a Manchester connection and comments that in the Lakes in 1849
Gaskell 'received us, as she always does, with that expression of heartfelt
cordiality . . .'. *Autobiography*, 274.

18. Ibid. 284.

19. Uglow, *Elizabeth Gaskell*, 232, says that Quillinan was renting Lesketh
How, the Davy's house, for the summer. This is incorrect. He had his own
house, Loughrigg Holme just across the valley from Rydal Mount, and it is
from there that he writes to Henry Crabb Robinson that he had first met
Elizabeth Gaskell at a party at the Davy's, that she was coming to tea with
him at his own house, and that he arranged the meeting with Wordsworth.
HCR: Corr., II. 698, 700, 705.

20. Edward Quillinan to Mrs H. N. Coleridge, 25 July 1849. WL. Quillinan
reports that Elizabeth Gaskell 'has been "a great pet" with the Arnolds,
Davys, Miss Martineau, & Mrs Fletcher'.

21. Ross D. Waller, 'Letters Addressed to Mrs Gaskell by Celebrated
Contemporaries', *Bulletin of the John Rylands Library*, 19 (1935), 133;
Uglow, *Elizabeth Gaskell*, 233.

22. Elizabeth Gaskell to Eliza Gaskell [12 May 1836]. *The Letters of Mrs
Gaskell*, ed. J. A. V. Chapple and Arthur Pollard (Manchester, 1966), 5–8.
Future citation to Elizabeth Gaskell as EG and her letters as *GL*.

23. Note to 'The Thorn' in *Lyrical Ballads* (1800). Sterling quotation from
Journals and Letters of Caroline Fox, 121.

24. EG to Mary Howitt [18 Aug. 1838]. *GL*, 33.

25. W to Henry Crabb Robinson [*c*.27 Apr. 1835]. *WL*, VI. 44, quoting
correctly the line EG slightly misquotes. How far the Wordsworth of this
line from *The Old Cumberland Beggar* was absorbed into serious
Victorian criticism is indicated by an article in the *Prospective Review*, 9
(30 Apr. 1853), 222–47, in which the anonymous author, reviewing *Ruth*,
sketches in a theory of the value of fiction, based on the 'deep truth of the
poet's words, "that we have all of us one human heart".' Edwin M. Eigner
and George J. Worth, eds., *Victorian Criticism of the Novel* (Cambridge,
1985), 85.

26. Henry Crabb Robinson 1825. Quoted G. E. Bentley, *Blake Records*
(Oxford, 1969), 544.

27. STC to Thomas Allsop, 8 Aug. 1820. *Collected Letters of Samuel Taylor
Coleridge*, ed. E. L. Griggs (6 vols; Oxford, 1956–71), V. 94.

28. Preface to *Lyrical Ballads* (1800). *Prose*, I. 124. W to Charles James Fox,
14 Jan. 1801. *WL*, I. 315.

29. STC to Robert Southey, 29 July 1802. *Collected Letters of Coleridge*, II.
830.

30. W to John Wilson [7 June 1802]; and to Edward Moxon, 13 June [1831].
WL, I. 352–8; V. 401.

31. In the letter to Mary Howitt Gaskell includes her husband in the project—
'We once thought of trying . . .', but on 29 May 1849 she refers to the
poem as 'a poem of mine'. *GL*, 82.

32. Quotations from Uglow, *Elizabeth Gaskell*, are pp. 237 and 3.

33. EG to George Smith, 1 March [1860]. *GL*, 602.

34. T. W. Thompson, *Wordsworth's Hawkshead*, ed. Robert Woof (London,
1970), p. xvi.

35. Fenwick Note to *Guilt and Sorrow*. *The Fenwick Notes of William Wordsworth*, ed. Jared Curtis (London, 1993), 62; letter W to John Kenyon, *c*.24 Sept. 1836. *WL*, III. 292.
36. W to STC, 22 May 1815. *WL*, III. 238.
37. Richard Parkinson, *The Old-Church Clock* (London, 1843). Parkinson dedicated his book to Wordsworth and reproduced the *River Duddon* memoir. Thanking Wordsworth for his permission, Parkinson explains that the book was written with the intention of 'instructing & delighting a humbler class of readers than can be expected to have access to the volumes in which the memoir now appears'. Letter 14 Mar. 1843. *WL*.
38. For its substantial, laudatory account of Wright's work the *Manchester Guardian* draws heavily on the comments of the prison inspector for March 1843 and December 1845.
39. Uglow, *Elizabeth Gaskell*, 265. Elizabeth Gaskell was vexatiously involved in a scheme to buy G. F. Watts's picture, *The Good Samaritan*, for Manchester in honour of Wright.
40. Quoted by A. W. Ward in the Knutsford edition of *Cranford* (London, 1906), p. xxv.
41. *Edinburgh Review*, 24 (Nov. 1814), 19.
42. *Nation*, 2 (22 Feb. 1866). Henry James, *Literary Criticism: Essays on Literature: American Writers English Writers* [The Library of America] (New York, 1984), 1019.
43. *Edinburgh Review*, 89 (1849), 402–35. W. E. Forster's review, mentioned in the next paragraph, is *Westminster and Foreign Quarterly Review*, 51 (1849), 48–63.
44. EG to Edward Chapman, 1 Jan. [1849], *GL*, 68.
45. EG to Edward Chapman, [?3 Jan. 1849] and to Miss Lamont, 5 January [1849]. *GL*, 69, 70.
46. EG to Mrs Greg, [?early 1849]. *GL*, 74.
47. See Handley's pioneering 'Mrs Gaskell's Reading: Some Notes on Echoes and Epigraphs in "Mary Barton" ', *Durham University Journal*, NS 28 (June, 1967), 131–8, and Michael Wheeler, *The Art of Allusion in Victorian Fiction* (London, 1979).
48. *The Moorland Cottage* (London, 1850). Quoted from *The Moorland Cottage and Other Stories*, ed. Suzanne Lewis (Oxford, 1995), 38–9. The 'World's Classics' edition of Elizabeth Gaskell is used as being the most accessible and the nearest we have at present to a reliable and well-annotated collected edition. The Wordsworth poem is 'Three years she grew in sun and shower'.
49. *Moorland Cottage*, ed. Lewis, p. xi.
50. *Cousin Phyllis and Other Tales*, ed. Angus Easson (Oxford, 1981), 62. An earlier version of the story was published as *Martha Preston* in *Sartain's Union Magazine*, 6 (1850), 133–8. *Half A Lifetime Ago* was published in *Household Words*, 12 (1855), 229–37, 253–7, 276–82. John Geoffrey Sharps, *Mrs Gaskell's Observation and Invention* (Fontwell, 1970), 243–8, discusses in some detail the development of the story's two versions. Martha Preston was the name of the farmer's wife the Gaskells stayed with during the Lake District holiday in which the meeting with Wordsworth took place.
51. EG to Charles Bosanquet [29 Aug. 1859]. *GL*, 569–72.

52. W to Charles James Fox, 14 Jan. 1801. *WL*, I. 314–15: 'In the two poems, "The Brothers" and "Michael" I have attempted to draw a picture of the domestic affections as I know they exist amongst a class of men who are now almost confined to the North of England. They are small independent *proprietors* of land here called statesmen . . . Their little tract of land serves as a kind of permanent rallying point for their domestic feelings, as a tablet upon which they are written which makes them objects of memory in a thousand instances when they would otherwise be forgotten. It is a fountain fitted to the nature of social man from which supplies of affection, as pure as his heart was intended for, are daily drawn.'

53. *The Prelude* (1805 text), VII. 211–18.

54. EG to Charles Bosanquet [29 Aug. 1859]. *GL*, 571.

55. Dorothy Wordsworth, *George and Sarah Green: A Narrative*, ed. E. de Selincourt (Oxford, 1936), 47. Dorothy Wordsworth refused to allow her narrative to be published, but its existence, and the Greens' story, was broadcast by De Quincey in 'Recollections of Grasmere', published in 1839 in *Tait's Edinburgh Magazine* and revised as 'Early Memorials of Grasmere' for *Selections Grave and Gay from the Writings of Thomas de Quincey* in 1854. Gaskell recommends De Quincey's essay to Bosanquet as part of his preparatory reading for his Lakes tour.

56. *My Lady Ludlow and Other Stories*, ed. Edgar Wright (Oxford, 1981), 343.

57. In 1814 Jeffrey had exempted Book I from most of his general excoriation of *The Excursion* and it continued to be the part of the poem that attracted most favourable comment. As noted in Chapter 3, later in the century it was published separately as *The Deserted Cottage* and as a text for school study. Arnold printed it as 'Margaret' in his selection.

58. *The Sexton's Hero* appeared in *Howitt's Journal of Literature and Popular Progress*, II (1847), 149–52. Quotations, which will not be separately referenced, are taken from *Moorland Cottage*, ed. Lewis, 101–10.

59. In *The Romantic Impulse in Victorian Fiction*, 136, Donald D. Stone writes of Gaskell: 'and if, like many Victorians, she seems oblivious to the Wordsworthian "burthen of the mystery," she shares the Wordsworthian sense of the burden of reality, a profound sympathy toward all who suffer and mourn and a realization of the tragic bounds of life'. The second half of this sentence is accurate, but the first makes an untenable distinction. The 'mystery' of Wordsworth's phrase from *Tintern Abbey* encompasses much more than just human suffering, but it certainly includes it.

60. Leslie Stephen, 'Wordsworth's Ethics', *Cornhill Magazine*, 34 (Aug. 1876), 206–26; Matthew Arnold, *Poems of Wordsworth* (London, 1879), pp. xix–xx.

61. EG to Mrs Greg [?early 1849]. *GL*, 74.

62. Angus Easson, *Elizabeth Gaskell* (London, 1979), 201.

63. Preface to *Lyrical Ballads* (1800). *Prose*, I. 126.

64. Preface to *Lyrical Ballads*. *Prose*, I. 124.

65. *A Dark Night's Work and Other Stories*, ed. Suzanne Lewis (Oxford, 1992), 167. Once the volume in which a story appears has been identified in the notes, no further reference for quotation will be given. The stories are short enough for the reader easily to find passages quoted.

66. Arthur Morrison, *Tales of Mean Streets* (London, 1894), 9.

67. *Cousin Phyllis and Other Tales*, ed. Angus Easson (Oxford, 1981), 80.
68. W to John Wilson, 7 June 1802. *WL*, I. 357.
69. W to Charles James Fox, 14 Jan. 1801. *WL*, I. 315.
70. Hilary M. Schor, *Scheherezade in the Marketplace: Elizabeth Gaskell and the Victorian Novel* (New York, 1992), 50.
71. Stone, *The Romantic Impulse*, 143.
72. *Mary Barton*, ed. Edgar Wright (Oxford, 1987), 70.
73. EG to Edward Chapman, 1 Jan. [1849]; to Miss Lamont, 5 Jan. [1849]; to Mrs Greg, [?early 1849]. *GL*, 68, 70, 74. The next quotations are from the Preface to *Mary Barton* and the letter to Mrs Greg.
74. In the letter to Mary Howitt [18 August 1838] Gaskell reports that her 'husband has lately been giving four lectures to the very poorest of the weavers in the very poorest district of Manchester, Miles Platting'. *GL*, 33. In *The Handloom Weavers* (Cambridge, 1969), 57, Duncan Bythell notes that Miles Platting was the focus for the Manchester remnant of the handloom trade.
75. *Fraser's Magazine*, 39 (April, 1849), 430.
76. Fenwick Note to *The White Doe of Rylstone*. Curtis, *The Fenwick Notes*, 33.
77. EG to Mrs Greg [?early 1849]. *GL*, 74.
78. Schor, *Scheherezade in the Marketplace*, 51, 50.
79. In his edition of *Ruth* for the 'World's Classics' series (Oxford, 1983), Alan Shelston identifies the quotations from 'Strange fits of passion I have known' (p. 210), 'Six months to six years added' (p. 312), and *Ode to Duty* (p. 142).
80. *Ruth*, p. xv.

5. WORDSWORTH AT FULL LENGTH: GEORGE ELIOT

1. George Eliot, 'The Modern "Hep! Hep! Hep!"', in *Impressions of Theophrastus Such* (Edinburgh, 1879), 322.
2. GE to Maria Lewis [21 June 1841]. *The George Eliot Letters*, ed. Gordon S. Haight (9 vols.; New Haven, 1954–78), I. 99. Future citation to *GEL*. Isaac Evans's visit is not recorded in the Rydal Mount Visitors Book, so one may surmise that he was one of the many, like the young couple who open Chapter 1 of this book, who filched a memento unannounced.
3. GE to Maria Lewis, 22 Nov. 1839, and to Charlotte Carmichael, 26 Dec. 1877. *GEL*, I. 34; VI. 439.
4. One of Eliot's earliest published writings, in the Coventry *Herald and Observer*, 5 Feb. 1847, is 'The Wisdom of the Child', a meditation on the theme of 'The Child is father of the Man', which is quoted. See *Essays of George Eliot*, ed. Thomas Pinney (London, 1963), 19–21. Future citation to *Essays*.
5. GE to Sara Sophia Hennell, 17 Jan. 1858 and GE Journal, 2–3 Feb. 1858. *GEL*, II. 423; 430.
6. GE must have had to work hard to win Lewes over to the poem. On its publication in 1850 he had reviewed *The Prelude* harshly: 'this poem must be regarded as an uninteresting performance, and an ambitious failure'.

Lewes conceded the claims made for Wordsworth as a certain sort of poet, 'but as a philosophic poet, we unhesitatingly pronounce him mediocrity itself'. *The Leader*, 17 *Aug.* 1850, 496–7. *Literary Criticism of George Henry Lewes*, ed. Alice R. Kaminsky (Lincoln, Neb., 1964), 78–81.

7. Thomas Pinney, 'George Eliot's Reading of Wordsworth: The Record', *Victorian Newsletter*, 24 (1963), 20–2, citing J. W. Cross, *George Eliot's Life: As Related in her Letters and Journals* (3 vols.; Edinburgh, 1885), I. 61. Ellis Yarnall, *Wordsworth and the Coleridges: With Other Memories Literary and Political* (New York, 1899), 101, records George Eliot in 1873 saying, 'I began to read Wordsworth when I was fifteen, and have gone on ever since with continually increasing pleasure.'

8. GE to Maria Lewis [22 Nov. 1839], *GEL*, I. 34.

9. GE to Maria Lewis, 1 Oct. 1840. *GEL*, I. 68. William Baker, *Some George Eliot Notebooks: An Edition of the Carl H. Pforzheimer Library's George Eliot Holograph Notebooks MSS 707, 708, 709, 710, 711* (4 vols.; Salzburg, 1976–85), vol. I. fo. 123. For the importance of this poem to the later George Eliot, see Karen B. Mann, 'George Eliot and Wordsworth: The Power of Sound and the Power of Mind', *Studies in English Literature*, 20 (1980), 675–94.

10. Benjamin Jowett to GE, 30 Dec. 1879. *GEL*, IX. 285: 'I love and value Wordsworth more as I get older. He makes you better and he expresses your own best thoughts and wishes in the best words. Yet he is a warning against being didactic which has taken from more than half his writings the true value and grace.'

11. GE to Frederic Harrison [19 Apr. 1880], *GEL*, VII. 261. Which editions of Wordsworth did GE actually read? The Wordsworth at full length acquired in 1839 was *The Poetical Works of William Wordsworth* (6 vols.; London, 1836–7). Her copy of *The Prelude* was the second edition of 1851, now in the Beinecke Library. William Baker has established that GE and Lewes also owned the 1841 six-volume Moxon edition, essentially a reprint of the 1836–7 edition, and *The Earlier Poems of William Wordsworth*, with Preface . . . by William Johnston (London, 1857). See William Baker, *The George Eliot–George Henry Lewes Library: An Annotated Catalogue of Their Books at Dr. Williams's Library, London* (New York, 1977), 253; 258, and *The Libraries of George Eliot and George Henry Lewes*. English Literary Studies Monograph 24 (University of Victoria, 1981), 120. According to Baker's edition of the notebooks already cited, there is evidence that late in life GE was using the six-volume Moxon 'Centenary Edition' of 1870. The one-volume edition she told Harrison she preferred could only have been one of the many reprints of the Moxon 1845 edition. Baker, *Libraries of George Eliot*, notes this and the existence of a two-volume edition, commenting that such were 'fairly common in the nineteenth century' (p. 120). This is not so. I know of no *two-volume* posthumous edition of Wordsworth before the gift-book in the *Miniature Library of the Poets, Poems of Wordsworth* (2 vols.; London, 1880). The only two-volume edition GE might have used would have been the handsome collected *Poems by William Wordsworth* (2 vols.; London, 1815).

12. Lord Acton to GE, 15 Apr. 1878. *GEL*, IX. 225.

13. GE to Maria Lewis, 22 Nov. 1839. *GEL*, I. 34.

14. W to STC, 22 May 1815. *WL*, III. 238.

15. See David Leon Higden, 'George Eliot and the Art of the Epigraph', *Nineteenth Century Fiction*, 25 (1970), 127–49.
16. For a detailed account of GE and Harrison, see T. R. Wright, *The Religion of Humanity: The Impact of Comtean Positivism on Victorian Britain* (Cambridge, 1986), 173–201. Harrison was not alone in thinking that Wordsworth's poetry could serve the Religion of Humanity. In a review of Arnold's selection of Wordsworth John Addington Symonds had remarked, after quoting *Tintern Abbey*, that the 'time may come, indeed may not be distant, when lines like these should be sung in hours of worship by congregations for whom the "cosmic emotion" is a reality and a religion'. *Fortnightly Review*, NS 26 (Nov. 1879), 687.
17. GE to Frederic Harrison, 15 Aug. [1866]. *GEL*, IV. 301. The point about the *Ode: Intimations* is obscured in most modern editions of Wordsworth. From the 1815 collection through to the final lifetime edition of 1849–50, the volumes of miscellaneous poems always concluded with the *Ode*.
18. F. W. H. Myers, *Century Magazine*, 24 (1881), 62. Quoted *GEL*, VI. 380.
19. GE to Charles Bray, 5 July 1859. *GEL*, III. 111. Preface to *Lyrical Ballads* (1802), *Prose*, I. 141.
20. *The Prelude*, I. 151–3. William Baker, *Some George Eliot Notebooks*, III. fo. 111.
21. STC, *Biographia Literaria*, ed. James Engell and W. Jackson Bate (2 vols.; Princeton, 1983), II. 136. It is important to note that this fault, Coleridge insists, is one 'of which none but a man of genius is capable'.
22. GE to Frederic Harrison [19 Apr. 1880]. *GEL*, VII. 262.
23. GE to John Blackwood, 12 November 1873. *GEL*, V. 459, referring to Alexander Main (ed.), *Wise, Witty, and Tender Sayings in Prose and Verse: Selected from the Works of George Eliot* (Edinburgh, 1872). Since this is not a general study of her art it would be inappropriate to list the numerous essays which discuss George Eliot's contention that her 'teaching' is integral to the structure of her novels. That it is an important issue (as it is not with, for example, Dickens or Trollope), was recognized early on by Edward Dowden in a brilliant article for the *Contemporary Review*, 20 (1872), 403–22; repr. in part in *A Century of George Eliot Criticism*, ed. Gordon S. Haight (London, 1966), 64–73.
24. *Adam Bede* was written from 22 Oct. 1857 to 16 November 1858. Wordsworth was read in February and July 1858, *The Excursion* being completed in February. See Pinney, 'George Eliot's Reading of Wordsworth', 21.
25. *The Excursion*, VI. 651–8, quoted as in *Adam Bede*, which differs in trifles from the final authorized text of the poem. Other quotations are lines 638–9 and 648–9, and in the next paragraph, 612.
26. 'Worldliness and Other-Worldliness: The Poet Young', *Westminster Review*, 67 (Jan. 1857), 1–42. *Essays*, 335–85. Quotation p. 385.
27. 'The Natural History of German Life' appeared in the *Westminster Review*, 66 (July, 1856), 51–79. See *Essays*, 266–99. All quotation in this paragraph, save for that from Wordsworth separately noted, is to be found in this essay. For a full study of the importance of Riehl to George Eliot see Suzanne Graver, *George Eliot and Community: A Study in Social Theory and Fictional Form* (Berkeley and Los Angeles, 1984). See also Deborah Heller Roazen, 'George Eliot, Wordsworth, and Peasant Psychology', *Research Studies* [Washington State University] 41 (1973), 116–78.

28. A favourite quotation of George Eliot's from *The Excursion*, I. 276, used in 'The Natural History of German Life', *Essays*, 288, and the description of St Oggs in *The Mill on the Floss*.
29. Many critics have of course touched on the connection between Wordsworth and George Eliot. The most notable studies to which I am conscious of being indebted (other than those mentioned separately in other notes) are, Mario Praz, *The Hero in Eclipse in Victorian Fiction*, trans. Angus Davidson (London, 1956); U. C. Knoepflmacher, *George Eliot's Early Novels: The Limits of Realism* (Berkeley and Los Angeles, 1968); Henry Auster, *Local Habitations: Regionalism in the Early Novels of George Eliot* (Cambridge, Mass., 1970); Jay Clayton, *Romantic Vision and the Novel* (Cambridge, 1987).
30. I date the beginning of Wordsworth's career as a poet from *Lyrical Ballads* (1798). He had published two poems in 1793, and written a good deal that remained unpublished, but it is clear that it was not until 1797–8 that he consciously recognized poetry as his future profession.
31. *Westminster Review*, 65 (Apr. 1856), 626. Most readily available in George Eliot, *Selected Essays, Poems and Other Writings*, ed. A. S. Byatt and Nicholas Warren (Harmondsworth, 1990), and *Selected Critical Writings*, ed. Rosemary Ashton (Oxford, 1992).
32. At the time of writing there is no Clarendon edition of *Adam Bede*. All page references in the text are from the World's Classics edition, ed. Valentine Cunningham (Oxford, 1996).
33. Charles Lamb to W [30 January 1801]. *The Letters of Charles and Mary Lamb*, ed. Edwin W. Marrs, Jr. (3 vols. continuing; Ithaca, NY, 1975–), I. 266.
34. *Prose*, I. 128–30.
35. 'Silly Novels by Lady Novelists', *Westminster Review*, 66 (Oct. 1856), 442–461. *Essays*, 300–24. The quotation in the next paragraph is p. 323.
36. *Prose*, I. 141.
37. *Essays*, 271.
38. Thomas Pinney, 'The Authority of the Past in George Eliot's Novels', *Nineteenth Century Fiction*, 21 (1966), 131–47; repr. George R. Creeger (ed.), *George Eliot: A Collection of Critical Essays* (Englewood Cliffs, NJ, 1970), 37–65.
39. W to Charles James Fox, 14 Jan. 1801. *WL*, I. 315.
40. *Saturday Review*, 26 Feb. 1859. Quoted from *George Eliot: The Critical Heritage*, ed. David Carroll (London, 1971), 74; Anne Mozley, *Bentley's Quarterly Review*, 1 (July 1859), ibid., 97; [W. Lucas Collins] anonymous review in *Blackwood's Edinburgh Magazine* 85 (Apr. 1859), 501.
41. Sheila M. Smith's *The Other Nation: The Poor in English Novels of the 1840s and 1850s* (Oxford, 1980) is a heavily documented account of attitudes to and attempts at representation of the poor in fiction. Smith gives details of how much Kingsley relied on blue-books and similar sources of information. She also points out how late in the day is George Eliot's call for a greater truthfulness in depictions of the life of the common people.
42. *Westminster Review*, NS 15 (Apr. 1859), 487.
43. *The Times*, 12 Apr. 1859. Quoted Carroll, *George Eliot: The Critical Heritage*, 77.

44. W to John Wilson [7 June 1802]. *WL*, I. 355.
45. Eliot uses this dramatic device again in the first chapter of *Felix Holt*, where Mrs Transome is described as having 'laughed at *Lyrical Ballads*' in her youth.
46. [*Essay on Morals*], 1798. *Prose*, I. 103.
47. Pinney, 'George Eliot's Reading of Wordsworth', 21.
48. Details of composition are given in *The Mill on the Floss*, ed. Gordon S. Haight [The Clarendon Edition of the Novels of George Eliot] (Oxford, 1980). Page references to this edition will be given in the text.
49. First quotation, Donald D. Stone, *The Romantic Impulse in Victorian Fiction* (Cambridge, Mass., 1980), 194. Second quotation, U. C. Knoepflmacher, 'Mutations of the Wordsworthian Child of Nature', *Nature and the Victorian Imagination*, ed. U. C. Knoepflmacher and G. B. Tennyson (Berkeley and Los Angeles, 1977), 419.
50. *The Prelude* (1850), I. 631–6.
51. Lines unused in *Michael*, printed in *Lyrical Ballads, and Other Poems, 1797–1800*, ed. James Butler and Karen Green (Ithaca, NY, 1992), 328.
52. Margaret Homans, 'Eliot, Wordsworth, and the Scenes of the Sister's Instruction' in her *Bearing the Word: Language and Female Experience in Nineteenth-Century Women's Writing* (Chicago, 1986), 120–52, has been seen rightly as a landmark examination of Eliot's allegiance to Wordsworth. Gary Hardy's, ' "Maggie's Shadow": Wordsworthian Tenets in *The Mill on the Floss*', *Meridian*, 4 (1985), 9–18, though less often cited, is also an important essay.
53. Basil Willey, *Nineteenth-Century Studies* (London, 1949), 205. Stone, *The Romantic Impulse*, 194.
54. The two letters quoted in this paragraph are John Blackwood to GE, 19 Feb. 1861, and GE's reply 24 Feb. 1861. *GEL*, III. 379, 382.
55. Ibid.
56. At the time of writing there is no Clarendon edition of *Silas Marner*. Page references in the text are from the World's Classics edition, ed. Terence Cave (Oxford, 1996).
57. Robert H. Dunham, '*Silas Marner* and the Wordsworthian Child', *Studies in English Literature*, 16 (1976), 645–59.
58. Peter Simpson argues the case persuasively in 'Crisis and Recovery: Wordsworth, George Eliot, and *Silas Marner*', *University of Toronto Quarterly*, 48 (1979), 95–114, that *Silas Marner* 'is indirectly a displaced portrait of the artist, a study of the growth of an artist's mind' (p. 100).
59. GE to John Blackwood, 4 Mar. 1861. *GEL*, III. 385.
60. See Deborah Roazen, '*Middlemarch* and the Wordsworthian Imagination', *English Studies*, 58 (1977), 411–25.
61. The passage was *The Excursion*, III. 850–5. See Gordon S. Haight, *George Eliot: A Biography* (Oxford, 1968), 527.
62. Benjamin Jowett to GE, 30 Dec. 1879, *GEL*, IX. 284.
63. Completed August 1867; published in *The Legend of Jubal and Other Poems* (Edinburgh, 1874), 240–2, as the last poem in the collection.
64. For an informative attempt, see Martha S. Vogeler, 'The Choir Invisible: The Poetics of Humanist Piety', in Gordon S. Haight (ed.), *George Eliot: A Centenary Tribute* (London, 1982), 64–81.

6. THE ACTIVE UNIVERSE:
ARNOLD AND TENNYSON

1. *The Prelude* (1850), II. 252–4.
2. Matthew to Frances Arnold, 4 Nov, 1873. *Letters of Matthew Arnold: 1848–1888*, ed. George W. E. Russell (2 vols.; London, 1895), II. 109. Future citation to *LMA: Russell*.
3. *The Excursion*, I. 943–53, quoted from the 1832 edition of Wordsworth which Arnold favoured.
4. In fact Arnold raises the question of the relation between truth in the pages of a book and truth in real life in his letter, when he remarks to his sister, 'One cannot say that dear old Wordsworth succeeded in complying with his own teaching when he lost Dora. Perhaps he was too old and had not his strength and spirits enough left to him. But he was right in his preaching for all that, and not in his practice.'
5. *Fortnightly Review*, NS 26 (Nov. 1879), 687.
6. *Influence of Natural Objects In Calling Forth and Strengthening the Imagination in Boyhood and Early Youth*. Published *The Friend*, 28 Dec. 1809, and subsequently in the 1815 *Poems*.
7. Francis Jeffrey, *Edinburgh Review*, 24 (Nov. 1814), 4; George Otto Trevelyan, *The Life and Letters of Lord Macaulay* (2 vols.; London, 1876), II. 279; John Morley, introduction to *The Complete Poetical Works of William Wordsworth* (London, 1888), p. lxiii; Matthew Arnold, introduction to *Poems of Wordsworth* (London, 1879), p. xix.
8. Waldo Hilary Dunn, *James Anthony Froude: A Biography* (2 vols.; Oxford, 1961–3), I. 74.
9. W. David Shaw, *The Lucid Veil: Poetic Truth in the Victorian Age* (London, 1987).
10. Basil Willey, 'Wordsworth Today', *Bicentenary Wordsworth Studies*, ed. Jonathan Wordsworth (Ithaca, NY, 1970), 267. Basil Willey was King Edward VII Professor of English at Cambridge and for many years chairman of the Wordsworth Trust. His account of his early life, with its Wordsworthian title, *Spots of Time: A Retrospect of the Years 1897–1920* (London, 1965), records in part the survival of essentially late Victorian attitudes to Wordsworth and literature more generally. 'Wordsworth in the Tropics' was published in Aldous Huxley's collection of essays, *Do What You Will* (London, 1929), 123–39.
11. Mark Roberts, *The Tradition of Romantic Morality* (London, 1973), 124.
12. 'Mr. Arnold's New Poems', *Fortnightly Review*, NS 2 (July–Oct. 1867), 427; 417.
13. Hopkins to Dixon, 7 Aug. and 23 Oct. 1886. *The Correspondence of Gerard Manley Hopkins and Richard Watson Dixon*, ed. Claude Colleer Abbott (London, 1935; 2nd rev. edn. 1955), 141; 147–8. For an exemplary reading of Hopkins's corrective response to Wordsworth see Donald Rackin, ' "God's Grandeur": Hopkins' Sermon to Wordsworth', *Wordsworth Circle*, 11 (1980), 66–73.
14. Matthew Arnold to Arthur Hugh Clough [?early December 1848]. *The Letters of Matthew Arnold*, ed. Cecil Y. Lang (1 vol. continuing; Charlottesville, Va., 1996–), 128. Future citation to *LMA*.

15. Park Honan, *Matthew Arnold: A Life* (London, 1981), 26, citing Mrs Mary Arnold's journal, 11 Feb. 1837.
16. Thomas Arnold to J. T. Coleridge, 5 Apr. 1832. *LMA*, 8.
17. Norman Wymer, *Dr Arnold of Rugby* (London, 1953), 148, citing Mrs Mary Arnold's journal.
18. Mrs Arnold's record quoted at length in F. V. Morley, *Dora Wordsworth: Her Book* (London, 1924), 107–18, and A. Dwight Culler, *Imaginative Reason: The Poetry of Matthew Arnold* (New Haven, 1966), 18.
19. *LMA*, I. 9.
20. Honan, *Matthew Arnold*, 39.
21. Emerson (1882; pub. 1883), in *The Complete Prose Works of Matthew Arnold*, ed. R. H. Super (11 vols.; Ann Arbor, 1960–77), X. 182. Future citation to *Arnold: Prose*. In 1872 Arnold included Wordsworth in a list of the four people from whom he had learnt 'habits, methods, ruling ideas, which are constantly with me . . .', the others being Goethe, Sainte-Beuve, and Newman. See *Unpublished Letters of Matthew Arnold*, ed. Arnold Whitridge (New Haven, 1923), 65.
22. Letter [24 May 1848]. *LMA*, 109.
23. Matthew Arnold to Mrs Mary Arnold, 7 Apr. 1866. *LMA: Russell*, I. 325.
24. *The Note-Books of Matthew Arnold*, ed. Howard Foster Lowry, Karl Young, and Waldo Hilary Dunn (London, 1952), 601.
25. Letter [early Feb. 1849]. *LMA*, 131. Honan, *Matthew Arnold*, 196.
26. See *The Fenwick Notes of William Wordsworth*, ed. Jared Curtis (London, 1993), pp. ix–xxi, for an account of the history of the manuscript of the notes.
27. I am grateful to Jonathan Wordsworth for permission to reproduce the lines from the book in his collection.
28. Arnold's words to Clough, [May 1850]. *LMA*, I. 172.
29. *Spectator*, 25 May 1850, p. 494. The poem is by 'H.M.R.'.
30. All quotations are from *The Poems of Matthew Arnold*, ed. Kenneth Allott (1965); 2nd edn., Miriam Allott (London, 1979). On first publication in *Fraser's Magazine*, 41 (June 1850), 630, *Memorial Verses* carried the full date of Wordsworth's funeral, 27 Apr. 1850.
31. In *Fraser's Magazine* 'Spirits dried up' read 'Spirits deep-crushed'.
32. Matthew Arnold, *The Yale Manuscript*, ed. S. O. A. Ullmann (Ann Arbor, 1989), 145.
33. 'Wordsworth retired (in Middle-Age phrase) into a monastery. I mean, he plunged himself in the inward life, he voluntarily cut himself off from the modern spirit'. *Heinrich Heine* (1863). *Arnold: Prose*, III. 121.
34. In a review of Nicholas Murray, *A Life of Matthew Arnold* (1996), *Times Literary Supplement*, 14 June 1996, Nicholas Shrimpton sounds a very important warning note to all commentators on Arnold, namely that we are ignorant 'of the dates of composition of most of the poems in Arnold's first two volumes'. Since my account of Arnold does not propose any sequence of development in his attitudes to Wordsworth, however, the hesitance of Kenneth Allott's conjectural dating for *Resignation* is not important, as it must be to a biographer.
35. U. C. Knoepflmacher, 'Dover Revisited: The Wordsworthian Matrix in the Poetry of Matthew Arnold', *Victorian Poetry*, 1 (1963), 17–26. See also the appendix on *Resignation* in Leon Gottfried, *Matthew Arnold and the*

Romantics (London, 1963). Knoepflmacher's remains the best treatment of the subject, but a substantial contribution is made by Thaïs E. Morgan, 'Rereading Nature: Wordsworth between Swinburne and Arnold', *Victorian Poetry*, 24 (1986), 427–39, who reads *Resignation* as 'a parody of the Victorians' Wordsworth rather than of any one Wordsworth poem in particular' (p. 434).

36. I have explored Wordsworth's revisitings in more detail in ' "Affinities Preserved": Poetic Self-Reference in Wordsworth', *Studies in Romanticism*, 24 (1985–6), 531–49.

37. Matthew Arnold to Mrs Clough, 22 January 1862. *The Letters of Matthew Arnold to Arthur Hugh Clough*, ed. Howard Foster Lowry (Oxford, 1932), 160.

38. Stephen Prickett, *Romanticism and Religion: The Tradition of Coleridge and Wordsworth in the Victorian Church* (Cambridge, 1976), 85.

39. David G. Riede, *Matthew Arnold and the Betrayal of Language* (Charlottesville, Va., 1988), 26.

40. At the earliest opportunity between September and November 1879 (the sequence of revision remains obscure), Arnold changed 'simple elementary affections' to 'simple primary affections'. Both versions echo key phrases from the Preface to *Lyrical Ballads* (1800), 'our elementary feelings' and 'great and simple affections'.

41. Wordsworth was appointed Poet Laureate in 1843, but he did not appear before the Queen until summoned to her ball in April 1845.

42. Alfred to Emily Sellwood Tennyson [6 Mar. 1851]. *The Letters of Alfred Lord Tennyson*, ed. Cecil Y. Lang and Edgar F. Shannon, Jr. (3 vols.; Oxford, 1982–90), II. 8. Future citation to *TL*. Quoted Robert Bernard Martin, *Tennyson: The Unquiet Heart* (Oxford and London, 1980), 358.

43. Tennyson in conversation with William Knight, early May 1890, quoted *TL*, III. 415.

44. W to Henry Reed, 1 July 1845. *WL*, VII. 688.

45. W to William Rowan Hamilton, 26 Nov. 1830. *WL*, V. 354.

46. Hallam Tennyson records his father in old age 'always greatly moved by "Yarrow Revisited," and particularly by the following stanza:

> And if, as Yarrow, through the woods
> And down the meadow ranging,
> Did meet us with unaltered face
> Though we were changed and changing:
> If, *then*, some natural shadows spread
> Our inward prospect over,
> The soul's deep valley was not slow
> Its brightness to recover.'

Alfred Lord Tennyson: A Memoir (2 vols.; London, 1897), II. 421–2. Future citation to *Memoir*. The copy of *Yarrow Revisited*, inscribed 'e dono amicissimi, E Fitzgerald', is in the Tennyson Research Centre. Nancie Campbell, *Tennyson in Lincoln: A Catalogue of the Collections in the Research Centre* (2 vols. continuing; Lincoln, 1971–), II. #2368. Tennyson's 1827 Wordsworth is in a private collection in America.

47. Martin, *Tennyson*, 202.

48. *Memoir*, II. 209.

49. Wilfrid Ward, *Aubrey de Vere: A Memoir* (London, 1904), 73.

50. *Memoir*, I. 209. The entry is incorrectly placed under 1842.
51. *Memoir*, II. 377. In 1832 *A Dream of Fair Women* opened with stanzas likening the poet to 'a·man, that sails in a balloon, | Downlooking sees the solid shining ground | Stream from beneath him . . .'. Ricks cites E. F. Shannon's suggestion that Tennyson's source 'was probably the participation of his friend Richard Monckton Milnes in a flight from Cambridge, 19 May 1829'. *The Poems of Tennyson*, ed. Christopher Ricks, 2nd edn, (3 vols.; Harlow, 1987), I. 479–80. Future citation to *Poems*.
52. *Memoir*, I. 265. Christopher Ricks, *Tennyson* (London, 1972), 151.
53. Ward, *Aubrey de Vere*, 73–74.
54. W to Henry Reed, 1 July 1845. *WL*, VII. 687–8.
55. *TL*, I. 193.
56. Edward Moxon to W, 31 July 1846. *WL*. W had quoted the Simplon Pass lines in the second of his railway letters to the *Morning Post*, 20 Dec. 1844, reprinted in the pamphlet *Kendal and Windermere Railway* (1845). *Prose*, III. 353–4. Now made public, this excerpt from Book VI of *The Prelude* was included in the single volume collected works of 1845. In the railway letter W introduced the lines as 'from a MS. poem in which I attempted to describe the impression made on my mind . . .', and dated them '1799', a further example of the way his readers were tantalizingly prepared for the eventual publication of the autobiographical work he had been mentioning since 1814.
57. *TL*, III. 66, 63. Tennyson had sent for a copy of *The Prelude* immediately on its publication on 27 July (not 20th as noted in *TL*) 1850. *TL*, I. 334.
58. *Memoir*, II. 69.
59. *Memoir*, II. 288 and 475. *TL*, III. 415.
60. *Memoir*, II. 504–5.
61. W to Sara Hutchinson, 14 June 1802. *WL*, I. 366–7.
62. *Memoir*, II. 70.
63. Locker-Lampson's account is in *Memoir*, II. 70. He draws not only on memory but on the copy of Wordsworth in his possession in which Tennyson made the revisions. See James D. Wilson, 'Tennyson's Emendations to Wordsworth's "Tintern Abbey" ', *Wordsworth Circle*, 5 (1974), 7–8.
64. The judgement 'ridiculous' is *Memoir*, II. 288. Since Hallam Tennyson is here reporting what his father said to him, not to Locker-Lampson, one must infer that Tennyson repeated his criticism of *Tintern Abbey* and that it was to him more than a matter just of 'amusement'.
65. Robert Woof (ed.), *Tennyson 1809–1892: A Centenary Celebration* (Grasmere, 1992), 43; Martin, *Tennyson*, 291.
66. Gwenllian F. Palgrave, *Francis Turner Palgrave: His Journals and Memories of His Life* (London, 1899), 217. Journal entry 1 Nov. 1888.
67. Quoted *Poems*, II. 232.
68. 'Conclusion', ll. 4–6, in *The River Duddon, A Series of Sonnets . . . And Other Poems* (London, 1820), 35.
69. Tennyson's tribute is recorded from two sources in the *Memoir*, in slightly differing phrasing. *Memoir*, II. 70 and 288.
70. James Anthony Froude, *Thomas Carlyle: A History of His Life in London 1834–1881* (2 vols.; London, 1884), I. 291.
71. W announced his plan to James Webbe Tobin, 6 Mar. [1798]. *WL*, I. 212. Kenneth Johnston, *Wordsworth and 'The Recluse'* (New Haven, 1984) is

the fullest consideration of the whole project. The forthcoming edition of *The Excursion* by Michael Jaye for the Cornell Wordsworth Series will provide a full account of the gestation of the only part of *The Recluse* completed.

72. *The Excursion*, I. 500. Shelley used the Wanderer's words at the close of the Preface to *Alastor*, dated 14 Dec. 1815.

73. All quotation from *In Memoriam* will be identified by section number in the Ricks edition of *Poems*.

74. First printed in *The Friend*, 25 (22 Feb. 1810). *Prose*, II. 52. Torturing reflections on the death of his brother five years earlier had wrung from Wordsworth a similar declaration: 'Why have we sympathies that make the best of us so afraid of inflicting pain and sorrow, which yet we see dealt about so lavishly by the supreme governor? Why should our notions of right towards each other, and to all sentient beings within our influence differ so widely from what appears to be his notion and rule, if everything were to end here? Would it be blasphemy to say that upon the supposition of the thinking principle being destroyed by death, however inferior we may be to the great Cause and ruler of things, we have *more of love* in our Nature than he has? The thought is monstrous; and yet how to get rid of it except upon the supposition of *another* and a *better world* I do not see.' W to Sir George Beaumont, 12 Mar. 1805. *WL*, I. 556.

75. *Poems*, I. 611, incorporating MS readings of lines between stanzas III and IV that were not published.

76. Laurie Magnus, *A Primer of Wordsworth, with a Critical Essay* (London, 1897), 189.

77. *Memoir*, I. 302–03.

78. For a deft unpicking of the science versus religion model propounded by Huxley and Tyndall, see Tess Cosslett (ed.), *Science and Religion in the Nineteenth Century* (Cambridge, 1984).

79. John Wyatt, *Wordsworth and the Geologists* (Cambridge, 1995).

80. *A Complete Guide to the Lakes, Comprising Minute Directions for the Tourist, with Mr. Wordsworth's Description of the Scenery of the Country, &c., and Three Letters upon the Geology of the Lake District*, by the Revd Professor Sedgwick. Edited by the Publishers (Kendal, 1842). A fourth letter was added for the 1846 edition. In opening Sedgwick claims that he and the poet 'subscribe to the same creed, that material science is only so far truly good, as it tends to elevate the mind of man', and that 'All Nature bears the impress of one great Creative Mind, and all parts of knowledge are, therefore, of one kindred and family'. *A Complete Guide to the Lakes*, 'Third Edition' (Kendal, 1846), 165. See also *Prose*, II. 390–1. For a succinct account of Sedgwick's involvement in the *Guide* see Jonathan Bate, *Romantic Ecology: Wordsworth and the Environmental Tradition* (London, 1991), esp. pp. 41–6, and Wyatt, *Wordsworth and the Geologists*.

81. W to John Wilson, 7 June 1801. *WL*, I. 355. It is worth noting that in Kingsley's 1872 address as President of the Chester Natural Science Society Wordsworth was recommended as a poet whose work did not conflict with geology, but rather acted as a frame of value for it: 'Go forth, dear friends, with microscope, hammer, dredge, and collecting box; find all you can, learn all you can. God speaks to you through physical facts; but do

not forget to take with you at times a volume of good poetry—say 'Wordsworth's Excursion,' above all modern poetry. For so you will have a spiritual tonic, a spiritual corrective . . .'. *Charles Kingsley: His Letters and Memories of His Life*, Edited by His Wife (2 vols.; London, 1890), II. 286.

82. Eleanor Bustin Mattes, *In Memoriam: The Way of a Soul* (New York, 1951) remains the seminal study of Tennyson's reading towards *In Memoriam*.

83. Hallam, who read an essay on the question, also voted 'No'. See *TL*, I. 43.

84. D. G. James focuses on the distinction in his very insightful British Academy Warton Lecture on English Poetry, *Wordsworth and Tennyson* (1950). *Proceedings of the British Academy*, 36.

85. Joanna E. Rapf, ' "Visionaries of Dereliction": Wordsworth and Tennyson', *Victorian Poetry*, 24 (1986), 376.

86. Kerry McSweeney, *Tennyson and Swinburne as Romantic Naturalists* (Toronto, 1981).

87. Tess Cosslett, *The 'Scientific Movement' and Victorian Literature* (Brighton, 1982), 47–8.

88. In a review of *The Excursion* which spread across the *Examiner* 21 and 28 Aug. and 2 Oct. 1814, Hazlitt observed that he wished it had been given 'the form of a philosophical poem altogether', and remarked that 'Even the dialogues introduced in the present volume are soliloquies of the same character, taking different views of the same subject. The recluse, the pastor, and the pedlar, are three persons in the same poet . . . the evident scope and tendency of Mr. Wordsworth's mind is the reverse of the dramatic' (pp. 542 and 555).

89. Christopher Ricks, *Tennyson* (London, 1972), 229.

90. *Memoir*, I. 303.

7. THE WORDSWORTH RENAISSANCE

1. Thomas Hardy, *Tess of the D'Urbervilles* (1891). Immediately preceding this quotation the narrator has been commenting on the plight of the Durbeyfield children, 'helpless creatures, who had never been asked if they wished for life on any terms, much less if they wished for it on such hard conditions as were involved in being of the shiftless house of Durbeyfield'.

2. John Ramsden Tutin, *The Wordsworth Dictionary of Persons and Places, with the Familiar Quotations from His Works (Including Full Index) and a Chronologically-arranged List of His Best Poems* (Hull, 1891).

3. Eleanor F. Rawnsley, *Canon Rawnsley: An Account of his Life* (Glasgow, 1923), 101.

4. John Wright, *The Genius of Wordsworth Harmonized With the Wisdom and Integrity of His Reviewers* (London, 1853). Quotations from pp. 10, 129.

5. January Searle [pseud. for George Searle Phillips], *Memoirs of William Wordsworth* (London, 1852), 24. The attack on Christopher Wordsworth is p. 223.

6. 'William Wordsworth', *National Review*, 7 (Jan. 1857), 1.

7. Alexander S. Patterson, *Poets and Preachers of the Nineteenth-Century* (Glasgow, 1862), 30–1.

8. The Moxon one-volume edition of 1845 carried a title-page illustration of Rydal Mount, engraved by William Finden from a design by G. Howse. Wordsworth disliked it and it was replaced for the 1847 and subsequent reissues with an engraving by T. H. Ellis after a design by Thomas Creswick, of Rydal Mount with three women and a girl child in the foreground.

9. Mrs Sara P. Green, who sent Wordsworth a quite fantastically adulatory letter dated 16 Feb. 1846, and a copy of her lecture, 'Poetry of Nature' [WL], ran a school in Charlestown, Mass. See James L. Mahoney, 'The Rydal Mount Ladies' Boarding School: A Wordsworthian Episode in America', *Wordsworth Circle*, 23 (Winter 1992), 43–8.

10. William Howitt, 'William Wordsworth', *Homes and Haunts of the Most Eminent British Poets* (2 vols.; London, 1847), II. 257–91. The Howitts, as their biographer puts it, 'worshipped' Wordsworth, whom they had known since 1831. See Carl Ray Woodring, *Victorian Samplers: William and Mary Howitt* (Lawrence, Kan., 1952), 66.

11. Christopher Wordsworth also gives an amount of space not earned by the quality of the verse to a poem by Maria Jane Jewsbury, first published in 1826, called *The Poet's Home*. *Memoirs of William Wordsworth* (2 vols.; London, 1851), I. 25–6.

12. STC to Thomas Poole, 14 Oct. 1803. *The Collected Letters of Samuel Taylor Coleridge*, ed. E. L. Griggs (6 vols.; Oxford, 1956–71), II. 1013. John Keats to Benjamin Robert Haydon, 8 Apr. 1818. *The Letters of John Keats 1814–1821*, ed. Hyder Edward Rollins (2 vols.; Cambridge, Mass., 1958), I. 265.

13. John Campbell Colquhoun, *Scattered Leaves of Biography* (London, 1864), 146–7; 163.

14. *The National Review*, 7 (Jan. 1957), 1–30. Revised as 'Wordsworth and His Genius' for *Essays: Theological and Literary* (2 vols.; London, 1871), II. 101–46.

15. Malcolm Woodfield, *R. H. Hutton: Critic and Theologian* (Oxford, 1986), 115.

16. Walter Bagehot, 'Wordsworth, Tennyson, and Browning; or, Pure, Ornate, and Grotesque Art in English Poetry', *National Review*, NS 1 (Nov. 1864), 27–67; repr. in *The Collected Works of Walter Bagehot*, ed. Norman St John Stevas, *The Literary Essays* (2 vols.; London, 1965), II. 321–66. Quotation from this edn., p. 365. Matthew Arnold, 'The Functions of Criticism at the Present Time', *National Review*, NS 1 (Nov. 1864), 230–51; repr. under later title 'The Function . . .' in *Lectures and Essays in Criticism* in *The Complete Prose Works of Matthew Arnold*, ed. R. H. Super (11 vols.; Ann Arbor, 1960–77), III (1962), 258–85.

17. *North American Review*, 100 (1865), 508–21. Quotation pp. 520, 521. For a full and thoughtful study of Clough's antipathy to Wordsworth, see Michael Timko, 'Wordsworth and Clough: Divine Reflections and Obvious Facts', *Victorian Poetry*, 24 (1986), 411–25.

18. First quotation from Algernon Charles Swinburne, 'Mr. Arnold's New Poems', *Fortnightly Review*, NS 2 (Oct. 1867), 424. Second from the introduction to *A Selection From the Works of Lord Byron* (London, 1866), p. xi. When Swinburne reprinted this piece in *Essays and Studies* (London, 1875), he disclaimed any intention of insulting Wordsworth, but

reaffirmed his belief that once Wordsworth lost his visionary delight in nature, he continued to write 'in the tone of a preacher to whom all the divine life of things outside man is but raw material for philosophic or theological cookery' (244–45). For a good account of Swinburne's shifting relation to Wordsworth see Antony H. Harrison, *Victorian Poets and Romantic Poems: Intertextuality and Ideology* (Charlottesville, Va., 1990).

19. 'Wordsworth: The Man and the Poet', *North British Review*, 41 (Aug. 1864), 3. The article was revised for Shairp's *Studies in Poetry and Philosophy* (Edinburgh, 1868), 1–115.

20. For a well-documented and brilliantly empathic analysis of the intellectual élite, see Stefan Collini, *Public Moralists: Political Thought and Intellectual Life in Britain 1850–1930* (Oxford, 1991). Many of its leading figures are also illuminated in John Gross, *The Rise and Fall of the Man of Letters: Aspects of English Literary Life Since 1800* (London, 1969).

21. The essays are as follows. Quotation from them, always from the earliest version, will not be identified by further notes, as it will be clear which essay is being referred to. Richard Holt Hutton, 'William Wordsworth', *National Review*, 4 (Jan. 1857), 1–30, revised as 'Wordsworth and His Genius', *Essays: Theological and Literary* (2 vols.; London, 1871), II. 101–46; Walter Pater, 'On Wordsworth', *Fortnightly Review*, NS 15 (Apr. 1874), 455–65, revised for *Appreciations* (London, 1889), 37–63; Stopford A. Brooke, 'Wordsworth', in *Theology in the English Poets* (London, 1874), 93–286; Leslie Stephen, 'Wordsworth's Ethics', *Cornhill Magazine*, 34 (Aug. 1876), 206–26, revised for *Hours in a Library. Third Series*, (London, 1879), 178–229; Matthew Arnold, 'Wordsworth', *Macmillan's Magazine*, 40 (July 1879), 193–204; Edward Caird, 'Wordsworth', *Fraser's Magazine*, NS 21 (Feb. 1880), 205–21; Aubrey de Vere, 'The Genius and Passion of Wordsworth', *Month and Catholic Review*, 38 (Apr. 1880), 465–89 and 39 (May, 1880), 1–30; 'The Wisdom and Truth of Wordsworth's Poetry', *Catholic World*, 38 (Mar. 1884), 738–54, 39 (Apr., May, and June 1884), 49–58, 201–16, and 335–55; both revised for *Essays Chiefly on Poetry* (2 vols,; London, 1887), I. 101–73, 174–264; John Campbell Shairp, *Aspects of Poetry. Being Lectures Delivered at Oxford* (Oxford, 1881), 1–65, 66–93; 'Wordsworth and "Natural Religion" ', *Good Words*, 25 (1884), 307–13.

22. For a helpful survey see Wendell Harris, 'Romantic Bard and Victorian Commentators: The Meaning and Significance of Meaning and Significance', *Victorian Poetry*, 24 (1986), 455–69.

23. For Stephen see Noel Annan, *Leslie Stephen: The Godless Victorian* (London, 1984). For the less familar figures treated here see Lawrence Pearsall Jacks, *Life and Letters of Stopford Brooke* (2 vols.; London, 1917); Wilfrid Ward, *Aubrey de Vere: A Memoir* (London, 1904); Sir Henry Jones and J. H. Muirhead, *The Life and Philosophy of Edward Caird* (Glasgow, 1921); William Knight, *Principal Shairp and His Friends* (London, 1888).

24. Walter Pater, 'Poems by William Morris', *Westminster Review*, NS 34 (Oct. 1868), 300–12.

25. Robert Buchanan, writing as Thomas Maitland, 'The Fleshly School of Poetry: Mr. D. G. Rossetti', *Contemporary Review*, 18 (Oct. 1871),

334–50, expanded in 1872 into pamphlet *The Fleshly School of Poetry and Other Phenomena of the Day* (London, 1872). For an account of the 'Fleshly School' controversy and a bibliography of contemporary materials, see William E. Fredeman, *Pre-Raphaelitism: A Bibliocritical Study* (Cambridge, Mass., 1965).

26. John Wordsworth to Walter Pater, 17 Mar. 1873. *Letters of Walter Pater*, ed. Lawrence Evans (Oxford, 1970), 13. For an account of the textual history of Pater on Wordsworth (unreliable in detail) see Samuel Wright, *A Bibliography of the Writings of Walter H. Pater* (New York, 1975).

27. Leslie Stephen, 'Art and Morality', *Cornhill Magazine*, 32 (July 1875), 91–101.

28. Leslie Stephen to Charles Eliot Norton, 5 Mar. 1876. *Selected Essays of Leslie Stephen*, ed. John W. Bicknell (2 vols.; Basingstoke, 1996), I. 170.

29. What the ethical approach could become is exemplified by James Fotheringham, *Wordsworth's "Prelude" As A Study of Education* (London, 1899). In this study, originating in a lecture to the Bradford Branch of the Teacher's Guild, Fotheringham reduces *The Prelude*—the key 'for the comprehension of [Wordsworth's] Ethic'—to a portmanteau of maxims.

30. The extent to which the quasi-religious wing of Wordsworthian apologetic constituted a line of authority now is suggested by W. H. Davenport Adams's genuflection in *Plain Living and High Thinking; or, Practical Self-Culture: Moral, Mental, and Physical* (London, 1880). In a section offering a practical course of study in English poetry he eulogizes Wordsworth, but says that most readers will need help. He advises them to turn to Robertson, Hutton, Stopford Brooke, George Brimley, and Principal Shairp.

31. William Knight, 'Wordsworth', *Studies in Philosophy and Literature* (London, 1879), 283–317. Lecture delivered May 1878. The volume also includes an 1879 lecture, 'Nature as Interpreted by Wordsworth', pp. 404–426.

32. Henry James on Stopford A. Brooke, *Theology in the English Poets, The Nation*, 20 (21 Jan. 1875) 41–2; repr. in Henry James, *Literary Criticism: Essays on Literature American Writers English Writers* [The Library of America] (New York, 1984), 770–5.

33. For an important account of Ruskin's interpretation of Wordsworth, see C. Stephen Finley, *Nature's Covenant: Figures of Landscape in Ruskin* (Philadelphia, 1992), 85–134.

34. The five papers comprising *Fiction, Fair and Foul* appeared in the *Nineteenth Century* between June 1880 and 1881. I quote from *The Works of John Ruskin*, ed. E. T. Cook and Alexander Wedderburn (39 vols.; London, 1903–12), XXXIV (1908), 263–397.

35. Matthew Arnold, 'Byron', *Macmillan's Magazine*, 43 (Mar. 1881), 367–77, afterwards Preface to *Poetry of Byron* (London, 1881). Reprinted with very helpful commentary in *English Literature and Irish Politics*, in Arnold, *Complete Prose Works*, ed. Super, IX (1973), 217–37. For a subtle reading of the interaction of Pater and Arnold and of the figure of 'Wordsworth' in it, see David J. DeLaura, 'The "Wordsworth" of Pater and Arnold: "The Supreme Artistic View of Life" ', *Studies in English Literature*, 6 (1966), 651–67.

36. Alfred Austin, review article in the *Quarterly Review*, 154 (July 1882),

53–82; repr. in *The Bridling of Pegasus* (London, 1910), 78–138, but omitting the concluding sentence which would have made Austin look very foolish by 1910: 'If, "when the year 1900 is turned, and our nation comes to recount her poetic glories in the century which has just then ended," any peer to Byron is named, Mr. Arnold may depend upon it, it will not be Wordsworth.'

37. Algernon Charles Swinburne, 'Wordsworth and Byron', *Nineteenth Century*, 15 (Apr. and May 1884), 583–609, 764–90; reprinted *Miscellanies* (London, 1886), 63–156. Swinburne's anger was fanned by Arnold's appropriation of his earlier praise of Byron's 'excellence of sincerity and strength', made in the preface to *A Selection From The Works of Lord Byron* (London, 1866) and reprinted in *Essays and Studies* (London, 1875), 238–58.

38. Richard Holt Hutton, 'Mr. Ruskin on Wordsworth', *Spectator*, 7 Aug. 1880, 1001–3. Hutton also plays the game of citing unimpeachable authority: 'If he [Ruskin] had taken the trouble to read Mr. Aubrey de Vere's fine essays in "The Month" on "The Genius and Passion of Wordsworth," we do not think he would have ventured to write this rather flippant and very obtuse criticism.'

39. In a letter of 22 Feb. 1878 William Wordsworth Jr. spelt out the details of income received from Ward, Lock. In the previous year half-share in the profits had amounted to only £63. 7s. 10d. In addition a royalty of one penny per copy was paid on sales of the *Moxon's Popular Poets* volume.

40. Negotiations between the executors and Knight lurched into crisis thanks to the disgraceful behaviour of Charles Wordsworth. William Jr. asked the Bishop to call on Professor Knight, his neighbour in St Andrews, to explain the situation. Too frightened or too idle to do so, Charles Wordsworth simply passed on to Knight William's letter which contained the phrase about 'ravenous requests'. Knight was deeply offended, as the tone of subsequent letters reveals, and he let William know it, driving him onto the defensive.

41. It is clear that this William Wordsworth, known in Wordsworthian circles as 'Bombay Bill', was the hope of the next generation. In his acknowledgements Grosart thanks 'Professor Wordsworth of Bombay' for his 'sympathetic and gladdening counsel throughout—augury of larger service ultimately, it is to be hoped' (I. p. xxxiv).

42. The information about the phantom edition for Longmans comes from a letter of 9 Sept. 1878 from Dowden to the Revd Thomas Hutchinson in the Wordsworth Library. For a brief account of Dowden see Terence Brown, *Ireland's Literature: Selected Essays* (Mullingar, 1988), 29–48. Brown surprisingly omits mention of Dowden's work on the poet of whom he wrote in 1890: 'No poet has been, or ever can be, to me quite what Wordsworth had been, for during many years I was lost in him.' Quoted H. O. White, *Edward Dowden 1843–1913. An Address Delivered in the Chapel of Trinity College Dublin, on Trinity Monday, 1943* (Dublin, 1943), 15.

43. William Knight (ed.), *The Poetical Works of William Wordsworth* (8 vols.; Edinburgh, 1882–6); complemented by *The Life of William Wordsworth* (3 vols.; Edinburgh, 1889); Edward Dowden (ed.), *The Poetical Works of William Wordsworth* [Aldine Edition] (7 vols.; London, 1892–93);

Thomas Hutchinson (ed.), _The Poetical Works of William Wordsworth_
[Oxford Edition] (London, 1895); the Hutchinson edition was also issued
in 1895 as a five-volume miniature set, available with a vellum carrying
case; William Knight (ed.), _The Poetical Works of William Wordsworth_
[Eversley Edition] (8 vols.; London, 1896).

44. Joseph Henry Shorthouse to George Macmillan, 1 Feb. 1893. _Life, Letters,
    and Literary Remains of J.H. Shorthouse_, Edited by His Wife [Sarah
    Shorthouse], 2 vols. (London, 1905), I. 322.
45. _Works of William Wordsworth_, ed. Dowden, I. xiv.
46. _Works of William Wordsworth_, ed. Knight (1896), I. p. xviii.
47. Letters from Dowden, Hutchinson, and Tutin are among the papers of
    Revd Thomas Hutchinson at the Wordsworth Library. Tutin was a
    bookseller, author, and Wordsworth collector. Private publications such as
    The Wordsworth Dictionary of Persons and Places and _An Index to the
    Animal and Vegetable Kingdoms of Wordsworth_ (Hull, 1892) might
    suggest that he was a crack-pot, but in fact he was within his limits a
    meticulous scholar, who impartially assisted Knight as well as Dowden.
48. For evidence of such pillage see Beth Darlington (ed.), _Home At Grasmere_
    (Ithaca, NY, 1977), 457–8.
49. Darlington, _Home at Grasmere_, 455–62, pièces together the full story.
    Knight saw the manuscript of the poem at least as early as 1885 and
    secured permission to publish it in his planned biography. Macmillan paid
    Knight for use in their Globe Edition of 1888 of the chronology of
    Wordsworth he had established and he discussed _The Recluse_ with the
    firm. Knight did not know, however, that Gordon Wordsworth had also
    granted them permission to publish the poem and he was dismayed when
    Macmillan anticipated his work by publishing _The Recluse_ separately in
    1888 and in the Globe Edition of the same year. Friends unwittingly
    rubbed salt into the wound by assuming that it was Knight who had
    prompted and facilitated the Macmillan edition. J. H. Shorthouse wrote to
    congratulate him on his part in 'this, as it seems to me, most important
    epoch-making publication'. _Life, Letters, and Literary Remains of J. H.
    Shorthouse_, Edited by His Wife [Sarah Shorthouse], I. 269. Knight agreed
    about the importance of _The Recluse_, but he had every reason for feeling
    cheated that it was not he who had first presented a text to the world.
50. Edward Caird, 'Wordsworth', 205–6.
51. All references to Knight's eleven volumes will be included in the text. Later
    references to the _Life_ will be as to volumes IX–XI.
52. The time was certainly ripe for a new biography. F. W. H. Myers
    contributed _Wordsworth_ to John Morley's 'English Men of Letters' series
    (London, 1881), but despite Myers's claim that his friendship with
    members of the family had given him privileged access to documents and
    information, his biography is the barest reworking of Christopher
    Wordsworth's _Memoirs_ and _The Prelude_.
53. Dowden and Hutchinson rejected Knight's arguments for chronological
    presentation and followed the poet's own classification, although they
    followed Knight in presenting a Wordsworth chronology in their editions.
54. Knight recognizes that the 'chronological method of arrangement . . . has
    its limits. It is not possible always to adopt it: nor is it necessary to do so, in
    order to obtain a new and a true view of the growth of Wordsworth's

mind' (I, p. xv). Exceptions are, for example, the sonnet sequences *The River Duddon* and *Ecclesiastical Sonnets*, where Knight acknowledges it would be absurd to dismember the sequences in order to honour the chronology of composition of given sonnets.

55. Dowden did print these poems, forcing Knight to follow suit eventually in the Eversley edition.

56. Knight admits his crime in vol. I of the Eversley edition, pp. lvii–lviii. In a letter to J. Dykes Campbell, 16 Sept. 1890, Knight mentions that John Wordsworth, Bishop of Salisbury, 'strongly . . . *interdicted* (so far as he could) the publication of the Somersetshire Tragedy. I am certain the Wordsworth family will do the same & I think it will be a *very sad business* if it ever sees the light' (private collection). Knight was quite correct in his assessment of family feeling. The poet's grandson Gordon Graham Wordsworth scissored the poem out of a manuscript notebook, but was sufficiently conscious of his duty to scholarship to leave in its place a typed note saying what he had done. For details of the poem and its disappearance see James Butler and Karen Green (eds.), *Lyrical Ballads, and Other Poems, 1797–1800* (Ithaca, NY, 1992), esp. pp. 459–63.

57. 'I am glad to hear you have found the Journals you took with you from Rydal to be of service, & readily consent to yr. inserting the extracts you therein wish for.' William Wordsworth, Jr., to William Knight, 25 Apr. 1882 (Cornell University Library). 'Rydal' refers not to Rydal Mount, but to William Wordsworth Jr's house, Stepping-Stones.

58. F. W. Bateson became *persona non grata* in Wordsworthian circles when in *Wordsworth: A Re-Interpretation* (London, 1954; 2nd rev. edn. 1956), he presented Wordsworth as anguished by the necessary suppression of all recognition that his 'love—it is the only word that can be used' (p. 143) for Dorothy had replaced his love for Annette Vallon. In his second edition Bateson acknowledged that some readers had been 'distressed and puzzled' by his 'hypothesis' and admitted that 'Perhaps the point might have been made with more circumspection', but he then compounded his offence by implying that Wordsworth's descendants had taken 'destructive precautions . . . with his manuscript remains' to ensure that the truth about the relationship between William and Dorothy could never be known (pp. vii–ix).

59. Dorothy Wordsworth, *The Grasmere Journals*, ed. Pamela Woof (Oxford, 1991), 61. All future references will be to this edition and entries identified either by date or page number in the text.

60. *Grasmere Journals*, 249–50. Helen Darbishire (ed.), *Journals of Dorothy Wordsworth* (London, 1958). In her revision of Darbishire (1971) Mary Moorman asserts of the erasures in the manuscript journals that they 'are almost certainly Knight's' (p. viii), but gives no reasons for her belief. It is striking that Ernest de Selincourt, who included many of the intimate passages Knight chose to omit in his *Dorothy Wordsworth: A Biography* (Oxford, 1933) and in his edition of the journals (2 vols.; London, 1941), did not recover the wedding-ring erasure.

61. William Knight (ed.), *Journals of Dorothy Wordsworth* (2 vols.; London, 1897).

62. In a fascinating article—exemplary in its economy and scrupulosity with evidence—James A. Butler relates how George McLean Harper negotiated

with Gordon Wordsworth to disclose the story of Wordsworth and Annette Vallon in his *William Wordsworth: His Life, Works, and Influence* (2 vols.; London, 1916), and reveals for the first time for how long other scholars had been aware of it. See 'The Duty to Withhold the Facts: Family and Scholars on Wordsworth's French Daughter', *Princeton University Library Chronicle*, 57 (1996), 287–307.

63. See *HCR: Books*, I. 248; I. 452; II. 454; II. 697–705.

64. W to Daniel Stuart, 7 Apr. 1817. *WL*, III. 374–6.

65. William Knight (ed.), *Letters of the Wordsworth Family From 1787–1855* (3 vols.; Boston, 1907). *Letters From the Lake Poets, Samuel Taylor Coleridge, William Wordsworth, Robert Southey, to Daniel Stuart* (London, 1889).

66. The evidence consists of a letter now in the Wordsworth Library from Ernest Hartley Coleridge to Gordon Graham Wordsworth, dated [?4] Nov. 1906. EHC sends a copy of the 'business details' in the letter and advises GGW that while it is certain that Knight has seen them, the original letter now being in the British Museum Library, he would not permit Knight to print them. Knight clearly wanted to print the whole letter in his forthcoming *Letters of the Wordsworth Family*.

67. George McLean Harper, *William Wordsworth: His Life, Works, and Influence*, I. p. vii.

68. A note amongst Gordon Wordsworth's papers now at WL. Quoted Butler, 'The Duty to Withhold the Facts', 291.

69. The publication of *Letters of John Keats to Fanny Brawne*, ed. Harry Buxton Forman (London, 1878; 2nd rev. edn. 1889) seriously damaged Keats's reputation, reawakening doubts about his 'manliness'. Sidney Colvin—the William Knight of Keats scholarship—not only voiced his dismay but omitted the letters from the edited collections he hoped would become standard. See J. R. MacGillivray, *Keats: A Bibliography and Reference Guide with an Essay on Keats' Reputation* (Toronto, 1949), pp. lxv–lxvi, and George H. Ford, *Keats and the Victorians: A Study of His Influence and Rise to Fame 1821–1895* (New Haven, 1944), 70–3.

70. In a letter of May 1891, quoted in John Sutherland, *Mrs Humphry Ward: Eminent Victorian Pre-eminent Edwardian* (Oxford, 1990), 192.

8. THE LAST DECADE: FROM WORDSWORTH SOCIETY TO NATIONAL TRUST

1. William Wordsworth, *Song at the Feast of Brougham Castle*, 162–4.

2. See letter 26 Sept. 1880 in which Dowden not only spells out what he sees as the aims of the Society but insists that once its task is done it should dissolve: 'I should not like the Club to languish, or to seek a factitious ground of existence in the curiosities of a scholarship which has exhausted all that is real and living.' *Letters of Edward Dowden and his Correspondents*, ed. Elizabeth D. Dowden and Hilda M. Dowden (London, 1914), 100.

3. *Transactions of the Wordsworth Society*, I (1882), 5. Under Knight's editorship the *Transactions* became substantial volumes, as they included not only the accounts of the annual meetings, but also scholarly papers,

bibliographies, collections of letters and so on. After the Society's demise Knight gathered together the best papers and addresses as *Wordsworthiana: A Selection From Papers Read to the Wordsworth Society* (London, 1889). To save further noting, quotation will be identified in the text by reference to a *Transactions* volume and page.

4. Bishop Wordsworth's words from the report in the *Spectator*, 16 Oct. 1880, of the foundation meeting of the Society. *Wordsworthiana*, p. xvii.

5. Ibid., p. xv.

6. Matthew Arnold to William Knight, 11 Mar. 1881. Pierpont Morgan Library.

7. Lord Selborne's commitment stemmed from his acknowledgement of Wordsworth's role in his life. In his privately printed *Memorials* he recounts a spiritual crisis in 1845, from which he was guided, in part, by Wordsworth's poetry. Roundell Palmer, Earl of Selborne, *Memorials* (2 vols.; Edinburgh, 1889–92), I. 257–8.

8. John Ruskin to William Knight, 24 June 1880. Pierpont Morgan Library.

9. Dowden's letter of 25 Apr. 1882 is in Cornell University Library. The Archbishop, Richard Chenevix Trench, made his contribution to Wordsworth studies with an edition of *The Sonnets of William Wordsworth: With an Essay on the History of the English Sonnet* (London, 1884).

10. Arnold, who was uneasy about being identified with any pressure group, however worthy, told George Wilson, Treasurer and Secretary to the Society, in a letter of 9 Oct. 1883, that he would not renew his subscription once his term of office had expired. Pierpont Morgan Library.

11. The 'Answer to Wordsworth's Sonnet Against the Kendal and Bowness Railway' deems it inevitable that the steam-car's noise will soon mingle with the sound of the cataract, but urges Wordsworth not to begrudge the labourer who will come to the Lakes 'To read these scenes by light of thine own lays'. *The Poetical Works of (Richard Monckton Milnes) Lord Houghton* (2 vols.; London, 1876), I. 267. Owen and Smyser note the appearance of the sonnet in the *Whitehaven Herald*, 30 Nov. 1844, but do not identify its author, the future President of the Wordsworth Society, *Prose*, III. 332.

12. Quoted Leon Gottfried, *Matthew Arnold and the Romantics* (1963), 233.

13. Lord Selborne [Roundell Palmer] to William Knight, 12 July 1880. Pierpont Morgan Library. When the *Selections* finally appeared Knight in fact followed Lord Selborne's advice. In a statement which is astonishingly evasive coming from a scholar who did have a sense of the importance of consistency and textual rectitude, Knight explained: 'an attempt has been made in this volume to select the best text, in the case of each poem included in it, although it would be impossible to state the ground on which the selection has been made'. *Selections from Wordsworth*, by William Knight and Other Members of the Wordsworth Society (London, 1888), pp. vi–vii.

14. Letter 6 Nov. 1886. Private collection.

15. This is a particularly surprising omission. It may be that space precluded excerpts or that Knight's appreciation of *The Prelude* was uncertain, but he certainly did not share Arnold's view that it was 'by no means Wordsworth's best work'. In the third edition of *The English Lake District As Interpreted in the Poems of Wordsworth* (Edinburgh, 1904), Knight

declared *The Prelude* 'by far the greatest work of its kind ever contributed to literature' (p. 216).

16. *Transactions*, VIII (1886), 16–17.

17. For a full account of Morris and Socialism see Fiona MacCarthy, *William Morris: A Life for Our Time* (London, 1994), esp. 462–588.

18. *Selections*, pp. vii–viii.

19. In 1915 Oxford University Press published *The Patriotic Poetry of William Wordsworth*, selected by Right Hon. Arthur H. D. Acland and a pamphlet *How We Ought to Feel About the War* by A. V. Dicey, in which the great constitutional lawyer repeatedly quotes Wordsworth. Dicey followed this by an edition of *The Convention of Cintra* in 1915, whose introduction draws attention to the significance of Wordsworth's thinking for the present, and in 1917 a collection of articles called *The Statesmanship of Wordsworth*, in which the final chapter is 'The Lessons for the Present War of Wordsworth's Statesmanship'.

20. The poem was first published in the *National Review*, 10 (Sept. 1887), 40–5 and later in *Wordsworth's Grave and Other Poems* (London, 1890).

21. Quotation from Dorothy Wordsworth to Lady Beaumont, 11 June 1805. *WL*, I. 598. For an account of the composition at Grisedale Tarn and thereafter see Stephen Gill, *William Wordsworth: A Life* (Oxford, 1989), 241–4.

22. Rawnsley was one of the young men who worked on Ruskin's famous road. Eleanor F. Rawnsley, *Canon Rawnsley: An Account of his Life* (Glasgow, 1923), includes a photograph of the work party. H. A. L. Rice, *Lake Country Portraits* (London, 1967), 122–42, gives an account of Rawnsley in the Lakes.

23. *Transactions*, VIII (1886), 79. The words quoted are Knight's paraphrase of the proposal.

24. Lawrence Pearsall Jacks, *Life and Letters of Stopford Brooke* (2 vols.; London, 1917), I. 57–8.

25. Ibid., II. 464.

26. *Dove Cottage: Wordsworth's Home From 1800–1808* (London, 1890), 14.

27. Documents relating to the purchase of Dove Cottage are in the WL. The make-up of the Provisonal Committee at 30 June 1891 is worthy of record. An asterisk denotes membership of the Executive Committee: Lord Tennyson, Duke of Argyll, Earl of Selborne, Bishop of Salisbury, Lord Coleridge, Sir John Lubbock, MP, Rt. Hon. J. Morley, MP, Sir F. Leighton, PRA, Sir Horace Davey, MP, Sir George Grove, DCL, Dean of St Pauls [the late], Dean of Salisbury, Revd Canon Ainger, Principal Caird, Professor Seeley, Professor Bradley, Professor F. T. Palgrave, Professor Dowden, Revd Dr Martineau, E. Burne-Jones, Esq., ARA., G. F. Watts, Esq., RA, *James Bryce, Esq., MP, F. W. H. Myers, Esq., *C. E. Mathews, Esq., Alfred Austin, Esq., *Rev. H. D. Rawnsley, William Watson, Esq., Mrs Oliphant, Miss Yonge, Mrs Ritchie, Mrs Humphry Ward, William F. Hills, Esq., Professor G. F. Armstrong, Mrs Armstrong. The Hon. Secretaries were Revd Stopford A. Brooke, Professor Knight, and William G. Brooke. George Lillie Craik of Macmillans was the Hon. Treasurer.

28. *Dove Cottage*, 15.

29. John Ruskin to William Knight, 3 Apr. 1883. Pierpont Morgan Library. Printed in part in *Transactions*, V. 4.

30. Wordsworth's *Guide* has a very complicated textual history. For a full account see *Prose*. II. 123–49. Page references in my text are to *Prose*, II. 155–253. The *Guide* is one of Wordsworth's masterworks and Jonathan Bate rightly observes, 'If we are to historicize Romanticism, we must bring the *Guide* from the periphery to the centre.' *Romantic Ecology: Wordsworth and the Environmental Tradition* (London, 1991), 42.

31. In 1810 the phrase was 'within the last forty years'. Over successive editions of the *Guide* Wordsworth had to alter the figure to continue to register that he is actually referring to the period roughly since 1770, his birthdate.

32. The letters were issued as a pamphlet *Kendal and Windermere Railway* (1845). Page references in my text are from *Prose*, III. 331–66.

33. As Owen and Smyser point out, *Prose*, III. 362–3, the assertion in the *Morning Post* that Wordsworth's special place in the Lake District and the honour due to 'the noblest poet of our time', ought to protect him personally from the 'intrusion' of a railway, was exactly the kind of special interest pleading the poet avoided and rightly saw as counter-productive.

34. Robert Somervell was a prominent businessman, founder of what became the 'K' shoe-making firm. After his marriage he moved to Windermere. For Ruskin's part in Somervell's business philosophy see *Robert Somervell: Chapters of Autobiography*, Edited with Additional Material by His Sons (London, 1935).

35. *The Works of John Ruskin*, ed. E. T. Cook and Alexander Wedderburn, 39 vols. (London, 1903–12), XXXIV. 135–6. Future citation to *Ruskin: Works*.

36. Robert Somervell, *A Protest Against the Extension of Railways in the Lake District*. With articles thereon reprinted from the "Saturday Review," &c. And a Preface by John Ruskin. (Windermere and London, 1876).

37. *Ruskin: Works*, XXXIV. 141. Previous quotation p. 138. Ten years later Ruskin's intensified hatred of railways produced what must be one of the most poetic denunciations ever of the steam monster: 'They are to me the loathsomest form of devilry now extant, animated and deliberate earthquakes, destructive of all wise social habit or possible natural beauty, carriages of damned souls on the ridges of their own graves' (Ibid. 604).

38. The main quotation is from Somervell, *A Protest*, 22 9. The second comes from a footnote on p. 23 in which Somervell refers to the excellent work being carried out in London by Octavia Hill's 'Society for the Diffusion of Beauty'. He warns that no one must suppose that such work, however, 'can supersede the necessity for a change in the condition of labour'. For Hill's thoroughly Ruskinian project, the 'Kyrle Society', see Gillian Darley, *Octavia Hill: A Life* (London, 1990), 179–84.

39. For a full account of the scheme, which includes Bateman's report, see Sir John Harwood, Kt., *History and Description of the Thirlmere Water Scheme* (Manchester, 1895). Harwood was Chairman of the Waterworks Committee.

40. *Manchester and Thirlmere Water Scheme. Statement of the Case of the Thirlmere Defence Association* (Windermere and London, n.d. [1877]). This pamphlet was also available in an illustrated edition designed to bring home to the reader just how beautiful the threatened site is.

41. See Darley, *Octavia Hill*, 184–6.

42. *Fors Clavigera*, Letter 82 (Oct. 1877). *Ruskin: Works*, XXIX. 226. Ruskin

also declared that the verdict on the scheme should be 'not that the Lake of Thirlmere should be brought to the top of the town of Manchester, but that the town of Manchester, or at least the Corporation thereof, should be put at the bottom of the Lake of Thirlmere'. Ibid. 225.

43. Arguments used *against* the opponents of the railway scheme were interestingly invoked by *The Times in favour* of Manchester's opponents. The Lakes must remain inviolate, it argued, because the artisan needs 'the one opportunity of tasting purer and more elevating pleasures than the conditions of his daily life render possible to him'. The scheme must be stopped, 'in the name of Utility rightly understood rather than of Beauty only'. Quoted J. D. Marshall and John K. Walton, *The Lake Counties: From 1830 to the Mid-Twentieth Century* (Manchester, 1981), 210.

44. Somervell, *The Manchester and Thirlmere Scheme*, 13–14.

45. *Hansard*, 12 Feb. 1878, col. 1524 and 1525. The final quotation is drawn from the Thirlmere Defence Association's statement of its aims in *Manchester and Thirlmere Water Scheme. Statement of the Case of the Thirlmere Defence Association*, 15.

46. Dorothy Wordsworth, *The Grasmere Journals*, ed. Pamela Woof (Oxford, 1991). Entries 6 Dec. 1800 and 4 May 1801.

47. William Wordsworth, *Benjamin the Waggoner*, ed. Paul F. Betz (Ithaca, NY, 1981), 118. A version of the lines had been written in the earliest composition for the poem in 1806.

48. *Manchester V. Thirlmere. The New 'Paradise Lost'. A Poem. Addressed to the People of England and Inscribed to the Thirlmere Defence Association* (Windermere and London, n.d. [1877/8]), p. 17.

49. William Knight, *The English Lake District As Interpreted in the Poems of Wordsworth* (Edinburgh, 1878). This little book went through many editions, but the text had to be revised to take account of the changes that Knight had forecast.

50. Harry Goodwin and Professor [William] Knight, *Through the Wordsworth Country* (London, 1887), 221–3.

51. For Somervell's own brief account of his campaigns see *Robert Somervell: Chapters of Autobiography*, 50–6.

52. There is some mystery about the later history of the 'Rock of Names'. Around 1984 it was 'rediscovered' and the fragments can now be seen at the Wordsworth Museum, Grasmere, set into an appropriate rock face.

53. *Transactions*, V (2 May 1883), 45. Further quotations are from this issue and will not be separately noted.

54. In its printed leaflet the Lake District Defence Society lists as members prominent figures whose names are familiar to anyone working on high Victorian culture—peers and MPs, critics, journal editors, poets and artists, clergymen, heads of colleges and public schools. But the handwritten list, now in the Cumbria Record Office, Carlisle, includes many others, not famous, industrialists, merchants, persons of property and influence, who, as Marshall and Walton observe, made available to the society 'a formidable body of influence, expertise and capital'. *Lake Counties*, 214.

55. Undated draft of letter to unknown recipient, addressed as 'My Lord'. Cumbria Record Office, Kendal. Rawnsley papers, WDX/422/2/1.

56. Ian Reid examines the ideological positioning of such statements in 'Patriotism, Natural Aristocracy and Manhood: The Import of English in

Two Lake Districts', *Literature and National Cultures*, ed. Brian Edwards (Deakin, 1988), 21–32.

57. The Kyrle Society was named after Pope's 'Man of Ross'. See Darley, *Octavia Hill*, 179–81.

58. See John K. Walton, 'The National Trust: Preservation or Provision?', *Ruskin and Environment: The Storm-Cloud of the Nineteenth Century*, ed. Michael Wheeler (Manchester, 1995), 144–64, for a forceful exposition of how much the National Trust, and Rawnsley, one of its founders, owed to Ruskin. Further detail is to be found in Graham Murphy, *Founders of the National Trust* (London, 1987).

59. *Ruskin: Works*, XXXIV. 604.

60. Rawnsley was well aware of the clash of private and public rights in the Lake District. In 1885 he led a large body of walkers to reopen a footpath to Latrigg which had been stopped up, a much-publicized action which further enhanced his standing as the local champion of the people's rights. Murphy, *Founders of the National Trust*, 69–100, gives a full account of Rawnsley's activities.

61. John K. Walton, *The National Trust*, 148.

62. See John Gaze, *Figures in a Landscape: A History of the National Trust* (London, 1988), which opens with a Prologue on 'The Patron Saint', Wordsworth. See also B. L. Thompson, *The Lake District and the National Trust* (Kendal, 1946).

Bibliography

This is not a comprehensive bibliography of the subject but a list of works consulted. To preserve some reasonable brevity all of the Victorian editions of Wordsworth mentioned in the main text are not separately listed, other than the most important ones edited by named scholars such as William Knight or Edward Dowden. The numerous periodical reviews, notices, and articles, from which only brief quotations have been taken and identified in the text or in the notes, are also not separately listed here.

ADAMS, W. H. DAVENPORT, *Plain Living and High Thinking; or, Practical Self-Culture: Moral, Mental, and Physical* (London, 1880).

ALLINGHAM, WILLIAM, *A Diary*, ed. H. Allingham and D. Radford (London, 1907).

ANDERSON, PATRICIA, and ROSE, JONATHAN, *British Literary Publishing Houses 1820–1965* (2 vols.; Detroit, 1991).

ANNAN, NOEL, *Leslie Stephen: The Godless Victorian* (London, 1984).

Anon., *Manchester V. Thirlmere. The New 'Paradise Lost'. A Poem. Addressed to the People of England and Inscribed to the Thirlmere Defence Association* (Windermere, n.d. [1877/8]).

ARNOLD, MATTHEW, *Letters of Matthew Arnold: 1848–1888*, ed. George W. E. Russell (2 vols.; London, 1895).

—— *Unpublished Letters of Matthew Arnold*, ed. Arnold Whitridge (New Haven, 1923).

—— *The Letters of Matthew Arnold to Arthur Hugh Clough*, ed. Howard Foster Lowry (Oxford, 1932).

—— *The Complete Prose Works of Matthew Arnold*, ed. R. H. Super (11 vols.) Ann Arbor, 1960–77).

—— *The Note-Books of Matthew Arnold*, ed. Howard Foster Lowry, Karl Young, and Waldo Hilary Dunn (London, 1952).

—— *Culture and Anarchy*, ed. R. H. Super (Ann Arbor, 1965).

—— *The Poems of Matthew Arnold*, ed. Kenneth Allott (London, 1965; 2nd edn. Miriam Allott, 1979).

—— *The Yale Manuscript*, ed. S. O. A. Ullman (Ann Arbor, 1989).

—— *The Letters of Matthew Arnold*, ed. Cecil Y. Lang (1 vol. continuing; Charlottesville, Va, 1996–).

AUSTER, HENRY, *Local Habitations: Regionalism in the Early Novels of George Eliot* (Cambridge, Mass., 1970).

AUSTIN, ALFRED, *The Bridling of Pegasus* (London, 1910).

BAGEHOT, WALTER, *The Collected Works of Walter Bagehot: The Literary Essays*, ed. Norman St John Stevas (2 vols.; London, 1965).

BAKER, WILLIAM, *The Libraries of George Eliot and George Henry Lewes*. English Literary Studies Monograph, 24 (University of Victoria, 1981).

BALDICK, CHRIS, *The Social Mission of English Criticism 1848–1932* (Oxford, 1983).

BALL, DOUGLAS, *Victorian Publishers' Bindings* (London, 1985).

BARRETT, ELIZABETH, *Elizabeth Barrett to Mr Boyd*, ed. Barbara P. McCarthy (London, 1955).

BATE, JONATHAN, *Romantic Ecology: Wordsworth and the Environmental Tradition* (London, 1991).

BATESON, F. W., *Wordsworth: A Re-Intepretation* (London, 1954; 2nd rev. edn. 1956).

BATHO, EDITH C., *The Later Wordsworth* (Cambridge, 1933).

BATT, RICHARD, *Gleanings in Poetry, with Notes and Illustrations* (London, 1836).

BAUER, N. S., *William Wordsworth: A Reference Guide to British Criticism, 1793–1899* (Boston, 1978).

BEER, JOHN, 'William Ellery Channing Visits the Lake Poets', *Review of English Studies*, NS 42 (1991), 212–26.

BEERBOHM, MAX, *The Poets' Corner* (London, 1904).

BLANSHARD, FRANCES, *Portraits of Wordsworth* (London, 1959).

BOURNE, Mrs, *Northern Reminiscences* (Whitehaven, 1832).

BOWDEN, JOHN EDWARD, *The Life and Letters of Frederick William Faber* (London, 1869).

BRIMLEY, GEORGE, 'Wordsworth', *Fraser's Magazine*, 44 (1851), 101–2, 106–18, 186–98.

BROOKE, STOPFORD, A., *Life and Letters of Frederick W. Robertson M.A.* (2 vols.; London, 1865).

—— *Theology in the English Poets* (London, 1874).

BROWN, DAVID BLAYNEY, WOOF, ROBERT and HEBRON, STEPHEN, *Benjamin Robert Haydon 1786–1846* (Grasmere, 1996).

BROWN, TERENCE, *Ireland's Literature: Selected Essays* (Mullingar, 1988).

BUCHANAN, ROBERT, *The Fleshly School of Poetry and Other Phenomena of the Day* (London, 1872).

BUCKLER, WILLIAM E., *Matthew Arnold's Books: Towards a Publishing Diary* (Geneva, 1958).

BUTLER, JAMES A., 'The Duty to Withhold the Facts: Family and Scholars on Wordsworth's French Daughter', *Princeton University Library Chronicle*, 57 (1996), 287–307.

BYTHELL, DUNCAN, *The Handloom Weavers* (Cambridge, 1969).

CAIRD, EDWARD, 'Wordsworth', *Fraser's Magazine*, NS 21 (Feb. 1880), 205–21.

CAMPBELL, NANCIE, *Tennyson in Lincoln: A Catalogue of the Collections in the Research Centre* (2 vols., continuing; Lincoln, 1971–).

CARLISLE, JANICE, 'J. S. Mill's *Autobiography*: The Life of a "Bookish Man" ', *Victorian Studies*, 33 (1989), 125–48.

CARROLL, DAVID, *George Eliot: The Critical Heritage* (London, 1971).

CASAGRANDE, PETER J., 'Hardy's Wordsworth: A Record and a Commentary', *English Literature in Transition*, 20 (1977), 210–37.

—— 'A New View of Bathsheba Everdene', in *Critical Approaches to the Fiction of Thomas Hardy*, ed. Dale Kramer (London, 1979), 50–73.

CHADWICK, OWEN, *The Victorian Church:* Part One: *1829–1859* (London, 1966; 3rd edn. 1971).

CHAUDHURI, NIRAD, C., *The Autobiography of an Unknown Indian* (London, 1951).

CLAYTON, JAY, *Romantic Vision and the Novel* (Cambridge, 1987).

CLOUGH, ARTHUR HUGH, *Selected Prose Works of Arthur Hugh Clough*, ed. Buckner B. Trawick (Tuscaloosa, Ala., 1964).

—— *The Oxford Diaries of Arthur Hugh Clough*, ed. Anthony Kenny (Oxford, 1990).

COLERIDGE, SAMUEL TAYLOR, *The Collected Letters of Samuel Taylor Coleridge*, ed. E. L. Griggs (6 vols.; Oxford, 1956–71).

—— *Biographia Literaria*, ed. James Engell and W. Jackson Bate (2 vols.; Princeton, 1983).

COLLINI, STEFAN, *Public Moralists: Political Thought and Intellectual Life in Britain 1850–1930* (Oxford, 1991).

COLQUHOUN, JOHN CAMPBELL, *Scattered Leaves of Biography* (London, 1864).

CONRAD, PETER, *The Victorian Treasure-House* (London, 1973).

COOPER, THOMAS, *The Life of Thomas Cooper: Written by Himself*, ed. John Saville (Leicester, 1971).

COSSLETT, TESS, *The 'Scientific' Movement' and Victorian Literature* (Brighton, 1982).

—— (ed.), *Science and Religion in the Nineteenth Century* (Cambridge, 1984).

COTTLE, JOSEPH, *Early Recollections, Chiefly Relating to the Late Samuel Taylor Coleridge* (2 vols.; London, 1837).

CROSS, JOHN W., *George Eliot's Life: As Related in Her Letters and Journals* (3 vols.; Edinburgh, 1885).

CULLER, A. DWIGHT, *Imaginative Reason: The Poetry of Matthew Arnold* (New Haven, 1966).

CUMMING, ROBERT DENOON, *Human Nature and History: A Study of the Development of Liberal Political Thought* (2 vols.; Chicago, 1969).

CUNNINGHAM, VALENTINE, *Everywhere Spoken Against: Dissent in the Victorian Novel* (Oxford, 1975).

CURTIS, JARED R., 'The Making of a Reputation: John Carter's Corrections to the Proofs of Wordsworth's *Poetical Works (1857)'*, *Texte*, 7 (1988), 61–80.

—— 'Matthew Arnold's Wordsworth: The Tinker Tinkered', *The Mind in Creation: Essays on English Romantic Literature in Honour of Ross G. Woodman*, ed. J. Douglas Kneale (Montreal, 1992), 44–57.

—— (ed.), *The Fenwick Notes of William Wordsworth* (London, 1993).

DARLEY, GILLIAN, *Octavia Hill: A Life* (London, 1990).

DAWSON, CARL, *Victorian Noon: English Literature in 1850* (Baltimore, 1979).

DAWSON, GEORGE, *Biographical Lectures*, ed. George St Clair (London, 1886).

DELAFONS, JOHN, 'A. B. Grosart, "A Prince of Editors": Tribute to a Victorian Scholar', *Bulletin of the New York Public Library*, 60 (1956), 444–54.

DELAURA, DAVID J., 'The "Wordsworth" of Pater and Arnold: "The Supreme Artistic View of Life" ', *Studies in English Literature*, 6 (1966), 651–67.

DE QUINCEY, THOMAS, 'Lake Reminiscences: From 1807–1830', *Tait's Edinburgh Magazine*, 6 (1839), 1–12, 90–103, 246–54.

DE SELINCOURT, ERNEST, *Dorothy Wordsworth: A Biography* (Oxford, 1933).

DE VERE, AUBREY, *Essays Chiefly on Poetry* (2 vols.; London, 1887).

DEWEY, ORVILLE, *The Old World and the New* (2 vols., New York, 1836).

DOUGLAS, Mrs STAIR, *The Life and Selections from the Correspondence of William Whewell, D.D.* (London, 1881).

DOWDEN, EDWARD, *Letters of Edward Dowden and his Correspondents*, ed. Elizabeth D. Dowden and Hilda M. Dowden (London, 1914).

DUNHAM, ROBERT, H., '*Silas Marner* and the Wordsworthian Child', *Studies in English Literature*, 16 (1976), 645–59.

Dunn, Waldo Hilary, *James Anthony Froude: A Biography* (2 vols.; Oxford, 1961–3).

EASSON, ANGUS, *Elizabeth Gaskell* (London, 1979).

—— 'Statesman, Dwarf and Weaver', in *The Nineteenth-Century British Novel*, ed. Jeremy Hawthorn (London, 1986), 17–29.

EIGNER, EDWIN M., and WORTH, GEORGE J., eds., *Victorian Criticism of the Novel* (Cambridge, 1985).

ELFENBEIN, ANDREW, *Byron and the Victorians* (Cambridge, 1996).

ELIOT, GEORGE, *Wise, Witty, and Tender Sayings in Prose and Verse: Selected from the Works of George Eliot*, ed. Alexander Main (Edinburgh, 1872).

—— *The Legend of Jubal and Other Poems* (Edinburgh, 1874).

—— *Impressions of Theophrastus Such* (Edinburgh, 1879).

—— *The George Eliot Letters*, ed. Gordon S. Haight (9 vols., New Haven, 1954–78).

—— *Essays of George Eliot*, ed. Thomas Pinney (London, 1963).

—— *Some George Eliot Notebooks: An Edition of the Carl H. Pforzheimer Library's George Eliot Holograph Notebooks MSS 707, 708, 709, 710, 711* (4 vols., Salzburg, 1976–85).

—— *The George Eliot-George Henry Lewes Library: An Annotated Catalogue of Their Books at Dr. Williams's Library, London*, ed. William Baker (New York, 1977).

—— *The Mill on the Floss*, ed. Gordon S. Haight (Oxford, 1980).

—— *Selected Essays, Poems and Other Writings*, ed. A. S. Byatt and Nicholas Warren (Harmondsworth, 1990).

—— *Selected Critical Writings*, ed. Rosemary Ashton (Oxford, 1992).

—— *Silas Marner*, ed. Terence Cave (Oxford, 1996).

—— *Adam Bede*, ed. Valentine Cunningham (Oxford, 1996).

ENGEN, RODNEY, K., *Dictionary of Victorian Wood Engravers* (Cambridge, 1985).

ERICKSON, LEE, 'The Egoism of Authorship: Wordsworth's Poetic Career', *Journal of English and Germanic Philology*, 89 (1990), 37–50.

FABER, FREDERICK WILLIAM, *Sights and Thoughts in Foreign Churches and Among Foreign Peoples* (London, 1842).

—— *Faber Poet and Priest: Selected Letters by Frederick William Faber from 1833–1863*, ed. Raleigh Addington (Cowbridge, 1974).

FABER, GEOFFREY, *Oxford Apostles: A Character Study of the Oxford Movement* (London, 1933; 2nd rev. edn., 1936).

FINLEY, C. STEPHEN, *Nature's Covenant: Figures of Landscape in Ruskin* (Philadelphia, 1992).

FLETCHER, Mrs [ELIZA], *The Autobiography of Mrs Fletcher*, ed. The Survivor of Her Family [Lady Richardson] (Edinburgh, 1875).

FORD, GEORGE H., *Keats and the Victorians: A Study of His Influence and Rise to Fame 1821–1895* (New Haven, 1944).

FOTHERINGHAM, JAMES, *Wordsworth's 'Prelude' As A Study of Education* (London, 1899).

FOX, CAROLINE, *Memories of Old Friends: Being Extracts from the Journals and Letters of Caroline Fox from 1835–1871*, ed. Horace N. Pym (London, 1882).

FREDEMAN, WILLIAM E., *Pre-Raphaelitism: A Bibliocritical Study* (Cambridge, Mass., 1965).

FROUDE, JAMES ANTHONY, *Thomas Carlyle: A History of His Life in London 1834–1881* (2 vols.; London, 1884).

FROUDE, RICHARD HURRELL, *Remains of the Late Reverend Richard Hurrell Froude, M.A.* (2 pts., each 2 vols.; London, 1838–9).

GASKELL, ELIZABETH, *The Letters of Mrs Gaskell*, ed. J. A. V. Chapple and Arthur Pollard (Manchester, 1966).

—— *Cousin Phyllis and Other Tales*, ed. Angus Easson (Oxford, 1981).

—— *My Lady Ludlow and Other Stories*, ed. Edgar Wright (Oxford, 1981).

—— *Ruth*, ed. Alan Shelston (Oxford, 1983).

—— *Mary Barton*, ed. Edgar Wright (Oxford, 1987).

—— *A Dark Night's Work and Other Stories*, ed. Suzanne Lewis (Oxford, 1992).

—— *The Moorland Cottage and Other Stories*, ed. Suzanne Lewis (Oxford, 1995).

GAULL, MARILYN, 'From Wordsworth to Dawin: "On to the Fields of Praise" ', *Wordsworth Circle*, 10 (1979), 33–48.

GAZE, JOHN, *Figures in a Landscape: A History of the National Trust* (London, 1988).

GILL, STEPHEN, *William Wordsworth: A Life* (Oxford, 1989).

—— 'Wordsworth's Poems: The Question of Text', *Review of English Studies*, NS 34 (1983), 172–90. Revised for *Romantic Revisions*, ed. Robert Brinkley and Keith Hanley (Cambridge, 1992), 43–63.

GOLDMAN, PAUL, *Victorian Illustrated Books 1850–1870: The Heyday of Wood-Engraving* (London, 1994).

—— *Victorian Illustration* (Aldershot, 1996).

GOMM, Sir WILLIAM MAYNARD, *Letters and Journals of Field-Marshal Sir William Maynard Gomm . . . 1799–1815*, ed. Francis Culling Carr-Gomm (London, 1881).

GOODWIN, HARRY, and KNIGHT, WILLIAM, *Through the Wordsworth Country* (London, 1887).

GOTTFRIED, LEON, *Matthew Arnold and the Romantics* (London, 1963).

GRAVER, SUZANNE, *George Eliot and Community: A Study in Social Theory and Fictional Form* (Berkeley and Los Angeles, 1984).

GRAVES, ROBERT PERCEVAL, *Recollections of Wordsworth and the Lake Country* (Dublin, 1869).

GROSS, JOHN, *The Rise and Fall of the Man of Letters: Aspects of English Literary Life Since 1800* (London, 1969).

HAIGHT, GORDON S. (ed.), *A Century of George Eliot Criticism* (London, 1966).

—— *George Eliot: A Biography* (Oxford, 1968).

HANDLEY, GRAHAM, 'Mrs Gaskell's Reading: Some Notes on Echoes and Epigraphs in "Mary Barton" ', *Durham University Journal*, NS 28 (1967), 131–8.

HARDY, FLORENCE EMILY, *The Life of Thomas Hardy* (2 vols.; London, 1933).

HARDY, GARY, ' "Maggie's Shadow": Wordsworthian Tenets in *The Mill on the Floss*', *Meridian*, 4 (1985), 9–18.

HARPER, GEORGE MCLEAN, *William Wordsworth: His Life, Works, and Influence* (2 vols.; London, 1916).

—— *Wordsworth's French Daughter* (Princeton, 1921).

HARRIS, WENDELL, 'Romantic Bard and Victorian Commentators: The Meaning and Significance of Meaning and Significance', *Victorian Poetry*, 24 (1986), 455–69.

HARRISON, ANTONY H., *Victorian Poets and Romantic Poems: Intertextuality and Ideology* (Charlottesville, Va., 1990).

HARWOOD, Sir JOHN, *History and Description of the Thirlmere Water Scheme* (Manchester, 1895).

HAZLITT, WILLIAM, *The Complete Works of William Hazlitt*, ed. P. P. Howe (21 vols.; London, 1930–4).

HIGDEN, DAVID LEON, 'George Eliot and the Art of the Epigraph', *Nineteenth Century Fiction*, 25 (1970), 127–49.

HILL, ALAN G., 'Wordsworth and his American Friends', *Bulletin of Research in the Humanities*, 81 (1978), 146–60.

HILTON, TIM, *John Ruskin: The Early Years 1819–1859* (New Haven, 1985).

HOMANS, MARGARET, *Bearing the Word: Language and Female Experience in Nineteenth-Century Women's Writing* (Chicago, 1986).

HONAN, PARK, *Matthew Arnold: A Life* (London, 1981).

HOPKINS, GERARD MANLEY, *The Correspondence of Gerard Manley Hopkins and Richard Watson Dixon*, ed. Claude Colleer Abbott (London, 1935; 2nd rev. edn., 1955).

HOUFE, SIMON, *The Dictionary of British Book Illustrators and Caricaturists, 1800–1914* (London, 1978; 3rd rev. edn. 1996).

HOUGHTON, LORD, *The Poetical Works of (Richard Monckton Milnes) Lord Houghton* (2 vols.; London, 1876).

HOWITT, WILLIAM, *Homes and Haunts of the Most Eminent British Poets* (2 vols.; London, 1847).

HUDSON, HENRY, N., *Studies in Wordsworth* (Boston, 1884).

HUTTON, RICHARD HOLT, *Essays: Theological and Literary* (2 vols.; London, 1871).

HUXLEY, ALDOUS, 'Wordsworth in the Tropics', *Do What You Will*, (London, 1929), 123–39.

JACK, IAN, *The Poet and His Audience* (Cambridge, 1984).

JACKS, LAWRENCE PEARSALL, *Life and Letters of Stopford Brooke* (2 vols.; London, 1917).

JAMES, D. G., *Wordsworth and Tennyson* (London, 1950).

JAMES, HENRY, *Literary Criticism: Essays on Literature: American Writers English Writers* [The Library of America] (New York, 1984).

JEFFREY, FRANCIS, *Edinburgh Review*, 11 (1807), 214–31.

—— *Edinburgh Review*, 24 (1814), 1–30.

—— *Edinburgh Review*, 25 (1815), 355–63.

—— *Edinburgh Review*, 37 (1822), 1–30.

JOHNSTON, KENNETH, *Wordsworth and 'The Recluse'* (New Haven, 1984).

JONES, Sir HENRY, and MUIRHEAD, J. H. *The Life and Philosophy of Edward Caird* (Glasgow, 1921).

KAPLAN, FRED, *Sacred Tears: Sentimentality in Victorian Literature* (Princeton, 1987).

KEATS, JOHN, *Letters of John Keats to Fanny Brawne*, ed. Harry Buxton Forman (London, 1878; 2nd rev. edn. 1889).

—— *The Letters of John Keats 1814–1821*, ed. Hyder Edward Rollins (2 vols.; Cambridge, Mass., 1958).

KEBLE, JOHN, *De Poetica Vi Medica: Praelectiones Academicae Oxonii Habitae* (2 vols.; Oxford, 1844); trans. E. K. Francis as *Keble's Lectures on Poetry* (2 vols.; Oxford, 1912).

KELLEY, MAURICE, 'The Recovery, Printing, and Reception of Milton's *Christian Doctrine*', *Huntington Library Quarterly*, 31 (1967), 35–41.

KENNY, ANTHONY, *God and Two Poets* (London, 1988).

KER, IAN, *John Henry Newman: A Biography* (Oxford, 1988).

KINGSLEY, CHARLES, *Charles Kingsley: His Letters and Memories of His Life*, edited by His Wife (2 vols.; London, 1877; 2nd rev. edn. 1890).

—— *Alton Locke, Tailor and Poet: An Autobiography*, ed. Elizabeth Cripps (Oxford, 1983).

KNIGHT, WILLIAM, *The English Lake District As Interpreted in the Poems of William Wordsworth* (Edinburgh, 1878; 3rd edn. 1904).

—— *Studies in Philosophy and Literature* (London, 1879).

—— *Principal Shairp and His Friends* (London, 1888).

—— (ed.), and Other Members of the Wordsworth Society, *Selections from Wordsworth* (London, 1888).

—— *The Life of William Wordsworth* (3 vols.; Edinburgh, 1889).

—— (ed.), *Wordsworthiana: A Selection From Papers Read to the Wordsworth Society* (London, 1889).

—— (ed.), *Letters From the Lake Poets, Samuel Taylor Coleridge, William Wordsworth, Robert Southey, to Daniel Stuart* (London, 1889).

KNOEPFLMACHER, U. C., 'Dover Revisited: The Wordsworthian Matrix in the Poetry of Matthew Arnold', *Victorian Poetry*, 1 (1963), 17–26.

—— *George Eliot's Early Novels: The Limits of Realism* (Berkeley and Los Angeles, 1968).

—— and TENNYSON, G. B. (eds.), *Nature and the Victorian Imagination* (Berkeley and Los Angeles, 1977).

LAMB, CHARLES AND MARY, *The Letters of Charles and Mary Lamb*, ed. Edwin W. Marrs, Jr. (3 vols. continuing; Ithaca, NY, 1975–   ).

LEADER, ZACHARY, *Revision and Romantic Authorship* (Oxford, 1996).

LEGOUIS, EMILE, *William Wordsworth and Annette Vallon* (London and Toronto, 1922).

LEVI, A. W., 'The "Mental Crisis" of John Stuart Mill', *Psychoanalytic Review*, 32 (1945), 86–101.

LEVINE, GEORGE, *Darwin and the Novelists: Patterns of Science in Victorian Fiction* (Cambridge, Mass., 1988).

LEWES, GEORGE HENRY, *Literary Criticism of George Henry Lewes*, ed. Alice R. Kaminsky (Lincoln, Neb., 1964).

LINDENBERGER, HERBERT, 'The Reception of *The Prelude*', *Bulletin of the New York Public Library*, 64 (1960), 196–208.

LIVEING, EDWARD, *Adventure in Publishing: The House of Ward, Lock 1854–1954* (London, 1954).

LOWELL, JAMES RUSSELL, *Among My Books: Second Series* (London, 1876).

MACAULAY, THOMAS BABINGTON, *The Letters of Thomas Babington Macaulay*, ed. Thomas Pinney (6 vols.; Cambridge, 1974–81).

MACCARTHY, FIONA, *William Morris: A Life for Our Time* (London, 1994).

MACGILLIVRAY, J. R., *Keats: A Bibliography and Reference Guide with an Essay on Keats' Reputation* (Toronto, 1949).

MACLEAN, CATHERINE MACDONALD, *Mark Rutherford: A Biography of William Hale White* (London, 1955).

McLEAN, RUARI, *Victorian Book Design and Colour Printing* (London, 1963; 2nd edn. 1972).

—— *Victorian Publishers' Book-bindings in Cloth and Leather* (London, 1974).

MACREADY, WILLIAM CHARLES, *Macready's Reminiscences, and Selections from his Diaries and Letters*, ed. Sir Frederick Pollock, Bart. (2 vols.; London, 1975).

McSWEENEY, KERRY, *Tennyson and Swinburne as Romantic Naturalists* (Toronto, 1981).

MAGNUS, LAURIE, *A Primer of Wordsworth, with a Critical Essay* (London, 1897).

MAHONEY, JOHN L., 'The Rydal Mount Ladies' Boarding School: A Wordsworthian Episode in America', *Wordsworth Circle*, 23 (1992), 43–8.

MAITLAND, FREDERICK WILLIAM, *The Life and Letters of Leslie Stephen* (London, 1906).

Manchester and Thirlmere Water Scheme. Statement of the Case of the Thirlmere Defence Association (Windermere and London, n.d. [1877]).

MANIER, EDWARD, *The Young Darwin and His Cultural Circle* (Dordrecht, 1978).

MANNING, PETER, *Reading Romantics: Text and Context* (New York, 1990).

MANTELL, GIDEON, *The Wonders of Geology* (2 vols.; London, 1838).

MARSHALL, J. D., and WALTON, JOHN K., *The Lake Counties: From 1830 to the Mid-Twentieth Century* (Manchester, 1981).

MARTIN, BRIAN W., 'Wordsworth, Faber, and Keble: Commentary on a

Triangular Relationship', *Review of English Studies*, NS 26 (1975), 436–42.

—— *John Keble: Priest, Professor and Poet* (London, 1976).

MARTIN, ROBERT BERNARD, *Tennyson: The Unquiet Heart* (Oxford, 1980).

MATTES, ELEANOR BUSTIN, *In Memoriam: The Way of a Soul* (New York, 1951).

MERRIAM, HAROLD, G., *Edward Moxon: Publisher of Poets* (New York, 1939).

MICHAEL, IAN, *The Teaching of English: From the Sixteenth Century to 1870* (Cambridge, 1987).

MILL, JOHN STUART, *The Earlier Letters of John Stuart Mill 1812–1848*, ed. Francis E. Mineka (2 vols.; Toronto, 1963).

—— *Essays on Ethics, Religion and Society*, ed. John M. Robson (Toronto, 1969).

—— *Autobiography and Literary Essays*, ed. John M. Robson and Jack Stillinger (Toronto, 1981).

—— *Journals and Debating Speeches*, ed. John M. Robson (2 vols.; Toronto, 1988).

MOIR, D. M., *Sketches of the Poetical Literature of the Past Half-Century* (Edinburgh, 1851).

MOORMAN, MARY, *William Wordsworth: A Biography. The Later Years 1803–1850* (Oxford, 1965).

MORGAN, THÄIS E., 'Rereading Nature: Wordsworth between Swinburne and Arnold', *Victorian Poetry*, 24 (1986), 427–39.

MORLEY, EDITH J., *The Life and Times of Henry Crabb Robinson* (London, 1935).

MORLEY, F. V., *Dora Wordsworth: Her Book* (London, 1924).

MORLEY, JOHN, introduction to *The Complete Poetical Works of William Wordsworth* (London, 1888).

MORRIS, JOHN N., *Versions of the Self: Studies in English Autobiography from John Bunyan to John Stuart Mill* (New York, 1966).

MORRISON, ARTHUR, *Tales of Mean Streets* (London, 1894).

MUMBY, F. A., *The House of Routledge 1834–1934* (London, 1934).

MYERS, F. W. H., *Wordsworth* (London, 1881).

NEWMAN, JOHN HENRY, *A Letter Addressed to the Rev. R. W. Jelf, D.D.* (Oxford, 1841).

—— (ed.), *Lives of the English Saints* (4 vols.; London, 1844).

—— *Apologia Pro Vita Sua*, ed. Martin J. Svaglic (Oxford, 1967).

OLLARD, S. L., *A Short History of the Oxford Movement* (London, 1915; 2nd rev. edn., 1932).

OWEN, W. J. B., 'Costs, Sales, and Profits of Longman's Editions of Wordsworth', *Library*, 5th ser. 12 (1957), 93–107.

PACKE, MICHAEL St JOHN, *The Life of John Stuart Mill* (London, 1954).

PALGRAVE, FRANCIS TURNER, *The Golden Treasury of the Best Songs and Lyrical Poems in the English Language*, ed. Christopher Ricks (London, 1991).

PALGRAVE, GWENLLIAN F., *Francis Turner Palgrave: His Journals and Memories of His Life* (London, 1899).

PALMER, D. J., *The Rise of English Studies* (London, 1965).

PALMER, ROUNDELL [Lord Selborne], *Memorials* (2 vols.; Edinburgh, 1889–92).

PARKINSON, RICHARD, *The Old Church Clock* (London, 1843).

PARRISH, S. M., 'The Whig Interpretation of Literature', *Text*, 4 (1988), 343–50.

PATER, WALTER, 'Poems by William Morris', *Westminster Review*, NS 34 (1868), 300–12.

—— *Appreciations* (London, 1889).

—— *Letters of Walter Pater*, ed. Lawrence Evans (Oxford, 1970).

PATTERSON, ALEXANDER, *Poets and Preachers of the Ninteenth Century* (Glasgow, 1862).

PEACH, LINDEN, *British Influence on the Birth of American Literature* (London, 1982).

PEEK, KATHERINE MARY, *Wordsworth in England: Studies in the History of His Fame* (Bryn Mawr, Pa., 1943).

PINNEY, THOMAS, 'George Eliot's Reading of Wordsworth: The Record', *Victorian Newsletter*, 24 (1963), 20–2.

—— 'The Authority of the Past in George Eliot's Novels', *Nineteenth Century Fiction*, 21 (1966), 131–47.

POSTON, LAWRENCE, ' "Worlds Not Realised": Wordsworthian Poetry in the 1830s', *Texas Studies in Literature and Language*, 28 (1986), 51–80.

PRAZ, MARIO, *The Hero in Eclipse in Victorian Fiction*, trans. Angus Davidson (London, 1956).

PRICKETT, STEPHEN, *Romanticism and Religion: The Tradition of Coleridge and Wordsworth in the Victorian Church* (Cambridge, 1976).

PRINGLE, THOMAS, *The Poetical Works of Thomas Pringle*, ed. Leitch Ritchie (London, 1839).

PYCROFT, JAMES, *A Course of Reading, Adapted to Every Taste and Capacity: With Anecdotes of Men of Genius* (London, 1844).

RAMSAY, E. B., *Two Lectures on the Genius of Handel* (Edinburgh, 1862).

RAPF, JOANNA E., ' "Visionaries of Dereliction": Wordsworth and Tennyson', *Victorian Poetry*, 24 (1986), 373–85.

RAWNSLEY, ELEANOR F., *Canon Rawnsley: An Account of his Life* (Glasgow, 1923).

REID, FORREST, *Illustrators of the Sixties* (London, 1928).

REID, IAN, 'Patriotism, Natural Aristocracy and Manhood: The Import of

English in Two Lake Districts', *Literature and National Cultures*, ed. Brian Edwards (Deakin, 1988), 21–32.

RICE, H. A. L., *Lake Country Portraits* (London, 1967).

RICHARDSON, ALAN, *Literature, Education, and Romanticism: Reading as Social Practice 1780–1832* (Cambridge, 1994).

RICKS, CHRISTOPHER, *Tennyson* (London, 1972).

—— *Essays in Appreciation* (Oxford, 1996).

RIEDE, DAVID G., *Matthew Arnold and the Betrayal of Language* (Charlottesville, Va., 1988).

ROAZEN, DEBORAH HELLER, 'George Eliot, Wordsworth, and Peasant Psychology', *Research Studies* [Washington State University], 41, (1973), 116–78.

—— '*Middlemarch* and the Wordsworthian Imagination', *English Studies*, 58 (1977), 411–25.

ROBERTS, MARK, *The Tradition of Romantic Morality* (London, 1973).

ROBERTSON, FREDERICK W., *Lectures and Addresses on Literary and Social Topics* (London, 1858).

ROBINSON, HENRY CRABB, *The Correspondence of Henry Crabb Robinson with the Wordsworth Circle*, ed. Edith J. Morley (2 vols.; London, 1927).

—— *Henry Crabb Robinson on Books and Their Writers*, ed. Edith J. Morley (3 vols.; London, 1938).

RUSKIN, JOHN, *The Works of John Ruskin*, ed. E. T. Cook and Alexander Wedderburn (39 vols.; London, 1903–12).

SCHNEEWIND, J. B., *Sidgwick's Ethics and Victorian Moral Philosophy* (Oxford, 1977).

SCHOR, HILARY M., *Scheherezade in the Marketplace: Elizabeth Gaskell and the Victorian Novel* (New York, 1992).

SEARLE, JANUARY [George Searle Phillips], *Memoirs of William Wordsworth* (London, 1852).

SHAIRP, JOHN CAMPBELL, *Studies in Poetry and Philosophy* (Edinburgh, 1868).

—— *Aspects of Poetry: Being Lectures Delivered at Oxford* (Oxford, 1881).

—— 'Wordsworth and "Natural Religion" ', *Good Words*, 25 (1884), 307–13.

SHARPS, GEOFFREY, *Mrs Gaskell's Observation and Invention* (Fontwell, 1970).

SHAW, W. DAVID, *The Lucid Veil: Poetic Truth in the Victorian Age* (London, 1987).

SHORTHOUSE, SARAH (ed.), *Life, Letters, and Literary Remains, of J. H. Shorthouse* (2 vols.; London, 1905).

SIMPSON, PETER, 'Crisis and Recovery: Wordsworth, George Eliot, and Silas Marner', *University of Toronto Quarterly*, 48 (1979), 95–114.

SMITH, CECIL WOODHAM, *Queen Victoria: Her Life and Times* (2 vols.; London, 1972).

SMITH, SHEILA, M., *The Other Nation: The Poor in English Novels of the 1840s and 1850s* (Oxford, 1980).

SOMERVELL, ROBERT, *A Protest Against the Extension of Railways in the Lake District* (Windermere and London, 1876).

—— *The Manchester and Thirlmere Scheme: An Appeal to the Public on the Facts of the Case* (Manchester, Windermere and London, n.d. [1877]).

—— *Robert Somervell: Chapters of Autobiography*, edited with Additional Material by His Sons (London, 1935).

STANSFIELD, ABRAHAM, 'Rambles in the West Riding (With a Glance at the Flora)', *Manchester Quarterly*, 2 (1883), 64–83 and 3 (1884), 155–72).

STEPHEN, LESLIE, 'Wordsworth's Ethics', *Cornhill Magazine*, 34 (Aug. 1876), 206–26.

—— *Hours in a Library. Third Series* (London, 1879).

—— *Selected Letters of Leslie Stephen*, ed. John W. Bicknell (2 vols.; Basingstoke, 1996).

STILLINGER, JACK, 'Textual Primitivism and the Editing of Wordsworth', *Studies in Romanticism*, 28 (1989), 3–28.

—— *Multiple Authorship and the Myth of Solitary Genius* (New York, 1991).

STONE, DONALD D., *The Romantic Impulse in Victorian Fiction* (Cambridge, Mass., 1980).

SUMNER, CHARLES, *Memoir and Letters of Charles Sumner*, ed. Edward L. Pierce (4 vols.; London, 1878–93).

SUTHERLAND, JOHN, *Mrs Humphry Ward: Eminent Victorian Pre-eminent Edwardian* (Oxford, 1990).

SWAYZE, WALTER, E., 'Early Wordsworthian Biography: Books and Articles Containing Material on the Life and Character of William Wordsworth that Appeared before the Publication of the Official Memoirs by Christopher Wordsworth', *Bulletin of the New York Public Library*, 64 (1960), 169–95.

SWINBURNE, ALGERNON CHARLES, 'Mr. Arnold's New Poems', *Fortnightly Review*, NS 2 (1867), 414–45.

—— *Essays and Studies* (London, 1875).

—— *Miscellanies* (London, 1886).

SWINGLE, L. J., *Romanticism and Anthony Trollope: A Study in the Continuities of Nineteenth-Century Literary Thought* (Ann Arbor, 1990).

TALFOURD, THOMAS NOON, 'An Attempt to Estimate the Poetical Talent of the Present Age', *Pamphleteer*, 5 (Feb. 1815), 413–71.

TAYLOR, DENNIS, 'Hardy and Wordsworth', *Victorian Poetry*, 24 (1986), 441–54.

TAYLOR, HENRY, *Autobiography* (2 vols.; London, 1885).

—— *Correspondence of Henry Taylor*, ed. Edward Dowden (London, 1888).

TENNYSON, ALFRED, *The Poems of Tennyson*, ed. Christopher Ricks (London, 1969; 2nd edn. 3 vols. Harlow, 1987).

—— *The Letters of Alfred Lord Tennyson*, ed. Cecil Y. Lang and Edgar F. Shannon, Jr. (3 vols.; Oxford, 1982–90).

TENNYSON, G. B., *Victorian Devotional Poetry: The Tractarian Mode* (Cambridge, Mass., 1981).

TENNYSON, HALLAM, *Alfred Lord Tennyson: A Memoir* (2 vols.; London, 1897).

THOMAS, WILLIAM, *The Philosophic Radicals: Nine Studies in Theory and Practice 1817–1841* (Oxford, 1979).

THOMPSON, B. L., *The Lake District and the National Trust* (Kendal, 1946).

TIMKO, MICHAEL, 'Wordsworth and Clough: Divine Reflections and Obvious Facts', *Victorian Poetry*, 24 (1986), 411–25.

TREMENHEERE, H. S., *I Was There: The Memoirs of H. S. Tremenheere*, ed. E. L. and O. P. Edmonds (Eton, 1965).

TRENCH, RICHARD CHENEVIX (ed.), *The Sonnets of William Wordsworth: With an Essay on the History of the English Sonnet* (London, 1884).

TREVELYAN, GEORGE OTTO, *The Life and Letters of Lord Macaulay* (2 vols.; London, 1876).

TUTIN, JOHN RAMSDEN (ed.), *Early Poems of Wordsworth* (London, 1889).

—— *The Wordsworth Dictionary of Persons and Places* (Hull, 1891).

—— *An Index to the Animal and Vegetable Kingdoms of Wordsworth* (Hull, 1892).

UGLOW, JENNY, *Elizabeth Gaskell: A Habit of Stories* (London, 1993).

ULLMANN, 'A "New" Version of Arnold's Essay on Wordsworth', *Notes and Queries*, 200 [NS 2] (1955), 543–4.

VISWANATHAN, GAURI, *Masks of Conquest: Literary Study and British Rule in India* (New York, 1989).

VOGELER, MARTHA, S., 'The Choir Invisible: The Poetics of Humanist Piety', in *George Eliot: A Centenary Tribute*, ed. Gordon S. Haight (London, 1982), 64–81.

VORZIMMER, PETER J., 'The Darwin Reading Notebooks (1838–60)', *Journal of the History of Biology*, 10 (1977), 107–53.

WALLER, ROSS D., 'Letters Addressed to Mrs Gaskell by Celebrated Contemporaries', *Bulletin of the John Rylands Library*, 19 (1935), 102–69.

WALTON, JOHN K., 'The National Trust: Preservation or Provision?', in *Ruskin and Environment: The Storm-Cloud of the Nineteenth Century*, ed. Michael Wheeler (Manchester, 1995).

WARD, WILFRID, *Aubrey de Vere: A Memoir* (London, 1904).
WATSON, WILLIAM, *Wordsworth's Grave and Other Poems* (London, 1890).
WHEELER, MICHAEL, *The Art of Allusion in Victorian Fiction (London, 1979).*
WHEWELL, WILLIAM, *The Elements of Morality, including Polity,* (2 vols.; London, 1845).
WHITE, DOROTHY V., *The Groombridge Diary* (London, 1924).
WHITE, GLEESON, *English Illustration: 'The Sixties' 1855–1870* (London, 1897).
WHITE, H. O., *Edward Dowden 1843–1913* (Dublin, 1943).
WHITE, JAMES, F., *The Cambridge Movement: The Ecclesiologists and the Gothic Revival* (Cambridge, 1962).
WHITE, NORMAN, *Hopkins: A Literary Biography* (Oxford, 1992).
WHITE, WILLIAM HALE, *The Autobiography of Mark Rutherford, Dissenting Minister,* edited by His Friend, Reuben Shapcott (London, 1881).
—— *Mark Rutherford's Deliverance: Being the Second Part of his Autobiography* (London, 1885).
—— *An Examination of the Charge of Apostasy Against Wordsworth* (London, 1898).
—— *Pages From a Journal* (London, 1900).
—— *More Pages From a Journal* (London, 1910).
—— *The Early Life of Mark Rutherford (W. Hale White)* (London, 1913).
WILKINSON, SAMUEL (ed.), *Contributions of William Wordsworth to the Revival of Catholic Truths* (Leeds, 1842).
WILLEY, BASIL, *Nineteenth-Century Studies* (London, 1949).
—— *Spots of Time: A Retrospect of the Years 1897–1920* (London, 1965).
—— 'Wordsworth Today', in *Bicentenary Wordsworth Studies,* ed. Jonathan Wordsworth (Ithaca, NY, 1970), 266–75.
WILSON, JAMES D., 'Tennyson's Emendations to Wordsworth's "Tintern Abbey" ', *Wordsworth Circle,* 5 (1974), 7–8.
WILSON, JOHN, *The Recreations of Christopher North* (3 vols.; Edinburgh, 1842).
WILSON, WRIGHT, *The Life of George Dawson* (Birmingham, 1905).
WISEMAN, NICHOLAS, *On the Perception of Natural Beauty by the Ancients and the Moderns* (London, 1856).
WOODFIELD, MALCOM, *R. H. Hutton: Critic and Theologian* (Oxford, 1986).
WOODRING, CARL, *Victorian Samplers: William and Mary Howitt* (Lawrence, Kan., 1952).
—— 'Wordsworth and the Victorians', in *The Age of William Wordsworth:*

Critical Essays on the Romantic Tradition, ed. Kenneth R. Johnston and Gene W. Ruoff (New Brunswick, 1987), 261–75.

WOOF, ROBERT, *The Lake District Discovered 1810–1850: The Artists, The Tourists, and Wordsworth* (Grasmere, 1983).

—— *Tennyson 1809–1892: A Centenary Celebration* (Grasmere, 1992).

WORDSWORTH, CHRISTOPHER, *Memoirs of William Wordsworth* (2 vols., London, 1851).

WORDSWORTH, DOROTHY, *Journals of Dorothy Wordsworth*, ed. William Knight (2 vols.; London, 1897).

—— *George and Sarah Green: A Narrative*, ed. Ernest de Selincourt (Oxford, 1936).

—— *Journals of Dorothy Wordsworth*, ed. Ernest de Selincourt (2 vols.; London, 1941).

—— *Journals of Dorothy Wordsworth*, ed. Helen Darbishire (London, 1958).

—— *The Grasmere Journals*, ed. Pamela Woof (Oxford, 1991).

WORDSWORTH, JONATHAN, *The Music of Humanity* (London, 1969).

WORDSWORTH, WILLIAM, *The Prose Works of William Wordsworth*, ed. Alexander B. Grosart (3 vols.; London, 1876).

—— *Poems of Wordsworth*, ed. Matthew Arnold (London, 1879).

—— *The Poetical Works of William Wordsworth*, ed. William Knight (11 vols.; Edinburgh, 1882–9). The last three vols. are the *Life of William Wordsworth*.

—— *The Poetical Works of William Wordsworth*, ed. Edward Dowden [Aldine Edition] (7 vols.; London, 1892–3).

—— *The Poetical Works of William Wordsworth*, ed. Thomas Hutchinson [Oxford Edition] (London, 1895).

—— *The Poetical Works of William Wordsworth*, ed. William Knight (8 vols., London, 1896).

—— *The Prose Works of William Wordsworth*, ed. William Knight (2 vols.; London, 1896).

—— *The Poetical Works of William Wordsworth*, ed. Ernest de Selincourt and Helen Darbishire (5 vols.; Oxford, 1940–9).

—— *The Prose Works of William Wordsworth*, ed. W. J. B. Owen and Jane Worthington Smyser (3 vols.; Oxford, 1974).

—— *The Fenwick Notes of William Wordsworth*, ed. Jared Curtis, London, 1993).

—— AND WORDSWORTH, DOROTHY, *Letters of William and Dorothy Wordsworth: The Early Years*, ed. Chester L, Shaver (Oxford, 1967); *The Middle Years, 1806–1811*, ed. Mary Moorman (Oxford,1969); The Middle Years, *1812–1820*, ed. Mary Moorman and Alan G. Hill (Oxford, 1970); *The Later Years, 1821–53*, ed. Alan G. Hill (4 vols.; Oxford, 1978–88); *A Supplement of New Letters*, ed. Alan G. Hill (Oxford, 1993).

WORDSWORTH FAMILY, *Letters of the Wordsworth Family from 1787–1855*, ed. William Knight (3 vols.; Boston, 1907).

WRIGHT, JOHN, *The Genius of Wordsworth Harmonized With the Wisdom and Integrity of His Reviewers* (London, 1853).

WRIGHT, SAMUEL, *A Bibliography of the Writings of Walter, H. Pater* (New York, 1975).

WRIGHT, T. R., *The Religion of Humanity: The Impact of Contean Positivism on Victorian Britain* (Cambridge, 1986).

WYATT, JOHN, *Wordsworth and the Geologists* (Cambridge, 1995).

WYMER, NORMAN, *Dr Arnold of Rugby* (London, 1953).

YARNALL, ELLIS, *Wordsworth and the Coleridges: With Other Memories Literary and Political* (New York, 1899).

ZALL, PAUL M., 'Wordsworth Edits His Editor', *Bulletin of the New York Public Library*, 66 (1962), 93–6.

Index